PHILOSOPHERS AT THE FRONT

geben können. Vielleicht wird u. b-
duld, deren gerade die frei-
dürfen. Ich weiss wie schwer
eine dura necessitas. Also
fort in Pflaum, ich brauche
eile! für diese Urlaub zu
keine Möglichkeiten. Ihr Dess.
[...] die nicht bereit etc. Hoff
[...]

Philosophers at the Front

Phenomenology and the First World War

Edited by

Nicolas de Warren & Thomas Vongehr

Leuven University Press

Contents

5   *Philosophers at the Front*

10   *Chronology of Significant Dates*

15   *The Husserl Family*
16   Edmund Husserl (1859-1938)
48   Malvine Husserl (1860-1950)
53   The Husserls in Time of War
56   Elisabeth („Elli") Husserl (1892-1981)
58   Gerhart Husserl (1893-1973)
59   Wolfgang Husserl (1895-1916)
60   Documents from the War
104   Letters of Condolence

116   *Philosophers in War*
117   The "Göttingen Philosophical Society"
119   Winthrop P. Bell (1884-1965)
129   Hedwig Conrad-Martius (1888-1966), Theodor Conrad (1881-1969)
134   Johannes Daubert (1877-1947)
147   Moritz Geiger (1880-1937)
152   Erich von Gündell (1854-1924)
156   Martin Heidegger (1889-1976)
164   Gustav Hübener (1889-1941)
168   Fritz Kaufmann (1891-1958)
176   Kurt Lewin (1890-1947)
180   Hans Lipps (1889-1941)
186   Karl Löwith (1897-1973)
190   Dietrich Mahnke (1884-1939)
200   Arnold Metzger (1892-1974)
209   Friedrich Neumann (1889-1978)
218   Max Scheler (1874-1928)
226   Edith Stein (1891-1942)

231   *The Fallen Ones*
232   Rudolf Clemens (1890-1914)
236   Waldemar Conrad (1878-1915)
240   Fritz Frankfurther (1889-1914)
242   Emil Lask (1875-1915)
250   Adolf Reinach (1883-1917)
266   Heinrich Rickert jr. (1891-1917)
270   Hermann Ritzel (1880-1915)

277   Select Bibliography
279   List of Sources
281   Index of Names
287   Colophon

Philosophers at the Front
Phenomenology and the First World War

In Erich Maria Remarque's *All Quiet on the Western Front*, Paul returns on leave from the frontline to visit his Gymnasium and enters a classroom during his former Professor's lecture. The elderly professor, whose name Kantorek thinly veils a reference to the founder of German philosophy, declares to his audience of students, caught in rapt attention, "there is no other duty now than to save the Fatherland!" As Paul enters the room, Professor Kantorek extends his hand in welcome, and exclaims to his former student, "you've come at the right moment!" Paul is urged to share his stories of heroic deeds, but describes instead, and much to Kantorek's consternation, the frontline experience of combat without any loftiness of spirit or elevated nobility. As he explains: "we live in the trenches out there, we fight, we try not to be killed, but sometimes we are. That's all." Prompted once again by Professor Kantorek, Paul retorts in anger, "I heard you in here, it's the same old stuff, making more iron men, making more young heroes, you still think that it's beautiful and sweet to die for your country, don't you!" Paul's indignation roundly accuses his Professor for filling the minds of his lost generation with the old Lie, *dulce et decorum est, pro patria mori*. As he bitterly remarks, "We used to think you knew, but with the first bombardment, we knew better."[1]

Remarque's indictment of the complicity of German academia in the "making of iron men" during the First World War remains as powerful today as when first published in 1929. His judgement issues a sharp condemnation of German university professors, writers, artists, and intellectuals who uncritically supported the German national cause in encouraging young men to sacrifice themselves for the nation. As the historian of ideas Ulrich Sieg writes, "young people became victims of an idealism that had been taught by no less than their university teachers."[2] Professors of philosophy played a critical and visible role in the formation of public wartime sentiment. With the outbreak of hostilities in August of 1914, German philosophers, with few exceptions, succumbed to what Kurt Flasch dubbed a "spiritual mobilization" (*geistige Mobilmachung*). As public advocates of the German Nation, *Kultur*, and *Geist*, the mainstay of German academic philosophy became weaponized in the service of the war. In numerous pamphlets, books, public speeches, and university lectures, philosophical discourse became transformed into instruments with which to pursue war by other, namely, intellectual means. This transformation of German philosophy into *Kriegsphilosophie* opened an intellectual front in parallel with the military frontline of trenches, barbed wire, and machine guns. Likewise, the war itself (and for German public awareness, especially the confrontation with France and England on the Western Front) became understood as an historical event of decisive philosophical significance, where nothing less than the identity of Germany and future of Europe was argued to be at stake. Within the first months of the conflict, the war rapidly took on a magnitude of meaning that exceeded political, military, and economic objectives. As Ernst Haeckl was quoted to have declared in an article published on September 20, 1914 in the *Indianapolis Star*: "There is no doubt that the course and character of the feared 'European War' [...] will become the first world war in the full sense of the word." That full sense of the word "war" included a war of ideas and a clash of civilizations. Under the banner of the "Idea of 1914," many philosophers and intellectuals argued that German *Kultur* with its unique characteristics (a "German" notion of freedom, the social organization of *Gemeinschaft*, the primacy of duty) had to be defended against the encroachments of civilization, utilitarianism, and rampant individualism.[3] As declared in public manifestos such the "Manifesto of the Ninety-Three" and "Die Erklärung der Hochschullehrer des Deutschen Reiches" (signed by over 3,000 professors), the German cause was deemed to be nothing less than higher culture and science. As Thomas Mann voiced in *Gedanken im Kriege* (1914), German war-efforts were necessary and justified, regardless of the costs, in order to defend against the dissolution of spirit, values, and life. As Mann declares, "How should the artist, the soldier in the artist, not have praised God for the collapse of a world of peace, of which he

---

1 This scene is depicted in the original 1930 film: https://www.youtube.com/watch?v=rSPj_G2yVz4&t=120s
2 Ulrich Sieg, *Aufstieg und Niedergang des Marburger Neukantianismus: die Geschichte einer philosophischen Schulgemeinschaft*, (Würzburg: Königshausen & Neumann, 1994), p. 377.
3 See Jeffrey Verhey, *The Spirit of 1914. Militarism, Myth and Mobilization in Germany*, (Cambridge: Cambridge University Press, 2000).

was so fed up, so very fed up! War! It was purification, liberation, what we felt along with a tremendous hope."⁴

*

This "spiritual mobilization" was not restricted to Germany alone.⁵ University professors, writers, philosophers, and scientists in other belligerent nations were equally called to arms. Yet, within this pan-European phenomenon, intellectual engagement for the war was especially vociferous in Germany. As the military historian Herfried Münkler remarks, "in no other country did the literature on the meaning of the war reach such a height as in Germany."⁶ This obsession with establishing the "spiritual" meaning of the war reflected the absence of public debate regarding the political aims of the war. Censorship of newspapers (although not as stringent for books) had been immediately imposed at the beginning of the war. This fixation on the meaning of the war also reflected the public role assigned to university professors (and intellectuals) as stewards and shapers of German National *Kultur* as well as the rise of their political influence since the beginning of the 20th century. This political role of German philosophers in the project of German national identity reached back to the first calls for German national consciousness, as most famously epitomized with Fichte's *Reden an die Deutsche Nation* (1808). In the decades leading up to the war, philosophy in particular became widely perceived as a pre-eminent cultural formation (*Bildung*), where professors of philosophy served as "spiritual educators" of the newly founded German Nation.⁷ This cultural engagement of philosophical thinking prior to 1914 - 1918 was forged in the crucible of the so-called *Kulturkrieg* that animated Germany culture after national unification in 1871.⁸ To a significant degree, the war arrived on the scene of an intellectual atmosphere already charged and mobilized, with many of the ideas re-energized and re-deployed during the war having already been formed beforehand.⁹

One hundred years later, much of this literature of *Kriegsphilosophie* reads like dispatches from an entirely alien time. The strangeness of this wartime philosophy, public engagement, and personal conviction bolsters the prevailing view that German philosophers during these years, with few exceptions, collectively succumbed to ideology and national chauvinism. Over the course of the war and across the modulation of public as well as private sentiments from expectation of victory (1914-1916) to pessimistic awareness of defeat (1916-1918), intellectual support of the war remained vibrant and vocal.¹⁰ It seems nearly impossible for us today to imagine the degree of spontaneous engagement by such philosophers during the opening weeks of the war (powerfully depicted in Remarque's novel) and fervor of the *Augusterlebnis* of 1914.¹¹ The German middle-class and university student populations were especially prone to this wave of war-enthusiasm. It is difficult to conjure the image of Rudolf Eucken, recipient of the Nobel Prize for Literature in 1908, and who enjoyed an international reputation on both sides of the Atlantic, delivering a public speech in Nurnberg "Die sittlichen Kräfte des Krieges" in November 1914 to a crowd of thousands.¹² In

---

4   Thomas Mann, *Gedanken im Krieg*, in: *Gesammelte Werke in dreizehn Bänden*, (Frankfurt: Fischer Verlag, 1974), Bd. XIII: 527 – 545; p. 531. "Wie hätte der Künstler, der Soldat im Künstler nicht Gott loben sollen für den Zusammenbruch einer Friedenswelt, die er so satt, so überaus satt hatte! Krieg! Es war Reinigung, Befreiung, was wir empfanden und eine ungeheure Hoffnung."

5   For the broader context, see Nicolas de Warren, "The First World War, Philosophy, and Europe," in: *Tijdschrift voor Filosofie*. 76, IV (2014): 715-737

6   Herfried Münkler, *Der Große Krieg: Die Welt 1914 bis 1918*, (Berlin: Rowohlt, 2013), p. 216.

7   See Ulrich Sieg, *Geist und Gewalt: Deutsche Philosophen zwischen Kaiserreich und Nationalsozialismus*, (Ulm: Carl Hanser Verlag, 2013).

8   See Barbara Besslich, *Wege in den „Kulturkrieg": Zivilisationskritik in Deutschland. 1890-1914*, (Darmstadt: Wissenschaftliche Buchgesellschaft, 2000).

9   See Helmut Fries, *Die große Katharsis. Der Erste Weltkrieg in der Sicht deutscher Dichter und Gelehrter*, Volume I: Die Kriegsbegeisterung von 1914: Ursprünge-Denkweisen-Auflösung; Volume II: Euphorie-Entsetzen-Widerspruch: Die Schriftsteller 1914-1918, (Konstanz: Verlag am Hockgraben 1994/1995)

10 For this periodization of two stages, see Klaus Schwabe, *Wissenschaft und Kriegsmoral: Die Deutschen Hochschullehrer und die Politischen Grundfragen des Ersten Weltkrieges*, (Göttingen: Musterschmidt Verlag. 1969).

11 A phenomenon that has received more measured historical appraisal and documentation, see Michael Neiberg, *Dance of the Furies: Europe and the Outbreak of World War I*, (Cambridge: Belknap Press, 2011)

12 Rudolf Eucken, *Die sittlichen Kräfte des Krieges, Daheim 50*, Heft 52 (Leipzig, 1914). For this lecture, see Kurt Flasch, *Die geistige Mobilmachung. Die deutschen Intellektuellen und der Erste Weltkrieg. Ein Versuch*, (Berlin: Alexander Fest Verlag, 2000), p. 15 ff.

contrast to this challenge of imagining such a level of popularity and prestige for a philosopher in his passion for war, it has arguably become all too evident for subsequent historians (and, indeed, even for a handful of contemporary observers, for example, Hermann Hesse's 1914 essay "O Freunde, nicht diese Töne!") that German philosophers during these years of conflict succumbed collectively to "self-deceit" and "ideology."[13] Such a judgment is bolstered by the strident manner in which wartime intellectuals pioneered forms of modern propaganda within an highly literate culture of mass media.[14] According to this established view, German philosophers were swept away by prevailing tides of nationalism and chauvinism into a collective form of naïveté and uncritical war hysteria. As stated in a recent history of the war, "much more than deceit and malice, it was naïveté and stupidity that determined the discussion of the war's aims [*among German intellectuals*]."[15] Yet, already in the words of the German Anarchist Gustav Landauer (killed in 1919 during the Bavarian Revolution), as he writes to his friend Fritz Mauthner: "Nothing (not even the field post) failed as miserably in this war as the German spirit."[16]

At the outbreak of war, phenomenological philosophy was a relatively new, yet thriving fixture of German academic philosophy. As with other philosophical movements (Neo-Kantianism, *Lebensphilosophie*), most members of the phenomenological movement, be it students or professors, engaged themselves in the war as volunteer soldiers, philosophical spokespersons, or supporters of the national cause at the home front. Whether as individuals or in terms of their ideas, whether publically in publications and lectures, or privately in letters and conversation, phenomenological philosophy was not immune to the "spiritual mobilization" of the war years.

Launched mainly on the basis of Edmund Husserl's self-styled "breakthrough work" of the *Logical Investigations* (1900/1901), the method and idea of phenomenology, as patiently re-worked and developed in Husserl's lecture courses at the University of Göttingen during the first decade of the 20th century, began to attract a cohort of dedicated and talented students: Adolf Reinach, Hedwig Conrad-Martius, Alexandre Koyré, Dietrich von Hildebrand, and Jean Hering, among others. What attracted this younger generation of philosophical minds, indeed, the next generation of German philosophy, is well attested to by Edith Stein. As she writes, "it must be said of Husserl that the manner in which he drew attention to the things themselves and educated [us] to grasp the things themselves in the clearest possible way and to describe them soberly and faithfully in a scientific manner, freed in knowledge from arbitrariness and arrogance, led to a simple, properly obliging and humble attitude of knowing. It also led to a liberation from prejudice and an unprejudiced willingness to accept insights."[17] When Stein herself arrived in Göttingen, this Golden Age of phenomenology seemed to have already passed. As she remarks in her autobiography, "I was twenty-one and all excited about everything that was going to happen to me. Dear old Göttingen! I think only people who were there between 1905 and 1914, in the brief flowering of the Göttingen School of phenomenology, can appreciate what that name contains for us."[18] While students gathered in the Göttingen Philosophical Society around Husserl's teaching, other gatherings of phenomenological students and research had emerged in Munich.[19] Mostly born after German unification in the 1880s and early 1890s, these students reached intellectual maturity along with Husserl's thinking in the decade before the First World

---

13 See Hermann Lübbe, *Politische Philosophie in Deutschland*, (Munich: DTV Deutscher Taschenbuch, 1974) and Sebastian Luft, "Germany's Metaphysical War. Reflections on War by Two Representatives of German Philosophy: Max Scheler and Paul Natorp," *Themenportal Erster Weltkrieg* (2007), URL: http://www.erster-weltkrieg.clio-online.de

14 See Fries, *Die große Katharsis. Der Erste Weltkrieg in der Sicht deutscher Dichter und Gelehrter*.

15 Münkler, p. 219.

16 Letter of November 2, 1914. *Gustav Landauer – Fritz Mauthner Briefwechsel 1890-1919*, (Berlin: C.H.Beck, 1994), p. 294. „Nichts (nicht einmal die Feldpost) hat in diesem Krieg so kläglich versagt wie der deutsche Geist."

17 Edith Stein, "Die weltanschauliche Bedeutung der Phänomenologie" (1930/31), in: ESGA 9 (2014), p. 156. "Von Husserl muß man sagen, daß die Art, wie er auf die Sachen selbst hinlenkte und dazu erzog, sie in aller Schärfe geistig ins Auge zu fassen und nüchtern, treu und gewissenhaft zu beschreiben, von Willkür und Hoffart im Erkennen befreite, zu einer schlichten, sachgehorsamen und darin demütigen Erkenntnishaltung hinführte. Sie führte auch zu einer Befreiung von Vorurteilen, zu einer unbefangenen Bereitschaft, Einsichten entgegenzunehmen."

18 Edith Stein, *Aus dem Leben einer jüdischen Familie. Kindheit und Jugend*, Edith Steins Werke, Bd. VII (Freiburg: Herder, 1965), p. 165.

19 For an useful overview, see Dermot Moran and Rodney Parker, "Resurrecting the Phenomenological Movement," in: *Studia Phaenomenologica*, XV (2015), p. 11–24.

War. This young gathering of students can be seen as belonging to what has been called the "generation of 1905," with their coming of age philosophically occurring against the backdrop of forebodings for a coming war: the Russian-Japanese War, the launch of the Naval arms race, the First Moroccan Crisis, and the Russian Revolution.[20]

Much debated among his students in the years immediately prior to the war, Husserl's "transcendental turn" marks a defining and contested transformation in this thinking; in its mature expression, as Husserl argued, phenomenology is transcendental phenomenology. In 1913, Husserl published (in his newly established "Yearbook for Philosophy and Phenomenological Research") this transcendental reformulation of his phenomenological project with *Ideen I*. The opening pages of Husserl's work brims with the optimism of establishing a new science called phenomenology and therewith, to renew philosophical thinking in the present age. This reformation of philosophy as a rigorous science through phenomenological means was already announced in his programmatic essay "Philosophy as a Rigorous Science" (1911), published in the Neo-Kantian Heinrich Rickert's (his colleague and friend) newly founded cultural journal *Logos*. On the personal level, Husserl began to realize that his systematic ambitions would extend beyond his own (already impressive) capacities and reach beyond his life time. Phenomenology became not only Husserl's philosophy and a movement, but a generational endeavor, where Husserl looked to his students and colleagues to expand and eventually accomplish his idea of philosophy. Phenomenology was a philosophy of the future with which Husserl envisioned the realization of the Western Idea of philosophy such that, as he writes in the first sentence of this *Logos* essay, the deepest theoretical and practical needs of humanity would be fulfilled: to attain a life in truth according to reason. In 1914, Husserl was 55 years old; his three children were beginning their university educations. In a letter from the summer of 1914, Husserl's wife, Malvine, writes to her daughter, with regard to a party at their home, "this 9th of July was one of the happiest days in my life." Husserl must have equally considered the future of phenomenology full of promise that summer as well.

*

Philosophers at the Front. Phenomenology and the First World War brings together a selection of letters, postcards, manuscripts, and other textual materials written during the First World War within the phenomenological movement. The aim of this volume is to present primary materials that document and give witness to the impact, reaction, and experience of members associated with phenomenological movement, with an emphasis on Edmund Husserl and his family. Given that philosophy is just as much a social form of existence as a theoretical enterprise, and given the sense in which the war mobilized the lives of individuals, their families and friends, this collection includes materials from professors, students, spouses, and children.

The aim of this volume is to document the texture of the life-world of phenomenology during the war years. What emerges from this collection is a nuanced image of the phenomenological movement during the First World War that renders visible one of the war's most notable and lasting effects, namely, the way in which established distinctions between "public university professor" and "private thinker," "institution" and "vocation," "rhetoric" and "argument," "teacher" and "student," "friend" and "colleague," and "ideology" and "philosophy" became contaminated, blurred, and transfigured. Encapsulated in these materials are the central questions of philosophy and politics, the public and the private, the personal and the professional, the institution and a vocation – questions that would, in different forms and contexts, continue to be tested throughout the 20th century.

These materials further reveal the complex and changing experience of the war from the frontline as well as at the home front, as chronicled through the expression of domestic concerns, philosophical speculation, political observation, gossipy exchange, mourning, optimism, and joy: indeed, the full spectrum of possible human reactions and responses. These documents possess an appeal and importance beyond the interest in phenomenology as a movement. The phenomenological movement, centered around the network of Husserl's students, was a relatively small group of in-

---

20 For this notion of the generation of 1905, see *Hugo von Hofmannsthal and the Austrian Idea*, translated and edited by David S. Luft, (West Lafayette: Purdue University Press, 2011), p. 3 ff.

dividuals, many of whom had formed close emotional, intellectual, and generational bonds. During the war, members kept in constant correspondence with each other by mail, and would, when circumstances allowed, visit each other, and generally sustained their friendships, professor-student relations, and collegial ties. This collection of materials offers an optic through which one can observe and track the fluid channels of discussion and information between the war front and the home front, as well as that grey zone of occupied territory (Husserl visits his wounded son, Wolfgang, at a field hospital in Belgium). What is revealed is how the war impacted a community of individuals – friends, family, colleagues – through the juxtaposition of the ordinary and the extra-ordinary, the exceptional and the mundane, the home-world and the alien-world. A life-world in miniature, in time of war, spread across geographical and temporal distances, appears here in print for the first time with *Philosophers at the Front*. In this life-world, we have those who served, those who were wounded, those who died, and those who stayed behind in a home-world where the war was ever present.

Given the vast amount of source material produced during the war by members of the phenomenological movement (letters, writings, post cards, books, etc.), our aim has not been to offer a comprehensive collection. We have, instead, selected materials based on intrinsic value and historical interest, giving a generous allowance for materials both significant and not so significant; even those materials that appear insignificant – a request for tobacco, a brief note of grief – are nonetheless in their insignificance significant. Individual materials are presented without any interpretation or commentary: the original German is given along with English translations. The German transcription of letters and other documents follows the original spelling.

*

The basis for this volume draws from materials first collected for the exhibition "From Ashes to Archives," curated by Clara Drummond, at the KU Leuven Central Library, February 20 - March 20, 2015.

All translations into English were done by the editors unless otherwise noted. Our translations have aimed to retain, when appropriate, the often informal, hurried, or idiomatic character of many of these documents.

We wish to express our gratitude to the following individuals for their assistance and advice in the preparation of this volume:

Prof. Julia Jansen, Director of the Husserl Archives Leuven; Prof. Ullrich Melle, President of the Husserl Archives Leuven; Dr. Rodney Parker, Dr. Christian Sternard, Dr. Robin Rollinger, Andrew Barrette, Dr. Kimberly Baltzer-Jaray, Malvine Bläßer, Richard Fleischmann, Dr. Alfred Denker, Dr. Joachim Feldes, Peter Neumann, Susan Iordanidis, David Mawhinney, Nataly Ritzel, and Prof. Hans Rainer Sepp.

Special thanks to Angelika Handschuck from the Universitätsarchiv in Göttingen as well as Dr. Nino Nodia and Annemarie Kaindl from the Bayerischen Staatsbibliothek for their engaged and timely help.

We wish to express our gratitude to the following institutions for their kind permission to include their materials in this volume:

Bayerische Staatsbibliothek München, Edith Stein Archiv, Karmel "Maria vom Frieden", Erzbischöfliches Archiv München, Husserl Archives Leuven, Ingarden Archiwum rodzinne Krzysztofa Ingardena, Institut für Zeitgeschichte München, Vittorio Klostermann Verlag, Landesarchiv Saarland, Martin-Heidegger-Archiv Stadt Meßkirch, Mount Allison University Archives, Nachlass Familie Ritzel, Niedersächsische Staats- und Universitätsbibliothek Göttingen, TU Darmstadt Berufspädagogisches Institut, Universitätsarchiv Göttingen, Universitätsbibliothek Freiburg, Universitätsbibliothek Heidelberg, Universitätsbibliothek Marburg, Universitäts- und Landesbibliothek Bonn, Universitätsbibliothek der Humboldt-Universität zu Berlin, University of New Brunswick (Archives & Special Collections).

Research for this volume was supported by a European Research Council Consolidator Grant (The Great War and Modern Philosophy – GRAPH) awarded to Prof. Nicolas de Warren. Our gratitude to Veerle De Laet and her excellent team at Leuven University Press for their enthusiasm for this volume. Our thanks as well to Stein De Cuyper for his assistance, as well as other staff members, who supported the ERC project for as long as it was allowed to continue at the Institute of Philosophy, KU Leuven.

Nicolas de Warren
Thomas Vongehr

Chronology of Significant Dates

1913
- Husserl publishes *Ideen I*

1914

June 28
Assassination of Archduke Franz Ferdinand of Austria and his wife Duchess Sophie in Sarajevo by Gavrilo Princip

July 31
The German Empire declares a state of war

August 1
Germany declares war on Russia

Husserl lectures on "Basic Questions on Ethics and Theory of Values"

August 2
Husserl's sons, Gerhart and Wolfgang, report as volunteers to the army and are assigned to the 3rd Company in the 234th Reserve Infantry Regiment

August 3
Germany declares war on France

August 4
Germany invades Belgium

1915
- Max Scheler publishes "The Genius of War and the German War"
- Hugo Münsterberg publishes "The Peace and America" (with an excerpt from a letter from Husserl)

February 20
Husserl's son, Wolfgang, wounded with gunshot to the lung

1916
- Max Scheler publishes "War and Construction"

February 21 – December 18
Battle of Verdun

March 8
Wolfgang Husserl killed in action during an attack on Fort Vaux (Verdun)

May 31
Naval Battle of Jutland

1917
- Dietrich Mahnke publishes "A New Monadology" and "The Will towards Eternity"
- Kurt Lewin publishes "War Landscapes"

April 24 – July 31
"Notes on Loose Paper" – manuscript written by Adolf Reinach at the front

April 6
America enters the war

August 8
Heinrich Rickert Jr. ("Heini"), the second eldest son of Heinrich and Sophie Rickert, killed in action

1918
- Husserl publishes an obituary for Adolf Reinach in Kant-Studien

January 30
Johannes Daubert receives the "Royal Military Service Order, 4th Class with Swords"

February 18
Moritz Geiger gives a lecture "Education after the War"

March 21
German Saint Michael Offensive on the Western Front

August 14
Husserl's student, the Canadian Winthrop P. Bell, is arrested on charges of anti-German statements in Göttingen. He remains for the duration of the war in an internment camp near Berlin

September 3
Martin Heidegger released from military duty due to a heart valve problem

September 6 – 10
German advance towards Paris halted at the Battle of the Marne

October 20 – 30
Husserl's sons participate in the Battle of Langemarck

October 21
Rudolf Clemens killed in action in Belgium

October 23
Husserl signs the "Declaration of Teachers of Higher Education in the German Empire"

November 22
Fritz Frankfurther killed in action in Flanders, Belgium

May 7
German U-Boat torpedoes the British passenger liner *Lusitania* off the Irish coast

May 17
Hermann Ritzel killed in action in Galicia

May 23
Italy enters the war

May 26
Emil Lask killed in action in Galicia (obituary published in Kant-Studien 15)

July 10
Waldemar Conrad dies due to "consequenes from excessive efforts in the medical services" (obituary in Kant-Studien 15)

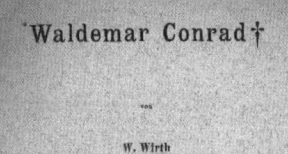

July 1 – November 18
Battle of the Somme

July 26
"Phenomenology of Foreboding" – Adolf Reinach's reflections on foreboding written in Embagneux (France)

August 27
Romania declares war on the Central Powers

September 9 – October 3
"Fragments for a religious-philosophical application" – manuscript written by Adolf Reinach at the front

November 7 – 8
Bolshevik Revolution

November 8 – 17
Husserl delivers for war veterans three lectures on Fichte's Ideal of Humanity (repeated on January 14 – 16, 1918 and on November 6, 7, and 9, 1918)

November 16
Adolf Reinach killed in action near Dixmuiden, Belgium

May 13
Husserl is awarded the "Prussian Service Cross for War Assistance" for his lectures on Fichte

September 25
Kurt Lewin (mistakenly) reported as killed in action

September 27
Allied forces break through the Hindenburg Line

November 3
Mutiny of the German Navy at the ports of Kiel and Wilhelmshaven

November 9
Kaiser Wilhelm seeks refuge in Holland

November 11
Armistice signed in Compiègne, France

November 28
Husserl signs a call against the abdication of the German Kaiser

„Der Krieg ist ‚eingeklammert'"

Brief von Edmund Husserl an Dietrich Mahnke, 2. XII. 1916

Freiburg i/B. 2. XII. 16
Lorettostr. 40 III
Lieber Freund!

Erst nach einer Monatspause ist es mir möglich eine ruhige Stunde für Sie zu erübrigen und Ihren lieben, herzergreifenden Brief zu beantworten. Meine erste Regung, als ich Ihre Handschrift sah, war die einer großen, tiefen Freude. Sie lebten also, obschon ich fast ein Jahr ohne Nachricht von Ihnen war. Von einer großen Sorge fühlte ich mich erlöst. Den Brief las ich dann mit tiefer Bewegung. Wie Schweres haben Sie mitgemacht, das ich in Ihrer anschaulichen Schilderung so ganz nachverstehen konnte. Es gieng mir nahe, daß schließlich Ihre Nerven versagten und Sie in die Heimat zurück mussten. Wie würde es mich freuen, zu hören, daß Sie sich in diesem Monat wieder voll gekräftigt haben und Ihre alte seelische Spannkraft, Ihren freudigen vaterländischen Optimismus, die alte Siegeszuversicht, wiedergewonnen haben. / Inzwischen hat sich ja auch die allgemeine Kriegslage gewendet, das Eingreifen Rumäniens, das uns als ein großes Unheil erschien, erwies sich eher als ein Segen, die neuen Siege, die baldige völlige Demütigung dieses verräterischen „Bundesgenossen" werden sicher zur Aufrichtung Ihrer Seele mitbeitragen. Dazu die erhebende Einmütigkeit des ganzen Volkes in der Übernahme der allg<emeinen> Hilfsdienstpflicht, im festen Willen alle Kräfte (endlich!) anzuspannen, um seine Zukunft zu erretten u. den gesicherten Frieden zu erkämpfen. Nun sieht auch die Schlacht im Westen sich anders an als vordem. Die Hekatomben sind nicht umsonst dargebracht u. das heldenhafte Ausharren im Höllenfeuer hat den Durchbruch verhindert, u. das kommt einem Siege gleich. Nun wird es immer besser werden, kein schädlicher Optimismus, keine Unterschätzung d<es> Feindes, wird wieder solche Situationen, wie die an der Somme im Juli möglich machen. Gott Lob wir spüren nun überall die eiserne Faust Hindenburgs. /

Sehr gerührt war ich, als ich las, daß Sie mir eine Schrift („Der Wille z<ur> Ewigkeit") widmen wollten. Vor einem Jahre wäre es mir vielleicht möglich gewesen, sie bei Niemeyer unterzubringen. Jetzt halte ich es für ausgeschlossen, bei den exorbitant gestiegenen Papier- u. Druckereipreisen. (In diesem Sommer kamen aber noch 2 Bände meines „Jahrbuchs f<ür> Philosophie u. phän<omenologische> Forschung" heraus.) Vielleicht senden Sie mir einmal Ihr Msc. ein, mich daran persönlich zu erfreuen. Haben Sie schon Gelegenheit gehabt den I. Bd. d<es> Jahrbuchs u. darin das I. Buch meiner „Ideen" zu studieren? Sie werden ersehen, daß ich im letzten Jahrzehnt sehr fortgeschritten bin. Die Grundgedanken arbeiteten schon damals, in Ihren Göttinger Semestern, in meinem Geiste, obschon ich noch nicht soweit war in den Vorles<un>gen darüber zu sprechen, vielmehr in diesen die alten Formulierungen / der L<ogischen> U<ntersuchungen> noch festhielt. Ich habe im folgenden Jahrzehnt gewaltig gearbeitet, trotz der großen Hemmungen durch die Gegnerschaft der Fakultät, bis zum Kriege hin. Ich war immerfort im Aufsteigen und Wachsen, ich gewann immer mehr die innere Sicherheit, auf guten, notwendigen Wegen zu sein, immer lebendiger, aber auch bedrückender, das Bewußtsein einer großen Mission, der ich meine geistigen Kräfte nur zu wenig angemessen fand. Immer näher traten mir dabei die metaphysischen Fragen, u. wenn meine Kräfte im Alter nicht versagen, hoffe ich die Fragen von Gott, Freiheit u. Unsterblichkeit umfassend bearbeiten zu dürfen.

Eine trübe Zeit liegt hinter mir. Zuerst der seelenlähmende Krieg, mit manchen tieftraurigen oder peinlichen Erfahrungen an Menschen u. Völkern; dazu Sorgen um meine beiden Jungens. Dann schwere Verwundung Wolfgangs, des Jüngeren, u. – das trübe Ende: der Tod dieses Lieblings. Zum 2ten Male ins Feld eingerückt, avancierte er rasch zum L<eutna>nt u. fiel dann an der Spitze seines Zuges vorgehend / bei dem ersten Sturme auf Vaux (8. März d. J.). Sein Grab liegt auf französ<ischer> Erde, immer noch im Feuer der feindl<ichen> Geschütze.

Wir waren gerade in der Übersiedlung nach Freiburg. Es war u. ist eine schwere Prüfung; besonders für meine Frau, die diesen Sohn über Alles liebte. Ich suchte Rettung u. Heilung in der Arbeit, die in den 2 Jahren d<es> Kriegs so wenig erfolgreich war. Der Zwang, den ich mir mit einem neuen 4st<ündigen> Colleg auferlegte, erwies sich als sehr wohlthätig, und seit den Ferien arbeite ich wieder ganz productiv am 2. Bd. meiner „Ideen". Ich habe mich innerlich von allen Kriegsirritationen befreit. Der Krieg ist „eingeklammert". Zur Unterstützung habe ich mir eine begabte Schülerin Dr Edith Stein als Privatassistentin verpflichtet u. sie hilft mir mit Fleiß u. Eifer. /

Doch ich erhalte Besuch u. schließe eilig ab.

Viele herzliche Grüße und freundschaftliche Wünsche für Ihre volle Gesundung. Hoffentlich darf ich Sie einmal wiedersehen.

Bitte lassen Sie ab u. zu von sich hören. Vielen Dank noch für die interessante Abhandlung über Ihren braven, gediegenen Cassmann.

Herzlichst
Ihr
EHusserl.

Mein älterer Sohn steht als Vicefeldw<ebel> in der Champagne. Circa 1/2 Jahr war er Krankheit halber in der Genesungscomp<anie> bzw. beim Offic<iers>kurs im Sennelager. Meine Tochter hat ihren Kriegsdienst als Hilfsschwester d<es> r<oten> Kr<euzes>.

"The war is 'bracketed'"

Letter of Edmund Husserl to Dietrich Mahnke, 2 December 1916

Freiburg i/B. 2 December 1916
Lorettostr. 40 III
Dear Friend!

Only after a month's pause is it now for me possible to snatch a quiet hour for you and answer your loving, heartbroken letter. My first impulse, when I saw your handwriting, was a great and profound joy. You are still alive, even though I was nearly a year without news from you. I feel released from a great anxiety. I then read your letter and was deeply moved. What hardships you have experienced, which I could so fully understand from your vivid description. It almost seemed to me that your nerves would finally break and that you would have to return back to the homeland. How it would make me happy to hear that your energy is fully regained this month and that your old emotional strength, your joyous patriotic optimism, and the old confidence in victory have returned to you. Meanwhile, the general situation of the war has also turned: the entrance of Rumania, which appeared to us as a great disaster, proved to be a blessing; the new victories, the imminent complete humiliation of this traitorous "companion," will surely contribute to the fortitude of the soul. To this end, the growing unanimity of the whole people in their assumption of the ge[neral] "service obligation," in the firm will to harness all forces (finally!) in order to save their future and to struggle for the securing of peace. The battle for the Western Front now also looks different than before. The hecatombs are not for nothing, the heroic perseverance in the fires of Hell has prevented the breakthrough and victory is soon to come. Things will only get better now, no harmful optimism, no under-estimation [of] the enemy, there will be once again be the situation, as it was made possible by the Somme in July. God be praised; we are now feeling Hindenburg's Iron Fist.

I was very touched when I read that you wanted to dedicate a book to me ("The Will for Eternity"). One year ago, I might have been able to bring your book to Niemeyer. But now, I think it is impossible given the exorbitant increase in paper & printing costs. (This summer, however, two volumes of my "Yearbook for Philosophy and Phenomenological Research" appeared.) Maybe you could send me your manuscript; that would give me great pleasure. Have you already had the opportunity to study the First Volume [of] the Yearbook and the First Book of my "Ideas"? You'll see that I have much advanced in the last decade. The basic thoughts I was already working-out back then in my mind, during your semesters in Göttingen, although I was not yet ready to speak about them in the lec[tures], but rather retained the old formulations of the researches from the L[ogical] I[nvestigations]. In the following decade, I worked enormously until the war, despite the great restrictions from the opposition of the faculty. I was always rising and growing. I was always gaining more and more in the inner certainty of being on the right and necessary paths, always thriving, but also more oppressive, in the awareness of being on a great mission, for which I found my spiritual powers to be too little. Metaphysical questions appeared thereby to be nearing even more closely, and if my forces do not fail me in old age, I hope to work-out thoroughly the questions of God, Freedom, and Immortality.

A bleak time is behind me. First of all, the soul-laming war, with much grief inducing or painful experiences for human beings and peoples; next, concern for my two boys. Then, the severe injury to Wolfgang, the younger, and the dismal end: the death of this loved-one. For the second time he entered the front, and quickly advanced to the [rank of] L[ieutenant] and then fell while leading his platoon in the assault on Vaux (March 8th of this year). His grave lies on French soil, still under fire from the enemy's guns.

We had just moved to Freiburg. It was & is a severe test; especially for my wife, who loved this son above everything else. I looked to work for salvation and healing, which was so unsuccessful in this second year [of] the war. The compulsion, which I imposed upon myself with a new 4-h[our] seminar, proved to be very beneficial, and since the holidays I have been working again very productively on the second volume of my "Ideas." I have freed myself internally from all these annoyances of the war. The war is "bracketed." For support, I have a gifted student, Dr. Edith Stein as a private assistant, who helps me with diligence and zeal.

I am getting a visit and must close quickly.

Many kind regards and friendly wishes for your full recovery. Hopefully, I'll be able to see you again.

Please send word now and again. Thank you for the interesting treatise on your brave and solid Cassmann.

Sincerely,
your
EHusserl.

My eldest son is serving as a Staff Sergeant in Champagne. For about half a year he was, due to illness, in the convalescent company as well as at the officier course in Sennelager. My daughter does her war service as an auxiliary nurse with the R[ed] C[ross].

Die Husserl-Familie
The Husserl Family

Malvine und Edmund Husserl mit den Kindern Gerhart (1893-1973), Wolfgang (1895-1916) und Elisabeth (1892-1981). Rechts: Husserls Bruder Heinrich mit seiner Frau Clotilde (Aufnahme ca. 1905)

Malvine and Edmund Husserl with their children Gerhart (1893-1973), Wolfgang (1895-1916), and Elisabeth (1892-1981). Right: Husserl's brother Heinrich with his wife Clotilde (photo circa 1905)

Von links: Jakob Rosenberg, Malvine Husserl, Wolfgang Rosenberg-Husserl, Dodo Husserl, Gerhart Husserl, Gabriele Husserl, Edmund Husserl, Elisabeth („Elli") Rosenberg-Husserl, Ruth Rosenberg-Husserl (Aufnahme 1929)

From Left: Jakob Rosenberg, Malvine Husserl, Wolfgang Rosenberg-Husserl, Dodo Husserl, Gerhart Husserl, Gabriele Husserl, Edmund Husserl, Elli Rosenberg-Husserl, Ruth Rosenberg-Husserl (photo 1929)

Edmund Husserl (1859-1938)

Edmund Husserl (ca. 1905)

Edmund Husserl (around 1905)

„1/August 1914. Erklärung des Kriegszustands"

"1 August 1914. Declaration of War"

Manuskriptseite aus Husserls Vorlesung über „Grundfragen zur Ethik und Wertlehre" (veröffentlicht in Husserliana XXVIII, S. 137). Am Rand des Blattes hat Husserl mit Rotstift das Datum der Vorlesung notiert: „1/Aug<ust> 1914 (Erklärung des Kriegszustands)"

Manuscript-page from Husserl's lecture course "Fundamental Questions in Ethics and Theory of Value" (published in Husserliana XXVIII, p. 137). On the margin of the page, Husserl noted in red pencil the date of his lecture: "1 August 1914. Declaration of War"

„Eine Zeit der Aufregungen – aber welch große Zeit"

Samstag Vormittag. 8/8. 1914
Lieber H\<einrich\>.

Deine Postkarte aus Flims ist erst gestern angekommen. Ist das eine Zeit der Aufregungen – aber welch große Zeit! Du kannst Dir nicht denken, was hier geleistet wird, wie großartig die Mobil\<isation\> von Statten geht. Diese ungeheuren Massen, die täglich kommen u. prompt eingekleidet werden u. etwa 1 Tag später als fertige Regimenter abfahren. Und dieser große Ernst, diese feste Entschlossenheit, diese Freudigkeit und Ruhe! Es sind gewaltige Erlebnisse. Alles ist von dem Geiste reinster Vaterlandsliebe u. Opferfreudigkeit erfüllt. Keine Thränen, keine Lamentationen; auch die Frauen sind freudig-ernst und thätig – ja selbst die Kinder leisten überall Dienste als Hilfen bei der Erndte, beim Vertheilen der Monturen, bei der Brotvertheilung, Auspacken etc. Unsere Jungens exerciren schon in Uniform die ganze Woche, Wolf heute schon 3h Morgens abkommandiert! Es haben sich schon 1100 Kriegsfreiwillige in G\<öttingen\> allein gemeldet (zur Linie); zum Landsturm sind alle von 17-45 J\<ahren\> einberufen u. werden von Sonntag ab eingekleidet. Es ist absolut sicher, daß wir / siegen: Diesem Geist, dieser Willensgewalt, kann jetzt wie 1813/4 keine Macht der Welt widerstehen! Ich freue mich, daß auch in Österr\<eich\> ein neuer guter Geist waltet – das ist Oe\<sterreich\>s Wiedergeburt! Heute ist alles gehoben durch die wichtige Nachricht, daß Lüttich im Sturm genommen sei. Überhaupt, die Nachrichten von allen Seiten zeigen, daß unsere Leute den alten großen Kriegsgeist haben. Also vorwärts! An sich kann man gar nicht denken, so sehr betroffen man im Privatleben ist. Jeder hat zu leisten. Elli u. Malv\<ine\> im Hilfsdienst, Fürsorge für die 2 Jungens, dazu Einquartierung m\<it\> Verpflegung, Ich Notexamina etc.
Wie gehts bei Euch?

Edmund.

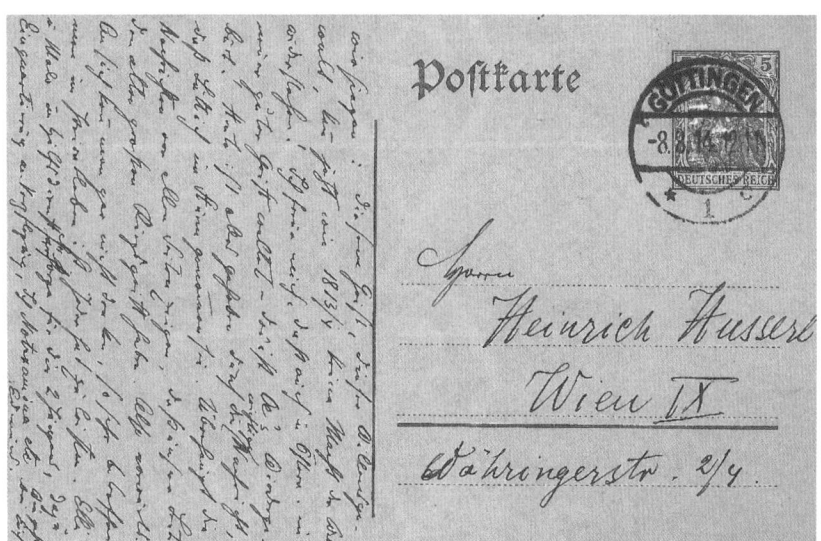

Postkarte von Edmund Husserl an seinen Bruder Heinrich, 8. VIII. 1914

Postcard from Edmund Husserl to his brother Heinrich, 8 August 1914

"What exciting times – but what a tremendous time"

Saturday, morning 8 August 1914
Dear H[einrich],

Your postcard from Flims only arrived yesterday. What an exciting time – but what a tremendous time! You can not imagine what is being done here, how tremendous the mobil[ization] is happening. These immense masses, arriving daily and promptly being uniformed and around one day later departing as complete regiments. And this great earnestness, this firm determination, this joy and calm! These are powerful experiences. Everything is inspired by the spirit of the purest love for the Fatherland and willingness for sacrifice. No tears, no lamentations; even the women are joyful, serious, and active, and even the children do their utmost to help with the harvest, with the distribution of field kits, with the distribution of bread, with unpacking, etc. Our boys are already training in uniform for the entire week, Wolfgang had to report for duty at 3 in the morning! 1,100 volunteers in G[öttingen] have already reported (for service); all 17 – 45 year olds have been called to the Landsturm and will receive their uniforms on Sunday. It is absolutely certain that we will be victorious: this spirit, this will-power, cannot resist, as with 1813/14, any power in the world! I am glad that a new good spirit is also prevailing in Aus[tria] – that is Aus[tria's] rebirth! Today everything is lifted up by the important news that Liege was taken by assault. Overall, the news from everywhere shows that our people possess the old great spirit of war. So, forward! One cannot think of oneself at all, that is how affected one is in one's private life. Everyone has to pull their share. Elli & Malv[ine] are serving in the auxiliary service, taking care of our 2 boys with quartering and accomodations, I have emergency exams.

How are things with you?

Edmund.

„Unser Glaube ist, daß für die ganze Kultur Europas das Heil an dem Siege hängt, den der deutsche ‚Militarismus' erkämpfen wird"

Wir Lehrer an Deutschlands Universitäten und Hochschulen dienen der Wissenschaft und treiben ein Werk des Friedens. Aber es erfüllt uns mit Entrüstung, daß die Feinde Deutschlands, England an der Spitze, angeblich zu unsern Gunsten einen Gegensatz machen wollen zwischen dem Geiste der deutschen Wissenschaft und dem, was sie den preußischen Militarismus nennen. In dem deutschen Heere ist kein anderer Geist als in dem deutschen Volke, denn beide sind eins, und wir gehören auch dazu. Unser Heer pflegt auch die Wissenschaft und dankt ihr nicht zum wenigsten seine Leistungen. Der Dienst im Heere macht unsere Jugend tüchtig auch für alle Werke des Friedens, auch für die Wissenschaft. Denn er erzieht sie zu selbstentsagender Pflichttreue und verleiht ihr das Selbstbewußtsein und das Ehrgefühl des wahrhaft freien Mannes, der sich willig dem Ganzen unterordnet. Dieser Geist lebt nicht nur in Preußen, sondern ist derselbe in allen Landen des Deutschen Reiches. Er ist der gleiche in Krieg und Frieden. Jetzt steht unser Heer im Kampfe für Deutschlands Freiheit und damit für alle Güter des Friedens und der Gesittung nicht nur in Deutschland. Unser Glaube ist, daß für die ganze Kultur Europas das Heil an dem Siege hängt, den der deutsche „Militarismus" erkämpfen wird, die Manneszucht, die Treue, der Opfermut des einträchtigen freien deutschen Volkes.

"Our conviction is that the future of European civilization depends on the victory gained by German 'militarism'"

We, the undersigned, teachers at the Universities and Technical Colleges of Germany, serve science and carry on the work of peace. We feel indignant, however, that the enemies of Germany, especially England, pretend that this scientific spirit is opposed to what they call Prussian Militarism and even mean to discredit us with such a distinction. The same spirit that rules the German army pervades the whole German nation, for both are one and we form part of it. Scientific research is cultivated in our army, and to it the army owes a large part of its successes. Military service trains the growing generation for all peaceful occupations as well, scientific work included. For military training fills them with a sense of duty and unselfishness, endowing them with that feeling of self-confidence and honour by which a really free man subordinates himself to the whole. This spirit is alive not only in Prussia, but it is the same all over Germany. It is the same in war and in peace. At this moment our army is fighting for the freedom of Germany and at the same time for all the blessings of peace and civilization. Our conviction is that the future of European civilization depends on the victory gained by German "militarism": i. e., by the discipline, loyalty, and devotion of a united and free German Nation.

Berlin, den 23. Oktober 1914.

Erklärung der Hochschullehrer des Deutschen Reiches.

Wir Lehrer an Deutschlands Universitäten und Hochschulen dienen der Wissenschaft und treiben ein Werk des Friedens. Aber es erfüllt uns mit Entrüstung, daß die Feinde Deutschlands, England an der Spitze, angeblich zu unsern Gunsten einen Gegensatz machen wollen zwischen dem Geiste der deutschen Wissenschaft und dem, was sie den preußischen Militarismus nennen. In dem deutschen Heere ist kein anderer Geist als in dem deutschen Volke, denn beide sind eins, und wir gehören auch dazu. Unser Heer pflegt auch die Wissenschaft und dankt ihr nicht zum wenigsten seine Leistungen. Der Dienst im Heere macht unsere Jugend tüchtig auch für alle Werke des Friedens, auch für die Wissenschaft. Denn er erzieht sie zu selbstentsagender Pflichttreue und verleiht ihr das Selbstbewußtsein und das Ehrgefühl des wahrhaft freien Mannes, der sich willig dem Ganzen unterordnet. Dieser Geist lebt nicht nur in Preußen, sondern ist derselbe in allen Landen des Deutschen Reiches. Er ist der gleiche in Krieg und Frieden. Jetzt steht unser Heer im Kampfe für Deutschlands Freiheit und damit für alle Güter des Friedens und der Gesittung nicht nur in Deutschland. Unser Glaube ist, daß für die ganze Kultur Europas das Heil an dem Siege hängt, den der deutsche „Militarismus" erkämpfen wird, die Mannszucht, die Treue, der Opfermut des einträchtigen freien deutschen Volkes.

Declaration of the professors of the Universities and Technical Colleges of the German Empire.

We, the undersigned, teachers at the Universities and Technical Colleges of Germany, are scientific men whose profession is a peaceful one. But we feel indignant that the enemies of Germany, especially England, pretend that this scientific spirit is opposed to what they call Prussian Militarism and even mean to favour us by this distinction. The same spirit that rules the German army pervades the whole German nation, for both are one and we form part of it. Scientific research is cultivated in our army, and to it the army owes a large part of its successes. Military service trains the growing generation for all peaceful occupations as well, scientific work included. For military training fills them with a sense of duty and unselfishness, endowing them with that feeling of self-confidence and honour by which a really free man subordinates himself to the whole. This spirit is alive not only in Prussia, but it is the same all over Germany. It is the same in war and in peace. At this moment our army is fighting for the freedom of Germany and at the same time for all the blessings of peace and civilization. We firmly believe that the future of European civilization depends on the victory gained by German „militarism": i. e. by the discipline, loyalty and devotion of a united and free German nation.

Prof. Dr. Jan Versluys.
Prof. Dr. Ernst Vogt.

Theologische Fakultät.
Lic. Paul Althaus.
Prof. D. Alfred Bertholet.
Prof. D. Nathanael Bonwetsch.
Prof. Wilhelm Bousset.
Prof. D. Karl Knoke.
Prof. D. Dr. Kühl.
Prof. D. Johannes Meyer.
Prof. D. Carl Mirbt.
Prof. D. Dr. Alfred Rahlfs.
Prof. D. Dr. Carl Stange.
Prof. D. Arthur Titius.

Rechts- und staatswissenschaftliche Fakultät.
Prof. Dr. Konrad Beyerle.
Prof. Georg Detmold.
Prof. Dr. Ferdinand Frensdorff.
Prof. Dr. Julius Hatschek.
Prof. Dr. Robert von Hippel.
Prof. Dr. Wilhelm Höpfner.
Prof. Dr. Karl Lehmann.
Prof. Dr. Karl Oldenberg.
Prof. Dr. Ernst Rabel.
Prof. Dr. Paul Schoen.
Dr. Otto Schreiber.
Prof. Dr. Heinrich Titze.
Otto Wolff.

Medizinische Fakultät.
Prof. Dr. Otto Damsch.
Dr. Ulrich Ebbecke.
Prof. Dr. Fritz Eichelberg.
Prof. Dr. Erwin von Esmarch.
Prof. Dr. Jacob Esser.
Prof. Dr. Friedrich Göppert.
Prof. Dr. Arthur von Hippel.
Prof. Dr. Eugen von Hippel.
Prof. Dr. Carl Hirsch.
Prof. Dr. Paul Jensen.
Prof. Dr. Philipp Jung.

Theologische Fakultät.
Prof. Lic. Dr. Friedrich Bosse.
Prof. D. Eduard, Freiherr von der Goltz.

Prof. Dr. Carl Watzinger.
Prof. Dr. Heinrich Weber.

25. Universität Göttingen.

Prof. Dr. Leopold Lichtwitz.
Prof. Dr. Gustav Körte.
Prof. Dr. Theodor Lochte.
Prof. Dr. Oswald Loeb.
Dr. Siegfried Loewe.
Prof. Dr. Friedrich Merkel.
Prof. Dr. Friedrich Port.
Prof. Dr. Hans Reichenbach.
Prof. Dr. Friedr. Jul. Rosenbach.
Prof. Dr. Ernst Schultze.
Prof. Dr. Max Voit.

Philosophische Fakultät.
Prof. Dr. L. Ambronn.
Prof. Dr. Friedr. Carl Andreas.
Dr. Wilhelm Behrens.
Prof. Dr. Gottfried Berthold.
Dr. Adolf Bestelmeyer.
Dr. M. Born.
Prof. Dr. Walther Borsche.
Prof. Dr. Karl Brandi.
Prof. Dr. Karl Busolt.
Prof. Dr. Alfred Coehn.
Prof. Dr. Gustav Cohn.
Prof. Dr. Paul Darmstaedter.
Dr. Bernhard Dürken.
Prof. Dr. Ernst Ehlers.
Prof. Dr. Paul Ehrenberg.
Prof. Dr. Ferdinand Fischer.
Dr. Otto Fischer.
Prof. Dr. Wilhelm Fleischmann.
Prof. Otto Freiberg.
Prof. Dr. Johannes Hartmann.
Dr. Erich Hecke.
Prof. Dr. David Hilbert.
Prof. Dr. Edmund Husserl.
Dr. David Katz.
Prof. Dr. Dr.-Ing. Felix Klein.
Prof. Dr. Alfred Koch.
Prof. Dr. Adolf von Koenen.

26. Universität Greifswald.

Prof. Dr. Johannes Hänel.
Prof. D. Dr. Johannes Haussleiter.
Prof. D. Dr. Julius Kögel.

Dr. Oswald Weidenbach.
Prof. Dr. Carl Wimmenauer.

Prof. Dr. Edmund Landau.
Prof. Dr. Franz Lehmann.
Prof. Dr. Enno Littmann.
Prof. Dr. Heinrich Maier.
Prof. Dr. Wilhelm Meyer.
Prof. Dr. Ludwig Mollwo.
Prof. Dr. Lorenz Morsbach.
Prof. Dr. O. Mügge.
Prof. Dr. G. E. Müller.
Dr. Kurt Müller.
Prof. Dr. Hermann Oldenberg.
Prof. Dr. Richard Pietschmann.
Prof. Dr. Max Pohlenz.
Prof. Dr. L. Prandtl.
Prof. Dr. R. Reitzenstein.
Prof. Dr. Eduard Riecke.
Dr. Fritz Roeder.
Prof. Dr. Carl Runge.
Dr. Hans Salfeld.
Prof. Dr. H. Alfr. Schmid.
Prof. Dr. Edward Schröder.
Prof. Dr. Conrad von Seelhorst.
Prof. Dr. Kurt Sethe.
Dr. Johannes Sielisch.
Prof. Dr. Hermann Th. Simon.
Prof. Dr. Walther Stein.
Prof. Dr. Albert Stimming.
Dr. Walther Suchier.
Prof. Dr. Gustav Tammann.
Prof. Dr. Bernhard Tollens.
Dr. H. Rausch von Traubenberg.
Dr. Rudolf Vogel.
Prof. Dr. Woldemar Voigt.
Prof. Dr. Hermann Wagner.
Dr. Otto Wallach.
Dr. Oskar Weigel.
Prof. Dr. Richard Weissenfels.
Prof. Dr. Paul Wendland.
Prof. Dr. Emil Wiechert.
Prof. Dr. Hugo Willrich.

Prof. D. Dr. Johannes Kunze.
Prof. D. Dr. Otto Procksch.
Lic. Erich Seeberg.
Prof. D. Dr. Friedr. Wiegand.

Zusammen mit 3000 Hochschullehrern unterzeichnet Husserl die „Erklärung der Hochschullehrer des Deutschen Reiches" vom Oktober 1914

Together with 3,000 university teachers, Husserl signed the "Declaration of the Professors from the Universities and Technical Colleges of the German Empire" in October 1914

„Dieses Bataillon der Gött<inger> Studenten u. Professorensöhne hatte bes<onders> an diesen Tagen furchtbare Verluste"

Lieber H<einrich>.

Ihr stellt Euch das Leben unsrer Jungens auch idyllischer vor als es leider ist. Sie sind unmittelbar in die schwersten Kämpfe dieses furchtbaren Krieges hineingestellt worden, seit dem 19ten X. sind sie im Kampf um Ypern u. Dixmuiden, in der vordersten Front. Sie erstürmten Roulers und stecken seit Wochen in den Gebieten von Rosebeke nah bei Ypern, immer im Gefecht, jetzt Tag u. Nacht in Schützengräben, den Feind oft kaum 100m vor sich; immerfort gehen die Granaten über ihre Köpfe, auch und besonders bei Nacht. Was sie da aushalten müssen u. Gott sei Dank ausgehalten haben, unglaublich. Wir haben von einem Verw<undeten> derselben Comp<anie> genaue Berichte. Einmal mußten sie 1 Tag u. Nacht in einem genommenen englischen Schützengraben im Grund-Wasser stehen, ohne sich bei dem mörderischen Feuer rühren zu können etc. Göttingen ist seit d 21./22. X. in großer Trauer; denn dieses Bataillon der Gött<inger> Studenten u. Professorensöhne hatte bes<onders> an diesen Tagen furchtbare Verluste. Wie Gerh<art> schreibt, waren am 27/X von der Comp<anie> (230-250 Mann) nur noch 110 da, am 30ten nur 90. Der gütige Himmel hat unsere Kinder beschützt, am 2/XI waren beide noch unverletzt u. gesund u. guten Muts. Wir waren natürlich schwer bedrückt, da wir bis zu den letzten Tagen ohne direkte Nachricht waren, keine Zeile! Jetzt kommen durcheinander Karten und Briefe, welche die ersten furchtbaren Eindrücke spiegeln u. zeigen, wie gut sie sich u. tapfer halten. Sie bekommen (nach der letzten Nachricht von Monatsanfang) alle paar Tage eine Ruhepause von 12 Stunden, um hinter der Linie in einem Bauernhause unter Dach mal schlafen zu können. Verpflegung ganz gut, gebessert durch die endlich ihnen zugekommenen (Chokoladen- etc.) Briefsendungen von uns. Auch für Cigaretten, sowie Latakiatabak sind sie empfänglich u. dankbar. Hoffentlich ist der Himmel weiter mit ihnen u. wird uns in diesem ungeheuren opfervollen Ringen der Sieg zu Theil.

Seid herzlichst mit allen Lieben umarmt.
Ed.

Postkarte von Edmund Husserl an seinen Bruder Heinrich, 8. XI. 1914

Postcard from Edmund Husserl to his brother Heinrich, 8 November 1914

"This battalion of Gött[ingen] students and professors' sons suffered esp[eciallly] during these days of horrific losses"

Dear Heinrich,

You imagine the life of our boys as more idylic than it sadly is. They presently find themselves put to the hardest battles in this terrible war, since the 19th of October they are fighting near Ypres and Dixmuiden on the front lines. They stormed Roulers and were stuck for weeks in combat in the area of Rosebeke near Ypres, and are day and night in the trenches, with the enemy often no more than 100 meters in front of them, the mortars are always flying over their heads, even and especially at night. What they there must endure and thank God what they have endured is unbelievable. We received an exact report from one of the wounded from the same company. Once they had to stand in groundwater for 1 day and night in a captured English trench, without being able to move during the murderous fire, etc. Göttingen is since the 21st and 22nd October in profound mourning; this battalion of Gött[ingen] students and professors' sons suffered esp[ecially] in these days of horrific losses. As Gerh[art] wrote, on the 27th of October only around 110 men from the company (230-250 men) were left, on the 30th, only 90. The gracious Lord has protected our children, on the 2nd of November, both were as yet unscathed and healthy and in good spirit. We were of course deeply depressed that we did not hear any direct news, not even a line, in the past few days. Now comes pell-mell cards and letters, in which the first terrible impressions are reflected and which show how brave and well they performed. They get (according to the last news from the beginning of the month) a break every few days for 12 hours, behind the lines in a peasant house under a roof [and are there] able to sleep. Food is very good, and made better with the packages (chocolates, etc.) which finally they have received from us. Even for cigarettes, such as Latakia tobacco, they are receptive and thankful. Hopefully, the Lord continues to be with them and hopefully we will be victorious in this tremendous struggle full of sacrifices.

With heartfelt embraces and much love,
Ed.

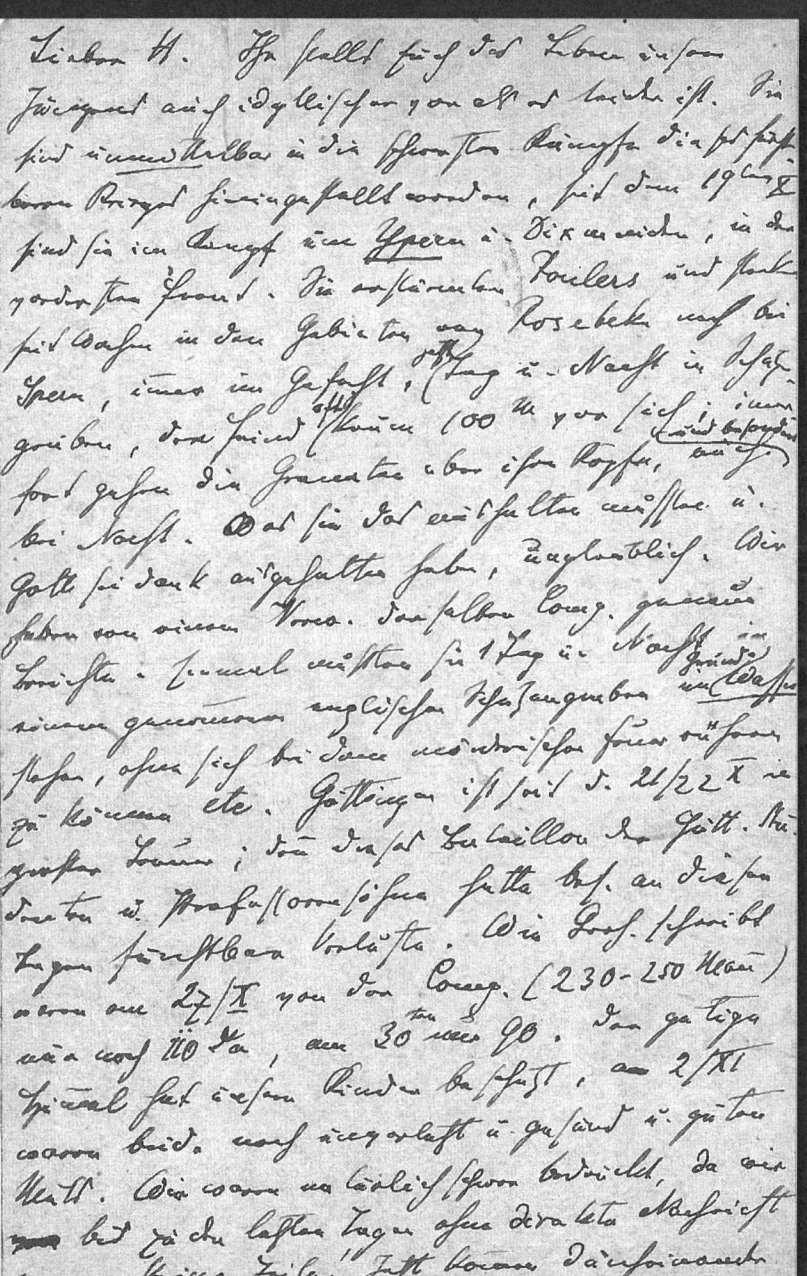

Edmund Husserl

„Ein Krieg des Volkes"

Die Menschen sind einander mit einmal nähergekommen, das Allzumenschliche, das die Menschen trennt, schmilzt dahin, Gemeinschaftsleid, Gemeinschaftsstolz, Gemeinschaftswille, kurz, lebendige Sozialität <ist> in einem Umfange da und wirkt in einem Umfange verbindend, wie man es kaum je geahnt und für möglich gehalten hätte. Das wirkt der „Militarismus", das wirkt der Krieg, der bei uns nicht ein Krieg volksferner Soldaten und Armeen ist, sondern ein Krieg des Volkes selbst, ein Krieg, in dem <aus> jeder Familie Männer mitkämpfen, in dem jede Familie ihre Todten, ihre Verwundeten, ihre Kranken, andererseits ihre kämpfenden, duldenden Helden hat. Das kann ein Engländer und auch ein Amerikaner nicht verstehen, oder nur sehr schwer verstehen. Er kann darum auch nur schwer verstehen die Einheit, die Sorge, Not, Leid bei den zurückgebliebenen Eltern, Geschwistern u.sw. schafft, und andererseits die Größe der Willensanspannung, die jede Familie zum inneren Mitkämpfer der Männer im Felde macht.

Briefentwurf von Husserl (an unbekannten Adressaten), ca. Ende 1914

Draft for a letter from Husserl (to an unknown recipient), around end of 1914

"A People's War"

People have become closer with each other, the all-to-human element, which separated people, melts away, a community of sympathy, a community of pride, and a common will, in short, a living sociality is present here to such a degree and tied together with such intensity, as one could not have suspected and believed to be possible. That is the effect of "militarism," that is the effect of the war, which is for us not a war of national foreign soldiers and armies, but a war of the people, a war in which men from every family fights along, and every family has their dead, their wounded, their sick, but also on the other hand, they have their fighting and enduring heroes. The British and also the Americans can barely understand, or can only understand with difficulty. They can therefore only hardly understand the unity, the concern, the danger, and the suffering produced in parents and siblings left behind, [but] on the other hand, the magnitude of the tension of the will, which makes of every family an inner fellow combatant with the men in the field.

„Kriegsferien 1914/15"

"War Holidays 1914-1915"

Husserls Exemplar von Leibniz „Hauptschriften zur Grundlegung der Philosophie". Auf der ersten Seite der Einleitung hat Husserl mit Bleistift notiert „Kriegsferien 1914/15. Weihn<achten> gelesen"

Husserl's copy of Leibniz "Main Writings on the Foundation of Philosophy." On the first page of the introduction Husserl noted in pencil: "War Holidays 1914-15. Read over Christmas"

„Ich habe seit dem 1. August mindestens acht Stunden den Tag dem Krieg gewidmet"

Cambridge Mass. 25. II. 15.

Sehr verehrter Herr Kollege:

Ihr Brief vom 29. I. hat mich – verhältnismäßig rasch – heute erreicht, und da heute Nachmittag bereits ein nordischer Dampfer abgeht und noch zwei Dutzend Briefe für ihn fertig werden sollen, so beschränke ich mich auf ein ganz kurzes Wort.

Der Fall Bell hat mich bereits seit September eingehend beschäftigt. Ich habe im Oktober der deutschen Botschaft in Washington eine ausführliche Darstellung eingereicht, mit genau dem gleichen Vorschlag, nämlich daß Bell sich verpflichtet, sofort nach Harvard zu gehn und hier zu bleiben. Der Botschafter hat es mit lebhafter Empfehlung an das Auswärtige Amt weitergesandt und auch ich habe es später noch in Berlin erwähnt, aber wir haben kein Wort von dort gehört. Es muß da irgend etwas Besonderes dahinterstecken; ich will <es> aber gerne noch einmal versuchen. Ich möchte übrigens bemerken, daß mein Kollege Perry, zu dem Bell hinwill, so ziemlich der maßloseste Beschimpfer Deutschlands hier im Universitätskreis ist; er spricht nie anders als von Deutschlands Schande und Verbrechen; ich habe den Verkehr abgeschnitten. Dagegen ist Royce wundervoll und reich an feinstem Verständnis.

Es ist eine Intensität der Spannung in den letzten Tagen, die kaum noch erträglich ist; der geringste Zwischenfall mit einem Unterseeboot mag hier zur Kriegserklärung führen. Ich habe seit dem 1. August mindestens acht Stunden den Tag dem Krieg gewidmet, und was ich vor den Kulissen tue, ist der kleinste Teil: und doch, wie unendlich viel mehr hätte getan werden sollen. Mein erstes Büchlein The War and America, das im September erschien, ist jetzt übrigens in Deutschland in der Tauchnitz Edition, und Ende März wird hier, und später bei Tauchnitz, die Fortsetzung: The Peace and America erscheinen. Ich erwähne das, weil Ihr Brief in seinen letzten Seiten eine so eindrucksvolle Ausprägung der Situation enthält, daß ich ein paar Absätze unter den Stimmen

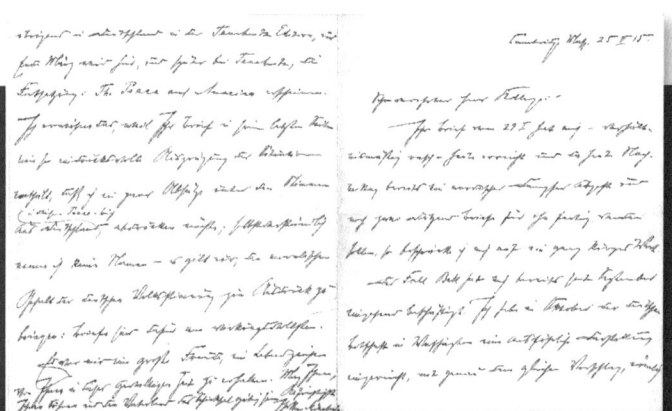

Brief von Hugo Münsterberg an Husserl, 25. II. 1915 (siehe zu „Bell", unten S. 120)

Letter from Hugo Münsterberg to Husserl, 25 February 1915 (see about "Bell", below p. 121)

aus Deutschland in diesem Peace-buch abdrucken möchte; selbstverständlich nenne ich keine Namen – es gilt nur, den moralischen Gehalt der deutschen Volksstimmung zum Ausdruck zu bringen: Briefe sind dafür am wirkungsvollsten.

Es war mir eine große Freude, ein Lebenszeichen von Ihnen in dieser gewaltigen Zeit zu erhalten. Mag Ihnen, Ihren Söhnen und dem Vaterland das Schicksal gütig sein.

Aufrichtigst
Ihr
Hugo Münsterbg.

Hugo Münsterberg (1863-1916), deutsch-amerikanischer Psychologe und Philosoph

Hugo Münsterberg (1863-1916), German-American psychologist and philosopher

"Since 1 August I have dedicated at least eight hours per day to the war"

Cambridge Mass. 25 February 1915

Dear colleague,

Your letter of January 29th has – relatively fast – reached me today, and that since this afternoon a Nordic steamboat is departing and I still have two dozen letters to finish before its departure, I will limit myself to a few words.

Bell's situation has concerned me intensely since September. I sent in October to the German Embassy in Washington a detailed assessment, with exactly the same recommendation, namely, that Bell commits himself to go immediately to Harvard and to stay here. The Ambassador forwarded [this] with an emphatic recommendation to the Foreign Ministry and, then, later even mentioned [this] in Berlin, but we have not heard a word since. Something peculiar must be happening behind the scenes; I will like to try one more time. I would like to mention by the way that my colleague Perry, who Bell wants to visit, is apparently the most shameless detractor against Germany here in the circle of the university; he speaks nothing other than about Germany's dishonour and crime; I have broken off contact. In contrast, Royce is wonderful and full of the finest understanding.

There is an intenstity of tension during these past days which is barely supportable; the slightest incident with a submarine could lead here to a declaration of war. I have since 1 August dedicated at least eight hours per day to the war, and what I do on the stage is the smallest part: and yet, how infinitely more should have been done. My first small book The War and America, which appeared in September, is now by the way in Germany in an edition from Tauchnitz, and end of March will be here, and then later, with Tauchnitz, the continuation will appear: The Peace and America. I mention this, because your letter in the final lines contained such an impressive characterisation of the situation, that I would like to print a few paragraphs from among the voices in Germany; of course, I will not name any names – the intention is only to bring to expression the moral content of the German People's spirit: letters are therefore most effective.

It was for me a great pleasure to receive a sign of life from you during these tumultous times. I hope that for you, your sons, and the Fatherland, destiny will be favorable.

Respectfully,
Yours,
Hugo Münsterbg.

„The Peace and America"

> Mit herzlichem Dank
> (s. Seite 222)
> von Hugo Münsterberg
>
> Cambridge Mass.
> Ostern 1915.

Auszug aus einem Brief von Husserl an Hugo Münsterberg (in englischer Übersetzung veröffentlicht in: Hugo Münsterberg, The Peace and America, New York and London 1915, S. 222-224). – Husserls Exemplar trägt die Widmung „Mit herzlichem Dank (s<iehe> Seite 222) von Hugo Münsterberg, Cambridge, Mass. Ostern 1915"

Excerpt from a letter from Husserl to Hugo Münsterberg (published in English translation in: Hugo Münsterberg, The Peace and America, New York and London 1915, 222-224). – Husserl's copy includes the dedication "With heartfelt thanks (see page 222) from Hugo Münsterberg, Cambridge, Mass. Easter 1915"

„Kriegssommer 1915"

Ausgewählte phän<omenologische> Probleme.
Gött<inger> Vorlesungen.
Kriegssommer 1915
1. Theil 1-42
[2. 43-69 in besonderem Umschlag]
Darin Argu<umente> z<um>
Transc<dendentalen> Idealism<us>

"War Summer 1915"

Selected phe[nomenological] problems.
Gött[ingen] lectures
War summer 1915
1 Part 1-42
[2. 43-69 in a special folder]
Argu[ments for] Transc[endental] Ideal[ism]

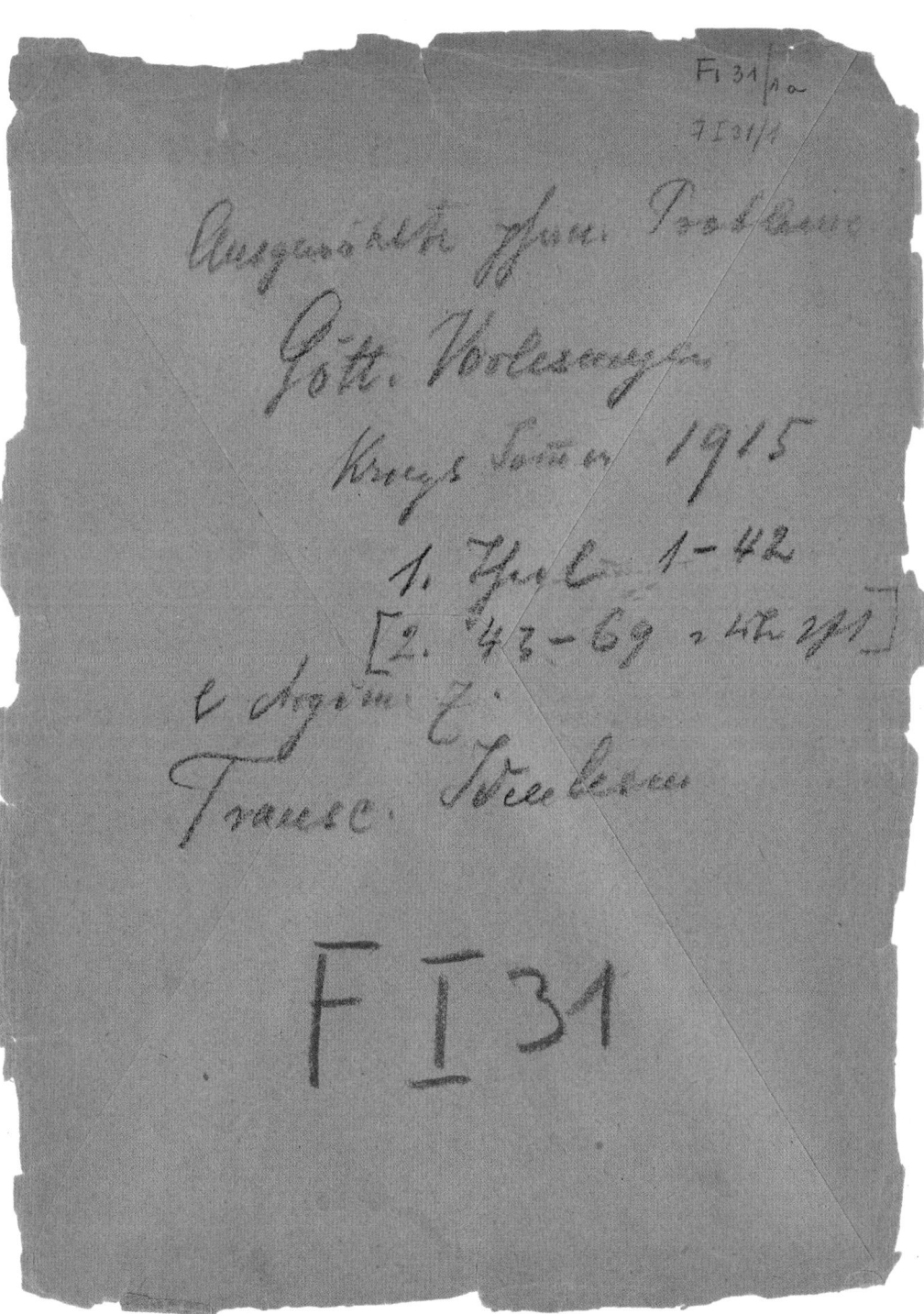

Umschlagsblatt von Husserls Vorlesung „Ausgewählte phänomenologische Probleme" aus dem Sommersemester 1915

Cover-page from Husserl's lecture "Selected Phenomenological Problems" from Summer Semester 1915

„War das Kriegspsychose?"

"Was that war psychosis?"

Am Rand eines Vorlesungs-Manuskripts notierte Husserl mit Blaustift: „Hier habe ich aber die ganze Lehre von der Intersubjektivität vergessen! Wie in der ganzen Vorlesung <von 1915>. War das Kriegspsychose?"

In the margin of a lecture-manuscript Husserl noted in blue-pencil: "Here I have forgotten the entire theory of intersubjectivity! As in the entire lecture-course <from 1915>. Was that war psychosis?"

„Erste Freiburger Zeit (Kriegszeit)"

Instinktives Tun. Triebhandlungen. Instinktive – erworbene Triebe. Instinktives Tun, „zwecklos". Folgen von Betätigungen, die in ihrer Einheit etwas zuwege bringen (als Einheit einer „Handlung"), was nicht vorher als Ziel vorgestellt war, weder anschaulich, noch unanschaulich. Das schließt nicht aus, dass wir sagen, die handelnde Instinktintention (die der Triebhandlung) sei fundiert in einer vorstellenden Intention, aber nicht in einer solchen, die im Voraus Bestimmtes (sei es auch nur allgemeinen Zügen nach Bestimmtes), im Voraus Bekanntes meint, sondern in dieser Hinsicht völlig unbestimmt ist, vielmehr Bestimmtheit erst durch die Erfüllung sich zueignet. Trotzdem ist die Vorstellung auf das in der Erfüllung ihr Zuzueignende „gerichtet" und auf nichts anderes, ebenso wie die Triebhandlung nicht Beliebiges realisiert, sondern immer wieder bei gleichem phänomenologischen Gehalt der Ausgangsintention „dasselbe", nämlich typisch Gleichartiges. Diese Gleichartigkeit ist vorgezeichnet durch die dunkle und unbestimmte Vorstellung. Wie ist es bei erworbenen Trieben? Es treibt mich zur Arbeit; oder inmitten der Arbeit fühle ich den Trieb hinauszugehen, mich in der Natur zu ergehen oder Klavier zu spielen und dgl. Hier mag es an einer klaren Vorstellung des Klavierspiels fehlen; mag die Vorstellung selbst eine völlig unanschauliche sein <…>

"First Period in Freiburg (Wartime)"

Instinctive doing. Drive comportments. Instinctive – acquired drives. Instinctive doing, "purposeless." Consequences of actions that bring about something in their unity (as the unity of an "action"), which was not previously represented as a goal, whether intuitively or non-intuitively. That does not exclude that we can say that the acting intention of instincts (belonging to the drive-comportment) could be founded in a representing intention, but not of that kind that [was] in advance something determinate (even if only in general traits according to something determinate), intends something in advance, but that in this regard is entirely indeterminate, and rather determination only is attained through fulfillment. Nonetheless, is the representation "directed" towards what it acquires in fulfillment and to nothing else, much as the drive-comportment does not realize anything arbitrarily, but is always in terms of phenomenological content the starting intention "the same," that is, typically the same. This homogeneity is characterized by the obscure and indeterminate representation. How is it with acquired drives? I am driven to work; or in the midst of the work, I feel the urge to go out into nature or to play the piano, and so on. There is here lacking a clear representation of piano playing; even if the representation itself may be entirely invisible [...]

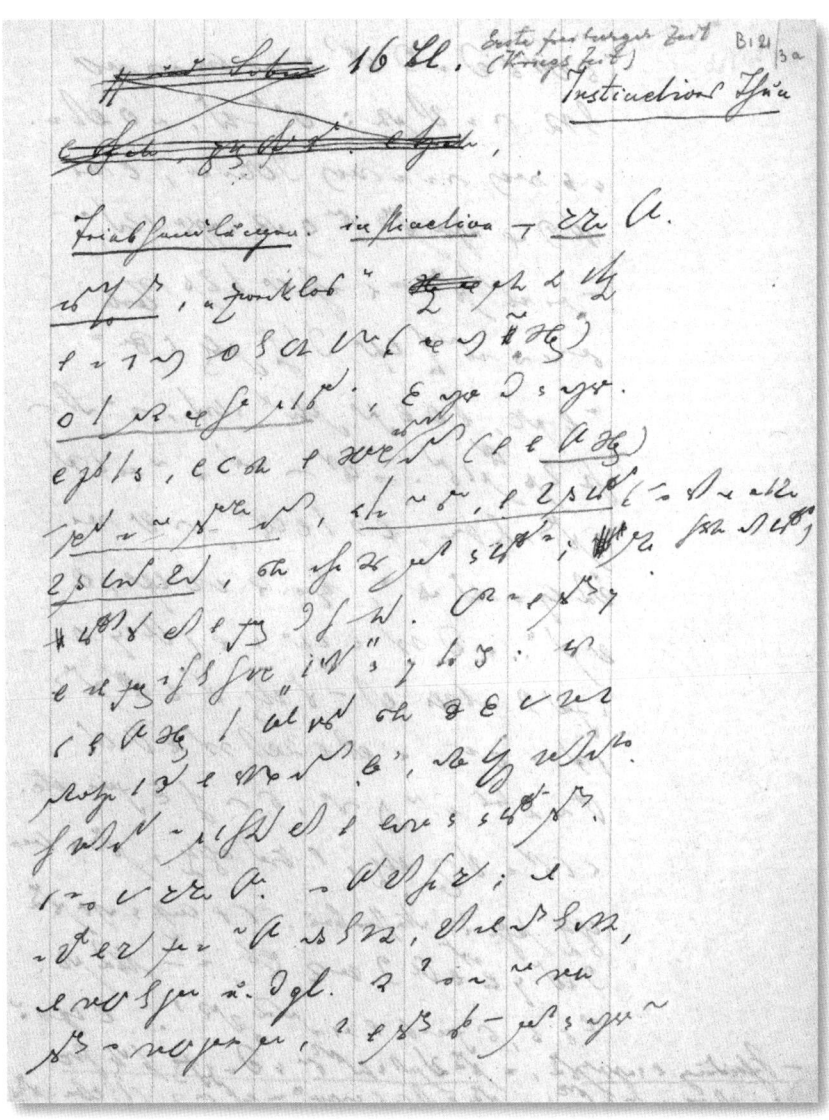

Erste Seite eines insgesamt 16 Blätter umfassenden Manuskripts von Husserl über „Instinktives Tun." An den oberen Rand hat Husserl mit Bleistift notiert: „Erste Freiburger Zeit (Kriegszeit)"

First page from 16 pages of a manuscript by Husserl on "instinctive doing." On the top margin Husserl noted in pencil: "First Period in Freiburg (Wartime)"

„Die beispiellose Verlogenheit der amerik‹anischen› Presse, die Schmutzfluth der Verläumdung"

Göttingen hoher Weg 7.
2. Juni 1915.

Liebe Flora!
Dein Brief aus dem Monat März kam mir mit einer unglaublichen Verspätung zu, u. da ich zudem in letzter Zeit sehr schwer zum Briefschreiben komme, so erhältst Du meine Antwort erst jetzt, nach Monaten. Ich habe mich über Deine Berichte über die Schulerfolge Deiner Kinder immer sehr gefreut, und ganz besonders über die Erfolge der höheren Studien. Daß Du Deine Kinder so ernst erzogen und, wie Du schon sagen darfst, Ihre Zukunft dauernd gesichert, ihnen höhere Lebensstellungen eröffnet hast bzw. ihr Streben dahin erfolgreich gelenkt hast – dessen darfst Du Dich mit Stolz rühmen und so hast Du Dir selbst ein glückliches Alter verdient. Daß Du Deine schweren Schicksale so getragen und zum Guten gewendet hast, erfüllt mich mit großer Hochachtung und Genugthuung. Es ist auch schön, daß Du so bescheiden schreibst und das feiner empfindenden Naturen peinliche Hinausgezerrtwerden in die / Publicität schreiender Zeitungssensationen als ein diesmal leider unvermeidliches Übel bezeichnest. Übrigens war mir der Zeitungsausschnitt amusant genug; auch als Kennzeichnung der unsympathischen Art amerikanischer Presse interessant.

Wenn Marguerite mathematische Wissenschaften studieren will, so kommt für sie wohl in erster Linie Göttingen in Betracht – es ist in diesen Fächern die z. Z‹t›. bedeutendste deutsche Universität u. wohl auch darin die erste der Welt. Auch in der Physik ist Göttingen sehr hervorragend, doch kämen darin auch andere Universitäten, wie Leyden, Berlin u.sw. in ernste Erwägung. Zwei Semester sind übrigens für ein Doktorat, worauf es wohl hinauslaufen soll, nicht ausreichend. Kommt M‹arguerite› nach Göttingen, so werde ich selbstverständlich alles thun, was ich irgend vermag, sie zu berathen u. zu fördern, selbstverständlich wird sie auch in meinem Hause als Deine Tochter herzliches Entgegenkommen finden. /

Schade ist freilich, daß ihr Stipendium nicht in die Zeit vor dem Kriege fiel: Wie viel Freundlichkeit hat man in Deutschland den vielen studierenden Amerikanern der U.S. entgegengebracht, wie hat man sie fast verhätschelt, geleitet von uralten, nie getrübten Sympathien, die Deutschland u. die Union verbanden. Dank der amerikan<ischen> „Neutralität", die tausenden und aber tausenden unserer herrlichen Jungens das Leben kostet, oder sie zu Krüppeln macht, sind unsere Gefühle für Amerika radikal geändert, u. das werden die herüberkommenden Studierenden in Form kühler Ablehnung wohl fühlen müssen. Die beispiellose Verlogenheit der amerik<anischen> Presse, die Schmutzfluth der Verläumdung, die unser Volk und Heer umspritzt, während es in unerhörten Heldenthaten u. Siegen einer Welt von Feinden Trotz bietet – u. das in dem gerechtesten Kampfe, den ein Volk je zu kämpfen hatte – ebenso / die Haltung der sog. amerik<anischen> Intelligenz u. seiner salbungsvollen Politiker – das werden wir, das wird die jetzt lebende Generation nicht mehr vergessen können. Ich wundere mich übrigens, daß Du, die in Begeisterung für deutsches Wesen und in Liebe für die altösterr<eichische> Heimat erzogen warst, kein Wort der Sympathie geäußert hast; und nach allem was ich schon vor dem Krieg über den Geist von Bryn-Mawr gehört habe, muß ich befürchten, daß Deine Töchter von dort aus alles, nur nicht Verständnis u. Liebe für die (wahrhaft große!) deutsche Art kennen gelernt haben. Vielleicht darf ich aber hoffen, daß Ihr Eltern Treue gehalten u. Eure Kinder auch darin recht erzogen habt, so daß sie sich ihrer deutschen Abkunft nicht schämen, sondern sich ihrer rühmen. Kommen sie herüber in gut deutscher Gesinnung, so werden sie hier natürlich überall herzlich willkommen sein u. nichts von den antiamerikanischen Reaktionen zu fühlen bekommen, die sonst nicht fehlen können. Inzwischen möge M<arguerite> auch nicht an der Übung in deutscher Sprache es ermangeln lassen und sich gehörig umthun im deutschen Geistesleben. Dann wird der Aufenthalt in D<eutschland> ihr ein / vielfältiger Gewinn fürs Leben sein.

Unseren Jungens geht es gottlob gut. Gerhart steht als Kriegsfreiwilliger von Anfang an bei Ypern und hat dort die schweren, ruhmvollen Kämpfe und unglaublichen Strapazen mitgemacht. Neben ihm kämpfte Wolfgang (der jüngere, 19jährige), der sich von seiner schweren Verwundung, die er Ende Februar erhalten hat (Lungenschuß), gut erholt und Mitte d.M. wieder in die Fronte ausrückt. Er ist Inhaber des eisernen Kreuzes.

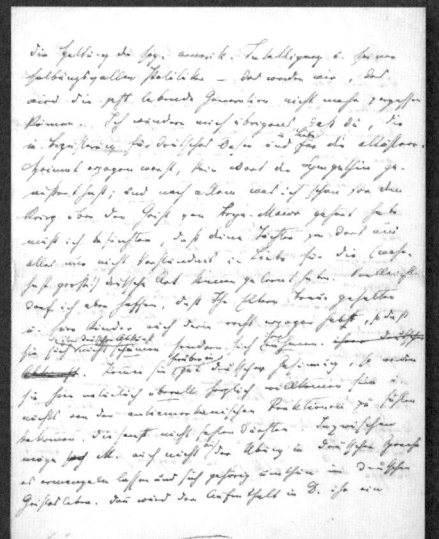
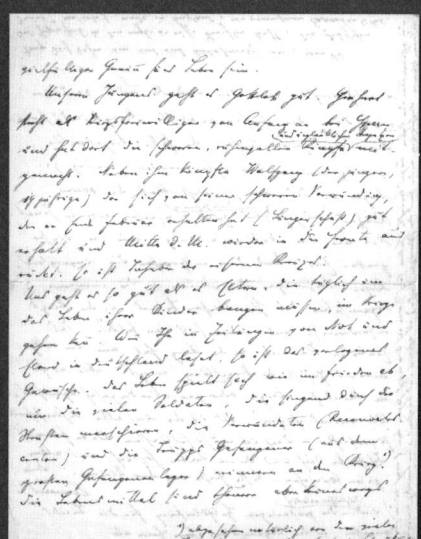

Brief von Husserl an Flora Darkow, 2. VI. 1915

Letter from Husserl to Flora Darkow, 2 June 1915

Uns geht es so gut als es Eltern, die täglich um das Leben ihrer Kinder bangen müssen, im Kriege gehen kann. Wenn Ihr in Zeitungen von Not und Elend in Deutschland leset, so ist das verlogenes Gewäsche. Das Leben spielt sich wie im Frieden ab, nur die vielen Soldaten, die singend durch die Straßen marschieren, die Verwundeten (Reconvalescenten) und die Trupps Gefangener (aus dem großen Gefangenenlager) erinnern an den Krieg.* Die Lebensmittel sind theurer, aber keineswegs / unerschwinglich geworden und die Leute verdienen viel durch die hochaufgeblühte Kriegsindustrie. Die Siegeszuversicht, der feste Siegeswille ist allgemein, die Opfer werden freudig getragen, u. das betrifft nicht bloß die oberen Klassen, es geht diese Gesinnung bis zum einfachen Arbeiter hinab. Nie war die Nation so einig, wie in dieser großen Zeit. Und dem entsprechen die unvergleichlichen Leistungen der Nation in der inneren Organisation des staatlichen Lebens u. der Kriegserfordernisse, und andererseits im Felde.** Das Eintreten Italiens in den Krieg hat nur ein allgemeines Gefühl der Verachtung erregt, aber nicht im Mindesten Sorge oder gar Niedergeschlagenheit. „Wir werdens schaffen", das ist die uns alle beherrschende Zuversicht. – Doch ich muß schließen, liebe Flora. Ich grüße Dich und Deine Lieben herzlich mit allen guten Wünschen. Beste Grüße von den Meinen.

Dein
Edmund.

Die officiellen deutschen Tagesberichte haben sich, wie ich Dir noch sagen kann (nach einer steten aufmerksamen Nachprüfung an Hand der schweizer Presse), als ehrlich und durchaus glaubwürdig erwiesen. Sorge Dich daher um uns und Altösterreich nie, wenn Du das Gegentheil in den engl<ischen> u. russ<ischen> Berichten liest. Die „deutschen Greuel" natürlich „made in England", ein vornehmer Exportartikel. /

* abgesehen natürlich von den vielen Trauerkleidern u. dem Ernste der Lebensstimmung
**und desgleichen natürlich in der großartigen Hilfsleistung für die Bundesgenossen, in der Organisation ihrer Heere etc.

"The unprecedented mendacity of the American press, the filthy deluge of defamation"

Göttingen hoher Weg 7.
2 June 1915.

Dear Flora!
Your letter from the month of March came to me with an unbelievable delay, and since I have been in these past days unable to find time to write letters, so you shall receive my answer only now, after some months. I am always very happy to hear your reports about your children's schooling, and especially about their sucess with their higher studies. That you have raised your children so seriously and, as you are right to have mentioned, have continuously secured their future, have opened up for them higher positions in life, or have guided their efforts successfully, you can proudly boast of this, and so you have for yourself earned a happy age. That you have borne your heavy fates and used them for good, fills me with great respect and satisfaction. It is also wonderful that you write so modestly, and that the subtler sentient natures are embarrassed to be dragged out into the publicity of screaming newspaper sensations as an unfortunate evil of this time. By the way, the newspaper excerpt was amusing enough; also as an indication of the unsympathetic nature of the American press.

If Marguerite wants to study mathematical sciences, so comes into immediate consideration for her Göttingen – it is in these disciplines at the moment the most significant German university and also the first in the world. Also in physics, Göttingen is very excellent, but so would enter into consideration other universities, for example Leyden, Berlin, etc. By the way, two semesters for a doctorat, what you are probably aiming for, are not enough. If Marguerite comes to Göttingen, I will of course do everything, what ever I can, to advise her and to mentor her, and naturally she would be warmly received as your daughter in my home.

It goes without saying that it is unfortunate that her stipendium did not occur in the time before the war: how much joy one had in Germany for the many American students coming from the US, we were so indulged by these students, defined by venerable and never over-shadowed sympathies, which bound together Germany and the Union. Thanks to American "neutrality," which cost lives of thousands upon thousands of our boys, or made them into cripples, our feelings for America has radically changed, and the students who come over here must feel this cold rejection. The unprecedented mendacity of the American press, with its filthy deluge of defamation, which colors our people, while the outrageous heroic deeds and victories of the world of enemies are passed over in silence, and that [against] the most rigtheous combat, in which a people have ever engaged, even the behaviour of the so-called American intelligence with its unctuous politicians [is something] which our present generation shall not forget soon. I wonder by the way, that you, in the enthusiasm for the German character and love for the old Austrian homeland where you grew up, have expressed not a word of sympathy; and after all what I have heard before the war about the spirit of Bryn-Mawr, I must fear that your daughters learned much there, but not an understanding and love for the (truly great!) German manner. Maybe I should hope, however, that her parents remained loyal and that your children were also properly educated so that they will not take shame in their German origin, but instead take pride. If they come over here with a good German attitude, of course, they will be here warmly welcomed everywhere, and they will feel nothing in the form of Anti-American reaction, which otherwise is not lacking. By the way, M[arguerite] will not lack for opportunities in the German language and will do well in partaking in German spiritual life. Her stay in Germany would thus be a manifold gain for her life.

Our boys are doing well, God be praised. Gerhart volunteered for the war from the begininng at Ypres and had to experience there tough and illustrious combat and unbelievable effort. Next to him fought Wolfgang (the youngest, 19 years), who received at the end of February a serious wound (shot in the lungs), and recovered well and will be sent back to the front at the middle of the month. He is the recipient of the Iron Cross.

We are doing as well as can be, as parents who must fear daily for the lives of their children in war. When you read in the newspapers of the hardships and misery in Germany, this is all lying non-sense. Life goes on just as in times of peace, only the many soldiers, who march through the streets singing, the wounded (and those recovering) and the captured troops (from the large prisoner of war camp) are reminders of the war.* Groceries are more expensive, but have not at all become prohibitive and people earn a good deal due to the booming war industry. The certainty of victory, the resolute will for victory is everywhere, and the sacrifices are joyfully endured, and this does not just affect the upper-class, for this spirit extends to the simple worker.

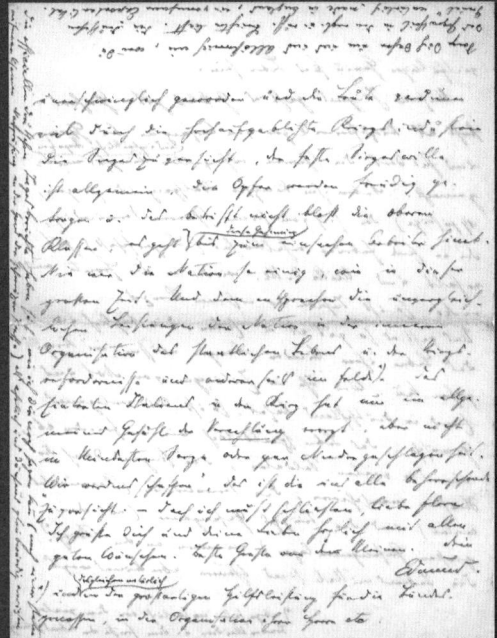

Never was a Nation so unified as in these great times. And in sync with the incomparable accomplishments of the Nation in the internal organization of State life and the demands of war, and on the other hand, on the front.** The entrance of Italy in the war has provoked a general feeling of mistrust, but not the least concern or even a sense of defeat. "We'll pull through," that is for everyone the dominant conviction. I must, however, come to a close, dear Flora. I send you my greetings and to your loved ones warmly all the best. Best wishes from mine.

Yours,
Edmund.

The official German daily reports have proved to be honest and quite credible, as I can report to you (after a constant careful validation by way of the Swiss press). Therefore, don't worry about us and old Austria, if you read the opposite in Engl[ish] and Russ[ian] reports. The "German abomination," of course, "made in England," a distinguished export article.

* apart from, of course, the many mourning clothes, the seriousness of life
** and likewise, of course, in the great aid to the Germans, in the organization of its armies, etc.

„Derselbe wahrhafte Krieg, der die Kämpfenden trennt, verbindet sie in der ethischen Gesinnung"

<...> werden unsere Geistesarbeiter mit verdoppelter Liebe dem langentbehrten Ideenreiche zustreben, und was sie dann an der geheiligten Heimstätte reiner Humanität erschaut, werden sie in glühendem Eifer hinübertragen in die verwüstete Kulturwelt: auf daß sie neu, und wie wir es alle ersehnen, in ungleich hellerer und reinerer Schönheit wiedererstehe. Werden wir ähnliche Erwartungen nicht für die Besten aus den übrigen, auch den uns feindlichen Völkern hegen dürfen? Sie alle, die dann sehnsuchtsvoll und frommen Sinnes den Tempel reiner Idealität betreten – von welchen der feindlichen Seiten sie auch kommen mögen – werden sich in ihm zusammenfinden als echte Gotteskinder, als Brüder im Geiste und der Wahrheit. In tiefer Scham der unerhörten Erniedrigungen gedenkend, die noch in diesem zwanzigsten Jahrhundert die Idee der Humanität erfahren konnte, werden in ihren Herzen leidenschaftliche Triebkräfte zum Aufbau einer neuen Menschheitswelt aufwärts streben, einer Welt, in der alle Nationen sich als freie Individualitäten entfalten und sich doch immerfort als verpflichtete Genossen eines ethisch organisierten Völkerverbundes fühlen. Diese Menschheit ist schon in uns geboren, soweit wir dem unum necessarium für diese Zeit gerecht werden. Was uns das Schicksal auszufechten heißt, wollen und werden wir als „wahrhafte Krieger" ausfechten. Was aber zudem notthut, ist es frei anzuerkennen: Derselbe wahrhafte Krieg, der die Kämpfenden trennt, verbindet sie in der ethischen Gesinnung. Also für sie – soweit sie vom Ethos des wahrhaften Krieges erfüllt sind – dürfen wir keinen Haß hegen, sondern nur Achtung. Wenn also Morgen der im voraus gesegnete Friede anbricht, wenn ausgefochten ist, was ausgefochten werden musste, dann können wir uns – wir alle, die dieses Geistes Kinder sind – den schöneren Aufgaben gemeinsamer Kulturarbeit wieder zuwenden, einander hilfreich die Hände reichen und uns an dem auf allen Seiten und unter wechselseitiger Förderung Errungenen freuen. – Könnte der Phänomenologe, dessen vornehmster Beruf es doch ist, nach den reinen Ursprüngen der Vernunft zu forschen, könnte er, der geschworene Feind aller Phrase, aller dumpfen Vorurtheile, aller Unklarheiten, aller sinnverwirrenden Leidenschaften, in diesen Dingen anders urtheilen? Lasst uns also jenen aufrechten, thatenfrohen Optimismus bekennen, der das Erbgut aller frei Geborenen ist. Der Hinblick auf die Fülle positiver Kräfte des Guten, die sich im Kriege in unzähligen Bekundungen eines echten Heroismus, einer edlen Nächstenliebe, auch einer ritterlichen Haltung gegen den Feind bewährten, giebt ihm einen festen Halt. Und ist dieser Optimismus, dessen Kern nicht schwächlich sentimentaler Glaube, sondern thatkräftiger ethischer Wille ist, nicht die Urquelle aller Verwirklichungen höchster socialer Güter?

Briefentwurf von Husserl (an unbekannten Adressaten), ca. 1917/1918

Draft for a letter from Husserl (to an unknown recipient), around 1917-1918

"The same genuine war, which separates the combatants, binds them in an ethical attitude"

[...] will our intellectual workers with double the love strive for the long wished realm of ideas, and what they then see in the holy homestead of pure humanity, they will carry over with glowing enthusiasm to the devastated world of culture, from which they might newly resurrect, as we all desire, an incomparably luminescent and pure beauty. Would we not have similar expectations for the best of the remaining nations, also for the nations, which are hostile against us? All those who enter the temple of pure idealism with ardent desire and virtuous sense – from what ever hostile side they might happen to come – will be united in this tempel as the true children of God, as brothers in spirit and truth. Mindful of the profound shame of unprecedented humiliations, which the Idea of Humanity experienced in this twentieth century, there will be kindled, striving upwards, in their hearts a passionate driving force for the construction of a new world of humanity, a world in which all nations unfold as free individuals, and yet always as compulsorily comrades in an ethically organized community of nations. This humanity has already been born within us as far as we are concerned, as the rightful *unum necessarium* for this time. Whatever fate might bring against us, we will and shall fight as "true warriors." But what is also necessary is freely to acknowledge that the same genuine war which separates the combatants, binds them in an ethical attitude. Thus for them, as far as they are filled with the ethos of genuine war, we must not hate, but only respect. When tomorrow blessed peace dawns, when what has been fought, what must be fought for – all of us who are children of this spirit – can turn back to the more beautiful tasks of common cultural work, and extend to each other helpful hands, and rejoice on all sides and in reciprocal challenge. Could the phenomenologist, whose most important vocation is to search for the pure origins of reason, could he, the sworn enemy of all empty phrases, of all dull prejudices, of all ambiguities, of all senseless passions, judge in such matters otherwise? Let us, then, confess to an upstanding and joyfully done optimism which is the inheritance of all those who are born of freedom. With regard to the abundance of positive forces of the good, which proved themselves in the war through countless declarations of genuine heroism, a noble charity, and a chivalrous attitude towards the enemy, give those [who are born free] a firm stance. And is this optimism, the core of which is not weak sentimental faith, but an active ethical will, not the source for all the realizations of the highest social goods?

Edmund Husserl

„Fichtes Menschheitsideal. (Kurse für Kriegstheilnehmer)"

3 Vorlesungen über Fichtes Menschheitsideal (Kurse für Kriegstheilnehmer (staatswissenschaftliche) der Universität Freiburg, 8.-17. Nov<ember> 1917) u<nd> 14.-16. I. 1918; 6., 7., 9. XI. <1918> wiederholt für Akademiker aus anderen philos<ophischen> Fak<ultäten>

"Fichte's Ideal of Humanity. (Course for Participants in the War)"

3 Lectures on Fichte's Ideal of Humanity (course for participants in the war (political science) at the University of Freiburg, 8 – 17 November 1917) and 14 – 16. I. 1918; 6, 7, 9. XI. <1918> repeated for academics from other philos[ophical] fac[ulties]

Umschlagsblatt von Husserls Vorlesungen über Fichte, die er 1917 und 1918 in Freiburg gehalten hat

Cover of Husserl's lectures on Fichte, which he held in Freiburg in 1917 and 1918

„Das preußische Verdienstkreuz für Kriegshilfe"

"Prussian Service Cross for War Assistance"

Der Minister des Kultus und Unterrichts.

Karlsruhe, den 22. April 1918.

Euer Hochwohlgeboren

beehre ich mich ergebenst in Kenntnis zu setzen, daß Seine Majestät der Kaiser und König von Preußen Allergnädigst geruht haben, Ihnen in Anerkennung Ihrer verdienstvollen Mitwirkung bei den von der Armee-Abteilung B veranstalteten Hochschulkursen das preußische Verdienstkreuz für Kriegshilfe zu verleihen.

Indem ich mich freue, Euer Hochwohlgeboren die genannte Auszeichnung übersenden zu können, spreche ich Ihnen meinen aufrichtigen Glückwunsch zu derselben aus. Gleichzeitig ersuche ich, den Empfang auf der beiliegenden Standesnachweisung, die ich ausgefüllt dem Ministerium zurückzusenden bitte, gefl. bescheinigen zu wollen. Das Besitz=

An Seine Hochwohlgeboren
Herrn Geh.Hofrat
Professor Dr.Husserl,
an der Universität
H e i d e l b e r g.

1918 erhält Husserl für seine „verdienstvolle Mitwirkung bei den von der Armee-Abteilung B veranstalteten Hochschulkursen <über Fichte> das preußische Verdienstkreuz für Kriegshilfe" verliehen.

In 1918, Husserl received the Prussian Service Cross for War Assistance for his "meritorious participation in the University courses organized [on Fichte] by the Army Division B"

„gerichtet auf einen reineren Idealen gemäßen Neubau des Staates u. der Nation"

Freiburg 28/XI 1918
Sehr verehrter Herr Kollege!
Ein Exemplar des Bonner Aufrufes hat gestern bei unserer Universität circuliert und ich habe dieses natürlich mit unterschrieben. Daher habe ich, das erübrigte sich ja dadurch, Ihre und Herrn Coll. Litzmanns nicht mit meiner Unterschrift versehen u. zurückgeschickt. Jedenfalls danke ich Ihnen herzlich und erwiedere Ihren sehr freundlichen Gruß. Möge die Bonner Action nun helfen. Allmälig muß, so möchte ich hoffen, die Vernunft u. Gerechtigkeit wieder zu praktischer Kraft erwachen. Wir wollen nicht versagen, da überall die innere Lähmung sich löst und ein neuer Strom von Energien in den Seelen zu pulsieren beginnt, gerichtet auf einen reineren Idealen gemäßen Neubau des Staates u. der Nation.
Ihr aufricht<i>g ergebener
EHusserl

"directed towards purer Ideals for the new construction of the State and the Nation"

Freiburg 28 November 1918
Dear colleague!
A copy of the appeal from Bonn circulated yesterday at our university and I naturally signed it. I therefore did not sign your and Herr colleague Litzmann's [copy of the pamphlet], because it was not necessary anymore, and thus sent it back. In any case, I thank you warmly and send you my friendly wishes. Let us hope that this action from Bonn might help. I would hope that reason and justice gradually awakens once again into being a practical force. We do not want to despair, because everywhere the inner paralysis slackens and a new stream of energy begins to pulse through souls, directed towards purer Ideals for the new construction of the State and the Nation.
Yours respectfully
EHusserl

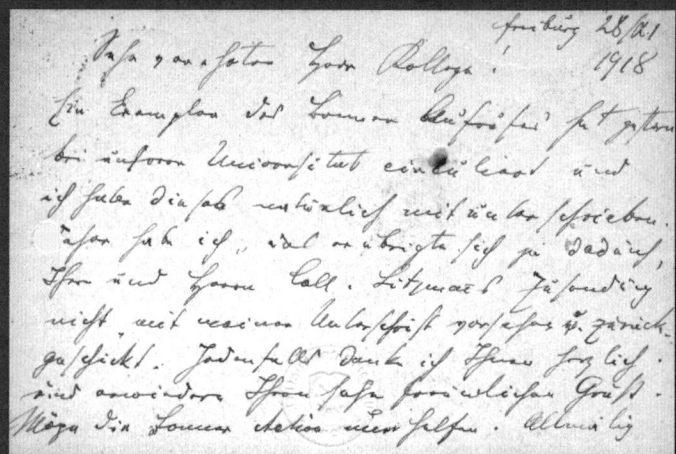

Husserl an Adolf Dyroff, 28. XI. 1918. – Es handelt sich wohl um Husserls Unterstützung für einen Aufruf, der sich gegen die Abdankung des deutschen Kaisers am 9. November 1918 richtet

Husserl to Adolf Dyroff, 28 November 1918. Most likely, Husserl supported an appeal against the abdication of the German Kaiser on November 9, 1918

Kriegsnotsemester 1919

Emergency War Semester 1919

Im ersten Halbjahr 1919 werden an der Universität Freiburg Kriegsnotsemester für Soldaten eingerichtet; siehe dazu die nebenstehenden Bemerkungen aus dem Vorlesungsverzeichnis: „Das Kriegsnotsemester für Kriegsteilnehmer bietet in allen Fakultäten die für einen geordneten Studienbetrieb erforderlichen Vorlesungen und Übungen; es soll den Kriegsteilnehmern als Studiensemester angerechnet werden, insofern sie durch Kriegsdienste an der normalen Vollendung ihrer Studien behindert waren, also einen zeitlichen Verlust erlitten haben."

In the first half of 1919 at the University of Freiburg, an emergency war semester was established for soldiers; see the accompanying remarks from the lecture catalogue: "The emergency war semester offers for participants in the war from all faculties all required lectures for an orderly course of studies; it should be counted for all participants in the war as a semester of studies, insofar as the normal completion of their studies was hindered by their war-service, and thus a loss of time."

Edmund Husserl

„Für die Unabhängigkeit des Geistes" – „die Hand zur Versöhnung"

"For the independence of spirit" – "the hand towards reconciliation"

Husserl unterzeichnet den Aufruf von Romain Rolland für die Unabhängigkeit des Geistes, der im September 1919 von der Liga zur Beförderung der Humanität verschickt wurde. Der Aufruf wurde von Husserl mit folgendem handschriftlichem Text weiter geleitet: „Herrn Prof. Bolza mit freundlichen Grüßen und der Bitte durch Unterschrift eventuell die Zustimmung zum Rolland'schen Aufruf auszudrücken und wenn möglich bei Gleichgesinnten Unterschriften zu sammeln und dann den Aufruf an mich gütigst zurückgehen zu lassen. 5. X. 19. EHusserl".

Die Liga zur Beförderung der Humanität, als die deutsche Gruppe einer weltumfassenden Organisation aller geistigen Arbeiter sieht ihre Aufgabe darin, ohne Rücksicht auf irgendwelche Parteirichtung diejenigen zu sammeln, denen daran liegt, die allgemein menschlichen und geistigen Beziehungen unter den Mitgliedern eines Landes und unter den Ländern verschiedener Sprache zu fördern; sie will ein nationales Comité für internationale Humanität sein.

Wir wollen nicht in den politischen Kampf eintreten, sondern meinen hier müsse jeder Einzelne, entsprechend seiner Weltanschauung vollkommen frei handeln. Wir wollen nur die Arena für diesen Kampf reinfegen und uns bemühen, dass dieser notwendige Kampf nicht mit den Mitteln der Lüge und der Gewalt, sondern nach Möglichkeit mit den Mitteln der Ueberzeugung und des Rechtes ausgefochten werde.

Jeder, der an die Kraft des Wortes und die Macht der Vernunft glaubt, der die Wahrheit und das Recht liebt, und in deren Verteidigung den einzigen Ausweg aus den jetzigen Wirrnissen sieht, ist daher als Mitstreiter willkommen. Wenn sich alle, die nur dem Geiste dienen wollen, vereinigen, dann wird dadurch die Grundlage zu jenem wahren Völkerbunde geschaffen, in dem keine Gewalt herrschen darf, sondern gleiches Recht gilt für alle Kulturinteressen der einzelnen Nationen.

Im besonderen aber wollen wir in Verbindung mit gleichstrebenden Vereinigungen des Auslandes (z.B. der unter Anatole France stehenden Gesellschaft Clarté in Frankreich) eine Vertretung aller geistig Strebenden sein, in der jeder den anderen achtet, auch wenn seine Ueberzeugung ihn zu anderem Ziele führt.

Eine bindende Verfassung haben wir noch nicht, wollen sie uns auch noch nicht geben! – Das soll erst die Gemeinschaft derjenigen tun, die sich zu dieser versöhnenden Aufgabe zusammentun werden. Wir wollen nur aufrufen und vorbereiten! – Um dies aber zu können, möge jeder, dem das angedeutete Ziel am Herzen liegt, seinen Namen senden – evtl. auf der Vorderseite der beiliegenden Karte – an die

Geschäftsstelle der
Liga zur Beförderung der Humanität
Berlin W., Uhlandstr. 145

Liga zur Beförderung der Humanität

Berlin, im September 1919

Sehr geehrter Herr!

Der umstehende Aufruf Romain Rollands ist auf seine Veröffentlichung in den Zeitungen hin bis jetzt von einer grossen Anzahl Deutscher unterzeichnet worden, von denen einige umstehend angeführt sind.

Da aber dieser Aufruf, mit dem uns Frankreich die Hand zur Versöhnung entgegenstreckt, und der im Ausland von einer grossen Zahl bedeutender Wissenschaftler und Künstler gebilligt wurde, nur dann seinen Zweck – der Völkerversöhnung zu dienen – wirklich erfüllen kann, wenn unter ihm so ziemlich alle Namen von gutem Klang in Deutschland stehen, haben wir den Aufruf an etwa tausend Männer und Frauen gesandt, die auf ihrem Gebiete führend sind, und bitten auch Sie, auf beiliegender Karte Ihre Unterschrift zu geben.

Falls Sie die Absicht des Aufrufs billigen, wären wir Ihnen dankbar, wenn Sie ihn unter Persönlichkeiten, die Ihnen geeignet scheinen, verbreiten würden; zumal wir uns bewusst sind, dass die von uns getroffene Auswahl der Adressaten keine erschöpfende und allgemeingiltige ist, sondern von unserer zufälligen und subjektiven Personenkenntnis abhängt.

Hochachtungsvoll

Professor Wilhelm Foerster
Bornim b. Potsdam

Husserl signed Romain Rolland's appeal for the independence of spirit, issued in September 1919 by the League for the Advancement of Humanity. The appeal was forwarded by Husserl with the hand-written note: "To Prof. Bolza with friendly greetings and the request to endorse with a signature Rolland's appeal and if possible to gather signatures from other supporters and then to send back to me. 5. X. 19. EHusserl."

„Ein Neues muß werden"

Erneuerung. Ihr Problem und ihre Methode

Erneuerung ist der allgemeine Ruf in unserer leidensvollen Gegenwart und ist es im Gesamtbereich der europäischen Kultur. Der Krieg, der sie seit dem Jahre 1914 verwüstet und seit 1918 nur statt der militärischen Zwangsmittel die „feineren" der seelischen Torturen und der moralisch depravierenden wirtschaftlichen Nöte gewählt hat, hat die innere Unwahrheit, Sinnlosigkeit dieser Kultur enthüllt. Eben diese Enthüllung bedeutet aber die Unterbindung ihrer eigentlichen Schwungkraft. Eine Nation, eine Menschheit lebt und schafft in der Fülle der Kraft, wenn sie von einem sie in Schwung haltenden Glauben an sich selbst und an einen schönen und guten Sinn ihres Kulturlebens getragen ist; wenn sie also nicht nur überhaupt lebt, sondern einem in ihren Augen Großen entgegenlebt und sich in ihren fortschreitenden Erfolgen in der Verwirklichung echter und sich steigernder Werte befriedigt. In solcher Menschheit ein würdiges Mitglied zu sein, für eine solche Kultur mitzuwirken, zu ihren herzerhebenden Werten beizutragen, ist das Glück jedes Tüchtigen und hebt ihn empor über seine individuellen Sorgen und Mißgeschicke.

Diesen Glauben, der uns und unsere Väter hob und der sich auf die Nationen übertrug, die wie die japanische sich erst in neuester Zeit der europäischen Kulturarbeit anschlossen, haben wir, haben weiteste Volkskreise verloren.

War er schon vor dem Kriege schwankend geworden, so ist er jetzt völlig zusammengebrochen. Als freie Menschen stehen wir vor dieser Tatsache; sie muß uns praktisch bestimmen.

Und danach sagen wir: Ein Neues muß werden; es muß in uns und durch uns selbst werden, durch uns als Mitglieder der in dieser Welt lebenden, sie durch uns und uns durch sie gestaltenden Menschheit. Sollen wir warten, ob diese Kultur nicht von selbst in ihrem Zufallspiel wertzeugender und wertzerstörender Kräfte gesunde? Sollen wir den „Untergang des Abendlandes" als ein Fatum über uns ergehen lassen? Dieses Fatum ist nur, wenn wir passiv zusehen – passiv zusehen könnten. Aber das können auch die nicht, die uns das Fatum verkünden. <...>

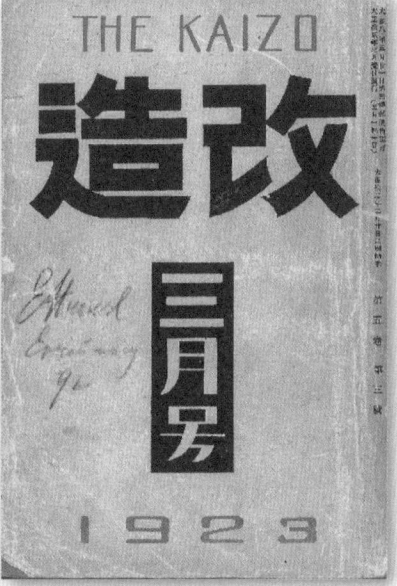

Husserls Exemplar der japanischen Zeitschrift „The Kaizo", in der er 1923 einen Artikel (deutsch und in japanischer Übersetzung) über „Erneuerung. Ihr Problem und ihre Methode" veröffentlichte

Husserl's copy of the Japanese journal "The Kaizo," in which he published in 1923 the article (in German and Japanese translation) "Renewal. Its Problem and its Method"

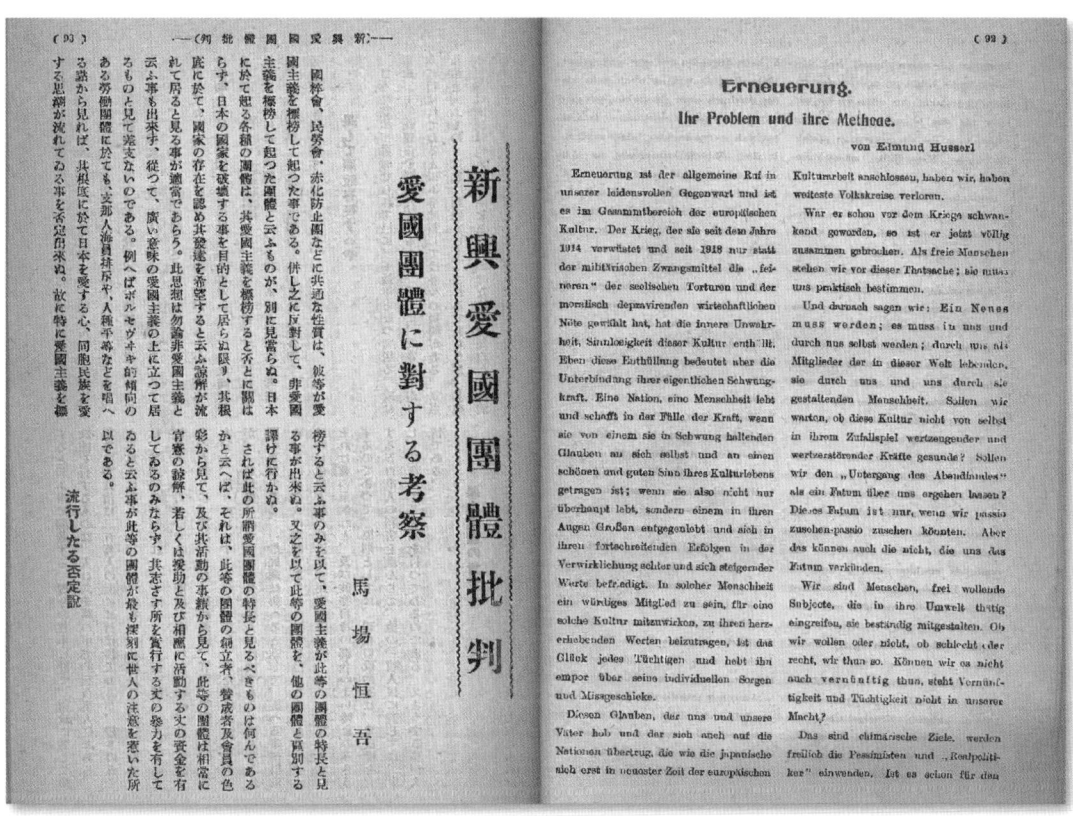

"Something new must occur"

Renewal. Its Problem and its Methods.

Renewal is the general call for our suffering times today and pervades the full range of European culture. The war, with its devastation since 1914 and which, since 1918, has chosen the "finer" [means] of psychological torture and morally depraved economic needs rather than military coercion, has revealed the inner untruth and meaninglessness of this culture. This revelation, however, means the suppression of its actual momentum. A nation, Humanity, lives and creates in the fullness of power, when it is sustained by a belief in itself as well as a beautiful and good sense of its cultural life; if it not only lives as such, but lives for something held great in its vision and for fullfilment in continuing success in the realization of genuine and ever increasing values. To be a dignified member in such humanity, to contribute to such a culture, to contribute in uplifting values, is the happiness of every capable person, and lifts him above his individual troubles and misfortunes.

This belief, which lifted us and our fathers, and which passed over to the nations which, like the Japanese, have only recently joined in European work of culture, has lost wide swaths of nationalities.

If this belief had already wavered before the war, it has now completely collapsed. As free human beings we stand before this fact; it must practically determine us.

And nonetheless we say: Something new must occur; it must become through us and in ourselves, through us as members of self-determining humanity living in this world. Should we wait to see if this culture will heal itself in its dice-game of value-creating and value-destroying forces? Shall we leave the "Decline of the West" as a fate hanging over us? This fate only is, when we passively watch – could only passively watch. But even this cannot be, for those who announce this fate. [...]

„Mit einer tiefen Abneigung gegen die idealistische Betriebsamkeit der Kriegsrhetorik <…> war diese Jugend großenteils zurückgekehrt"

Seit der Wende dieses Jahrhunderts ist in Deutschland und im besonderen in der akademischen Jugend das Wiedererwachen eines tiefen, in der innersten Persönlichkeit verwurzelten Interesses an der Philosophie zu beobachten. Die Leiden der Kriegsjahre haben es noch mächtig entfacht. Als die Generation der Schützengräben die lange verödeten Lehrsäle füllte, da galt ihr Studieneifer nicht etwa ausschließlich der spezialwissenschaftlichen Ausbildung für die erwählten besonderen Berufe. Wider Erwarten gehörten die an Hörer aller Fakultäten sich wendenden philosophischen Vorlesungen mit zu den besuchtesten. Für den philosophischen Lehrer war der Anblick dieser neuen Hörerschaften tief ergreifend. Aus leuchtenden Augen sprach eine glühende Sehnsucht nach den ewigen Ideen, welche den Sinn der Welt und des Menschenlebens in sich tragen. Die eifrige Mitarbeit in den überfüllten Seminaren erwies mindest für einen beträchtlichen Teil dieser Hörerschaft, daß sie in der Philosophie nicht bloß Selbstvergessenheit suchte gegenüber der harten Not der Gegenwart, daß sie sich nicht bloß emportragen lassen wollte von den schönen philosophischen Weltdichtungen, von der Rhetorik großer Systeme und großer Worte; was sie vielmehr wünschte, war Anleitung zu selbständiger wissenschaftlicher Arbeit, zum Zweck einer auf sicheren Fundamenten gegründeten, kritisch freien Stellung gegenüber dem Überlieferten. Mit einer tiefen Abneigung gegen die idealistische Betriebsamkeit der Kriegsrhetorik, ja selbst mit einem starken Mißtrauen gegen die in den Dienst der Kriegspropaganda gestellten philosophischen, religiösen, nationalen Ideale war diese Jugend großenteils zurückgekehrt. Aus dem unentwirrbaren Durcheinander von Wahrheit, frommer Lüge, frecher Verleumdung, von echten und verfälschten Idealen und Gefühlen / wollte sie herauskommen. Radikale Wahrhaftigkeit in Wort und Tat war ihr Wille. Eine neue Welt im Geiste reiner Wahrhaftigkeit wollte sie um sich bauen. Die Philosophie war für sie die wissenschaftliche Stätte radikaler Selbstbesinnungen. In diesen Kreisen, inmitten des politischen, nationalen, religiösen, künstlerischen, philosophischen Chaos, das jetzt Deutschland und dem weiteren Horizont nach europäische Kultur heißt, hat sich auch eine neue philosophische Bewegung rasch verbreitet, die sich die „Phänomenologische" nennt. In der „Transzendentalphänomenologie", einer neuen, schon um 1900 zum ersten Durchbruch gekommenen philosophischen Grundwissenschaft und -methode, sieht sie nichts minderes als einen Heilsquell, aus dem unsere entartete Kultur sich allmählich erneuern, durch den gesundend sie zu einer wurzelechten, ihres tiefsten Sinnes bewußten und ihn erfüllenden Kultur werden kann. <…>

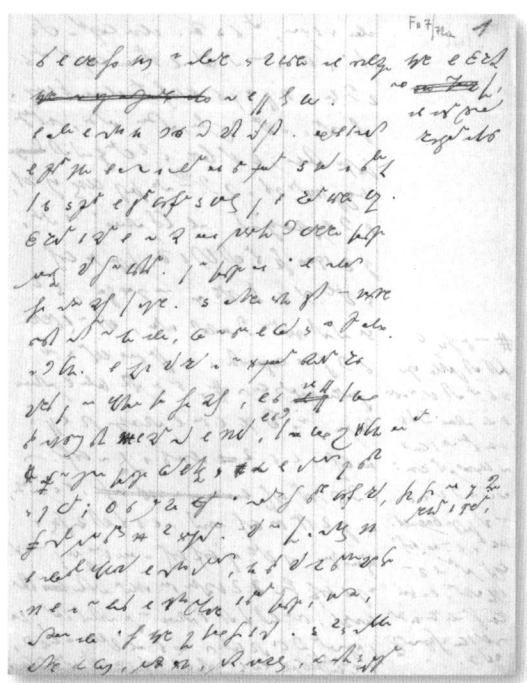

"With a deep aversion against the idealistic activity of war rhetoric [...] this youth largely returned home"

Since the turn of this century, in Germany and especially among the academic youth, the re-awakening of a profound, and deeply rooted within the person, interest in philosophy is to be observed. The sufferings of the war-years have aroused it powerfully. As the generation of trenches filled the long disrespected lecture halls, their [desire for studies] was not only exclusively for the special scientific education for selected particular vocations. Against all expectations, philosophical lectures were among the most frequented by auditors from all faculties. For the philosophical teacher, the sight of these new audiences was profound. From glowing eyes spoke a glowing desire for the eternal ideas which carry the meaning of the world and human life. The zealous collaboration in the overcrowded seminars proved at least for a considerable part of this audience that in philosophy they were not merely seeking self-forgetfulness against the tough hardship of the present, that they did not merely want to be carried away by beautiful philosophical world poetry, by the rhetoric of great Systems and big words; what they wished for was a guide towards independent scientific work, for the purpose of a critically free attitude, based on secure foundations, against the tradition. With a deep aversion against the idealistic activity of war rhetoric, and even with a stronger mistrust of the philosophical, religious, and national ideals placed at the service of war propaganda, this youth largely returned home. They wanted to emerge from the inextricable confusion of truth, pious lies, insolent slander, genuine and adulterated ideals and feelings. Radical truthfulness in word and deed was their volition. They wanted to build a new world in the spirit of pure truthfulness. For them, philosophy was the scientific site for radical self-awareness. In these circles, in the midst of political, national, religious, artistic, and philosophical chaos, now called Germany and the wider horizon of European culture, a new philosophical movement called "phenomenology" spread rapidly. In "Transcendental Phenomenology," a new philosophical fundamental science and method, which had already come to an early breakthrough in 1900, [they] see nothing less than a source of healing from which our degenerate culture is gradually being renewed, by which it might heal into a genuinely grounded culture, in its most profound sense self-aware and fullfilled. [...]

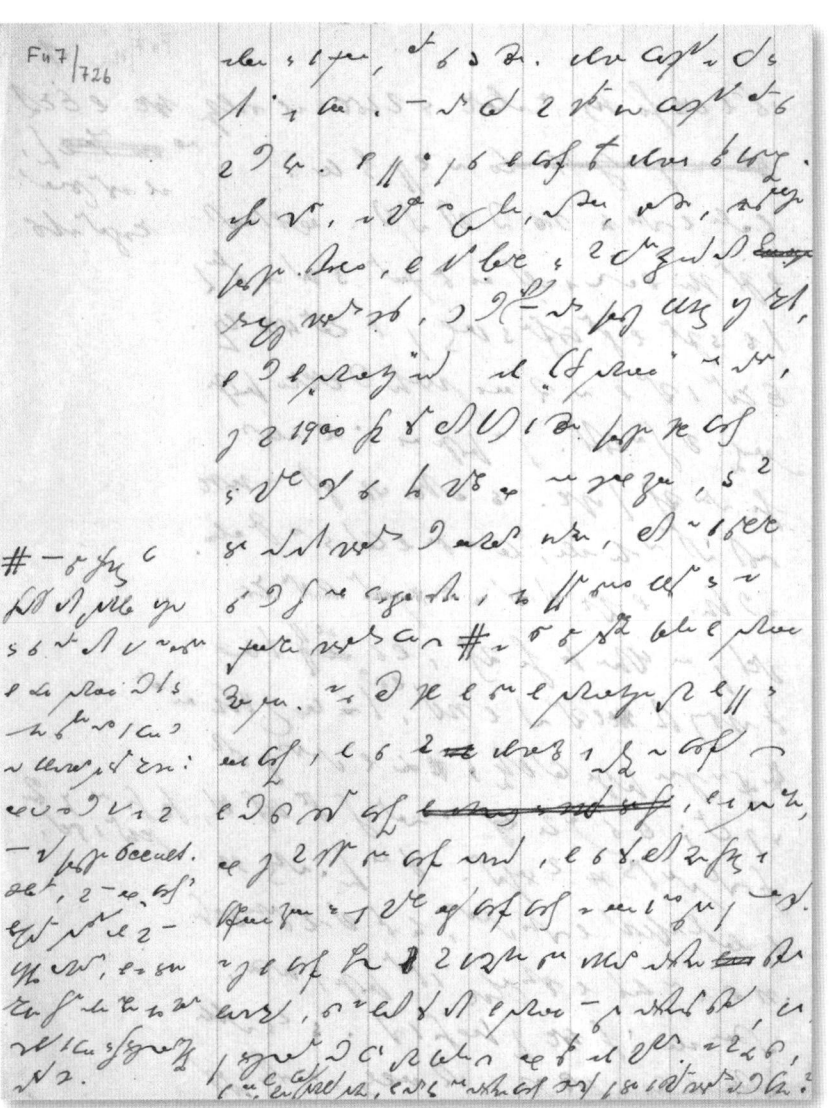

Manuskript von Husserl – Anfangsteil einer früheren Fassung seines „Kaizo"-Aufsatzes über Erneuerung

Husserl's manuscript – the beginning section of an early version of the first Kaizo article on renewal

Malvine Husserl (1860-1950)

Aufnahme etwa 1905

Around 1905

Aufnahme etwa 1939

Around 1939

„Dieser 9. Juli war einer meiner glücklichsten Tage"

Göttingen 16. Juli 1914
Liebe Elli.

Ich wollte Dir schon seit einigen Tagen immer schreiben, aber Himmel u. Erde hatten sich dagegen verschworen – die furchtbare Hitze, die ein Gewitter gestern Abend etwas gemildert hat, und Mangel an Zeit, das irdische Hindernis. Dies war diesmal deshalb so unüberwindlich, weil wir letzten Donnerstag eine große Gesellschaft hatten – 22 Personen –, was doch vor- u. nachher ziemlich zu thun giebt; dann war Amalie gleich darauf krank, lag sogar zu Bett und zu alledem reifte das Obst so rasch, daß man gezwungen war trotzdem einzumachen. Auch heute stand ich den ganzen Vormittag mit beiden Mädchen beim Herd u. schreibe trotz Müdigkeit, um die Wäsche, die Du wahrscheinlich brauchst, nicht ohne Geleitwort abgehen zu lassen.

   Die Gesellschaft war wirklich sehr schön ausgefallen. Herrlicher Abend, die Tafel sehr einheitlich geputzt, gutes Essen u. Trinken und beinahe lauter angenehme, jedenfalls gut zusammenpassende Menschen. Den Glanzpunkt bildete für mich Littmann, der mich zu Tisch führte. Wir waren vor dem Essen im Garten, u. schon auf dem Wege zum Speisezimmer fieng er an (ich nahm mir vor, Wolfgangs Namen nicht zu nennen) vom Bubi zu sprechen. Wie günstig er über ihn denkt, hatte ich trotz meiner eigenen guten Meinung nicht zu hoffen gewagt. Er sagte, W<olfgang> wäre weitaus der Beste von den hiesigen Leuten u. überhaupt der begabteste seiner bisherigen Schüler. Seine Receptivität, seine Auffassung etc. sei hervorragend u. wenn seine Productivität sich ebenso erweise, könnte man das Höchste von ihm erwarten. Er verrate z. B. beim Übersetzen unglaublichen wissenschaftlichen Instinct etc. etc. Littmann konnte garnicht aufhören, man sah ihm an, wie glücklich er selbst darüber ist, so einen Jungen für seine Wissenschaft zu haben. Er war jetzt in Straßburg u. hat mit Nöldecke (neben Wellhausen die größte Größe, aber sehr alt) über Wolf gesprochen. Dieser wird für Wolf ein entsprechendes Colleg lesen, wenn er übernächsten Winter zu ihm kommt.

   Dieser 9. Juli war einer meiner glücklichsten Tage. Littmann u. Goepperts u. noch einige blieben bis 1/4 2 Uhr u. ich gieng

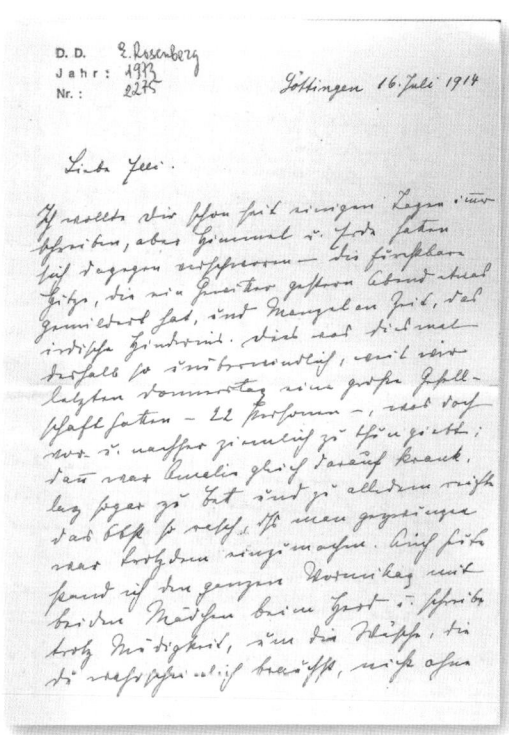

Brief von Malvine Husserl an ihre Tochter Elisabeth („Elli"), 16. VII. 1914

Letter of Malvine Husserl to her daughter Elisabeth ("Elli"), 16 July 1914

mit einem unbeschreiblichen Gefühl zu Bett. Was kann eine Mutter auch inniger beglücken, als wenn sie Gutes von ihren Kindern hört.

   So freue ich mich auch sehr, daß Du von Tante Lucy so wol gelitten bist und so erfüllte und freudige Briefe schreibst. Fahr nur damit so fort, ich würde sonst sehr traurig sein. Jensens lesen mit u. Nina, die neulich da war, bat auch darum. Grüße habe ich Dir von tausend Leuten zu sagen. Fr<au> Hirsch (die am 9. auch bei uns waren), Reinach, Beyerles etc. etc.

   Grüße das ganze liebe Haus und sei herzlich umarmt
   Mama.

   Die Leibwäsche kommt erst nächste Woche. Wenn Du Freitag Abend noch Wäsche schickst, so bekommst Du sie mit der Leibwäsche nächsten Donnerstag.

"This 9th of July was one of the happiest days in my life"

Göttingen 16 July 1914
Dear Elli,

I've wanted to write you for some days now, but heaven and earth conspired against me – the terrible heat, which became milder yesterday after a thunder-storm, and the lack of time, earthly impediments. This time it became so unavoidable, because we hosted a larger company – 22 people – which keeps you pretty busy before and after; and then Amalie became immediately sick, and even had to stay in bed, and on top of all that, the fruit ripened so quickly that one is nonetheless compelled to can them. Even today I was standing the entire morning with both girls at the stove and write despite my tiredness, so as not to send the laundry, which you probably need, without writing a few accompanying words.

The party was really very successful. Wonderful evening, the table very nicely laid-out, good food and drink and almost everywhere pleasant people, who mostly got along well with each other. The high-point was for me Littmann, who took me aside to the table. We were before the meal in the garden and already on the way to the dining room when he began (I decided not to drop Wolfgang's name) to speak about Bubi. How favorably he thinks of him, I would have never imagined, despite my own good opinion. He said that W[olfgang] was by far the best from the present people and over-all the most talented of his past students. His receptivity, his understanding, etc., are said to be excellent and if his productivity likewise demonstrates itself, one could expect from him the greatest. He confided, for example, that he possesses an unbelievable scientific instinct for translation, etc., Littmann could not stop, one saw him, how happy he was to have such a young man for his science. He was just in Strasbourg and spoke about Wolf with Nöldecke (along with Wellhausen, the greatest of the great, but very old). He would read for Wolf an appropriate lesson, when he comes to him the winter after next.

This 9th of July was one of the happiest days in my life. Littmann and Goepperts and the others stayed until a quarter past 1 in the morning and I went to bed with an indescribable feeling. What could make a mother more happy inside, when she hears so much good about her children.

I am so happy that your aunt Lucy likes you so much and that you write so fulfilling and joyful letters. Keep on doing this, as I would otherwise be very sad. The Jensens are reading the letters too, and Nina asked for them as well. Greetings I have to send you from a thousand people. Frau Hirsch (who was also here on the 9th), Reinach, Beyerles, etc., etc.

Greet the whole dear house and be warmly embraced,
Mama

The undergarments will only come next week. If you still send laundry on Friday evening, you will get it with the linen next Thursday.

„Also es ist wirklich Krieg"

Liebe Elli.

Also es ist wirklich Krieg u. es ist schrecklich, daß es so kommen mußte. Aber weil es eben mußte, empfindet man zunächst jene Erleichterung, die auch der Ausbruch eines gräßlichen Unwetters auslöst, das einer unerträglichen Schwüle das ersehnte Ende macht. Wir sind sehr erregt u. haben die beiden letzten Nächte kaum geschlafen, erst heute früh erfuhren wir die Kriegsgewißheit.

Unter diesen Umständen halte Dich jeden Moment zur Heimreise bereit u. fahre – das ist Dein strikter Auftrag – mit Fr<au> Runge nach Göttingen. Wenn Deutschland auch mit hineingezogen wird, dürfte Fr<au> R<unge> wol sofort heimkehren. Gerhart hat auch schon entsprechende Order. Schreibe gleich, wie Fr<au> R<unge> sich das denkt.

Da ich Dich mit Geld für alle Fälle versehen will, so schicke ich 200 M., wovon Du die Pension, Stunden bezahlen u. das Übrige zu verrechnen hast.

Grüße Tante Lucy, Frau Runge und das ganze liebenswürdige Haus herzlichst von mir.

Mama

"So, it's really war"

Dear Elli,

So it's really war and it is terrible that it had to come to this. But because it had to happen, we are now experiencing the kind of relief which occurs with the burst of a terrible storm, which brings an end to an unbearable humidity. We are very excited and have scarcely slept during the last two nights, but we only learned of war's certainty this morning.

Under these circumstances, keep yourself ready at any moment for the journey home, ride – this is your strict request – with Frau Runge to Göttingen. Since Germany is also brought in [the war], Frau Runge will probably return immediately. Gerhart has already received marching orders. Write immediately what Frau Runge thinks about this.

Since I want to provide you with money for all eventualities, I send 200 Marks, from which you can pay the pension, the hours, as well as settle what remains.

Greetings to Aunt Lucy, Frau Runge, and the whole amiable house of mine.

Mama

Postkarte von Malvine Husserl an ihre Tochter Elisabeth („Elli"), 26. VII. 1914

Postcard from Malvine Husserl to her daughter Elisabeth ("Elli"), 26 July 1914

Malvine Husserl

„Was macht Trude u. was sagt sie zu Wolfgang als Soldat?"

"What's Trude up to and what does she say about Wolfgang as a soldier?"

Liebe Clotilde,
ich danke Dir vielmals für Deinen herzlichen Brief. Inzwischen habt Ihr Edmunds Karte u. die von Elli erhalten, außerdem aus der z. Th. copierten Feldbriefpost der Jungens alles für Euch Interessante erfahren. Heute erhielten wir eine Nachricht v<om> 4., daß sie mit ihrem Regiment abgelöst würden u. nach beinahe 14tägigem Aufenthalt im Schützengraben nach Rosebeke marschierten, wo sie vorläufig in Reserve liegen u. gut gefüttert werden u. exercieren. Ein Bett haben sie seit 4 1/2 Wochen nicht gesehen, sind aber glücklich in einer Scheune auf Stroh schlafen zu können. Sie fühlen sich wol u. brennen darauf wieder ins Gefecht zu kommen.

Wir freuen uns sehr, daß es Deinem Bruder gut geht, wo steht er eigentlich?

Also hab vielen Dank für Deine Zeilen u. seid beide herzlichst gegrüßt. Was macht Trude u. was sagt sie zu Wolfgang als Soldat? Sie hat doch die Photogr<aphie> gesehen?

Deine treue
Malvine

Dear Clotilde,
I thank you so much for your kind letter. You have since received Edmund's postcard as well as one from Elli, as well as some copied letters of the boys from the front where you can learn many interesting things. We received today news from the 4th that they have been detached from their regiment and after almost 14 days of being stationed in the trenches, they will march to Rosebeke, where they will for the time being remain in reserve, and will be well fed and will train. They have not seen a bed in 4 and half weeks, but are happy that they can sleep in a barn on straw. They are doing well and are itching to return to combat.

We are very happy that your brother is doing well, where is he actually?

So many thanks for your lines and we greet you both sincerely. What's Trude up to and what does she say about Wolfgang as a soldier? Has she seen the photo?

Yours faithfully,
Malvine

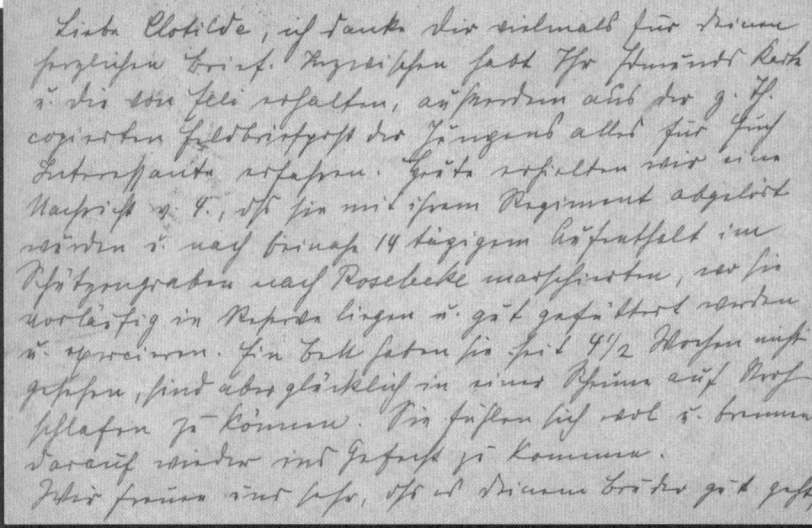

Postkarte von Malvine Husserl an Clotilde Husserl (Frau von Husserls Bruder Heinrich), 12. XI. 1914

Postcard from Malvine Husserl to Clotilde Husserl (wife of Husserl's brother, Heinrich), 12 November 1914

Die Husserls im Krieg

The Husserls in Time of War

Gerhart und Wolfgang Husserl in Uniform zu Beginn des Krieges

Gerhart and Wolfgang Husserl in uniform at the start of the war

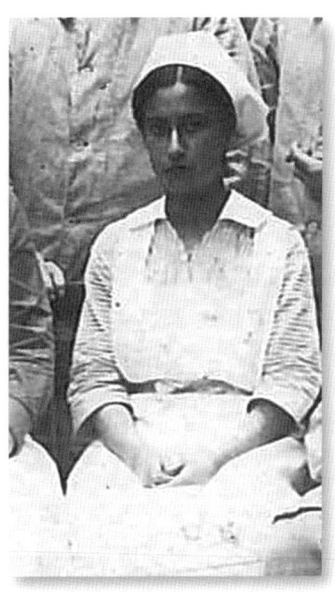

Elli Husserl als Krankenschwester im Lazarettdienst 1915

Elli Husserl as nurse serving in a field-hospital

„Die Söhne des Philosophen Husserl im Weltkrieg"

Die Söhne des Philosophen Husserl im Weltkrieg.

Der jetzt in Kiel beurlaubte Professor Gerhart Husserl meldete sich zusammen mit seinem Bruder Wolfgang am 2. August 1914 freiwillig beim Göttinger Infanterieregiment und wurde mit fast allen seinen Freunden und Schulkameraden der 3. Kompanie des Res. Inf. Regt 234 zugeteilt, das Anfang Oktober vor Ypern geworfen wurde und die berühmten Stürme bei Langemarck zwischen dem 20. und 30. Oktober und am 10. Nov. mitmachte. Im Februar <19>15 wurde Wolfgang durch einen Lungensteckschuss verwundet und unter Lebensgefahr von Gerhart und 2 Kameraden aus dem feindlichen Feuer getragen, der eine erhielt dabei einen Beckenschuss. Etwa ein Jahr später wurde Gerhart Husserl, der sich durch besonders aktives Handeln bei Patrouillen usw. ausgezeichnet hatte (Leutnant und Eisernes Kreuz I), durch einen Kopfschuss schwer verwundet. Nach glücklicher Operation (Trepanation der Hirnschale und Entfernung der Granatsplitter in Sedan) wurde er nach vielmonatlicher Lazarettbehandlung als dauernd nur garnisondienstfähig dem Ersatzbataillon Kassel als Gerichtsoffizier zugeteilt. Inzwischen hatte sich Wolfgang Husserl, kaum genesen, aufs Neue ins Feld gemeldet. Um den Feldzug in Gemeinschaft mit seinem ehemaligen Gymnasialprofessor, Hauptmann d. R. Henkel, mitmachen zu können, ließ er sich von den 234 zum Res. Inf. 19 versetzen, das dem Armeekorps des Kommandeur General von Gündell unterstellt war, und vor Verdun lag. Hier fiel Wolfgang Husserl 20jährig beim Sturm auf Fort Vaux als Offizier an der Spitze seines Zuges am 8. III. 16. 2 Jahre nachdem sein einziger Bruder gefallen war, als der Krieg im Frühjahr 1918 in sein letztes verzweifeltes Stadium gerückt war, ging Gerhart Husserl wieder freiwillig ins Feld. Da er infolge der verletzten Hirnschale keinen Stahlhelm tragen durfte, rückte er mit der Feldmütze bei seinem alten Infant. Regiment, den 234, als Kompanieführer ein, wurde gleich Regimentsadjutant und machte die verlustreichen Kämpfe bei … mit, bei denen er vorübergehend auch ein Bataillon führte. Am 30. September 1918 wurde er ein 2. Mal durch Kopfschuss verwundet, diesmal büßte er die Sehkraft des linken Auges auf immer ein. Die Erholung ging schwer und langsam vor sich, der militärische Zusammenbruch Deutschlands und die Hungersnot erschwerten die Rekonvaleszenz und verzögerten sie immer wieder. Dennoch gelang es <Gerhart> Husserl nach vielen Monaten wieder, sich mit ganz ungewöhnlicher Energie zur Durchführung seiner juristischen Ausbildung aufzuraffen und seinen Doktor und Assessor sogar mit Auszeichnung zu bestehen. Husserl, der sich nie politisch betätigt und keiner Partei angehört hat, ist diese Woche auf Grund des Gesetzes zur Wiederherstellung des Berufsbeamtentums beurlaubt worden.

"The sons of the philosopher Husserl in the Great War"

Husserl's Sons in the Great War.

The presently furloughed professor Gerhart Husserl reported with his brother Wolfgang on August 2, 1914 as volunteers to the Göttingen Infantry Regiment and were assigned with most of all their friends and school comrades to the 3rd company of the Reserve Infantry Regiment 234, which was thrown at the beginning of October in the fighting at Ypres and the celebrated attack at Langemarck between the 20th and 30th of October and November 10th. In February 1915, Wolfgang was wounded with a bullet through the lungs and brought back from enemy fire in critical condition by Gerhart and two comarades, one of whom thereby received a gunshot wound in the pelvis. About one year later, Gerhart Husserl, who was rewarded because of his outstanding actions during patrols, etc. (Lieutenant and Iron Cross First Class), was severely wounded with a bullet in the head. After a successful operation (trepanation of the skull and removal of shell fragments in Sedan) he was assigned after many months of care at a field hospital to the reserve-battalion in Kassel as a court officer, and was only able to do his duty in garrison. Meanwhile, Wolfgang Husserl, who had barely recovered, once again entered the front. To serve in the field with his former professor from the Gymnasium, Hauptmann in the Reserves Henkel, he was allowed to transfer from the 234th to the 19th Reserve Infantry, which was serving in the Army Corps of Commander General von Gündell, positioned in front of Verdun. There, Wolfgang Husserl fell in combat, 20 years old, during the attack on Fort Vaux as officer at the head of his platoon on March 8, 1916. 2 years after his only brother had fallen, when the war had moved to its last desperate stage in the spring of 1918, Gerhart Husserl again voluntarily entered the field. Since he could not wear a steel helmet on account of his injured skull, he went to the front with his old cap from his former Infantry Regiment, the 234th, as a company commander, and became immediately a regimental adjutant, and participated in the costly battles at [...] where he temporarily led a battalion. On September 30, 1918, he was wounded a second time by a gunshot to the head, and this time permanently lost sight of the left eye. The recovery was difficult and slow, the military collapse of Germany and the famine made the convalescence difficult and prolonged it longer. Nevertheless, after many months, [Gerhart] Husserl succeeded in returning, with his unusual energy, to complete his juridical education and cobble together his Doctorate and even became an Assessor with distinction. Husserl, who had never been politically active and has not belonged to any party, has been suspended this week on the basis of the law for the restoration of the professional civil service.

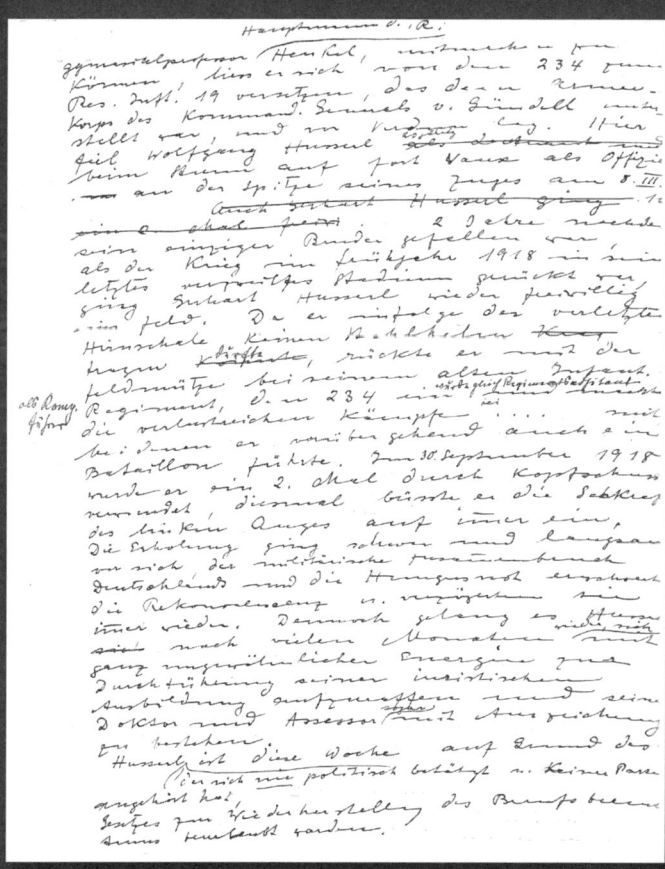

Aufzeichnung von Husserls Tochter Elisabeth vom April 1933 über ihre Brüder, Wolfgang und Gerhart, während des 1. Weltkrieges

Notes by Husserl's daughter Elisabeth from April 1933 about her brothers Wolfgang and Gerhart during the First World War

Elisabeth („Elli") Husserl (1892-1981)

Elli mit ihrem Vater, Sommer 1921 in St. Märgen

Elli with her father, Summer 1921 in St. Märgen

„Alle warten mit ruhiger Zuversicht auf das Ende des Krieges"

"Everyone is waiting with calm confidence for the end of the war"

Göttingen 8. Nov. <1914>
Lieber Onkel Heinrich,
Vielen Dank für Deine l<iebe> Karte (an Papa), ich will Dir gleich noch einmal die Feldadresse der Jungens schreiben: Kriegsfreiwillige Husserl, 26. Res. Armeekorps, 51. Res. Division, 234. Res. Inf. Reg. 3. Bataillon, 11. Kompanie. Das ist alles. Du darfst Dich nicht wundern, dass sie dir noch nicht geschrieben haben, wir selbst haben 3 Wochen lang keine Nachricht von ihnen gehabt, jetzt auf einmal kommen Briefe u. Karten, z.T. solche, die noch Mitte Okt. geschrieben sind. Daraus kannst Du sehen, dass sie nicht etwa gemütlich hinten in Reserve stehen, sondern in der Front, wo darf ich auf dieser offenen Karte nicht schreiben, aber ich schicke heute der l<ieben> Grossmama Abschriften der bisher eingelaufenen Feldpostsendungen, die für Euch alle bestimmt sind u. woraus Ihr sehen könnt, wie es steht. Wir sind sehr glücklich, dass unsere beiden bis jetzt noch ganz gesund sind u. hoffen dass es so bleibt. – Wir haben hier sehr viele Gefangene, Hunderte von Engländern, die manchmal in grossen Trupps durch die Strassen zur Arbeit marschieren, sie wohnen in den neuen Baracken, die im Süden der Stadt wie Pilze aus der Erde geschossen sind. Sonst ist nicht viel vom Krieg zu merken, das ganze Leben u. alle Arbeit geht wie sonst, alle warten mit ruhiger Zuversicht auf das Ende des Krieges. Dir, der l<ieben> Tante Clotilde und der Trudel herzl<iche> Grüssi von Deiner Elli.

Viele Grüße von d<en> Eltern.

Göttingen, 8 Nov. [1914]
Dear Uncle Heinrich,
Thank you for your l[ovely] card (to Papa), I want to write you immediately with the postal-field address of the boys: Wartime volunteers Husserl, 26th Res. Armeekorps, 51st Res. Division, 234th Res. Inf. Reg., 3rd Battalion, 11th Company. That's all. You must not be surprised that they have not yet written to you, for three weeks we have had no news from them, and now all at once cards and letters are coming, i.e., those written in the middle of October. From this you can see that they are not in the reserve, but at the front, which I am not allowed to write on this open card, but I am sending today to d[ear] Grandmama copies of the field mails sent to us, which will be important for you all, and where you can see how things stand. We are very happy that both of them are still quite healthy, hope it remains so. We have a great many prisoners here, hundreds of Englishmen, who sometimes march through the streets to work in large squads. They live in the new barracks, which sprang up from the earth like mushrooms in the south of the city. Otherwise, not much of the war is registered, all of life and work goes on as usual, everyone is waiting with calm confidence for the end of the war. To you, d[ear] Aunt Clotilde and Trudel your Elli sends w[arm] little greetings.
Elli.

Best wishes from the parents.

Elisabeth Husserl an ihren Onkel Heinrich Husserl, 8. XI. 1914

Elisabeth Husserl to her uncle Heinrich Husserl, 8 November 1916

Elisabeth („Elli") Husserl

Gerhart Husserl (1893-1973)

Gerhart Husserl zusammen mit seinem Vater (um 1930)

Gerhart Husserl together with his father (around 1930)

Gerhart als Soldat (zu Beginn des Krieges)

Gerhart as a soldier (at the beginning of the war)

Wolfgang Husserl (1895-1916)

Wolfgang zu Beginn des Krieges

Wolfgang at the beginning of the war

Nach seiner ersten Verwundung im Februar 1915

After his first wounding in action in February 1915

Aus den Kriegsbriefen der Husserl-Söhne (1914-1916): „Zickzackreise!"

From the war-letters of Husserl's sons (1914-1916): "Zigzag journey!"

Zum 70. Geburtstag ihrer Mutter (am 7. März 1930) und zum Gedenken an den 14. Todestag ihres jüngeren Bruders, Wolfgang, der am 8. März 1916 vor Verdun gefallen war, fertigte Elli Husserl eine etwa 140 Seiten zählende Schreibmaschinen-Abschrift der während der Kriegsjahre 1914-1916 geschriebenen Briefe ihrer Brüder Wolfgang und Gerhart an. Die originalen Briefe sind wahrscheinlich zusammen mit der persönlichen Habe der Familie Husserl bei einem Brand im Hafen von Antwerpen 1940 vernichtet worden.

On the occasion of the 70th birthday of their mother (March 7, 1930) and in commemoration of the 14th anniversary of the death of Wolfgang Husserl (who died at Verdun on 8 March 1916), Elli Husserl produced an extensive typewritten transcript (about 140 pages) from written letters of her brothers during the war. The original letters no longer exist; they were probably destroyed together with other personal possessions of the Husserl family during a fire in the port of Antwerp in 1940.

Grupont (Belgium), 14 October 1914, 9 in the morning
Dear Elli!
What a zigzag journey! From Cologne South to Euskirchen, then North-West via Düren to Malmedy, where we ate on German soil at 11 o'clock at night. Then continued to Libramont (South-West) and now again North-West, who knows where. Wonderful morning, magnificent wooded area with Bavarian Landsturm troops. We might spend the night in Liège or Namur or France. So far, we've been riding for 45 hours, and washing now always a blessing.

Gerhart

15 October 1914
Dear Parents!
On our return trip through Belgium yesterday we came to Namur, which looks beautiful. Traces of the siege are not many, we only saw trenches, a shot-up fort, and burnt houses. We're riding unbelievably slowly, since every few hours a military train comes by. Three times a day we are mostly fed with pea soup.
Belgium makes a cultivated impression and the landscapes are very appealing, especially Belgian Luxemburg. The entire land is teeming with nice Landsturm troops, the railroad is entirely German. Yesterday we encountered a train with captured Francstireurs. We had just detrained and readied our weapons. We are in Grammont (between Brussels and Ghent).

Wolfgang

Grupont (Belgien)   14.10.14.
9h morgens

Liebe Elli!

Das ist eine Zickzackreise! Von Cöln südl. nach Euskirchen, dann nordw. über Dühren nach Malmedy, wo wir um 11h nachts zum letzten Mal auf deutschen Boden verpflegt wurden. Dann weiter bis Libramont (s.w.) u. nun wieder nord w., wer weiss, wohin. Wundervoller Morgen, prachtvolle waldige Gegend mit bayrischen Landsturmleuten. Vielleicht sind wir die Nacht in Lüttich oder Namur oder Frankreich. Bis jetzt fahren wir schon 45 Stunden, ja, und waschen ist auch nur mehr eine Glücksache.

Gerhart.

15.10.14.

Liebe Eltern!

Auf unserer Rundreise durch Belgien kamen wir gestern Nachmittag nach Namur, das sehr schön liegt. Die Spuren der Belagerung sind nicht zahlreich, wir sahen nur Schützengräben, ein zerschossenes Fort und verbrannte Häuser. Wir fahren mit unglaublicher Langsamkeit, da alle paar Stunden ein Militärzug fährt. Drei mal am Tag werden wir meistens mit Erbsensuppe abgefüttert.

Belgien macht einen kultivierten Eindruck u. ist landschaftlich reizvoll, besonders Belg. Luxemburg. Das ganze Land wimmelt von netten Landsturmleuten, die Eisenbahn ist ganz deutsch. Gestern begegneten wir einem Zug gefangener Franctireurs. Eben steigen wir aus und setzen die Gewehre zusammen. Wir befinden uns in Gramont (zw. Brüssel und Gent).

Wolfgang.

Gerhart Husserl an seine Schwester Elli, 14. X. 1914, und Wolfgang Husserl an seine Eltern, 15. X. 1914 (Abschrift der Schwester)

Gerhart Husserl to his sister Elli (14 October 1914), and Wolfgang Husserl to his parents (15 October 1914)

„Das ist heute der 7te Tag der Schlacht bei Langemarck" – „Ringsum verbrannte Gehöfte, tote Kühe, platzende Schrapnells, dazwischen Leib an Leib wir Brüder"

Bei Langemark nördlich Ypres, Westflandern 26.1o.14.

Das ist heute der 7. te Tag der Schlacht bei Langemark. Man hat sich daran gewöhnt, wenn nicht gerade Granaten in nächster Nähe einschlagen bleibt man unbekümert. Der Schützengraben, den wir uns gester ausheben ,ist gut 1,m tief, und indem ich darin sitzend schreibe, lasse ich seelenruhig vereinzelte Gewehrkugeln darüberhin pfeifen. Seit 4 Tagen bin ich mit circa 5o anderen aus dem Kompagnieverband gekommen und als Deckung der Artillerie zugeteilt,d.h. wir befinden uns zu 2o Mann in der Nähe der Geschütze von zwei Batterieh,dazu bestimmt,im Falle eines plötzlichen Angriffes die im Nahkampf unbrauchbaren Kanonen zu verteidigen... Ich hätte nie gedacht,daß Artillerie eine so üble Sache für den betreffenden Teil ist,bis wir es neulich,am Tage unserer Feuertaufe,gründlich merkten.

Roulers war von uns genommen worden,erst hat die Artillerie die wenigen feindlichen Truppen vertrieben, dann drang die Infanterie über Barrikaden und von Franktireuren besetzte Häuser stürmend,in den Ort ein. Es war erstaunlich die langen Reihen von Kanonen,Menschen und Pferden in einer Stadt zu sehen,die kaum geringer an Bewohnerzahl als Göttingen jetzt ganz verwüstet lag. Licht kam aus brennenden Häusern,die weil aus ihnen geschossen wurde, oder Patronenvorräte in ihnen gefunden wurden, in Flammen aufgingen. Den Tag darauf war es bei der Einnahme des Dorfes Poelkapelle, daß wir ganz harmlos ohne erhebliche Sicherung einrückend,noch nicht einmal ausgeschwärmt, aus den Häusern hageldichtes Gewehrfeuer empfingen, dem bald das Aufschlagen der Granaten sich beigesellte. Die meisten Kugeln pfiffen über unsere Köpfe, aber immerhin kostete uns dieser Tag zwei Tote und mehrere Verwundete. Unser Korps entbehrt schmerzlich der Artillerie, die das Gelände ganz anders aufklären würde, als es jetzt geschehen kann. In den eigentlichen Wurstkessel kamen wir am 21.,der für unser Bataillon ein dies ater war. Feuer aus besetzten Häusern und Artilleriefeuer richteten großen Schaden an . Das Gräßliche war, wir konnten uns gar nicht wehren,denn von Feinden war auch absolut nichts zu se Zwei Stunden im Schützengraben,während Schrappnelle und Granaten z.T. der eigenen Artillerie platzen,das war nicht gerade gemütlich. Schließlich zog sich das Bataillon zurück. Ein Flieger hatte unsere Rückzugslinie ausgekundschaftet und flugs flog in unsere Kompagniekolonne ein Schrapnell, das immensen Schaden anrichtete. Acht Tote un etwa 25 Verwundete auf einen Schlag. Daß Wolfgang und ich völlig unversehrt geblieben bis heute , ist ein Wunder. In unserer Korporalschaft sind allein vier Tote und fünf Verwundete... Da eine ander Division eingesprungen war,konnte das Regiment und die Artillerie den Vormarsch noch am selben Abend wieder aufnehmen,den organisiert zu haben das Verdienst unseres Bataillonsadjutanten (des langen Kerls)war, der dafür das eiserne Kreuz erhielt. Als wir am späten Abend mit Blutgeruch,hungrig,müde, ganz verschreckt zurückzogen,der Major zitternd und totenst, der Adjutant zu Rad mit dem Gewehr über der Schulter, rief dieser : "Kinder, wir haben Unglück gehabt,wollen die Scharte wieder auswetzen!" , ja da war einem ganz toll zu Mute. Seitdem liegen wir im Feuer und haben doch fast keinen Schuß abgegeben.... Man muß eben mit den Kanonen vorher möglichst alles zusamen schießen und den Rest der Häuser mit dem Bajonett stürmen. Ganz unermeßlichen Schaden tun uns die alle Augenblicke erscheinenden feindlichen Flieger, denen wir manchen Verlust verdanken.... Es geht im ganzen entschieden vorwärts,unser Armeekorps hat die Aufgabe die Stellung zu halten,da die weiterdringenden Flügel den Feind umklammern sollen, daher macht er hier immer Durchbruchsversuche,die bis jetzt immer abgewiesen wurden. Diese Nacht wurde ein halbes Dorf von feindlicher Artillerie in Brand geschossen,ein fabelhaftes Schauspiel. Bei alledem führen wir unser gleichmäßiges Leben.... Manchmal schnallt man 24 Stunden lang nicht einmal das Koppel ab.

Wolfgang schreibt weiter :

.... Obgleich wir wiederholt vom Feind mit Kugeln und Granaten be-

"Today is the 7th day of the Battle of Langemarck" – "All around, burned farms, dead cows, bursting shrapnel, in between body to body us brothers"

At Langemarck, north of Ypres, West Flanders, 26 October 1914
Today is the 7th day of the Battle of Langemarck. One has gotten used to it; if shells are not falling-down in the near vicinity, one remains unconcerned. The trenches, which we dug-out yesterday, are a good 1 meter deep, and as I write sitting here, I let pass in tranquility the sporadic rifle-bullets whistle by. 4 days ago, I came [here] with about 50 others from the company and was assigned to protect the artillery, that is, we are 20 men near the guns of two batteries, destined to defend these useless cannons in close combat, in the event of a sudden attack ... I would have never thought that artillery was so bad a thing for the part in question, until we recently soundly recognized this, on the day of our baptism of fire.

Roulers has been taken by us, first the artillery had driven out the few enemy troops, then the infantry, storming over barricades and houses occupied by Francs-tireurs, entered the town. It was astonishing to see the long rows of cannon, men, and horses in a city that has just as many inhabitants as Göttingen, and which is now almost devastated. Light came from burning houses, which, since shots were fired from them or supplies of cartridges were found, burst into flames. The next day, when the village of Poelkapelle was taken, we were approaching, and had not yet swarmed up, without taking any harm and in considerable security, then suddenly we received a hail of gunfire from the houses, which soon were silenced through a barage of artillery. Most of the bullets whistled over our heads, but this day cost us two dead and several wounded. Our corps is painfully lacking in artillery, which would open up the terrain much more, as now can be done. We found ourselves in a genuine sausage kettle on the

Aus den Kriegsbriefen der Husserl-Söhne: 26. u. 27. X. 1914
(Abschrift der Originalbriefe durch deren Schwester)

From the war-letters of Husserl's sons: 26 and 27 October 1914
(typewritten copy by their sister)

21st, which was for our battalion a disaster [a black day]. Gunfire from occupied houses and artillery fire caused great damage. The horrible thing was, we could not defend ourselves at all, because nothing could be seen of the enemy. Two hours in the trench, while shrapnel and shells, some times from our own artillery, exploded, that was not exactly cozy. Finally, the battalion withdrew.

An aviator had exposed our retreat, and suddenly flew into our company [some] shrapnel, which caused much harm. Eight dead and about 25 wounded in one fell swoop. That Wolfgang and I have remained completely unscathed is to this day a miracle. In our Corporal's command, there are alone four dead and five wounded ... Then another division jumped in, the regiment and the artillery could resume the advance that same evening, the organization of which was the merit of our Battalion Adjutant (the tall guy), who received for this the Iron Cross. When we retired in the late evening, with blood-smell, hungry, tired, quite frightened, and the Major shivering and deadly-pail, the Adjutant came over with counsel with his rifle slung over his shoulder; he shouted: "Boys, we have been unlucky, let us get over this!," yes, everyone was entirely silent. Since then, we have been under fire, but have almost not fired anything ... One must indeed shell as much as possible in advance and assault the rest of the houses with bayonette. Enemy airplanes, which appear at any moment, are of immeasurable harm to us, to which we owe many losses ... On the whole, things are moving decidedly forward, our Army Corps has the task of keeping the position, as the advancing wings are supposed to close-up the enemy, so he always makes breakthrough-attempts, which have always been defeated thus far. This night, half of a village was fired upon by enemy artillery, what a fabulous spectacle. In all of this, we lead our regular lives. ... Sometimes we can't even unbuckle our waist belts for 24 hours.

[Wolfgang continues:] Although we were repeatedly fired upon by the enemy with bullets and artillery, we could feel a bit relieved. We have had no more losses, and could sometimes satisfy our greedy hunger. Everywhere close-by are farmsteads where sometimes a few men are detached to get food and often enough it happens that, just when the soup is simmering, artillery shakes us up or the battery changes its position, and we must leave. Exceptionally pleasant and in camaraderie, we stand with our brothers from the cannons [field kitchen, Gulasch-Kanone]. If they have too much, they give some of their surplus to us, and we at times given them some. Brilliant are their officers ...

27 October 1914
Dear, dear parents!

The field-post arrived today! How fortunate, to hear from the homeland, for which our ardent desires long. Ah, how wonderful it must be [to be] with you all once again in Göttingen. We are once more with the company, around 110 men and are positioned in the most forward trench. Day and night a few hundred meters from the enemy. You know that Stimming und Götting are dead, and most likely also Bernhard Runge. My best comrades are either wounded or dead. The officers from our battalion all have received the Iron Cross ... All around, burned farms, dead cows, bursting shrapnel, in between body to body us brothers.

Sincerely, Gerhart

„Wolfgang hat heute Morgen um 7 ¼ Uhr einen Gewehrschuss bekommen"

Liebe Eltern !   Poel- Kapelle ,Bataillons-
                                  stab 2o.2.15. 1o h morgens

Nun ist der Augenblick gekommen,wo der Krieg auch in unser Haus ganz roh und konkret sein Zeichen gräbt und ich möchte Euch bitten,eingedenk zu sein dessen,was Ihr so oft beteuert habt,daß das Vaterland und sein Wohl unser alles und eines ist.Im Vertrauen darauf schreibe ich ganz wahrheitsgetreu Eurer ruhigen Auffassung gewiß.

Wolfgang hat heute morgen um 7 1/4 Uhr einen Gewehrschuß bekommen. Er blieb bei vollem Bewußtsein. Man verband ihn sofort. Der Schuß ging durch die Schießscharte und drang unter dem linken Schulterblatt ein.Ich und 2 andere brachten ihm gleich heraus.Wolf war imstande den ganzen beschwerlichen Weg bis zur Barrikade zu gehen Von da holten ihn die Sanitäter mit der Bahre hierher,wo ihn der Unterarzt sofort aufs neue untersuchte.Nach dessen Urteil,das er mir sofort ganz unverhohlen abgab auf meine Bitte ist Lebensgefahr auf Grund des Schusses nicht vorhanden.Die Verwundung ist unten in der linken Lunge,aber die Prognosen für Heilung sind bei Lungenschüssen aller Erfahrung nach sehr günstig, Ihr dürft also das Beste hoffen. Wolfgang befindet sich natürlich in mattem Zustande und hat Atem-schwierigkeiten,sonst jedoch keinerlei Schmerzen.Heut abend holt ihn der Krankenwagen ab und er kommt höchstwahrscheinlich in das Res. Feldlazarett 87 in Ostneukerke.Ich bleibe bis Abend hier. Vorläufig liegt er sehr komfortabel hier im Hause. Er läßt Euch grüssen.

Liebe Eltern,es ist natürlich sehr traurig,daß wir zwei jetzt so getrennt werden,aber das ist dieser furchtbare Krieg.Ich kann jetzt nicht viel schöne Worte machen,habe auch jetzt keine Zeit,der Brief soll gleich nach Roulers fahren.Seid guten Mutes !

            In herzlicher Liebe
                        Gerhart.

P.S. Ein Kamerad,der Wolf mit herausführte ,wurde noch unterwegs leicht verwundet.

            Diktat:

Liebe Eltern !   Ostnieuwkerke bei Roulers
                            in Westflandern 21.2.15.

Ich bin am 2o. 2. morgens 8 h durch einen Gewehrschuß im Rücken verwundet worden.Ich wurde sofort vom San. Untffz.verbunden. Ich hatte noch soviel Kraft zu Fuß nach Poel-Kapelle zu gehen gelei-tet von meinem Bruder und 2 Kameraden. Der Unterarzt erklärte meinen Verband für gut und ließ mich durch einen Sanitätskompagniewagen nach dem Res.Feldlaz.87 (Res.Div.51) schaffen.Das Geschoß trat im Rücken ein,verletzte die Lunge leicht und die Knochenhaut einiger Rippen und blieb unter der Haut stecken,heute morgen wurde es raus-geschnitten. Ich war durch Aether betäubt,die Operation ist gut und schmerzlos verlaufen.Sowie ich mich besser fühle,schreibe ich

Aus den Kriegsbriefen der Husserl-Söhne an die Eltern: 20.-22. II. 1915 (Abschrift der Originalbriefe durch deren Schwester)

From the war-letters of Husserl's sons: 20-22 February 1915 (typewritten copy by their sister)

```
ausführlicher.
                Herzliche Grüße
                        Euer Wolfgang.
Gruß erlaubt sich Kriegs-fr.Gefr. Fritz Lederer.

Liebe Eltern !                    Ostneukerke 22.2.15.
       Eben komme ich aus dem Res. Feldlaz.87,wo ich Wolfgang im Bette
schlafend vorfand....Das einzig beschwerliche ist ihm das ewige auf
dem Rücken liegen. Die Atembeschwerden sind schon ganz gering.Die
ersten 2 Tage spuckte er bei Husten etwas Blut,doch ist das jetzt
auch fast vorbei....Der Transport hierher muß sehr unangenehm gewe-
sen sein. Nun liegt er wohlgeborgen vor feindlichen Geschossen in
einem hellen Saale unter lauter guten , hilfsbereiten Menschen.Das
Lazarett ist mit allen neuzeitlichen Einrichtungen ausgestattet und
sicher so gut wie jedes im Inlande. Man hat ihn gestern morgen oper-
riert,d.h. die Kugel herausgenommen.Sie saß links vorne dicht unter
den Rippen.Der Schuß ging also durch den Brustkorb,hat aber keine
Rippe ernstlich lädiert und die Lunge auch nur leicht angeritzt.Die
Schußwirkung war infolge des Durchschlagens des Geschosses durch
die Deckung stark herabgemindert.Das Geschoß selbst,das Wolfgang
aufbewahrt,ist französisch und hat folgende verbogene Form:
       Von Lebensgefahr keine Rede.Bei ganz glatter Heilung ist
Wolf in 14 Tagen bis 3 Wochen bereits Rekonvalescent.
       Komplikationen durch Eiterung, Entzündung sind natürlich
immer möglich,würden aber auch nicht ohne weiteres sehr bedenklich.
Man wird ihn jedenfalls mindestens 2 Wochen hier behalten,da Trans-
porte bei solchen Verletzungen stets gefährlich sind....
       Ihr seht also liebe Leute,es steht alles zum besten und wir
können Gott danken,daß alles so gekommen ist. Ein großes Glück war
vor allem,daß es gelang ,ihn gleich morgens aus dem Graben und sogar
ins Lazarett zu kriegen.Möglich war das nur infolge des famosen Ver-
```

```
haltens der beiden freiwilligen Begleiter  Landwehrmann Wagner und
Kriegsfr. Steup. Es war ganz hell und wir wurden bemerkt und übel
beschossen.Steup hat dabei einen Lendenschuß erhalten,der glückliche
weise (direkt am Rückenmark vorbei!) ungefährlich  und nur Fleischuß
ist,aber doch lange brauchen wird.Der gute Junge liegt auch hier im
selben Lazarett und ist guten Mutes.Wagner ist über 30 Jahre  und
gewiß verheiratet.Beide sind (auf mein persönliches Verwenden) so-
fort dem Regiment zum eisernen Kreuz eingereicht und bekommen es
gewiß.-Der Anteil der Kompagnie ist sehr groß.Alles ließ ihn grüßen,
er wird genug Besuche bekommen !
        Mir gehts meist gut,ich habe Freude an der Führung der Corp-
ralschaft und komme mit dem Compagnieführer auch etwas näher zusam-
men.Wenn ichs weiter gut mache,habe ich keine schlechten Aussichten.
Wir sind in Poel-Kapelle mit großer Mühe untergekommen. Das Nest wi
immer mehr zerschossen und immer stärker belegt. Um 12 h (wirkamen
9) hatte ich glücklich meine Leute untergebracht.Man kann nun ein
paar Tage schlafen. Ah !
                Auf Wiedersehen
                                        Gerhart.
```

"Wolfgang received a gun-shot wound this morning at 7:15"

Dear parents!
Poelkapelle, battalion, 20 February 1915, 10 in the morning
The moment has now arrived when the war also etches its sign coarsely and concretely into our home, and I would please ask you to keep in mind, what you so often have asserted, that the Fatherland and its well-being be our one and only. I write to you confidently and truthfully, assured of your calm composure.
  Wolfgang was shot this morning at 7:15. He remained fully conscious. He was immediately bandaged. The gun-shot went through the firing crenel and then under the left shoulder blade. I and 2 others brought him out right away. Wolf was able to go all

the difficult way to the barricade. From there, medical personnel brought him with the stretcher, where the assistant doctor immediately examined him again. After his assessment, which he immediately gave me without issue at my request, there is no danger of life with this gun-shot. The wound is under the left lung, but the prognosis for healing is very favorable for lung shots of all kinds, so you can hope for the best. Wolfgang is naturally in a weak condition and has difficulty breathing, but otherwise no pain. This evening the hospital transport will pick him up, and he is most likely going to the Reserve Field Station in Oostnieuwkerke. I'll stay here until the evening. For the time being, it is very comfortable here in the house. He sends you his greetings.

Dear parents, it is, of course, very sad that we two are now so separated, but there you have it, this terrible war. I can't write many beautiful words now, don't have time at the moment, the letter will go straight to Roulers. Be of good cheer!

In heartfelt love.
Gerhart
P.S.: A comrade who led Wolf back was lightly wounded on the way.

Oostnieuwkerke near Roulers in West Flanders, 21 February 1915
Dear parents!
I was wounded at 8 o'clock in the morning by a rifle shot in the back. I was immediately joined by the medical under-officer. I still had enought strength to walk on foot to Poelkapelle, accompanied by my brother and two comrades. The assistant physician declared that my dressing was good and let me be taken by a medical transport to the Reserve Field Hospital 87 (Reservedivision 51). The bullet entered in the back, injured the lungs slightly, the bones of some ribs, and remained stuck under the skin, this morning it was cut out. I was put under with ether, the operation went well and was painless. When I'll feel better, I'll write in more detail.
Kind regards, Your Wolfgang
Greetings from war-volunteer Fritz Lederer.

Oostnieuwkerke, 22 February 1915
Dear parents!
I've just come from the Reserve Feld Hospital 87, where I found Wolfgang sleeping in bed. ... The only complaint is that he must forever rest on his back. The respiratory problems are already very slight. For the first two days he coughed-up some blood, but this is now almost over. ... The transportation here must have been very unpleasant. Now he is well-protected from enemy fire in a bright room among good and helpful people. The hospital is equipped with all modern facilities and just as good as those in country [Germany]. He was operated on yesterday morning, i.e., the bullet was removed. It sat deep under the ribs on the left side. The bullet went through the chest-cavity, but did not seriously damage the rib and the lungs were only slightly scratched. The effect of the shot was greatly diminished as a result of the bullet being thrown through the cover [of the uniform]. The bullet itself, which Wolfgang keeps, is French and has the following bent form:

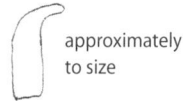 approximately to size

There's no talk of it being life-threatening. With smooth healing, Wolf will already regain his health in 14 days to 3 weeks. Complications because of suppuration, inflammation are, of course, always possible, but would not be very serious. He'll nonetheless be kept here for at least 2 weeks, since such wounds are always dangerous when transported. ...

So, you see dear people, it's all for the best, and we can thank God that everything has come about so. It was very fortunate that it was managed to get him out of the trench early in the morning and even to the hospital. That was only possible because of the brilliant actions of the two voluntary companions, Landwehrmann Wagner and war-volunteer Steup. It was very bright and we were noticed and shot up badly. Steup received a gunshot in the loin, but luckily (directly past the spinal cord!) not dangerous and only a flesh wound, but will still take a good amount of time. The good boy is also here in the same hospital and is in good spirits. Wagner is over 30 years [old] and certainly married. Both of them (per my personal suggestion) were immediately recommended to the Regiment for the Iron Cross and get it surely. – The company's share is very large. Everyone sent their greetings, he'll receive enough visits!

I'm generally well, I'm pleased with the leadership of the Corporal's command and have gotten close with the company leader. If I continue to do it well, I'll not have any bad prospects. We went to Poelkapelle with great effort. The nest becomes ever more fired upon and even more vigorously bombarded. At 12 o'clock (we arrived at 9) I happily accommodated my people. One can now sleep for a few days. Ah!

Goodbye, Gerhart

„Also wäre das doch herrlich, wenn Papa hierher käme"

Grüße die deutschen Bücher und Bäume und Häuser!
        An alle herzlichst
                    Gerhart.

Liebste Mama!   Feldlaz.87. 3.3.15.
....Die Wunden sind schon zu. Bin froh,daß ich mit einer so leichten Sache weggekommen bin,wenn ich hier Verwundungen sehe,bei denen einem die Haare zu Berge stehen und was die Aermsten für Schmerzen auszustehen haben! Wollte Gott dieser elende Krieg wäre bald zu Ende!Gestern war G. nach Roulers,um Besorgungen für mich zu machen...
              Heil ! Wolfgang.

Liebe Mama!   5.3.15.
Teile Dir auf Deinen Brief vom 27. und auf Deine Karte vom 28. mit,daß ich selbstverständlich ruhig im Bett liege. Ich bin auch viel zu schwach,um mich viel zu bewegen und aufzurichten.Du brauchst verdammt nicht zu denken,daß ich hier zu früh weggeschickt werde. Die Aerzte sind sehr vorsichtig.Gestern besuchte mich der Leutnant noch mal.Heute abend geht die Komp. wieder in den Graben. Passow war gestern auch da. Sonst nichts Neues.
                Wolfgang.
Habe die Aepfel etc. erhalten.

Liebe Eltern!   6.3.15.
Ueber mein Befinden ist nichts zu sagen,es geht mir weiter gut. Ich habe jetzt auch wieder Appetit.... Wenn Papa mich abholt, was sehr schön wäre,sollte er doch gleich nach hier nach Ostnieuwkerke kommen,das nur eine Stunde Wegs von Roulers entfernt ist.Das müßte für Papa doch sehr interessant sein,den Betrieb so dicht hinter der Front kennen zu lernen und besonders das Donnern unsrer schweren Artillerie,die gar nicht so weit von hier steht,zu hören.Man kann an einer bestimmten Stelle den Kirchturm von Poel-Kapelle und von Westroosebeke sehr schön sehen.Wenn dann gerade die Sonne untergeht, sieht das fein aus.Also wäre das doch herrlich,wenn Papa hieherkäme. Ich benütze jetzt die Gelegenheit,um verschiedenen Leuten zu schreiben. Dicke Briefe kann ich allerding nicht loslassen,ist mir zu mühsam.Ich denke natürlich fortwährend an zu Hause.Hoffentlich findet Ihr mich nicht zu rauh. Das wird man aber im Kriege.Ich glaube und hoffe,daß ich in 2 Monaten wieder im Felde bin,wenn jetzt die Wunden schon geheilt sind.Sollte ich aber felddienstunfähig werden, dann will ich auch gänzlich dienstunfähig sein.Zu Garnisondienst habe ich gar keine Lust.Grüße an Jensens,Frau Oldenberg.Eben war der General von Kleist wieder da.
                Wolfgang.

Liebste Mama!   Res. Feldlaz.87. 9.3.15.
Habe gestern Deinen Brief vom 1. und den vom 4. erhalten. Vielen Dank für die schönen Bonbons,die ich heute bekam. G. besuchte mich und überzeugte sich von meinem gleichmäßig guten Befinden.Wenn ich nur nach Göttingen komme! Da ich doch keine ärztliche Behandlung mehr brauche,wird hoffentlich das Gesuch bewilligt. Herr Littmann hat mir einen sehr netten Brief geschrieben.Bedaure wirklich sehr, von G. getrennt zu sein.Wir hatten als Brüderpaar in der Komp. große Berühmtheit erlangt und wurden andauernd verwechselt und auch von Leuten,die uns nicht kannten für Brüder erklärt,was seine Vorteile und Nachteile hatte. So wurde ich z.B. einmal,als ich von der Küche Essen holte,mit dem Bemerken von dem Unteroff. vom Dienst weggeschickt ich wäre schon mal dagewesen,dabei war es " mein Bruder".Wenn man alle Sachen zusammen hat,ist das für beide Teile praktisch.
                Wolfgang.

Liebste Mama!   Feldlaz.87 7.3.15.
Sende Dir zu Deinem Geburtstag,der heute ist,allerherzlichsten Glückwunsch. Ich hoffe,daß Du ihn , wo Du weißt,daß es Gerhart und mir so gut geht und wir in Dankbarkeit an Dich denken,

"It would be therefore wonderful if Papa came here"

Dear parents! 6 March 1915
There is nothing to report about my condition, I am still well. I've now regained my appetite. ... If Papa picks me up, which would be very nice, he should come straight to Oostnieuwkerke, which is only an hour away from Roulers. It might be very interesting for Papa to get to know the operation so close behind the front, and especially the thunder of our heavy artillery, which is not so far from here. You can see very beautifully from a certain vantage-point the church tower of Poelkapelle and Westroosebeke. When the sun begins to go down, it looks very fine. So it would be therefore wonderful if Papa came here. I now use the opportunity to write to different people. Long letters I still cannot pull-off, since these are too troublesome. I am, of course, always thinking about home. Hopefully you will not find me too raw. Such is how one becomes in war. I believe and hope that I shall be back in the field in two months, when the wounds become healed. But if I am declared unfit for the field, then I shall also be entirely discharged from field service. I do not want to go to the garrison.

Greetings to Jensens, Mrs. Oldenberg. General von Kleist was just again here.
Wolfgang

Dearest Mama!
Reserve Feld Hospital 87, 9 March 1915
I received yesterday your letter from the 1st and the 4th. Many thanks for the wonderful bonbons, which I got today. G[erhart] visited me and was convinced about my stable condition, all things considered. If only I could come to Göttingen! Since I do not need any more medical treatment, the request will be hopefully granted. Mr. Littmann wrote me a very nice letter. I really regret that I am separated from Gerhart. We enjoyed a great reputation in the company as a pair of brothers and were mistaken for each other, and even people who did not know us, declared us to be brothers, which had both its advantages and disadvantages. I'll give an example: once, as I was getting something to eat from the kitchen, I was sent back by a service officer with the remark that I had already been there, but it was "my brother." When you have all things together, that's convenient for both of us.
Wolfgang

Aus den Kriegsbriefen der Husserl-Söhne: 6. u. 9. III. 1915
(Abschrift der Schwester)

From the war-letters of Husserl's sons, 6 and 9 March 1915
(typewritten copy by their sister)

„Fahre 12.40 mit Dzug nach Köln"

Liebe Malvine.
Ich bin von der Bahn mit Auto zum Generalkomm<andeur> gefahren, und ohne daß ich erfahren hätte, ob aus Thielt eine Antwort und Erlaubnis eingetroffen wäre, sagte mir der betreffende Officier von gestern, daß ich den Passierschein sogleich ausgestellt erhalten werde. Das ist auch geschehen. Ich habe mich beim Generalgouvernement in Brüssel morgen zu melden wegen der Weiterreise. Ich fuhr gleich zurück zum Bahnhof. Fahre 12.40 mit Dzug nach Köln. Die Fahrkarte habe ich schon nach Herbesthal (Grenze nach Aachen, wo ich 1 Stunde Aufenthalt habe). Ich komme 2.56 Br<üssel> an. Von Köln fahre ich circa 8h früh ab.

So ist alles gut vonstatten gegangen. Ich werde hier wieder auf dem Bahnhof Mittag essen.
Ich umarme und grüße Dich und alle tausendmal.

Dein
Edm.
Hauptpostamt, 11h Vormittag.

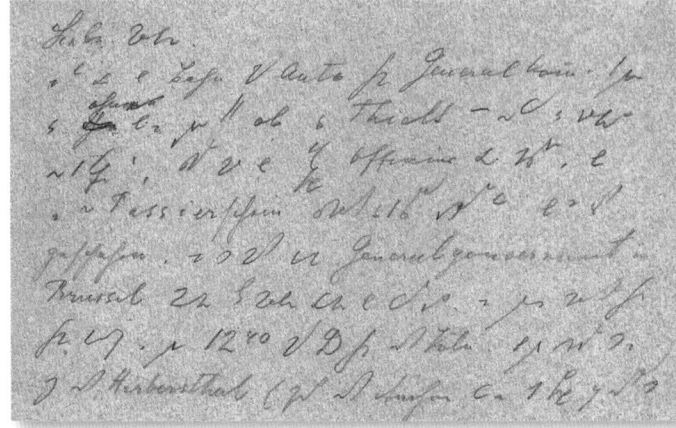

"Taking the 12:40 D-train to Cologne"

Dear Malvine,
I rode by car from the train to General Headquarters, and without knowing whether there had been any permission given from Thielt, the responsible officer told me yesterday that I would receive the pass at once. This has now happened. I have to report to the General Government in Brussels tomorrow because of my continuing journey. I then drove back to the station. Taking the 12:40 D-train to Cologne. The ticket I have already to Herbesthal (border with Aachen, where I have a 1 hour stay). I arrive at 2:56 in Br[ussels]. From Cologne I leave early around 8:00 am.

So everything went well. I will have lunch here again at the station.
I embrace and greet you and all a thousand times.
Your,
Edm.
Main Post Office, 11 in the morning.

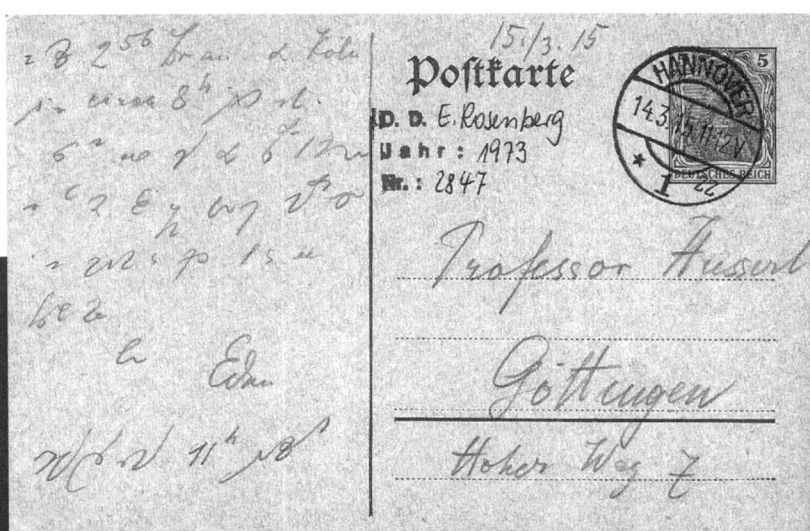

Postkarte von Husserl an seine Frau Malvine, 14. III. 1915. Husserl befand sich auf dem Weg nach Belgien, um seinen am 20. II. 1915 durch Lungenschuss verwundeten Sohn Wolfgang zu besuchen und auf dem Krankentransport nach Deutschland zu begleiten.

Postcard from Husserl to his wife Malvine, 14 March 1915. Husserl was on his way to Belgium to accompany his son Wolfgang on the medical transport train, who had been wounded on 20 February 1915 with a gunshot wound to his lung.

„Ob mich da Gert erwartet?"

Mont<a>g Abend
L<iebe> M<alvine>.
Ich kann erst 7.02 früh nach O<ostnieuwkerke> bzw. Roulers fahren und bin dann 7.51 abends in R<oulers>!!
Im Gouvernement ist man von rührender Freundlichkeit. Amtlich wurde nach Laz<arett> 87 telegr<aphiert> u. meine Ankunft angekündigt. Ob mich da Gert erwartet? Ein wenig habe ich mich in der Stadt umgesehen, na was man so in 2/3 Stunden kann. Unsympathisch, protzig, interessant doch.
Tausend Grüße
Dein
Edmund

Postkarte von Husserl an seine Frau Malvine, 19. III. 1915. – Husserl reist über Brüssel, um seinen Sohn Wolfgang im Lazarett in Belgien zu besuchen.

Postcard from Husserl to his wife Malvine, 19 March 1915. – Husserl passes through Brussels on his way to visit his son Wolfgang in a military hospital in Belgium.

"Is Gert expecting me there?"

Mond[ay] Evening

D[ear] M[alvine],
I can only leave early at 7:02 am for O[ostnieuwkerke] as well as Roulers and then I'm only at 7:51 in the evening in Roulers!!
Those in the government are of touching kindness. Hospital 87 was officially tele[graphed] in order to announce my arrival. Is Gert expecting me there? I looked a little around the town, which one can do in 2-3 hours. Unsympathetic and pretentious, but not uninteresting.
Thousand greetings
Your
Edmund

„Vor 1 Woche können wir Wolfgang nicht zuhause haben"

9h Ab<en>d
L<iebe> Malvine!
Auf Wunsch W<olfgang>s bleibe ich noch morgen hier. Das Gesuch um Überweisung ist an das Res<erve>L<azarett> Dortmund zu richten. Beigelegt muß sein die Bescheinigung des R<eserve>L<azaretts> Göttingen (dieselbe, die wir dem Gesuch nach Thielt beigelegt haben). Bitte lasse Dir das ausstellen, damit ich bei meiner Rückkunft sogleich das Gesuch schreiben kann. W<olfgang> ist außerordentlich schön und gut hier untergebracht und hat ungeheuren Appetit. Es kommt daher nicht auf einen Tag an. Er ist sehr vergnügt. Der Arzt sagt, er muß ohnehin jetzt einige Tage noch zu Bett liegen. Vor 1 Woche können wir W<olfgang> nicht zuhause haben.
Dein
Edm.

Res<erve>laz<arett> Kronenburg, wo Wolfg<ang> untergebracht ist. Sehr schön und behaglich. Ich habe noch kein Hotel, ich hatte immerfort mit dem Laz<arett> zu tun. Es dauerte Stunden, bis ich es eruirt hatte. W<olfgang> hat die Fenster in diesen schönen Garten

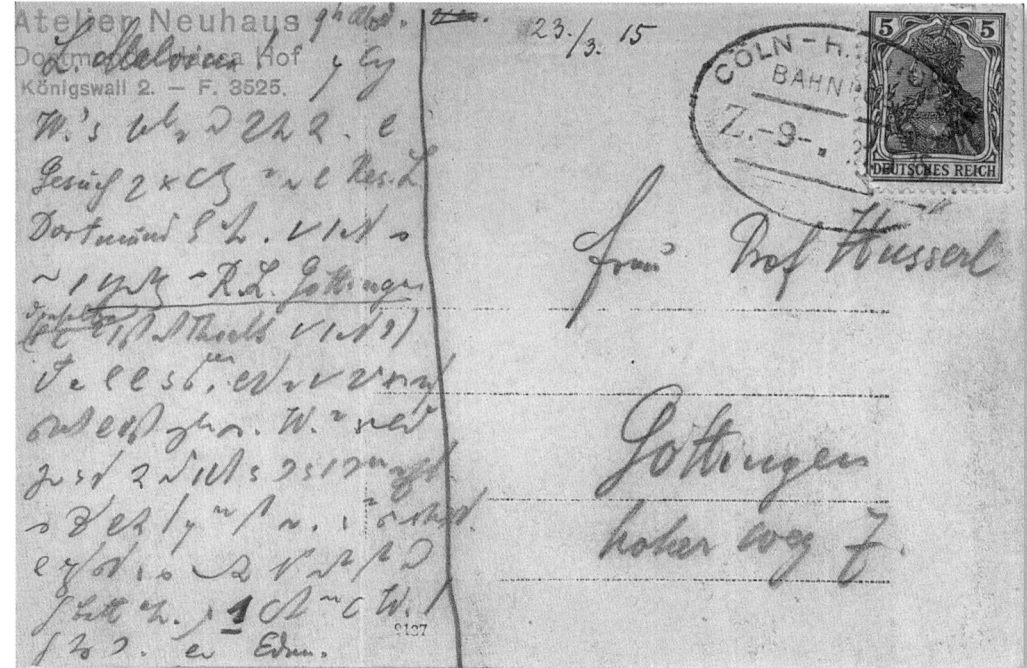

Postkarte von Husserl an seine Frau Malvine, 21. III. 1915

Postcard from Husserl to his wife, Malvine, 21 March 1915

"We can't expect to have Wolfgang home before 1 week"

9:00 evening
Dear Malvine!
At Wolfgang's request, I'll stay here until tomorrow. The application for transfer is to be addressed to the Reserve Hos[pital] in Dortmund. It must be accompanied by the certificate of the R[eserve] H[ospital] in Göttingen (the same one which we submitted in request to Thielt). Please let this be issued, so that I can write the request upon my return. W[olfgang] is extraordinarily beautiful and well taken care of here and has an incredible appetite. It doesn't depend on the day. He is very well in comfort. The doctor says that he must without question remain in bed for some more days. We can't expect to have W[olfgang] home before 1 week.
Your
Edm.

Res[erve] Hos[pital] Kronenburg, where Wolfg[ang] is housed. Very nice and comfortable. I still don't have a hotel. I was always busy at the hospital. It took hours until I could find it. W[olfgang] has a window over-looking this beautiful garden.

„Hurra!
Eben war Papa da"

Liebste Mama!
16. 3. <19>15

Hurra! Eben war Papa da. Er kam gestern Abend 7.51 <Uhr> in Roulers an. Gerhart bekam Urlaub und holte ihn von der Bahn ab. Beide übernachteten im Hotel Bourgogne. Wenn Gerhart Urlaub erhält, bleibt Papa bis Sonntag da, wo das Regiment wieder in den Graben geht. Ich lasse mich dann nach Roulers ins Kriegslazarett überführen. Es wäre ja langweilig für Papa, wenn er jeden Morgen mit dem Lokalzug nach hier herüber fahren sollte. Ich freue mich außerordentlich über Papas Besuch und dass unser beider Wunsch in Erfüllung gegangen ist. Ich habe übrigens vom kommandierenden General das Eiserne Kreuz bekommen. Sage bitte niemandem etwas.

Herzlichst, Wolfgang
Ich schreibe jetzt nicht mehr.

Liebe Malvine!
Donnerstagvormittag <18. 3. 1915>

Gestern also den Tag über bei Wolf-Ritter des Kreuzes, das ihm vom komm<andierenden> General persönlich überreicht wurde. – Alle möglichen hohen und niederen Militärs gesprochen, nämlich auch der Divisionär ließ sich mir vorstellen (oder umgekehrt) und erkundigte sich sehr fr<eundlich> nach Wolf, besonders zwei Mal auch der Regimentskommandeur, ein wahrer Kavalier. ... Wolf sieht sehr gut aus, stark abgemagert, noch etwas schwach, sehr guter Dinge. Mittags aß ich als Gast der Gerhart'schen Kameradschaft das Mannschaftsessen. Die Jungen (Hippel etc.) gesprochen. Göppert traf ich, als ich zum Zügle ging, das ich dadurch versäumte, erhielt dann aber vom Divisionsstab einen zweirädrigen Wagen nach Roulers, wo ich zum 2. Mal übernachtete. Gerhart erhielt Urlaub bis Samstag, und ich hoffe so lange in R<oulers> bleiben zu können – wenn nicht der Lazarettzug früher abgeht. Gerhart sehr gut aussehend. ...

Herzliche Grüße,
Edmund und Gerhart

Aus den Kriegsbriefen der Husserl-Söhne: Wolfgang Husserl an seine Mutter, 16. III. 1915; Edmund und Gerhart Husserl an Malvine Husserl, 18. III. 1915

From the war-letters of Husserl's sons: Wolfgang Husserl to his mother, 16 March 1915; Edmund and Gerhart Husserl to Malvine Husserl, 18 March 1915

"Hurray!
Papa was just here"

Dearest Mama!
16 March [19]15

Hurray! Papa was just here. He came yesterday evening at 7:51 in Roulers. Gerhart received leave and picked him up from the train. Both spent the night at Hotel Bourgogne. If Gerhart receives leave, Papa will stay until Sunday, when the regiment must go back to the trenches. I will then be transported to the military field hospital in Roulers. It would be boring for Papa, if he had to come over here every morning with the local train. I am very happy with Papa's visit and that both of our wishes have been fulfilled. By the way, I have received the Iron Cross from the commanding General. Please do not tell anyone about this.

Yours,
Wolfgang
I will not write any more.

Dear Malvine!
Thursday morning [18 March 1915]

Yesterday all day with Wolf, Knight of the Cross, which was personally given to him by the com[manding] General. – Spoke with all kinds of high and low ranking military figures, and was even presented (or he was presented to me) to the Divisional Commander, who asked about Wolf in a friendly manner, and even the Regimental Commander asked twice, a real trooper ... Wolf looks very good, very emaciated, still a little weak, all very good. At noon, I ate as a guest of Gerhart's comrades. Spoke with the boys (Hippel and others). I met Göppert as I was going to get the local train, which I therefore missed, but then got from the Divisional Staff a two-wheel car to Roulers, where I stayed overnight for the second time. Gerhart received leave until Saturday, and I hope to be able to stay in R[oulers] for as long – if the hospital train does not leave earlier. Gerhart looks very good ...

Best regards,
Edmund and Gerhart

„Über das schwere Unglück, das Mirbts getroffen hat, bin ich aufs Tiefste erschüttert"

Liebste Mama!
26. Juli 1915

… Über das schwere Unglück, das Mirbts getroffen hat, bin ich aufs Tiefste erschüttert. Mit Heinz M. war ich gerade vor einem Jahr viel zusammen. Wie kommt es, dass Karli doch Soldat wird? Hat er sich freiwillig gemeldet? …

Nun habe ich Dir auch Trauriges mitzuteilen. Die Kompanie hat Freitagnacht durch Schrapnells beim Schanzen wieder Verluste gehabt, 1 Toten und 2 sehr schwer verwundet; ferner ist von uns jener nette elsässische Kriegsfreiwilliger, von dem ich schrieb, hoffnungslos schwer verwundet.

Herzliche Grüße,
W.

Heinz Mirbt (ein Freund von Wolfgang Husserl) fiel am 13. VII. 1915. Die Aufnahme zeigt ihn auf seinem Pferd wenige Tage vor seinem Tod. Er war der Sohn von Carl Theodor Mirbt (1860-1929), seit 1912 in Göttingen Professor für Kirchengeschichte und Missionswissenschaft, dessen Buch „Quellen zur Geschichte des Papsttums und des Römischen Katholizismus" die Widmung trägt: „Dem Gedächtnis meines Sohnes Heinz Mirbt, Student der Theologie, gefallen als Kriegsfreiwilliger am 13. Juli 1915."

Heinz Mirbt, friend of Wolfgang Husserl, fell on 13 July 1915. The photo shows him on his horse a few days before his death. He was the son of Carl Theodor Mirbt (1860-1929), since 1912 Professor of Church History and Missionary Studies in Göttingen, whose book "Sources on the History of the Papacy and Roman Catholicism" bears the dedication: "The memory of my son Heinz Mirbt, student of theology, fallen as a volunteer on July 13, 1915."

*Aus den Kriegsbriefen der Husserl-Söhne:
Wolfgang Husserl an seine Mutter, 26. VII. 1915*

*From the war-letters of Husserl's sons:
Wolfgang Husserl to his mother, 26 July 1915*

"The terrible misfortune that has befallen the Mirbts has touched me profoundly"

Dearest Mama!
26 July 1915

… The terrible misfortune that has befallen the Mirbts has touched me profoundly. I was just last year often together with Heinz M. How did it happen that in fact Karli became a soldier? Did he volunteer? …

I now have something sad to communicate. The company suffered once again casualties on Friday night from shrapnel while working on the entrenchment. 1 dead and 2 severely wounded. Additionally, one of our very nice war-volunteers from Alsace, whom I have written about, is hopelessly gravely wounded.

Heartfelt wishes,
W.

Aus dem Kriegstagebuch von Wolfgang Husserl, 30. Mai – 28. Juni 1915

Tagebuch vom 30. Mai bis 28. Juni 1915

Sonntag, den 30. Mai wurde ich als geheilt und felddienstfähig vom Reservelazarett Göttingen entlassen.

Montag, den 31. Mai. Fahrt zum Ersatzbataillon (II. Ersatzbataillon des I.R. 107) nach Eisenach. Während der Reise und dort treffe ich viele Kameraden. Ich melde mich auf der Schreibstube der 5. Kompanie und übernachte in der Stadt bei Privatleuten (Kathrinenstr. 10).

Dienstag, 1. Juni. Um 6 ¾ Revierdienst. Es wird mir und allen, die aus Lazaretten kommen, 14 Tage Erholungsurlaub zudiktiert. Um 9 Uhr Angabe der Personalien auf <der> Schreibstube. Einreichung des Urlaubscheines. Dann antreten. Einteilung in Korporalschaften. Ich 10. Kompanie, Korporalschaftsführer Kriegsfreiwilliger Gefreiter Danert. Löhnung. Mittagessen in der Stadt. Um 2 Uhr hole ich mir meinen Urlaubschein mit Fahrschein hin und zurück ab. Abfahrt 3.16 <Uhr> Bebra – Göttingen. Abends komme ich an. Große, freudige Überraschung. Bei uns ist geflaggt.

2. Juni bis 16. Juni (Erholungsurlaub). Ich höre regelmäßig bei Bertholet Psalmen und beschäftige mich mit Kriegsliteratur. Ernst von Hippel auf Urlaub in Göttingen. Am 9. Juni *dies academicus*. Prachtvolle Rede von Herrn Runge (Mathematik und Kultur). 142 Studenten, 5 Dozenten gefallen. Während der 14 Tage herrscht immer schönes Wetter, zum Teil große Hitze. Am Montag, den 14., Hippels zu einer Bowle bei uns.

Mittwoch, den 16. Zum zweiten Mal Abschied. Viele Geschenke. Vormittag noch bei Littmann im Kolleg. Ich fahre mit Mama nach Eisenach. Wohnen im Thüringer Hof. Melde mich auf Schreibstube und frage beim Bataillonsbüro wegen Überweisung an das Korps von Gündell R.I.R. 19 nach. Erfahre aber nichts. Am nächsten Tag

Donnerstag, 17. Morgens mache ich keinen Dienst. Spaziergang auf die Wartburg. Nachmittags ärztliche Untersuchung. „Haben Sie irgendwelche Beschwerden?" „Nein." „Gut." F<reitag>, dann auf Schreibstube kommen. Meldung ans Bataillon: Der Kriegsfreiwillige Husserl von Urlaub zurückgekehrt. Löhnung, Verpflegungsgeld 13, 80 M<ark>. Empfang Drillichzeug, harmloser Appell, darin Brustbeutel vergessen! Abends zusammen mit Runge im Zimmermannshotel.

18. Juni. 16 Uhr Marschübung nach der Hohen Sonne; bemühte mich, mit dem abends abgehenden Transport mitzukommen. Mama hindert mich. Nachmittags Geländeübung.

Sonnabend, 19. Juni. Vormittags Marschübung Tiergarten (Menagerie), nachmittags Neueinteilung der Kompanie, wir essen im Tiergarten zu Abend. Ich wohne nicht mehr im Hotel, sondern Mühlhäuserstr. 4 bei Dekorationsmaler Hahn zusammen mit einem Kameraden aus der 11. Kompanie.

Wolfgang Husserls Kriegstagebuch vom 30. Mai - 28. Juni 1915 (Schreibmaschinenabschrift seiner Schwester). – Einige Wochen nach seinem Lungenschuss (22. Februar 1915) wird Wolfgang in einem Reservelazarett in Göttingen untergebracht. Ende Mai 1915 als gesund und felddienstfähig entlassen, kommt er zunächst in ein Ersatzbataillon nach Eisenach. Dort beginnt er dies Tagebuch zu schreiben.

Wolfgang Husserl's war diary from May 30 to June 28, 1915 (as type-written from his sister). – A few weeks after his lung wound (on February 22, 1915), Wolfgang was lodged in a Military Hospital in Göttingen. At the end of May 1915, he was released healthly and ready to service in the field, and was then sent for a replacement battalion in Eisenach, where he began to write this diary.

Sonntag, 20. Juni. 12 Uhr Appell durch den Oberleutnant, der 10 Minuten dauert. Wir essen im Hotel. 3.16 <Uhr> fährt Mama.

Montag, 21. Juni. 2 Stunden Kartoffelschälen, dann Löhnungsappell. Um 3 Uhr werde ich feldmarschmäßig eingekleidet (Unteroffizier Brühl). Keine Waffen. Nach Empfang von 3,48 Mark Verpflegungsgeld in Marsch gesetzt. Eisenach nach Metz über Göttingen, Metz, Baroncourt. Abfahrt 7.09 <Uhr>, in Bebra übliche Pause. Telegraphiere nach Hause: Komme 12.25 in Göttingen an.

Dienstag, 22. Juni. Ich fahre 2.48 weiter, Frankfurt 8.54 <Uhr> an. Logiere, nachdem von der Bahnhofskommandantur Erlaubnis erhalten zum Verlassen derselben, am Markte. Esse im Restaurant daselbst, Siegesläuten wegen Lemberg. Hurra!

Mittwoch, 23. Juni. Abfahrt 7.34 nach Metz, von da nach Longuyon, esse in der Kantine. Warte von 3 bis 6 <Uhr> auf den Zug nach Baroncourt. Das L<onguyon> ist ein zerschossenes Nest. Komme 6.46 in Baroncourt an, gehe von da nach Bouligny zum Stab der 9. Reserve-Division. Der Major bestimmt, ich solle ½ 10 mit 2 Offiziersstellvertretern im Auto zum Regiment herausfahren nach Etain. Werden dort vom Regimentsadjutanten in Empfang genommen, vom Regimentskommandeur begrüßt, gefragt wie lange im Felde gewesen etc., werden der 10. Kompanie zugeteilt. Ein

From Wolfgang Husserl's War Diary, 30 May – 28 June 1915

Diary from 30 May to 28 June 1915

On Sunday, May 30th, I was discharged as healthy and ready for service in the field from the military hospital in Göttingen.

Monday, May 31st. Drove to the replacement battalion (II Replacement battalion of the 107th Infantry Regiment) to Eisenach. During the trip, I meet many comrades. I reported at the office of the 5th company and spent the night in the city with local residents (Kathrinenstr. 10).

Tuesday, June 1st. Around 6:45 am reveille duty. For all those, like myself, who are returning from hospital, given 14 days of rest. Around 9:00 am, distribution of personal gear in the secretarial office. Submission of pass for holidays. Then falling into order and divided into platoons. I, in the 10th Company, under Corporal Commander, war volunteer Danert. Wages. Lunch in the city. Around 2:00 pm, I get my holiday pass with a return train ticket. Departure 3:16 [pm] to Bebra - Göttingen. In the evening I arrive. Great, joyful surprise. We've hung flags at our place.

2 June to 16 June (rest and relaxation holiday). I regularly listen to Psalms at Bertholet's and read war literature. Ernst von Hippel on holiday in Göttingen. On 9 June dies academicus [academic day]. A splendid speech by Mr. Runge (Mathematics and Culture). 142 students, 5 lecturers were killed in action. During the past 14 days, always nice weather, in some cases very hot. On Monday the 14th, Hippel came over to our place to drink some wine-punch.

Wednesday, the 16th. For the second time departure. Many gifts. In the morning with Littmann at the seminar. I am going to Eisenach with Mama. Staying at the Thüringer Hof. Reported to the secretarial office and inquired with the Battalion Office about the transfer to Gündell's Corps [and] the 19th Infantry Regiment. Haven't heard anything yet. On the next day

Thursday, the 17th. I do not have any duty in the morning. Stroll to the Wartburg. In the afternoon, medical examination. "Do you have any complaints?" "No." "Good." F[riday], then to the office. Message from the Battalion: the war-volunteer Wolfgang returned from leave. Pay, boarding allowance 13, 80 M[arks]. Received drills, harmless roll call, forgot my chest bag! In the evening together with Runge in the Zimmermannshotel.

18th of June. 4 pm, training march to the Hohe Sonne; tried to get the evening departing transport. Mama prevents me. Afternoon training ground exercises.

Saturday, June 19th. In the morning, training march to the zoo (the menagerie), in the afternoon, new assignments to a company, we ate at the zoo in the evening. I'm no longer staying in the hotel, but in Mühlhäuserstrasse 4 with the decorative painter Hahn along with a comrade from the 11th Company.

Radfahrer bringt mich nach Rouvers, wo die Kompanie in Ruhe ist. Kompanie ist zum Schanzen weg, stellte mich dem Kompaniefeldwebel und Leutnant und Kompanieführer vor. Wurde freundlich aufgenommen, nach Henkel gefragt. Schlafe bei der 9. Korporalschaft mit Matratze und Decken. Ort liegt gänzlich in Trümmern, nur Kirche erhalten.

Donnerstag, 24 .Juni. Aufnahme in die Stammrolle. Gewitter. 3h strammes Exerzieren, harmloses Granatfeuer (15 cm) hauptsächlich nach der Kirche.

Freitag, 25. Juni. Von nun an habe ich jeden Morgen um 8 Uhr in Etain beim Einjährigenunterricht beim Leutnant von Scheelinger zu sein, ein echter aktiver Leutnant, sehr famos. Nachmittag üblicher Dienst. Verpflegung ist gut. Schicken Essen von der Küche, die hier stationiert ist, Zigarren, dreimal täglich Kaffee.

Sonnabend, 26. Juni. Morgens Unterricht, Kommandieren üben. Die Kompanie hat währenddessen Besichtigung durch den Divisionskommandeur Guretzky, sonst kein Dienst.

Sonntag, 27. Juni. Kein Unterricht, nachmittags Biertrinken auf der Wiese unter schönen Pappelbäumen.

Montag, 28. Juni. Jahrestag des Mordes von Sarajevo. Morgens wie gewöhnlich, nachmittags exerzieren. Wir schlafen trotz der schrecklichen Fliegenplage. Wetter meist schön. Mitunter starke Niederschläge.

Sunday, June 20th. 12:00 am roll-call with the Lieutenant, lasted 10 minutes. We ate at the hotel. 3:16 [pm] Mama leaves.

Monday, June 21st. 2 hours of potato peeling, then roll-call for pay. Around 3:00 pm I am out-fitted in a uniform for field operations (non-commissioned officer Brühl). No weapons. After receiving 3.48 Marks for food money on the march. Eisenach to Metz via Göttingen, Metz, Baroncourt. Departure at 7:09 am, made the usual break in Bebra. Telegraphed home: Arrive at 12:25 pm in Göttingen.

Tuesday, June 22nd. I continue at 2:48 pm, Frankfurt 8:54 pm. Lodging, after receiving permission from the train-station commander to leave, at the Market. Ate in the restaurant there, Victory bells for Lemberg. Hooray!

Wednesday, June 23rd. Departure 7:34 am to Metz, from there to Longuyon, ate in the canteen. Wait for the train to Baroncourt from 3 to 6 o'clock. L[onguyon] is a shot-up place. Arrive in Baroncourt at 6:46 pm, and go from there to Bouligny to the Staff of the 9th Reserve Division. The Major decides I should go out to the Regiment around 9:30 with 2 officer representatives in the car to Etain. Was received there by the regimental adjutant, greeted by the regimental commander, asked how long in the field, etc., and assigned to the 10th Company. A cyclist takes me to Rouvers, where the company is resting. The company went to work on the entrenchment, so I presented myself to the company Staff Sergeant and Lieutenant and company commander. Was received kindly, asked about Henkel. Slept with the platoon on a mattress and [with] blankets. Place is entirely in ruins, only church preserved.

Thursday, June 24th. Fell into ranks for roll-call. Thunderstorm. 3 hours of strenuous exercise, harmless artillery fire (15 cm) mainly around the church.

Friday, June 25th. From now on I have to be in Etain at eight o'clock every morning for first-year instruction with Lieutenant Scheelinger, a genuinely active Lieutenant, very brilliant. Afternoon, usual service. Food is good. Food sent over from the kitchen that is stationed here, cigars, three times a day coffee.

Saturday, June 26th. Teaching in the morning, practice commanding. The company has inspection by the Commander-in-Chief, Guretzky, but otherwise no duty.

Sunday, June 27th. No instruction, in the afternoon beers on the meadow under beautiful poplar trees.

Monday, June 28th. Anniversary of the murder in Sarajevo. In the morning, as usual, training in the afternoon. We sleep despite the terrible plague of flies. Weather mostly nice. With occasional thunderstorms.

„Dass es ihm an Eifer und soldatischem Mut gefehlt hat, kann ich nicht gut annehmen"

"I can't really accept that he lacked zeal and military courage"

Darf ich es wagen, mich als besorgter Vater an den Sohn eines von mir hochgeschätzten früheren Kollegen zu wenden? Es fällt mir auf, dass mein in Ihrer Kompanie stehender Sohn <Gerhart> schon seit langer Zeit sehr kärgliche Berichte sendet, in denen eine niedergedrückte Stimmung unverkennbar ist. Es hängt offenbar damit zusammen, dass er, ungleich vielen seiner gleichaltrigen und jüngeren Studienkollegen, nicht avanciert ist und er scheint sich dessen geradezu zu schämen, dass er, nachdem er den Krieg von Anfang mitgemacht und bei vielen Gelegenheiten seine Tapferkeit erwiesen hat, mit dem E<isernen> K<reuz> übergangen worden ist. Sollte gegen ihn etwas vorliegen? Dass es ihm an Eifer und soldatischem Mut gefehlt hat, kann ich nicht gut annehmen. So sprach mir z.B. der Vater eines seiner verwundeten Kameraden im vorigen Winter schriftlich seinen Dank dafür aus, dass mein Sohn dem seinen im ersten großen Gefechte des R<e>g<imen>ts das Leben gerettet, als er ihn mitten im Kugelregen unter Preisgabe der eigenen Deckung aus dem Felde geholt und in Sicherheit gebracht hat. Natürlich muss mein Sohn seine Zurücksetzung jetzt doppelt empfinden, da sein jüngerer Bruder, der nach Wiederherstellung von seiner Verwundung in das 19. Res<erve>-R<e>g<imen>t gekommen ist, in wenigen Monaten vom Musketier zum Leutnant befördert ist.

Wenn ich denke, mit welcher Begeisterung mein Sohn am ersten Mobilmachungstage sich als Freiwilliger gemeldet und wie gern er alle Mühen des Krieges getragen hat, so bekümmert es mich sehr, dass unter den gegebenen Verhältnissen seine Freudigkeit dahinzuschwinden droht.

Ich möchte zum Schluss noch nachdrücklich betonen, dass der einzige Zweck dieses Briefes eine streng vertrauliche Anfrage ist, ob in dem militärischen oder persönlichen Verhalten meines Sohnes <alles> einwandfrei ist.

Should I dare, as a concerned father, turn to the son of a former colleague, whom I have esteemed? It struck me that my son, Gerhart, who has been serving in your company, had long been sending very meager reports, in which a depressed mood is unmistakable. It is obviously connected to the fact that, unlike many of his student peers of the same age and even younger, he has not advanced [in rank], and he seems to be ashamed of the fact that, having fought in the war from the outset, and having shown his bravery on many occasions, he has been passed over for the I[ron] C[ross]. Might there be anything against him? I can't really accept that he lacked zeal and military courage. For example, the father of one of his wounded comrades last winter wrote in gratitude for the fact that my son saved his life during the first major combat of the Regiment, as he saved him from the field, leaving any cover, amidst a rain of bullets and brought him to safety. Of course, my son must now feel his being kept back even more, given that his younger brother, who, after recovering from his wounds has arrived with the 19th Re[serve] Re[giment], was in a few months promoted from Private to Lieutenant.

If I think with what enthusiasm my son reported on the first mobilization day as a volunteer, and how gladly he had borne all the troubles of the war, I am very much troubled by the fact that, under these circumstances, his joy is bound to disappear.

I would like to emphasize, finally, that the sole purpose of this letter is a strictly confidential question as to whether the military or personal conduct of my son is free from [any] reprimand.

Entwurf eines Briefes von Husserl an Hermann Ebbinghaus jr., ca. Herbst 1915 (siehe auch unten, S. 215). – Leutnant Ebbinghaus war ein Sohn des 1909 verstorbenen Psychologen Hermann Ebbinghaus

Draft for a letter from Husserl to Hermann Ebbinghaus Jr. around Fall 1915 (see also below, p. 215). – Lieutenant Ebbinghaus was the son of the psychologist Hermann Ebbinghaus (died in 1909)

"Hier schicke ich Dir eine Teilaufnahme meines Lazaretts, in dem ich seit d. 1. Sept. bin"

16. IX. <19>15
Lieber Onkel Albrecht!
Hier schicke ich Dir eine Teilaufnahme meines Lazaretts, in dem ich seit d. 1. Sept. bin. Von Gerhart u. Wolfgang haben wir gute Nachrichten. Von Wolfgang heute wieder ein längerer interessanter Brief. Hoffentlich ist Euch die Sommererholung gut bekommen!
Herzl. Grüsse Euch allen von Eurer Elli

"Here I send you a small portrait of my hospital where I am since 1 September"

16 Sept. [19]15
Dear Uncle Albrecht!
Here I send you a small portrait of my hospital, where I am since 1 September. Regarding Gerhart & Wolfgang, we have good news. From Wolfgang today again a longer and interesting letter. Hopefully, the summer vacation has served you well!
Warm Greetings to all of you, your Elli

Postkarte von Elli Husserl an Gustav Albrecht, 16. IX. 1915

Postcard from Elli Husserl to Gustav Albrecht, 16 September 1915

„So schön, dass wir drei uniformiert sind"

Liebe Elli!

Etain, den 14. 1. 1916

Gestern erhielt ich aus Karlsruhe die Nachricht, dass Papa den Ruf nach Freiburg angenommen hat. Die Gefühle, die ich habe, sind gemischt. Zunächst freue ich mich sehr, dass Papa eine Anerkennung seiner Arbeit auch in dieser Form zuteil wurde. Aber bedauerst Du nicht auch, dass wir unser schönes Haus, unsere zahlreichen Bekannten und Freunde, kurzum unsere Heimat verlassen müssen? Es tut mir leid, dass ich, wenn ich diesen Krieg glücklich überstehe, nicht nach Göttingen, sondern nach dem fremden Freiburg zurückkehren soll. Na, die Freude des Wiedersehens wird aber, denke ich, solche Gedanken gar nicht aufkommen lassen. Was wird nun aus Dir werden? Wirst Du in Göttingen Deine Verwundeten weiter pflegen? Du weißt nicht, wie stolz ich auf Dich bin. So schön, dass wir drei uniformiert sind. Ich glaube, Du hast es viel schwerer als wir hier draußen im friedlichen Stellungskrieg. Ich sitze hier in einem ebenso schönen Zimmer wie zu Hause, schlafe in einem richtigen Bett, habe elektrisches Licht, mehr Bedienung, sehr gutes Essen und leider Gottes in der letzten Zeit sehr wenig zu tun. Man muss sich schämen, wenn man bedenkt, wie gut man es hat <...>

"So nice that all three of us are in uniform"

Dear Elli!

Etain, 14 January 1916

Yesterday I received news from Karlsruhe that Papa has accepted the call to Freiburg. My feelings are mixed. I am, of course, very pleased that Papa has received recognition for his work in this form. But don't you regret that we have to leave our beautiful home, our numerous friends, in short, our homeland? I am sorry that if I happily survive this war, that I shall not return to Göttingen, but to strange Freiburg. Well, the joy of reunion will not, I think, allow such thoughts to arise at all. What will become of you? Will you continue to care for your wounded in Göttingen? You do not know how proud I am of you. So nice that all three of us are in uniform. I think you've got it a lot harder than us out here in this peaceful trench warfare. I'm sitting here in a beautiful room like one at home, sleeping in a proper bed, with electrical lighting, good service, excellent food, and unfortunately very little to do these past days. When one thinks about how good one has it here, one can't help but feel ashamed [...]

Aus den Kriegsbriefen der Husserl-Söhne: Wolfgang Husserl an seine Schwester, 14. I. 1916

From the war-letters of Husserl's sons: Wolfgang Husserl to his sister, 14 January 1916

„Es grüßt Dich herzlichst Deine Tante Hilbert"

Käthe und David Hilbert (im Hintergrund der Mathematiker Ernst Hellinger), um 1905

Käthe und David Hilbert (in the background the mathematician Ernst Hellinger), around 1905

Gött<ingen,> 27. Februar <1916>
Liebster Wolfgang!

Ich habe mich herzlich gefreut gestern Abend endlich wieder mal von Dir zu hören! Danke Dir sehr für Deine Karte und schicke Dir hier ein Paar Kartenbriefe, damit Du möglichst bald wieder ein Paar Worte schreibst. Gleichzeitig kriegst Du Deine Zigaretten. Hoffentlich bleibt Ihr noch in Eurer alten Stellung. Schrieb ich Dir eigentlich, daß ich von Littmann einen Vortrag hörte über Ägypten. Ich sah ihn zum ersten Mal. Hier ist jetzt endlich schönes klares Winterwetter und Schnee, wir haben es benutzt um einen Ausflug nach <…> zu machen, dabei mußte ich lebhaft an unsre Wanderung nach der <…> denken. Das unternehmen wir, wenn Du uns das nächste Mal besuchst, Wolfgang. Es grüßt Dich herzlichst Deine Tante Hilbert.

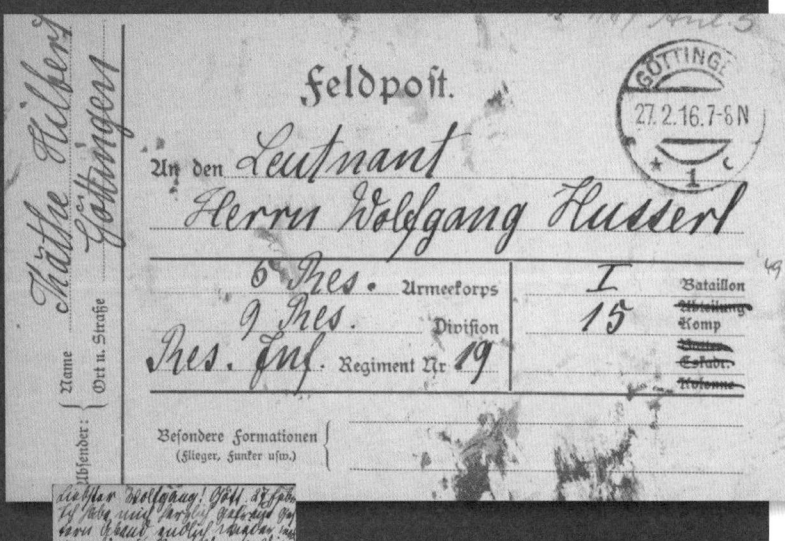

Feldpostkarte von Käthe Hilbert an Wolfgang Husserl, 27. II. 1916

Field postcard from Käthe Hilbert to Wolfgang Husserl, 27 February 1916

"Warm greetings from your Aunt Hilbert"

Gött[ingen], 27 February [1916]
Dearest Wolfgang!

I was very happy yesterday evening to finally have heard from you again! Thank you very much for your card and I am sending you here a few letter-cards, so that you can write again a few words as soon as possible. At the same time you'll get your cigarettes. Hopefully, you'll still remain in your old position. I write to you actually [to say] that I saw Littmann for the first time. Here, it's now beautiful with clear winter weather and snow, [so] we took this opportunity to go on an excursion to […] and I vividly remembered our walks together to […]. We'll have to make this hike when you visit us the next time, Wolfgang. Warm greetings from your Aunt Hilbert.

„Jetzt ist die Herrlichkeit zu Ende. Ich muss aufhören zu schreiben. Los geht's!"

6.3.1916

Vor dem Abmarsch nach dem 15 Minuten entfernten Ouvrage d' Hardaumont

Liebe Eltern!

Kaum hat man sich irgendwo eingerichtet, muss man wieder weg. Unsere Stellung und Unterkunft hatten wir recht nett ausgebaut, da wurde gestern III./19 von III./6 abgelöst. Gestern Morgen rückten wir hier an diesen steilen, kahlen Berghang, einige 100 Meter vom Walde entfernt, wo wir nur Gräben u. Erdlöcher für einen Zug vorfanden. Also wieder einbuddeln! Es war wenigstens Tag und schönes Wetter, so dass am Abend alles tadellos untergebracht war. Man hebt einen 1,50 m tiefen Graben aus, buddelt in Brust- und Rückenwehr gegenüber Löcher, wo Kopf u. Beine hinkommen, bespannt das Ganze mit Zelten, dann ist die Sache fertig. Etwas Holzwolle als Streu wurde geliefert. Aus dem Walde konnte man sich Holz holen, aus dem ¾ Stunde entfernten Orte Bezonvaux Bretter, Heu u.a. Heute bekamen wir Dachpappe geliefert. Essen u. Kaffee kann bei Tage geholt werden – ein großer Vorteil. Ich hatte mit meinem Vizefeldwebel zusammen ein recht hübsches Loch gebaut und tüchtig mit daran geschafft. Die Decken bilden Stämme, die ich im Walde schlagen ließ. Wir schliefen heute Nacht prächtig auf Reisig, Holzwolle und Heu in einem Sack. In der Wand ließ ich in die Erde einen Kamin bohren. So können wir auch feuern. Wände mit alten Tüchern bespannt. Jetzt ist die Herrlichkeit zu Ende. Ich muss aufhören zu schreiben. Los geht's!

7.3.1916

Nun schreibe ich vom Hardaumont aus der Ouvrage, die besteht aus 2 betonierten Kasematten, die kreisförmig umstellt sind, anschließend daran Lauf- und Schützengräben. Wir liegen in fürchterlicher Enge in stickiger Luft und Hitze in den beiden Kasematten, die grässlich schmutzig sind. Es ist wie damals auf den Heuböden in Flandern – wenn man das Lokal verlassen will, muss man über so und so viele Arme, Köpfe, Beine steigen. Man muss aber immer drin bleiben, da man draußen vor den häufigen heftigen Feuerüberfällen der feindlichen Artillerie nie sicher ist. Wir liegen nahe am Feinde, wir auf der Kuppe des Berges, der Feind am Hang. Heute Nacht wurden die Franzosen durch 50 aus allen Kompanien des Bataillons sich gemeldeten Freiwilligen unter Führung von Hauptmann Henkel und zweier Offiziere aus einem Sappenkopf vertrieben und 23 Gefangene gemacht. Hauptmann Henkel ist am Arm und Hals durch Handgranatensplitter nicht schwer verwundet. Heute schießt sich die schwere Artillerie wieder mal ein. Morgen soll ein vermutet noch heftigeres Konzert als am 2. März auf Vaux und Umgebung beginnen. Hoffentlich sind die Kerls dann mürbe und der Sturm gelingt. Die Artillerie ist durch Munition und Geschütze bedeutend verstärkt. Daher die Verzögerung in den Operationen.

Deinen Brief liebe Mama vom 29. 2. und 2. 3. erhalten. Vielen Dank! Gestern konnte ich mich in Ermangelung von Wasser in reiner Wäsche waschen, dank der beiden erhaltenen Pakete. Schmutzig bin ich fürchterlich. Ich glaube, Du würdest mich als Deinen Sohn verleugnen. Ich brauche Kerzen und Batterien.
W.

Draufschrift:
Herzlichen Gruß sendet Vizefeldwebel Müller, derzeitiger Bettnachbar des Herrn Leutnant.

"The glory is now over. I have to stop writing. Here we go!"

6 March 1916

Before leaving for Ouvrage d'Hardaumont 15 minutes away

Dear parents!

No sooner have we set up somewhere, we leave again. We had built our position and accommodations quite nicely, but yesterday we were relieved by the III/19 and III/6. Yesterday morning we came to this steep, bare mountain slope, a few hundred meters from the woods, where we discovered trenches and foxholes for a platoon. And so back to digging-in. There was a least day-light and nice weather, so that in the evening everything was impeccably arranged. You dig up a trench 1.5 meters deep, and dig holes into the front parapet and revetment, where your head and legs go, cover the entire thing with a tarp, and then it's finished. Wood shavings were delivered. From the woods, we can get wood, and from the town of Bezonvaux, about 45 minutes away, we received wood wool as straw. Today we were supplied with roofing. Food and coffee can be brought-up by day – a great advantage. Together with my Staff Sergeant, I efficiently dug-out a very nice foxhole. The roof is build from [tree]-trunks, which we felled from the woods. We slept tonight splendidly on sticks, wood shavings, and hay in a sack. In the wall I had a small fireplace hollowed out in the ground. So we can also fire. Walls are tied together with old cloths. The glory is now over. I have to stop writing. Here we go!

Die beiden Briefe, die Wolfgang kurz vor seinem Tod (8. März) an die Familie geschickt hat, wurden später von seiner Mutter abgeschrieben und an Freunde weitergeleitet. – Auf der Abschrift hat sie notiert: „Wolfgangs letzter Brief. Angekommen bei uns am 13. März, einen Tag nach der Todesbotschaft."

Both letters, which Wolfgang sent to this family shortly before his death (8th March), were later copied by his mother and sent to friends. In her copy, she noted: "Wolfgang's final letter. Arrived to us on March 13th, one day after news of his death."

"Am 8. März fiel für sein Vaterland"
"On March 8th died for his fatherland"

7 March 1916

Now I am writing from the Ouvrage at Hardaumont, which consists of two concrete encasements, which are circular in form, followed by parallel and protecting trenches.* We are lying in terrible confines with stuffy air and heat in both encasements, which are hideously filthy. It's much like as it was on the haylofts in Flanders – if one wants to leave this place, you have to climb over so many arms, heads, legs. But one must always remain here, because one is never safe outside from the frequent volleys of fire from the enemy artillery. We are close to the enemy, we are on the crest of the mountain, the enemy on the slope. Tonight, the French were chased away with 50 volunteers from every company in the battalion under the command of Captain Henkel and two officers from the sap-head and [we] bagged 23 prisoners. Captain Henkel was not severely wounded on his arm and neck by hand grenade splinters. Tomorrow, a more aggressive action will most likely be undertaken against Vaux and its surroundings than on March 2. Hopefully the boys are feeble and our attack will be successful! The artillery is significantly reinforced with ammunition and guns. Hence, the delay in the operations.

Your letter, dear Mama, from Feb. 29 and Mar. 2 received. Many thanks! Yesterday I could wash myself [despite] the lack of water with new laundry, thanks to the two packages received. I'm terribly dirty. I think that you would not recognize me as your son. I need candles and batteries.
W.

Inscription:
cordial greeting from Lance Sergeant Müller, presently bed neighbor of the Lieutenant.

* Translator's Note: The Ouvrage at Hardaumont is a protected set of reinforced trenches for infantry situated in front of the Fort of Douaumont at Verdun.

Todesanzeige für Wolfgang Husserl.

Obituary for Wolfgang Husserl. "On March 8th, our beloved son and brother Wolfgang Husserl, Reserve Lieutenant in the 19th Reserve Infantry Regiment, bearer of the Iron Cross, fell at the head of his unit in the assault on Verdun, at the age of 20…"

„Darunter Leutnant Ladenburg und Leutnant Husserl. Letzterer war sofort tot"

Nachmittagskämpfe 12-6 nachm.
12 mittags! Die Stunde des Angriffs war gekommen.

Am weitesten rechts in der Linie der Angreifer tauchte die 15. Ko<mpanie> aus den Deckungen hervor. In einem Sprung erreicht sie den Rand der Schlucht, die nach dem Ostrande von Dorf Vaux hinweist. Jetzt stürzen die Schützen den Hang hinunter, um die Tiefe der Schlucht zu gewinnen. Zwei MG. und zwei Flammenwerfer sind bei ihnen. In einem Abstande von 100 m folgt die Schützenlinie der 12. Ko.

Die 15. Ko. wendet sich südwärts gegen Vaux. Da erhält sie starkes Infanterie- und MG.-Feuer. Starke Verluste bei beiden Kompagnien treten ein. Doch der tapfere, umsichtige Kompagnieführer der 15., Ob<er>l<eutnan>t Alt, weiß sich zu helfen. Hören wir ihn selbst:

Aus einem Brief des Oblts. Alt (24.5.16):

„Nach imposanter Artillerievorbereitung ging unser Sturm los. In einem Lauf viele 100 m die Schlucht herunter. An Atempause dachte niemand, bis ein MG und ein quer durch die Schlucht sich hinziehender Graben Halt geboten. Das Feuer dieses MG und der Grabenbesatzung kostete mich im Handumdrehen etwa 80 Mann, darunter Lt. Ladenburg und Lt. Husserl. Letzterer war sofort tot. Wir bekamen kein Artilleriefeuer. Die feindliche Artillerie konnte nichts sehen; es wurde ihr von unserer ein Staub- und Rauchvorhang vorgezogen. Mit Hülfe eines MG hielt ich dann den feindlichen Graben nieder, was glänzend gelang. Arbeitete mich dann mit dem Rest der Kompagnie in die Flanke des feindlichen Grabens auf halbem Hange vor. Sah dann die Franzosen im Graben kauern und knallte sie schulterwehrweise zusammen. Nur fünf Gefangene machten wir; das Andere – 70-80 Mann – sind die Sühne gewesen für meine Opfer. Als ich in den

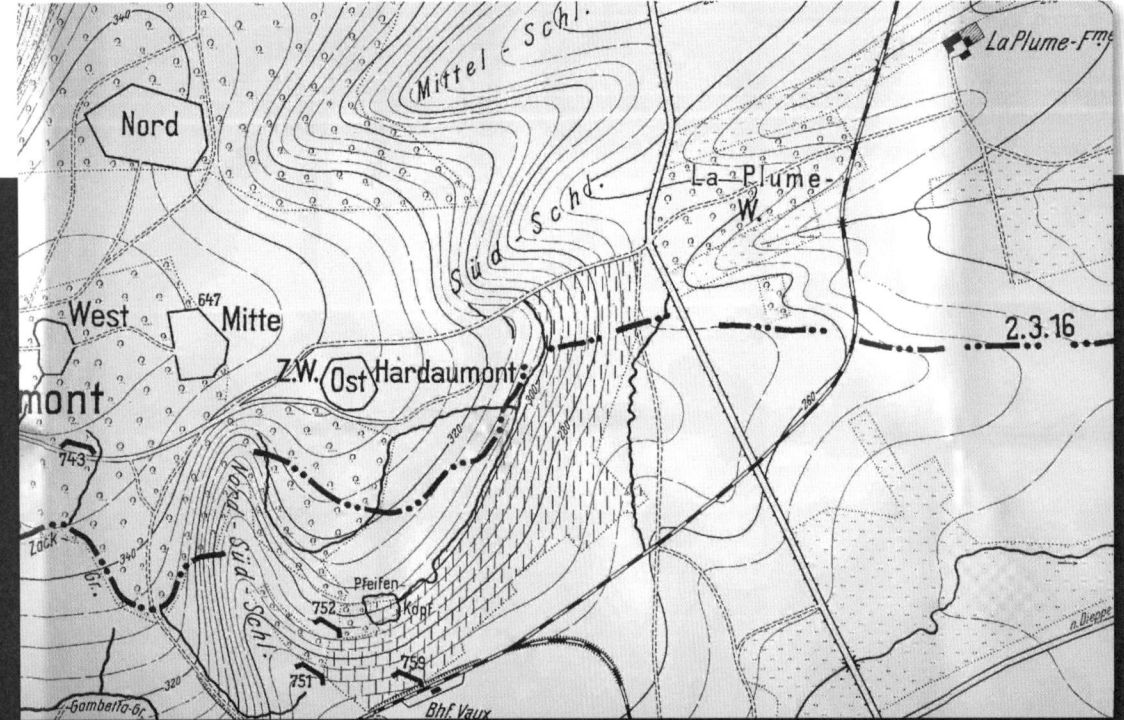

Karte zur Schlacht um Fort Vaux, bei der Wolfgang Husserl am 8. III. 1916 fiel

Map of the battle for Fort Vaux where Wolfgang Husserl fell at 8 March 1916

Graben stieg, stand ich neben dem französischen MG. Der Schütze war tot. Wir warfen die Leichen heraus, so dass sie vom Dorf Vaux zu sehen waren. Zeit 1.50! Zu dieser Zeit kam der Pfeifenkopf in die Hand der anderen Kompagnien. Die Jäger rechts von uns – wie das ganze III. Korps – waren zu dieser Zeit endgültig abgewiesen. Ich saß am Schluchtausgang und wartete, dass die Kompagnien vom Pfeifenkopf herabstiegen. Es geschah erst 6 abends!"

Schilderung der Todesumstände von Wolfgang Husserl durch einen seiner Vorgesetzten, Oberleutnant Alt, in: Geschichte des Reserve-Infanterie-Regiments Nr 19 im Weltkriege 1914-1918: Nach d. amtl. Kriegstagebüchern u. persönl. Berichten u. Aufzeichn., bearb. Alexander Schwencke, Oldenburg i. O. 1926 (Erinnerungsblätter deutscher Regimenter Bd. 124), S. 127.

Description of Wolfgang Husserl's death according to First Lieutenant Alt in: Geschichte des Reserve-Infanterie-Regiments Nr 19 im Weltkriege 1914-1918: Nach d. amtl. Kriegstagebüchern u. persönl. Berichten u. Aufzeichn., bearb. Alexander Schwencke, Oldenburg i. O., 1926 (Erinnerungsblätter deutscher Regimenter vol. 124), p. 127.

"Among them Lieutenant Ladeburg and Lieutenant Husserl. The latter was instantly killed"

Afternoon battles 12 – 6 afternoon.
Midday. The hour of the attack has come.

On the far right in the line of attack, 15th Company sprang forward from cover. In one bound, they reached the edge of a ravine, which points to the eastern edge of Vaux village. Now, the riflemen descend the slope to win the bottom of the gorge. Two machine-guns and two flame-throwers are with them. At a distance of 100 meters follows the defensive line of the 12th Company.

15th Company turns southwards against Vaux. Receives intense infantry and machine-gun fire. Heavy losses for both companies. But the brave and prudent company commander of the 15th, First Lieutenant Alt, knows how to do things. Let us listen from him ourselves:

From a letter from First Lieutenant Alt (24 May 1916):

"After an impressive artillery preparation, our attack was unleashed. In one rush, many hundred meters down the gorge. No one thought of taking a break until a machine-gun in a trench stretching across the gorge stopped us. The fire from this machine-gun and the occupying troops [in the trench] cost me around 80 men, including Lieutenant Ladenburg and Lieutenant Husserl. The latter was instantly killed. We did not receive any artillery fire. Enemy artillery couldn't see anything; we were shielded by a curtain of dust and smoke. With the help of a machine-gun, I then pinned-down the enemy's trench, which succeeded splendidly. I then worked with the rest of the company up the enemy's flank moat half-way up. Then saw the French cower in the moat and pounded them from the trench embankment. We only bagged five prisoners; the other 70-80 men atoned for my own sacrifices. When I got into the ditch, I stood next to the French machine-gun. The gunner was dead. We threw out the bodies so that they could be seen from the village of Vaux. Time 1:50 pm! At this time the Pipe Head (*Pfeifenkopf*) came into the hands of other companies. The *Jägers* to our right – as was the entire III Corps – were finally ejected at this time.* I sat at the mouth of the gorge, waiting for the company to descend from the Pipe Head (*Pfeifenkopf*). It happened only at 6 in the evening."

* Translator's Note: *Jäger* refers here to a French unit of *chasseurs à pied*, a type of light infantry.

„Im Grab unseres Wolfgang …“

Über Wolfgangs Grabstätte nach Mittheilungen des Leutnant Lehrer: Im Grab unseres Wolfgang mitbegraben Unteroffizier Feldmann. In der Nähe, etwa 6m östlich, liegt Leutnant Ladenburg. Direkt bei Wolfgangs Grab das des Leutnant Rothe. Ganz in der Nähe ein Massengrab, in dem 21 Deutsche und einige Franzosen begraben liegen.

"In the grave of our Wolfgang ..."

Regarding Wolfgang's gravesite, according to the communications of Lieutenant Lehrer: In the grave of our Wolfgang buried with him Non-Commissioned Officer Feldmann. Nearby, about 6 meters to the east, is Lieutenant Ladenburg. Immediately next to Wolfgang's grave is the grave of Lieutenant Rothe. Very close to a mass grave in which 21 Germans and some Frenchmen are buried.

x Wolfgangs Grabstätte nach Mittheilungen des Ltn. Lehrer …

Im Grab unseres Wolfgang mitbegraben Uoff. Feldmann.

In der Nähe etwa 6 m östlich liegt Ltn. Ladenburg.

direkt bei W's Grab das des Ltn. Rothe

ganz in der Nähe ein Massengrab, in 2 21 Deutsche u. einige Franzosen begraben liegen.

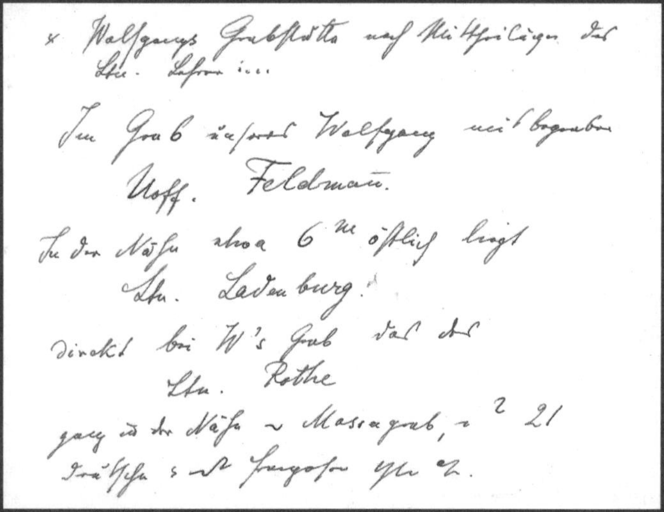

Husserls Notiz über die Lage des Grabes seines Sohnes Wolfgang bei Verdun, ca. 1916

Husserl's note about the position of his son Wolfgang's grave at Verdun, around 1916

„Kann man je über den Verlust eines solchen Menschen hinwegkommen?“

Freiburg 21. 4. 16
Lieber Gerhart.

Papa hat Dir als Ostergruß das Stundenbuch von Rilke geschickt u. ich sandte Dir einen Kuchen u. eine Wurst. Hoffentlich kommt alles gut in Deine Hände u. macht Dir Freude. Die beiden Bücher aus der Univ<ersitäts>Bibliothek kannst Du jetzt nicht haben, da die Bibliothek bis 27. geschlossen ist. Hat es dann noch einen Sinn, sie Dir zu schicken?

Gestern habe ich mich endlich entschlossen, Wolfgangs Koffer u. Sack auszupacken. Wie liebevoll er sich alles u. jedes aufbewahrt hat, ich kann Dir nichts sagen. Kann man je über den Verlust eines solchen Menschen hinwegkommen? Seine Bücher, die er immer mit sich führte, reden eine gute Sprache: Thukydides, Horaz, Neues Testament, Biblia hebraica, Mörikes, Goethes u. Heines Gedichte, Faust. Dazu alle möglichen militärischen Bücher.

Das schöne Wetter wird Dir in Hönebach besonders lieb sein. Oder fährst Du über die Feiertage wirklich nach Göttingen? Schade, daß Freiburg so weit weg ist.

Wie wird es sich mit dem Curs entscheiden?

Herzliche Grüße von

Mama

"Can one ever get over the loss of such a person?"

Freiburg 21 April 1916
Dear Gerhart,

Papa has sent you as an Easter greeting Rilke's Book of Hours and I am sending you cake and a sausage. Hopefully, everything will find its way into your hands safely and make you happy. You can't have at the moment the two books from the uni[versity] library, since the library is closed until the 27th. Would it then make any sense to send them to you?

Yesterday, I finally decided to unpack Wolfgang's trunk and pack. How carefully he kept everything, I can't express to you. Can one ever get over the loss of such a person? His books, which he always carried with him everywhere, speaks volumes about him: Thucydides, Horace, New Testament, Biblica Hebraica, Mörikes', Goethe's, Heine's poems, Faust. And all kinds of military books.

The beautiful weather will be especially pleasing to you in Hönebach. Or do you really go to Göttingen over the holidays? Too bad Freiburg is so far away.

When will your course be decided?

Warm greetings,
Mama

Feldpostbrief von Malvine Husserl an ihren Sohn Gerhart, 21. IV. 1916

Field postcard from Malvine Husserl to her son Gerhart, 21 April 1916

„Der erste Schmerz, den er uns bereitet hat, war sein Tod"

Freiburg i/Br. Lorettostr. 40
1. Mai.

Meine lieben Freunde.
Ihr habt mir so lieb und herzlich geschrieben, daß ich Euch dafür danken möchte, wenn mir auch das Briefschreiben sehr schmerzlich ist. Wenn innige Theilnahme Trost bringen kann, dann müßte man sich sehr getröstet fühlen; was aber ist im Stande, einen solchen Verlust zu erleichtern? Ich lebe so ganz in meinem theuern Wolfgang und kann es noch immer nicht fassen, daß er wirklich dahin ist, daß so ein herrlicher Mensch ausgelöscht ist für alle Zeiten. Nicht wir allein haben so unendlich viel verloren, jeder der ihm näher stand / und die wolthuende Harmonie dieser reinen und reichen Persönlichkeit auf sich wirken ließ, betrauert sein frühes Hinscheiden. Neben diesen hohen menschlichen Eigenschaften besaß er auch eine ungewöhnliche wissenschaftliche Begabung. Seine akademischen Lehrer – u. er hatte die bedeutendsten Deutschlands – sagen übereinstimmend, er wäre im ersten Semester weiter gewesen als andere im achten. O Gott, was für Hoffnungen sind dahin! Wie waren wir reich u. wie verarmt sind wir jetzt! Ich werde es nie verwinden, wenn ich auch alle meine Pflichten wieder aufnehme und die äußere Fassung längst wieder gewonnen habe. Mir war Wolfgang / nicht nur der Sohn, sondern mein bester Freund, mein Berater, die Verwirklichung aller Träume von einer edlen hohen menschlichen Persönlichkeit. Er hat uns keinen Augenblick seines Lebens betrübt, seine Entwicklung war eine ungestörte Linie nach oben. Der erste Schmerz, den er uns bereitet hat, war sein Tod.

Ach, wie könnte ich noch lange von ihm erzählen und nur Erhebendes, Gutes, Schönes. Unter Tausenden und Abertausenden entsteht einmal ein solch herrliches Menschenkind, und das muß mit 20 Jahren sterben, beinahe ehe es gelebt hat. Aber nein, er hat so intensiv gelebt, daß er unsterblich ist. Uns u. allen, die ihn kannten, hat er nur Freude ins Dasein / gebracht und als Soldat hat er Glänzendes geleistet. Seine Vorgesetzten, der kommandierende General, der Reg<iments->Kommandeur, Bataillons- u. Komp<anie>führer, alle alle schrieben uns, was für ein vorbildlicher Offizier u. was für ein vortrefflicher Kamerad er gewesen u. wie heldenhaft er in den Tod gegangen war.

Euch hat er auch sehr geliebt, Euch und Eure Kinder. Wie hatte er sich vor zwei Jahren mit Elli angefreundet!

Gerhart ist wieder felddienstfähig geschrieben u. wartet bei seinem Ersatz-Bataillon auf weitere Verwendung. Elli kommt heute aus Gött<ingen>, wo sie ihr Schwesternexamen abgelegt hat, zu dauerndem Aufenthalt hieher. Morgen fängt das Semester an, Edmund freut sich darauf.

Seid herzlich umarmt
Malvine

Brief von Malvine Husserl an Familie Gustav Albrecht, 1. V. 1916

Letter from Malvine Husserl to the family of Gustav Albrecht, 1 May 1916

"The first pain he has caused us is his death"

Freiburg i / Br. Lorettostr. 40
May 1.

My dear friends,
You kindly wrote so affectionately that I would like to thank you, even though the letter is very painful to me. If intimate sympathy can bring comfort, then one should feel very comforted; but what is capable of alleviating such a loss? I live so completely for my dear Wolfgang and still can't fathom that he is really gone, that such a wonderful person has been extinguished forever. It is not only us who have lost so infinitely much, but those who were close to him and who gained from him the beneficial harmony of his pure and vibrant personality, mourn his premature departure. In addition to these elevated human qualities, he also possessed an unusual scientific talent. His academic teachers (and he had the most reknown in Germany) were all unanimous, he was far more advanced in his first semester as others in their eighth. Oh God, what hopes have now disappeared! How were we rich and how impoverished we are now! I'll never get over it, even if I assume again all of my duties and even long after I gain back my outwards composure. Wolfgang was for me not only a son; he was my best friend, my advisor, the realization of all dreams for a noble and elevated human person. He never caused distress for one moment in his life, his development ran [along] an undisturbed line upwards. The first pain he has caused us is his death.

Oh, how I could contine to talk about him for so long and [talk only] about what is sublime, good, beautiful. Among thousands and thousands of thousands, such a glorious child is born, [who] must die at the age of twenty, just about as he was about to live. But no, he lived so intensively that he is immortal. To us and everyone who knew him, he only brought joy into existence, and as a soldier he performed brilliantly. His superiors, the commanding general, the commanders, battalion- and company commanders, everyone of them, all of them, wrote to us about what an exemplary officer he was, what an excellent comrade he had been, and how heroically he was in meeting his death.

He also loved you very much, you and your children. How he was so happy with Elli two years ago!

Gerhart was declared again to be fit for field-service and waits with his replacement battalion for further use. Elli now comes from Gött[ingen], where she has taken her nurses' exam, and will remain here. Tomorrow starts the semester, Edmund looks forward to it.

Be warmly embraced,
Malvine

„Wenn wir alle u. er noch einmal das Glück eines Wiedersehens gehabt hätten!"

Freiburg i./Br. Lorettostr. 40
9. Mai 1916

Liebe Frau Hilbert.

Endlich habe ich die Entschließung aufgebracht, Ihnen die gewünschten Schriftstücke abzuschreiben und sende sie mit dem <…> gleichzeitig ab. Das rote Portemonnaie, das Sie Wolfgang geschenkt hatten, und das er so gerne hatte, ist nicht zurückgekommen. In Saarbrücken, Ende November, trug er es noch u. zeigte mir mit Bedauern, wie er es schon abgenutzt habe. So schickte ich ihm Weihnachten ein neues u. dieses haben wir jetzt wieder bekommen.

Liebe Frau Hilbert, Sie und nur Sie sollen aber doch ein Andenken haben, das mit Ihrem geliebten Wolfgang innig verbunden gewesen ist.

Ich schicke Ihnen seine Erkennungsmarke, die er bis 8 Tage vor seinem Tode getragen hat. Warum er sich von mir eine andere, kleinere, ausbat, weiß ich nicht. Jedenfalls ließ ich am 23. Februar eine neue Erkennungsmarke bei Knauer anfertigen, die er am 1. März erhalten u. angelegt hat. Diese Marke ist mitten durchschossen, das war der Schuß in sein braves tapferes Herz.

Wenn Sie einmal für ein paar Tage nach Freiburg kämen, so wäre es mir das Woltuendste in meiner hoffnungslosen Sehnsucht nach meinem Kind. Mit niemanden könnte ich mich über das, was er war und was man an ihm lieben musste, mehr verstehen als mit Ihnen.

Malvine Husserl

Auf der Photographie sehen Sie sein Zimmer in Etain, das er als Laufgrabenoffizier bewohnte u. das er sich mit seiner liebevollen Art mit allen möglichen Sachen behaglich ausgestattet hatte. Wie stolz schrieb er von jeder Kleinigkeit! Auf dem Tische liegen seine gezeichneten Pläne, Lineal u. Bleistift. Die Aschenschale ist aus einem Granatstück.

Unter den Sachen, die wir wiederbekamen, ist so vieles, wovon man ohne die tiefste Erschütterung nicht sprechen kann.

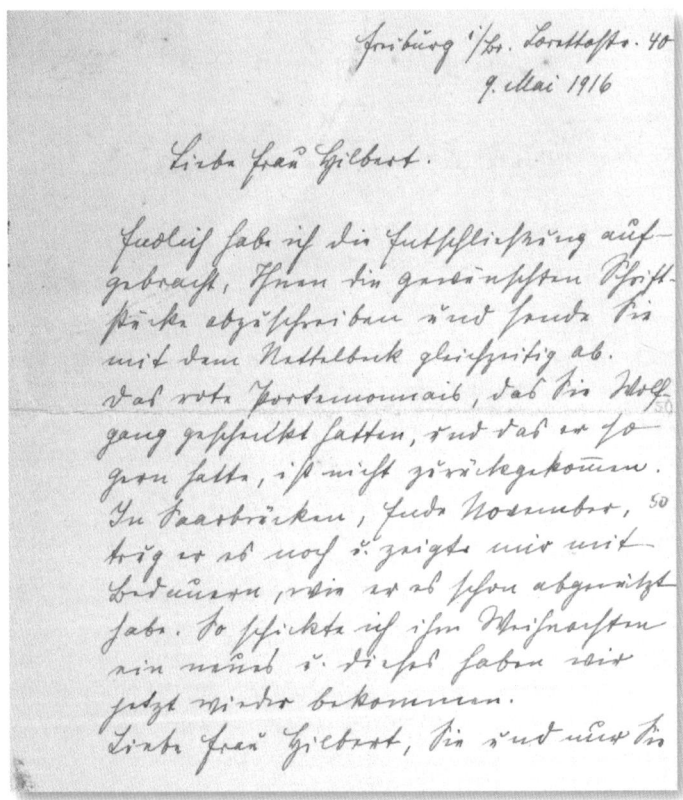

Brief von Malvine Husserl an Käthe Hilbert, 9. V. 1916 (mit beigelegtem Photo von Wolfgang Husserl; auf der Rückseite hat Malvine Husserl notiert „aufgenommen den 1. Febr. 1916 in seinem Zimmer in Etain")

Letter from Malvine Husserl to Käthe Hilbert, 9 May 1916 (with a photo of Wolfgang Husserl. On the reverse side, Malvine Husserl noted "taken on Feb. 1 1916 in his room in Etain")

Aufzeichnungen über den Sturmangriff, Befehle aus den letzten Stunden seines theuren Lebens.

Sein Urlaubsgesuch v. 27. Jan<uar>, befürwortet v. Regimentskommandeur u. dann von der Division nicht genehmigt. Wenn wir alle u. er noch einmal das Glück eines Widersehens gehabt hätten!

"If all of us, and he, would have had once again the happiness of a reunion!"

Freiburg i./Br. Lorettostr. 40
9 May 1916

Dear Frau Hilbert,

Finally, I have made the resolution to transcribe for you the wished for writings and to send them with […] to you immediately. The red wallet that you had given to Wolfgang, which he liked so much, did not come back. In Saarbrücken, at the end of November, he still carried it, showed it to me with regret at how he had already worn it out. So I sent him a new one for Christmas and this has now been returned to us.

Dear Frau Hilbert, you and only you should have a memento that is intimately connected to your beloved Wolfgang.

I will send you his identification tag, which he carried until 8 days before his death. Why he wanted from me another, smaller one, I don't know. In any case, I had a new identification tag made for him at Knauer's on February 23, which he received on March 1 and wore. This tag was shot through the middle, that was the shot in his brave, gallant heart.

If you would come to Freiburg for a few days, so would this be for me the best possible thing for my desparate longing for my child. With no one else could I come to understand more about what he was and what one loved about him than with you.

Malvine Husserl

On the photograph you see his room in Etain, where he was housed as a trench officer and which he arranged in the most comfortable manner in his caring ways with all sorts of things. How proud he was to write about every detail! On the desk there are his sketched plans, ruler and pencil. The ashtray is made from a piece of artillery.

Among the things which we received back, there are so many things, of which one can't speak without being deeply moved. Sketches for an assault, commands from the final hours of his dear life.

His holiday request of 27 Jan[uary], which had been approved by the Regimental Commander and then not approved from the Division. If all of us, and he, would have had once again the happiness of a reunion!

„Am 10. März wurde er begraben, ein Kreuz aus einer Munitionskiste mit Inschrift wurde auf das Grab gesetzt"

Brief von Malvine Husserl an Käthe Hilbert, 5. I. 1917

Letter from Malvine Husserl to Käthe Hilbert, 5 January 1917

Hinterzarten i/Schwarzwald, 5.1.1917

Liebe Frau Hilbert,

Ihr Brief von Viznau ist gerade an Wolfgangs Geburtstag angekommen und in meinem Schmerz war es mir doch eine wehmüthige Freude zu wissen, daß Sie diesen Tag so tief miterleben. Ihr Verhältnis zu dem geliebten Kind war ja auch ein ganz besonderes, er liebte Sie wie eine zweite Mutter und Sie haben dieses seltene Menschenherz mit seiner Güte, seinem Schwunge, seiner Schlichtheit verstanden. Darum weiß ich, daß Sie mein furchtbares Unglück ganz ermessen können, und daß Sie selbst unter diesem Verlust schwer leiden. Er war eben etwas ganz Besonderes. Wenn Sie daran denken, welche Freiheiten er sich Ihnen gegenüber gestattete, so müssen Sie doch sagen, Sie würden dies bei jedem anderen für unmöglich halten – bei Wolfgang freute es einen nur. Jede seiner Lebensäußerungen war schön, weil sie aus einer goldig klaren reizvollen Natürlichkeit herausgeboren wurde. Ich kann sagen, dass er mir nie einen traurigen Moment im Leben bereitet hat, er war 20 Jahre lang mein Glück und meine Freude. Und daß das alles unwiederbringlich ewig dahin ist! Und man lebt weiter! Vor einigen Wochen hatten wir einen erschütternden Besuch. Ein Regimentskamerad von Wolf, ein Leutnant Kästner von der 1. Komp<anie>, die ihn beerdigt hat, kam zu uns. Wie viele schöne Stunden er in heiteren und ernsten Gesprächen mit Wolf verlebt hat, wie er zu der gereiften Klugheit u. Güte des um so viel jüngeren Kameraden aufgeblickt hat, wie allseitig beliebt er gewesen war und wie allen die Thränen über die Wangen liefen, als sie den Leichnam dieses jungen Helden im argen Feuer in die Erde senkten – das und anderes erzählte der Off<i>z<ier> unter Thränen. Daß er Wolfgangs Freundschaft besessen habe, rechne er sich als den schönsten Gewinn seines Lebens an. Am 10. März wurde er begraben, ein Kreuz aus einer Munitionskiste mit Inschrift wurde auf das Grab gesetzt, auf dem Abhang zwischen ouvrage d' Hardaumont u. Vaux.

Wie schmerzlich getroffen waren wir von dem Verluste dieses Geländes. Wie zerstampft und zerschossen ist jetzt dort jeder Zoll Boden u. von dem Grabe ist gewiß keine Spur mehr vorhanden. –

Wir sind für den Haupttheil dieser Ferien hier herauf in einen hochgelegenen Bergort des so nahen Schwarzwaldes gegangen. Weihnachten u. Neujahr ohne das Kind, dabei Gerhart im vordersten Graben in der Champagne, da war eine Flucht in die Natur noch das Allerbeste.

Elli konnte uns leider nur für einen Tag besuchen, ihre Lazareththätigkeit ließ sie nicht los. Morgen fahren wir zurück, es ist nur eine Stunde Bahnfahrt. Wie glücklich könnte man in dieser Stadt mit der unvergleich<lich> herrlichen Umgebung leben, wenn die Gegenwart nicht so fürchterlich wäre. Diese Antwort der Entente mit ihrer Verlogenheit ist eine üble Einleitung des neuen Jahres. Welche Ströme Blut werden da noch fließen!

Es grüßt Sie herzlich
Ihre
Malvine Husserl

"He was buried on March 10, a cross made from an ammunition box with an inscription was placed on the grave"

Hinterzarten in the Black Forest, 5 January 1917

Dear Frau Hilbert,

Your letter from Viznau just arrived on Wolfgang's birthday, and in my pain it was for me nonetheless a wistful pleasure to know that you are also feeling for this day so deeply. Your relationship to the beloved child was a very special one; he loved you as a second mother, and you understood this precious human heart with its kindness, verve, and simplicity. That is why I know that you can fully appreciate my terrible misfortune, and that you yourself suffer deeply from this loss. He was something special. When you think of what freedoms he allowed himself with you, so you must admit, that you would think this impossible with anyone else –in the case of Wolfgang, this kind of behavior only made us happy. Each expression of this life was beautiful, because born from a golden clear and charming naturalness. I can state that he never made for me a sad moment in [my] life, he was for 20 years my happiness and joy. And all of this is irretrievably gone forever! And one lives on! A few weeks ago we had a shocking visit. One of Wolfgang's regimental comrades, a Lieutenant Kästner from the First Company, who buried him, came to us. How many beautiful hours in cheerful and serious conversations he spent with Wolf, how he looked up to the mature intelligence and goodness of the other much younger comrade, how popular he had been all around, and how tears ran down everyone's faces as they lowered the corpse of the young hero under terrible fire into the ground [earth] this and other things the Officer recounted in tears. That he had Wolfgang's friendship, he reckoned as the most beautiful gain of his life. He was buried on March 10, a cross made from an ammunition box with an inscription was placed on the grave, on the slope between the Ouvrage of Hardaumont and Vaux.

How painfully we were affected by the loss of this area. How smashed up and shot up is now any marker of territory and there is surely no more trace of the grave.

We have gone up here for the main part of this vacation to a high mountain village in the vicinity of the Black Forest. Christmas and New Year without our child, with Gerhart in the forward trenches in the Champagne – an escape into nature was still for us most welcome.

Elli could regrettably only visit us for one day, she wasn't able to abandon her activities at the field hospital. Tomorrow we drive back, it is only an hour's train ride. How happy one could live in this town with its incomparably lovely surroundings, if the present were not so awful. This reply of the Entente with its mendacity is a bad introduction of the New Year. What streams of blood will still flow!

Warm wishes,
Your,
Malvine Husserl

„Ich vernehme, daß Ihr Herr Sohn die hohe Auszeichnung des Eisernen Kreuzes I. Klasse empfangen hat"

Berlin, Reichstag, den 27. April 1917.
Hochverehrter Herr Kollege!

Hier in Berlin zur Wahrnehmung meiner parlamentarischen Pflichten weilend, vernehme ich, daß Ihr Herr Sohn, der Leutnant der Res<erve> Husserl, die hohe Auszeichnung des Eisernen Kreuzes I. Klasse empfangen hat.

Gestatten Sie, daß ich meiner Freude über diese besondere Ehre Ausdruck verleihe und ihm, sowie Ihnen von Herzen Glück wünsche, hoffend, daß es ihm vergönnt sein möge, in nicht zu ferner Zeit gesund und heil in die liebe Heimat zurückzukehren.

Mit vorzüglicher Hochachtung und mit kollegialem Gruße
Prof. v. Schulze-Gaevernitz
M<itglied> d<es> R<eichstags>

"I discovered that your son has received the highest distinction of the Iron Cross First Class"

Berlin, Reichstag, 27 April 1917.
Esteemed Colleague!

Here in Berlin, while lingering in the exercise of my parliamentary duties, I discovered that your son, Lieutenant in the Res[erves] Husserl, has received the high distinction of the Iron Cross First Class.

Permit me to express my joy on this special honor and [I] wish him, much as you must wish from your heart, that he will be allowed in the not too distant future to return safe and secure to his beloved homeland.

Yours sincerely, and with collegial greetings,
Prof. v[on] Schulze-Gaevernitz
M[ember] [of the] R[eichstag]

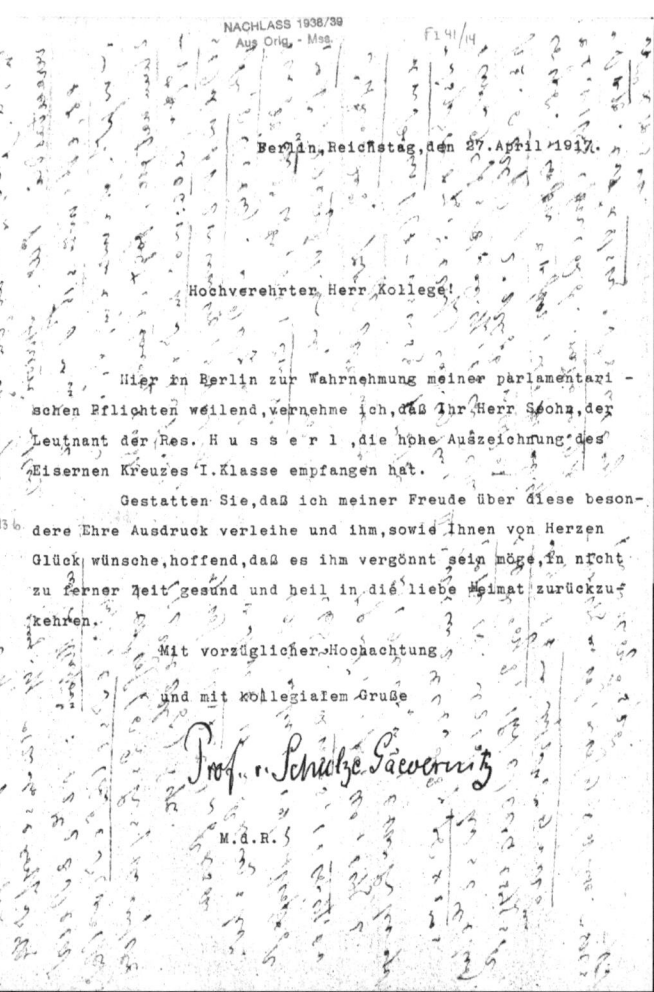

Gerhart von Schulze-Gaevernitz an Husserl, 27. IV. 1917. Husserls Sohn Gerhart hatte kurz zuvor das Eiserne Kreuz erhalten.

Gerhart von Schulze-Gaevernitz to Husserl, 27 April 1917. Husserl's son Gerhart received the Iron Cross shortly before.

„Du weißt wohl schon, daß unser über alles geliebter Wolfgang in den Kämpfen um Verdun 1916 gefallen ist, in reiner Hingabe für sein Vaterland"

Freiburg in Baden 27. Sept<ember> 1919.
Lorettostr. 40.

Liebe Flora!

Nach Jahren wieder ein Brief von Dir – und leider berichtet er wenig Erfreuliches! Ich glaube aber doch, daß Ihr drüben in Amerika es noch herrlich habt im Vergleich mit uns und daß Ihr bisher gar keine Vorstellung habt u. haben könnt von den physischen und noch mehr seelischen Leiden, die das deutsche und deutsch-österreichische Volk seit einem Jahre erdulden müssen – davon abgesehen, daß es schon in den vorangegangenen Jahren so viel Elend gab, daß man eine Steigerung kaum für möglich hielt. –

<...>

Du weißt wohl schon, daß unser über alles geliebter Wolfgang in den Kämpfen um Verdun 1916 gefallen ist, in reiner Hingabe für sein Vaterland. Unser Gerhart war 2mal schwer verwundet und verlor zuletzt die Sehkraft eines Auges. Elli war während der ganzen Kriegszeit im Dienst des r<oten> Kreuz, über 3 Jahre davon im harten Lazarettdienst als Hilfsschwester. Jetzt studiert sie weiter als Kunsthistorikerin, Gerhart fürs jurist<ische> Doktorat.

In den Zeitungen habt Ihr seit Jahren lesen können, was für edle Seelen die Engl<änder>, Franzosen, Ital<iener>, Amerikaner sind u. was für abgründig verderbte die Deutschen u. Österr<eicher>. Auch viele Dokumente, die das „beweisen". Wir haben dafür nur ein bitter-trauriges Lächeln u. freuen uns übrigens, daß es drüben allmälig bei einzelnen wahrhaftigen Menschen dämmert, u. so wird ja einmal die Sonne der Wahrheit aufgehen.

Auf mir liegen, u. besonders in diesem Jahre, so schwere Arbeitslasten, daß ich kaum ein Stündchen finde für mich zu sein u. mich frei vom Drang der Pflichten zu fühlen. Ich konnte Dir wirklich nicht früher schreiben.

<...>

Von den Wiener Lieben habe ich nicht oft Nachrichten, ich kann eben selbst nur gar selten schreiben. Ich denke, daß Du jetzt mit ihnen in direkte Verbindung treten kannst. Sie leiden natürlich schwer unter dem Zusammenbruch, der wohl auch ihre materielle Lage gefährdet. Man wird am Ende mit den Staatspapieren, drüben wie hier, die Zimmer tapezieren können. Ich muß sagen, daß ich mir, für uns, daraus nicht viel mache. Man verhungert nicht so leicht und wir alle haben Freude an der Arbeit. Possierlich ist es ja, daß Handarbeit jetzt so viel besser gelohnt wird als Geistesarbeit. Doch wie immer, ich lebe in meiner Philosophie u. sehe mit Genugthuung, wie sie junge Herzen bewegt u. für ein wahrhaftiges, reines Leben begeistert. Meine Kinder sind aber so, daß sie sich im Leben sicher durchsetzen werden. – Leider hast Du es im nahenden Alter besonders schwer – aber sorge Dich nicht zu sehr und besonders nicht um Deine Kinder. Sie sind, ich höre es mit Freude, tüchtig, also werden sie ihren Weg machen. Leid thut mir, daß Ihr so fern seid u. ich so gar nichts thun kann, zu fördern.

Es grüßt Dich herzl<ich> u. sendet alle guten Wünsche – sowie auch Malvine –

Dein Cousin
Edmund

Auszüge aus einem Brief von Husserl an Flora Darkow, 27. IX. 1919

Selections from a letter of Husserl to Flora Darkow, 27 September 1919

"You may well know, our dearly loved Wolfgang was killed in combat at Verdun in 1916 in pure devotion to his Fatherland"

Freiburg, in Baden, Germany, 27 September 1919.
Lorettostr. 40

Dear Flora!

After many years, another letter from you – and unfortunately your letter reports of little that is pleasing! I believe, however, that you are still having a wonderful time in America in comparison to us and that you can't imagine, nor could you, the physical and even more so, the spiritual, sufferings, which the German and the German-Austrian peoples have endured in one year, apart from the fact that there was so much misery in the preceding years that an increase was scarcely seen as possible.

[...]

You may well know, that our dearly loved Wolfgang was killed in combat at Verdun in 1916 in pure devotion to his Fatherland. Our Gerhart was severely wounded twice, and recently lost the sight of an eye. Elli served for the duration of the war in the Red Cross, more than 3 years in tough hospital service as an auxiliary nurse. Now she is continuing to study art history, Gerhart [is studying] for the juridical PhD.

In the newspapers you have been able to read for years now what noble souls the Eng[lish], the French, the Ital[ians], the Americans have been and what for profoundly corrupted [souls] the Germans and Aust[rians] [have been]. Also many documents that "prove" this. We have only a bitter-sad smile for this and rejoice, by the way, that it out-there gradually dawns upon some truthful people, and so will the sun of truth rise once again.

I am burdened, and especially this year, with such a heavy load of work, that I can hardly find even a small hour for myself and to feel myself free from the compulsion of duty. I really could not write to you sooner.

[…]

From the Viennese loved ones, I don't have frequent news, I myself can write only rarely. I think you can now enter into direct contact with them. Of course, they suffer severely from the collapse, which is likely to endanger their material situation. At the end of the day, one can only carpet the room with the state-currency, here as over there. I must say that for me, for us, I don't really care much about it. One does not starve so easily and we all take joy in work. It's funny indeed that handwork is now better payed than intellectual work. But as always, I live in my philosophy and see with satisfaction how it moves young hearts and animates [them] for a truthful and pure life. My children are such that they will persevere in life. Unfortunately, you will have it particularly hard in the coming age, but don't worry too much about it and especially not about your children. They are, so I hear with joy, efficient, so they'll make their own way. I am sorry that you are so far away, and that I can do nothing at all to further encourage [you].

Warm greetings and best wishes – as well as from Malvine –

Your cousin,
Edmund

„Der Kummer um unseren gefallenen Wolfgang bleibt aber lebendig"

Freiburg i. Br. 31. Okt<ober> 1923
Liebe Flora.

Länger darf Dein lieber Brief v<om> 4. Okt<ober> nicht unbeantwortet bleiben, und da Edmund momentan sehr angestrengt mit der Vorbereitung seines diese Woche beginnenden Collegs beschäftigt ist, übernehme ich es mit aufrichtiger Freude, Dir zu schreiben.

<…>

Inzwischen ist ja der vollständige Zusammenbruch des einst durch seine Wolgeordnetheit vorbildlichen Deutschland erfolgt. Alle materiellen Verbesserungen, die man vom preuß<ischen> Ministerium erhalten hätte, wären dahin u. wir säßen im Alter in Berlin wie in einem Labyrinth. So sind wir ganz froh, hier in dem kleineren Städtchen geblieben zu sein. Wie es in Deutschland aussieht, ist Euch wenigstens teilweise durch die Zeitungen bekannt. Man lebt ohne den kleinsten Vorblick in die nächsten Tage. Es ist schon schrecklich, wird aber noch schrecklicher werden bei den unerschwinglichen Preisen u. der Knappheit der Lebensmittel. Die Franzosen haben eine ungeheuerliche Blutschuld auf sich geladen, die Jahrhunderte nicht abwaschen können. Wenn nur Amerika zur Erkenntnis der wahren Sachlage käme! Aber schließlich kann niemand in unserem verfehmten Lande auf Hilfe von außen rechnen, die Politik hat leider kein Ethos. Gottseidank sind die einzelnen Menschen von anderer ethischen Gesinnung. Und so gab uns Dein Brief mit der warmen Herzlichkeit und Marguerites rührende Hilfsbereitschaft einen neuen Beweis dafür.

Eigentlich wollten wir dieses Geschenk nicht annehmen u. Marg<uerite> mit herzlichem Danke zurückschicken. Aber dies schien uns eine zu wenig zarte Handlung u. so wollen wir mit Hinblick auf ihren versprochenen Besuch bei uns die 5 $ annehmen u. zur Anschaffung von Winterkartoffeln (die Bauern nehmen nur Devisen in Zahlung, obwol es verboten ist) u. Butter verwenden. Wir hoffen aber ganz bestimmt, daß Marg<uerite>, sowie sich die hiesigen Verhältnisse gebessert haben, ihren Plan wahr macht. Wir werden uns aufrichtig freuen, sie bei uns zu begrüßen u. ihr die Wege für die Fortführung ihrer Studien zu ebnen. Wenn nicht eine böse Wendung in unseren Verhältnissen eintritt (die Staatsbeamten sind ja bei einem bankerotten Staate immer in Gefahr) u. wir die Wohnung halten können, dann kann Marg<uerite> so lange bei uns wohnen, als es ihr lieb ist. Das ist alles ernsthaft gemeint.

Nun wollte ich Dir, liebe Flora, noch mitteilen, daß Gerhart am 10. Septb<e>r in aller Stille in Göttingen geheiratet hat, u. zwar die Tochter von Geheimrat Tammann, Prof<essor> f<ür> physik<alische> Chemie in G<öttingen>. Gerhart ist Hilfsrichter am Landgericht in G<öttingen>, u. da ihm ein Teil der großen Dienstwohnung seines Schwiegervater<s> überlassen wurde, kann er von seinem Gehalt einfach leben. So haben wir zwei verheiratete Kinder, der Kummer um unseren gefallenen Wolfgang bleibt aber lebendig.

Herzlichste Grüße Dir, Deinem Mann u. Deinen Töchtern, insbesondere Marguerite

Deine Cousine
Malvine

"The grief for our fallen Wolfgang still remains vivid"

Freiburg i. Br. 31 Oct[ober] 1923
Dear Flora,

No longer should your lovely letter from October 4 remained unanswered, and since Edmund is presently extremely preoccupied with the preparation of his seminars, which begin this week, I have taken it upon myself with sincere pleasure to write to you.

[...]

In the meantime, the complete collapse of Germany has occured, which once exemplified the essence of an orderly state of affairs. All the material improvements, which one would have received from the Prussian Ministry, are now gone, and [had Husserl accepted a position in Berlin] we would be sitting there in old age living as in a labyrinth. We are thus quite glad to have stayed here in a small town. How things are looking for Germany, is partly known to you from newspapers. You live without the slightest foresight about the coming days. It is indeed terrible, but will become even more terrible with the prohibitive prices and scarcity of food. The French have taken upon themselves an incredible blood guilt, which with the centuries will not be washed away. If only America would come to recognize the true nature of the situation! But in the end, no one can count on outside help in our confounded country, unfortunately politics has no ethos. Thank goodness, individual persons are of a different ethical attitude. And so your letter in its heartfelt cordiality and Marguerite's touching willingness to help gave us a new proof for this.

In truth, we did not want to accept this gift and [wanted] to return it to Marg[uerite] with heartfelt gratitude. But this would have seemed less than appreciative and so we want in view of your promised visit with us to accept the $5 and use it for the procurement of winter potatoes (the peasants only accept cash in payment, although it is forbidden) and butter. We especially hope that Marg[uerite], as soon as the present conditions have improved, can make good on her plans. We would sincerely look forward to welcoming her here and pave the way for the continuation of her studies. If there is no evil turn in our circumstances (state officials are always in danger in a bankrupt state), we can hold onto the appartment, then Marg[uerite] can live with us for as long as she pleases. This is all meant seriously.

Now, I wanted to tell you, dear Flora, that Gerhart has married in Göttingen on the 10th of September the daughter of Privy Councilor Tammann, Prof[essor] for Physical Chemistry in Göttingen. Gerhart is an auxiliary judge at the regional court in Göttingen, and since he was given part of the spacious service apparment from his father-in-law, he can live from his salary alone. So we have two married children, the grief for our fallen Wolfgang still remains vivid.

Sincere greetings to you, your husband and your daughters, especially Marguerite.

Your cousin,
Malvine

Auszüge aus einem Brief von Malvine Husserl an Flora Darkow, 31. X. 1923

Selections from a letter of Malvine Husserl to Flora Darkow, 31 October 1923

Beileidsbekundungen des Militärs

Brief des kommandierenden Generals des 5. R. A. K. <Es handelt sich um Erich von Gündell (1854-1924), General der Armeeeinheit, in der auch Husserls Sohn bis zu seinem Tod diente. 1912 hatte von Gündell bei Husserl studiert. Er stand mit der Familie Husserl in näherem Kontakt.>:

12. März 1916

Hochverehrter Herr Professor.
Es thut mir von ganzem Herzen leid, dass ich Ihre gütigen Zeilen vom 8. d. mit der schmerzlichen Nachricht von dem Heldentod Ihres braven Sohnes beantworten muß. In derselben Stunde, in der ich Ihren Brief empfing, erhielt ich die Gewißheit, daß Ihr Sohn am 8. März von einem Schuß in den Kopf und einem anderen in das Bein getroffen, seine Treue gegen sein Vaterland mit dem Tode besiegelt hat. Er ist beerdigt worden zwischen dem Ouvrage d' Hardaumont u. dem Dorfe Vaux am Hange der Schlucht nördlich Vaux in der Nähe eines zerstörten feindlichen Geschützes. <...> Ihnen u. Ihrer Frau Gemahlin spreche ich mein innigstes Beileid aus; ich fühle mit Ihnen den ganzen Schmerz um den lieben Sohn, der so schöne Hoffnungen in sein Grab mitgenommen hat. Wir alle trauernden Eltern können unseren einzigen Trost in der Hoffnung finden, daß unsere Heldensöhne nicht umsonst dahingehen, sondern daß unsere Opfer gebracht werden müssen zum Segen des Vaterlandes. <…> Von Herzen wünsche ich, daß Ihr ältester Sohn Ihnen gesund erhalten bleiben möge.

    Meine dankbaren Wünsche begleiten Sie nach Freiburg in den neuen Wirkungskreis; bei meinen philosophischen Studien werde ich Ihrem Namen oft begegnen; ich würde es als ein Glück ansehen, auch unsere persönlichen Beziehungen dereinst erneuern zu können.

    In aufrichtiger Teilnahme an Ihrem Schmerze bin ich in unveränderlicher Verehrung
Ihr sehr ergebener
von Gündell.

*

Brief des Regimentskommandeurs des R. I. R. 19 <Oberstleutnant Smalian>:

13. März 1916

Euer Hochwolgeboren muß das Regiment die traurige Nachricht geben, daß der Leutnant Wolfgang Husserl am 8. d<es> M<onats> in den Kämpfen bei Vaux vor Verdun den Heldentod gefunden hat.

    Das Regiment bittet Euer Hochwolgeboren unter dem Ausdruck der aufrichtigsten Theilnahme versichern zu dürfen, daß das Andenken dieses tapferen Offiziers allezeit im Regiment in hohen Ehren gehalten werden wird. Sein Name wird bei uns fortleben, sein Beispiel fortwirken.
Smalian
Oberstleutnant u. Reg. Kommandeur

*

Brief des Kommandeurs <Hauptmann Henkel> des III. Bataillons, einen Tag vor Wolfgangs Tod schwer verwundet:

Nürnberg, Lazareth. 29. März 1916

Hochgeehrter Herr Professor, hochgeehrte gnädige Frau.
    Wie ich von meiner Frau u. einem Kameraden erfahren habe, ist Wolfgang am 8. vor Vaux gefallen. Ich habe ihn am 6. abends zuletzt gesehen u. gesprochen. Es war mir, als ob mir etwas zustoßen sollte. Ich wollte ihm darum einen letzten Gruß nach Hause auftragen, nahm aber davon Abstand, um ihn nicht zu beunruhigen. Wir nahmen Abschied. Er blickte mich aus seinen großen Augen freudig an, legte die Hand zum Gruße an den Helm, reckte sich auf, drückte die ihm dargebotene Rechte und erwiderte meinen Gruß auf fröhliches Wiedersehen so wie ein Mann den Gruß eines Mannes beantwortet. „Auf fröhliches Wiedersehen" waren seine letzten Worte.

    Er wußte, daß er mit dem Bataillon etwas Großes und Schweres erleben würde. Sein feuriger Mut freute sich auf diese Stunde.

Nun ist er von uns gegangen. Seine Seele, die das Böse nicht kannte, hat das Reich gesucht, wo das Gute und die Gerechtigkeit herrschen. Er ist selig.

Wir aber trauern u. vermissen ihn. Er war der Stolz und die Freude seiner Soldaten und Kameraden, Ihnen, den Eltern und der Familie war er mehr! Sie allein wissen, wie schwer sein Verlust wiegt. Gott sei bei Ihnen in Ihrem Schmerz.

Ich bitte um Entschuldigung, daß ich diesen Brief diktiere, da ich selbst noch nicht schreiben kann.
In herzlicher Antheilnahme bleibe ich,
Ihr
Henkel

*

Brief des Kompanieführers <Oberleutnant Alt> der 15. Komp<anie>:

Senon 12. III. 1916

Sehr geehrter Herr Professor!
Am 8. März führte die Kompagnie den Sturm, vom Ouvrage d'Hardaumont vorgehend, durch die Schlucht nach dem Dorfe Vaux aus. Der tapere 2. Zug, den Ihr Herr Sohn führte, kam dabei in Flankenfeuer und mußte schwer leiden. Nach Gottes Ratschluß ist er als tapferer Führer vor seinem Zuge um 12^{15} Mittags den Heldentod gestorben. Ich erlaube mir mein herzlichstes Beileid auszusprechen.

Durch eine Infanteriekugel am Kopfe verwundet, war er sofort todt. Die 1. Komp<anie> (Leutnant v. Gilsa) hat ihn begraben, in der Nähe des französischen Panzergeschützes, das sich in der Mitte der Schlucht befindet.

Seinen Koffer und Kleinigkeiten, die er bei sich trug, werden Ihnen zugehen. Sofort sende ich seinen Ring, der aus einem Geschoßzünder hergestellt ist, und den er sehr gern trug.

Sein nettes Wesen hatte ihm im Regiment viele Freunde verschafft. Wir betrauern umso mehr diesen schmerzlichen Verlust.
Ergebensten Gruß
Alt
Oberleutnant u. Komp<anie>führer 15/19 R.I.R.

*

Brief des Oberjägers Giesemann, der uns durch eine Karte vom 12. mittheilte, daß er die Briefe gefunden hat u. den wir um nähere Auskunft baten:

29. April 1916

Werte gnädige Frau.
Danke Ihnen bestens für die Antwort und Anerkennung auf mein Schreiben.

Ihr Herr Sohn war am Kopf und Brust verletzt, letzere hat seinen sofortigen Tod zur Folge gehabt, wie man deutlich erkennen konnte.

Herr Leutnant muß im Begriff gewesen sein, die Höhe zu erreichen, denn er lag am Abhang mit der Front nach dem Feinde, den rechten Arm vorgestreckt. Ich erkläre es mir so: Herr Leutnant ist mit seinen Leuten vorgestürmt mit erhobenem Arm, hat den Schuß bekommen und ist vornüber gefallen und sofort todt gewesen.

Die Verletzungen hatten den Körper nicht im geringsten entstellt. Es ist anzunehmen, daß die Verwundung von der Artillerie <Anmerkung von Malvine Husserl: „sicher nicht der Fall"> hervorgerufen ist, doch kann ich dies nicht bestimmt behaupten.
Indem ich Ihnen mein herzlichstes Beileid ausspreche, grüßt
Conrad Giesemann
Oberjäger Jägerfeldbat. 3, 6. I. Div. III. A.K.

*

Vizefeldwebel Müller aus Wolfgangs Zug, der am 9. März verwundet wurde u. den ich am 3.4. im Lazareth in Karlsruhe besuchte, sagte mir Folgendes:

Wolfgang ist stolz und glücklich ohne jede Todesahnung in den Tod gegangen. In der Nacht vom 7. zum 8. März hat er mit einem Theil seiner Leute die feindlichen Drahtverhaue durchschnitten. Als er zurückkam, schlug er dem Vizef<eldwebel> auf die Schulter u. rief: „Nun Müller freuen Sie sich, die Bahn ist frei und morgen geht's zum Sturm". Unter den fürchterlichsten Entbehrungen haben sie die letzten zwei Wochen verbracht, Kälte u. Nässe u. Sturm, ohne Obdach und Tag u. Nacht in den Kleidern u. Stiefeln. „Mein Herr Leutnant war immer vergnügt und hat uns alle obenauf gehalten. Überall hat er selbst mit Hand angelegt" u. dabei rannen dem reifen Mann dicke Thränen über die Wangen.

Statements of condolence from the military command

Letter from the Commanding General of the 5th R. A. K. [Erich von Gündell (1854-1924), the General of the Reserve Army Corps in which Husserl's son, who was killed on March 8th, 1916, served, studied with Husserl in 1912 and remained in close contact with Husserl's family.]:

12 March 1916
Esteemed Professor,
It is with heartfelt sorrow that I answer your honorable lines from the 8th with the painful news of the heroic death of your brave son. In the same hour that I received your letter, I was given the assurance that your son received on March 8th a gunshot wound to the head and another wound to the leg, his loyalty to the Fatherland being sealed with his death. He was buried between the Ouvrage of Hardaumont and the village of Vaux on the slopes of the ravine north of Vaux, near destroyed enemy artillery. [...] Allow me to express my heartfelt condolences to you and your wife; I feel with you all the pain for the dead son, who took away with him to his grave such beautiful hopes. All of us as parents in mourning can find our only consolation in that our heroic sons have not died in vain, but that our sacrifices must be made for the blessing of the Fatherland. [...] With all my heart, I wish that your eldest son may remain safe and secure for you.

My grateful wishes accompany you to Freiburg in this new sphere of activity; in my philosophical studies, I often encounter your name; I would regard it as a blessing to be able to renew our personal relations sometime.
In sincere sympathy for your pain, I remain forever in esteem,
Your very devoted,
von Gündell

*

Letter of the Regimental Commander [First Lieutenant Smalian] of the R. I. R. 19 [Infantry Reserve Regiment]:

13 March 1916
Your Honor, it is with deep regret that the Regiment must inform you that Lieutenant Wolfgang Husserl on the 8th o[f this] m[onth] in combat near Vaux at Verdun met a hero's death.

The regiment allows itself to express to your Honor the most sincere sympathy, that the memory of this brave officer will always be held in high regard in the regiment. His name will continue to live with us, his action will remain exemplary.
Smalian
First Lieutenant and Regimental Commander

*

Letter from the Commander [Captain Henkel] of the III Battalion, one day after Wolfgang's death:

Nuremberg, hospital. 29 March 1916
Most Esteemed Professor, highly esteemed Madame,
As I learned from my wife and my comrades, Wolfgang was killed on the 8th in front of Vaux. I last saw him and talked with him on

Malvine Husserl hat die Beileidsbriefe, die die Familie von Vorgesetzten und Kameraden ihres verstorbenen Sohnes erhalten hat, abgeschrieben und diese Abschrift dann mit kurzen Erläuterungen an Käthe Hilbert geschickt; die originalen Briefe sind nicht mehr vorhanden.

Malvine Husserl copied the condolence letters for her dead son, which the family received from officers and comrades, and sent these copies with a brief explanation to Käthe Hilbert. The original letters no longer exist.

the evening of the 6th. It was as if something had struck me. I wanted to send with him a last greeting home, but decided to refrain from asking him, in order not to disturb him. We took leave of each other. He looked at me joyfully with his large eyes, laid his hand in greeting on the helmet, stood up, and squeezed his outstretched hand into mine and replied to my salutation for a happy reunion as would a man answering the greeting of another man. "Until our next pleasant reunion," were his last words.

He knew that he would experience something great and tremendous with the battalion. His ardent courage rejoiced for this hour.

Now he has left us. His soul, which knew no evil, sought the kingdom where goodness and righteousness prevail. He is blessed.

But we grieve and miss him. He was the pride and joy of his soldiers and comrades, for you, parents and family, he was more! You alone know how heavy his loss weighs. God be with you in your pain.

I apologize to have dictated this letter, since I cannot yet write. In my heartfelt sympathy,
Your,
Henkel

*

Letter from Company Commander [First Lieutenant Alt] of the 15th Company:

Senon 12 March 1916
Dear Professor!
On the 8th of March, the company carried-out an assault, moving from the Ouvrage of Hardaumont, through the ravine towards the village of Vaux. The brave second platoon, which your son commanded, came upon flanking fire and suffered heavily. According to God's will, he died a heroic death in brave command of his platoon around 12:15 midday. I would like to express my heartfelt condolences.

Wounded by an infantry [rifle] shot to the head, he was dead immediately. The 1st Company (Lieutenant v. Gilsa) buried him, near the French armored artillery, which is in the middle of the ravine.

His trunk and belongings, which he carried with him, will go to you. I'll immediately send his ring, made from a bullet case, and which he loved to wear.

His pleasant nature attracted many friends in the regiment. We shall mourn this painful loss all the more.
Highest regards,
Alt
First Lieutenant and Company Commander, 15/19 R.I.R.

*

Letter from the Oberjäger Giesemann, who informed us through a [post]card from the 12th that he found the letters and whom we then asked for further information:

29 April 1916
Respected, dear Madame,
Thank you very much for the reply and acknowledgment of my communication.

Your son was wounded in the head and chest, the latter killed him immediately, as one could clearly see.

The Lieutnant was close to reaching the top of the hill, for he lay on the slope facing the enemy in front, with his right arm stretched forward. My understanding is as follows: the Lieutenant had rushed forward with his men with his arm raised high, was shot, fell forward, and was immediately killed.

The injuries did not disfigure the body in the least. One can assume that the wounding came from the artillery fire [remark by Malvine Husserl: "was certainly not the case"], but I can't assert this for sure.
With heartfelt sympathy, greetings,
Conrad Giesemann
Oberjäger Jägerfeldbat. 3, 6. I. Div. III. A. K.

*

Staff Sergeant-Major Müller from Wolfgang's platoon, who was wounded on March 9th, in the hospital in Karlsruhe, told me this:

Wolfgang went to his death proudly and happily without any premonition of death. In the night of 7th to 8th of March, he cut through the enemy wire with some of his men. When he came back, he slapped the Staff-Sergeant on the shoulder and shouted, "Well, Müller, be happy, the way is clear for you to attack tomorrow." Among the most terrible deprivations he endured over the past two weeks, cold and wetness and storm, without shelter and day and night in his clothes and boots. "The Lieutenant was always happy and kept us all [cheered] up. He was always engaged to help with his work." And therefore thick tears run down the face of the mature man.

Kondolenzbrief von Franz Brentano

70 Orellistr., Zürich, den 6. April 1916.

Lieber Freund!
Mit innigster Teilnahme erfuhr ich, welch schwerer Schlag Sie und Ihre verehrte Frau getroffen. Diejenigen, von welchen ich die Nachricht erhielt, wussten mir so viel Rühmliches von Ihrem Sohne zu erzählen, dass sein Tod als ein noch viel schwererer Verlust sich darstellt. Dennoch muss gerade in dem Gedanken an alles, was ihn vor so vielen anderen jungen Männern auszeichnete, ein gewisser Trost für Sie liegen. Die wehmütige Erinnerung an ihn wird für immer ein wahres Gut für Sie sein. Unsere Zeit ist reich an Leiden und spricht zu uns mit überzeugender Kraft von der Nichtigkeit des diesseitigen Lebens, wenn es nicht als Vorbereitung für ein jenseitiges diente. Dahin werden Sie nun die Blicke zu richten, sich noch mehr aufgefordert fühlen und wenn irgend jemand, so können Sie vertrauen, dass in dem jenseitigen Teile des Gottesreiches Ihr geliebter Sohn der Segnungen einer göttlich-väterlichen Fürsorge sich erfreut. Auch das möge Ihnen den Schmerz der Trennung lindern.

Meine Frau vereinigt den Ausdruck ihres herzlichsten Beileids mit dem meinigen.
Freundschaftlich ergeben

Ihr
F. Brentano

Condolence letter from Franz Brentano

70 Orellistr., Zurich, 6 April 1916.

Dear friend!
With most sincere sympathy, I learned what a great blow has befallen you and your esteemed wife. Those from whom I received the news spoke with so much praise of your son, which made his death an even greater loss. Nevertheless, in the memory of everything that distinguished him from so many other young men, there must be a certain consolation for you. The wistful memory of him will forever be a true good for you. Our time is rich in suffering and speaks to us with convincing force from the emptiness of life on this side, if it did not serve as a preparation for a life beyond. Your regard can now look in this direction, and feel itself even more called upon, and if anyone, so can you rest assured, that in the part beyond within God's Kingdom, your beloved son rejoices in the blessings of divine-fatherly care. Let this also alleviate the pain of separation.

My wife joins me in the expression of our heartfelt condolences.
In friendship,

Your,
F. Brentano

Franz Brentano (1838-1917)

70, Orellistr. Zürich, den 6. April 1916.

Lieber Freund!

Mit innigster Teilnahme erfuhr ich, welch schwerer Schlag Sie und Ihre verehrte Frau getroffen. Diejenigen, von welchen ich die Nachricht erhielt, wussten mir so viel Rühmliches von Ihrem Sohne zu erzählen, dass sein Tod als ein noch viel schwererer Verlust sich darstellt. Dennoch muss gerade in dem Gedanken an alles, was ihn vor so vielen anderen jungen Männern auszeichnete, ein gewisser Trost für Sie liegen. Die wehmütige Erinnerung an ihn wird für immer ein wahres Gut für Sie sein. Unsere Zeit ist reich an Leiden und spricht zu uns mit überzeugender Kraft von der Nichtigkeit des diesseitigen Lebens, wenn es nicht als Vorbereitung für ein jenseitiges diente. Dahin werden Sie nun die Blicke zu richten, sich noch mehr aufgefordert fühlen und wenn irgend jemand, so können Sie vertrauen, dass in dem jenseitigen Teile des Gottesreiches Ihr geliebter Sohn der Segnungen einer göttlich-väterlichen Fürsorge sich erfreut. Auch das möge Ihnen den Schmerz der Trennung lindern.

Meine Frau vereinigt den Ausdruck ihres herzlichsten Beileids mit dem meinigen.

Freundschaftlich ergeben
Ihr

F. Brentano

Brief (Kopie) von Franz Brentano an Husserl, 6. IV. 1916

Letter (copy) of Franz Brentano to Husserl, 6 April 1916

Kondolenzbrief von Paul Natorp

Marburg 29. März 1916.

Verehrter Herr Kollege!

Da ich einmal in Ihr schönes häusliches Leben hineinblicken durfte und durch den Verkehr Ihrer lieben Tochter in unserem Hause der persönliche Zusammenhang zwischen uns erhalten blieb, so berührt es uns besonders schmerzlich, zu erfahren, daß die harte Zeit in Ihr häusliches Glück nun so grausam eingegriffen hat. Was könnten wir Ihnen zum Trost sagen, das Sie sich nicht längst selbst gesagt hätten? Alles was wir tun können, ist, Sie unsrer herzlichsten Teilnahme zu versichern.

    Auch wir haben unsre Opfer bringen müssen. Mein zweiter Sohn wurde gleich im Beginn des Krieges durch Kopfschuß sehr schwer verletzt, ein Wunder, daß er mit dem Leben davonkam. Recht<s>seitige Lähmung blieb zurück, das Geschoß saß fest im Hinterkopf. Die Genesung ging anfangs zwar langsam, aber stetig weiter – geriet dann ins Stocken. Man mußte endlich sich entschließen das Geschoß zu entfernen, auch die Schläfenwunde, die es im Durchgang gerissen, wieder zu öffnen. So hatte m<ein> Sohn von neuem hintereinander zwei äußerst schwere Operationen durchzumachen. Dadurch sind nahe, sehr ernste Gefahren beseitigt u. für weitere Heilung bessere Vorbedingungen geschaffen. Wie weit sie gelingen wird, ob er seinen Beruf (er hatte grade vorher das Referendarexamen bestanden) ausfüllen kann u. wann, ist noch sehr ungewiß. Der ältere Bruder hat erst vor Verdun Schwerstes mit durchgemacht, mußte seiner Nerven wegen zurückgeschickt werden, wurde dann in Garnisonsdienst auf einem Fort vor Metz verwendet, es ging wieder nicht, so ist er jetzt hier, zeitig dienstuntauglich, erholt sich anscheinend gut, ob er aber seine ganze Arbeitsfrische wiedererlangen wird, ist ebenfalls unsicher. Ich halte mich durch Arbeit aufrecht, glaube darin auch gut vorwärts zu kommen, bin aber noch ziemlich weit von irgendeinem Abschluß.

    Ihre Berufung nach F<reiburg> hat mich umso mehr gefreut, da ich nach früheren Vorgängen die Vorstellung gewonnen hatte, daß man Sie da unten nicht wolle. Ich hätte eher gedacht, daß man Sie nach München rufen werde. Aber in mancher Hinsicht mag Fr<eiburg> sogar vorzuziehen sein.

    Die Meinigen alle lassen Ihnen u. den Ihrigen ihre herzliche Teilnahme ausdrücken.

In herzlicher Ergebenheit

Ihr
P. Natorp

Condolence letter from Paul Natorp

Marburg, 29 March 1916.

Dear colleague!
Given that I once had the privilege of seeing your beautiful domestic life and through the interaction with your lovely daughter in our house was able to continue our personal connection, it is particularly painful for us to learn that hard times have now so gruesomely entered into your domestic happiness. What could we ever say for consolation, which you have not already said to yourself? All we can do is assure you of our most heartfelt sympathy.

Even we have brought upon ourselves sacrifice. My second son was very badly wounded at the beginning of the war with a gun-shot wound to the head, a miracle that he walked away with his life. Paralysis of the right-side remains nonetheless, the bullet lodged firmly in the back of the head. Recovery is proceeding slowly, but steadily, and then stalled. It was finally decided to remove the bullet and also open once again the head-wound, which was torn open by the bullet's passage. My son had to endure anew two difficult operations one after the other. But with these [operations], very serious dangers have been eliminated, and improved conditions for continued recovery has been made. How far this will succeed, whether he can still fulfill his profession (he had previously passed the trainee lawyer exam) is still very uncertain. The older brother has to endure terrible things at Verdun, and was then sent back because of his nerves, and was then deployed in garrison duty in a fort near Metz, but that didn't go any further, so he is now here, temporally declared unfit for duty, and is apparently recovering well, but whether he will regain entirely his vitality for work is equally uncertain. I maintain myself through work, believe to have moved forward in my work, but am still far from any kind of conclusion.

Your call to F[reiburg] was all the more pleasing to me, since I had been under the earlier impression that they did not want you down there. I would have rather thought that you would have been called to Munich. But, in some respects, Fr[eiburg] may even be preferable.

Our hearfelt sympathies from my family to you and yours.

In heartfelt condolence,

Your
P. Natorp

Paul Natorp (1854-1924)

Brief von Paul Natorp an Husserl, 29. III. 1916

Letter from Paul Natorp to Husserl, 29 March 1916

„In den Tod gieng er mit Freudigkeit"

Freiburg i/B. Lorettostr. 40
22. 4. 16.

Hochverehrter Herr Kollege!
Wir danken Ihnen vom Herzen für Ihren gütigen und wohlthuenden Brief anlässlich des Todes unseres jüngeren Sohnes. Ich bitte Sie auch Ihrer verehrten Frau Gemahlin unseren Dank zu übermitteln.

Der Verlust dieses Kindes traf unsere ganze Familie sehr schwer. Es war der erklärte Liebling aller: ein frischer, heiterer, warmherziger, durchaus auf das Gute gerichteter Junge, dessen Charakterentwicklung nie einen Wunsch offen ließ. Auf seine wissenschaftliche Entwicklung setzte College Littmann große Hoffnungen. Wir konnten ihn nie anders denken als inmitten eines weiten, schönen, fruchtreichen Lebenshorizonts. Dieser Tage kam sein Feldkoffer zurück, darunter seine letzten literarischen Begleiter: Horaz, T<h>ukydides (sc. im Orig<inal>). Göthes Faust m<it> Urfaust, Schillers Gedichte u. Dramen, Mörike u.dgl. Dazu Biblia Hebraica, Evangelien: Deutsche Barbaren! In den Tod gieng er mit Freudigkeit. Wenige Tage vorher schrieb er überglücklich, daß sein 19. Res<erve>-R<e>g<imen>t nun endlich in die erste Linie gezogen worden sei. Er fiel am 8ten März bei dem ersten, erfolgreichen Sturm auf Vaux an der Spitze seines Zuges, von mehreren Kugeln getroffen.

Mein älterer Sohn, der seit Anfang des Krieges (ein halbes Jahr lang Schulter an Schulter mit dem jüngeren – bis dieser schwer verwundet ausschied) vor Ypern gekämpft hatte, ist, vor etwa 10 Wochen, wegen geschwächter Gesundheit in die Genesungskomp<anie> seines Ersatzbataillons zurückgeschickt worden und thut jetzt Dienst in Eisenach. Nächstens soll er einem Officierskurs überwiesen werden.

Mit Ihren Söhnen, verehrter Herr College, haben Sie und Ihre Frau Gemahlin auch sehr Schweres durchgemacht. Ich

"He went to his death in joy"

Freiburg i / B. Lorettostr. 40
22 April 1916

My esteemed colleague!
We sincerely thank you for your kind and benevolent letter on the occasion of the death of our youngest son. I would also like to extend my thanks to your honorable wife.

The loss of this child affected our whole family very hard. He was the cherished darling for us all: a vital, cheerful, warmhearted, well-directed boy whose character development never left anything to be desired. Colleague Littmann had placed great hope on his scientific development. We could never think of him differently, always in the midst of a wide, beautiful, and fruitful horizon of life. Today, his field trunk came back to us, with among other things, his literary companions: Horace, Thucydides (in the original), Göthes Faust w[ith] Urfaust, Schiller's poems and dramas, Mörike, and the like. And the Biblia Hebraica, Gospels: German barbarians! He went to his death in joy. A few days before, he wrote with great happiness that he had been called up to the front line. He died on the 8th of March during the first, successful assault on Vaux at the head of his platoon, hit by several bullets.

My eldest son, who had fought since the beginning of the war at Ypres (for half a year shoulder to shoulder with the youngest until he left with a grave wound), has been sent back about 10 weeks ago to a replacement battalion due to his weak health, and is now serving in Eisenach. He should shortly be transferred to an officer training course.

As for your sons, dear colleague, you and your wife have also endured terrible things. I thank you for your letters, which I have read with heartfelt sympathy. I attach here the expression of the most heartfelt wishes and hopes.

That your vigorous nature could react to these difficult and profoundly shocking experiences, not only as a father, but as a patriot and philosopher, during this unholy war, with fruitful labor and beneficial public declarations, gives me much pleasure to hear. Unfortunately, I do not have as much praise for myself. At

danke Ihnen für Ihre Mittheilungen, die ich mit inniger Theilnahme gelesen habe. Ich knüpfe daran den Ausdruck herzlichster Wünsche und Hoffnungen.

Daß Ihre kräftige Natur auf die schweren, nicht nur den Vater, sondern auch den Patrioten und Philosophen tief ergreifenden Erlebnisse während dieses unheilvollen Krieges mit fruchtbringender Arbeit u. mit segensreichen öffentlichen Bekundungen reagieren konnte, das zu hören freute mich sehr. Von mir kann ich leider so Rühmliches nicht sagen. Ich war unglücklicher Weise zu Kriegsbeginn zwar in gutem Arbeitsschwung, aber schon (in Folge der Überarbeitung während mehrerer Jahre) bei geschwächten Kräften, so daß ich die tiefen Erregungen minder gut überwand und zeitweise die Fähigkeit zu productiver Arbeit einbüßte. So kamen alle meine Entwürfe ins Stocken, wie sehr ich mich abmühte. Es ist damit allmälig besser geworden und ich hoffe, zumal jetzt angeregt durch völlig neu ausgearbeitete Collegien, größere Fortschritte machen zu können.

Wie viel hätte ich mit Ihnen über Zeit u. Ewigkeit zu sprechen. Es thut mir wohl zu wissen, daß ich mich mit Ihnen in den großen praktischen Fragen Eins fühlen kann, bzw. daß ich Ihren praktischen Impulsen, wie schon in früheren Jahren, herzlich zustimmen kann.

Von unserer Elli, die sich Verehrung und Liebe für Ihre Familie treu bewahrt hat, kann ich keinen Gruß beifügen: Sie ist noch im Helferinnendienst des r<oten> Kreuz in Göttingen zurückgehalten u. wird hoffentlich bald dem hiesigen Dienst überwiesen werden.

Ich drücke Ihnen und Ihrer verehrten Gemahlin in alter Verehrung die Hände.

EHusserl

---

the beginning of the war, although I was in the full swing of work, I regrettably found myself quickly with weakened endurance (as a consequence of over-work over many years), so that the profound agitations could not be over-come, and I temporarily lost the capacity for productive work. So all my projects came to a standstill, as I was struggling. It has thus gradually become better, and I hope, especially now, to be able to make greater progress by means of entirely newly developed seminars.

How much I have to talk to you about time and eternity. I am happy to know that I can feel at one with you with regard to the great practical questions, as well as that I can warmly agree with your practical motivations, as with earlier years.

Concerning our Elli, who remains devoted and full of love for your family, I cannot add a greeting: she is still detained as an assistant for the Red Cross in Göttingen and will hopefully be soon transferred to our local service.

In venerable honor, I extend my hands to you and your wife.
EHusserl

Dankesbrief von Husserl an Paul Natorp, 22. IV. 1916

Thank You letter from Husserl to Paul Natorp, 22 April 1916

Kondolenzbrief von Alexander Pfänder

München. d<en> 21. Mai 1916.
Leopoldstr. 70/II

Lieber Herr Professor!
Für Ihre werte Karte besten Dank. Nehmen Sie noch nachträglich mein herzlichstes Beileid zu Ihrem schweren Verluste entgegen. Erst vor ein paar Tagen erfuhr ich von Herrn Daubert, der augenblicklich auf Urlaub hier ist, die Bestätigung der gerüchtweise vernommenen Trauerbotschaft.–

Da ich annehme, daß die Sache eilt, so will ich Ihrer Bitte sogleich nachkommen und Ihnen aus dem Stegreif meine Meinung über Kollegen Ettlinger entwerfen. Ich kenne E<ttlinger> seit seinem ersten Studiensemester, früher sehr genau, seit längeren Jahren dagegen nur aus der Ferne. Er war ein im Grunde ehrlicher, fleißiger, ernster und nach eigener Erkenntnis strebender Mensch. Etwas nüchtern, bedenklich und ein wenig mißtrauisch <…>

Letter of condolence from Alexander Pfänder

Munich, 21 May 1916
Leopoldstr. 70/II
Dear Professor!
Many thanks for your precious letter. Please accept my belated and heartfelt sympathy for your difficult lost. I received confirmation of this sad communication, which I had heard through the grape vine, only a few days ago from Herrn Daubert, who is at the moment on vacation.

Since I assume that the situation is urgent, I would like with your permission to return to the matter at hand and spontaneously give you my own opinion regarding my colleague Ettlinger. I have known Ettlinger since the first semester of studies, and even earlier for a number of years, but only from a distance. He was in principle a very honest, efficient, serious, and on his own account, a person driven to know things on his own. Somewhat sober, reflective, and somewhat skeptical by nature […]

Erste Seite eines Briefes von Alexander Pfänder an Husserl, 21. V. 1916

First page of a letter from Alexander Pfänder to Husserl, 21 May 1916

Alexander Pfänder (1870-1941), Aufnahme aus den 1930er Jahren

Alexander Pfänder (1870 – 1941), photograph from the 1930s

Kondolenzbrief von Georg Simmel

Straßburg 10. IV. 16
Verehrter Freund!

Durch Jonas Cohn, den ich zufällig in der Eisenbahn traf, habe ich erfahren, daß nun auch Ihr Sohn ein Opfer des Weltschicksals geworden ist. Jedes Wort, das man darüber sagen wollte, wäre eine Entweihung. Aber nehmen Sie u. Ihre Frau von mir u. der meinigen einen Händedruck an u. glauben Sie an unsre tiefe u. innige Teilnahme.

Immer
Ihr
Simmel

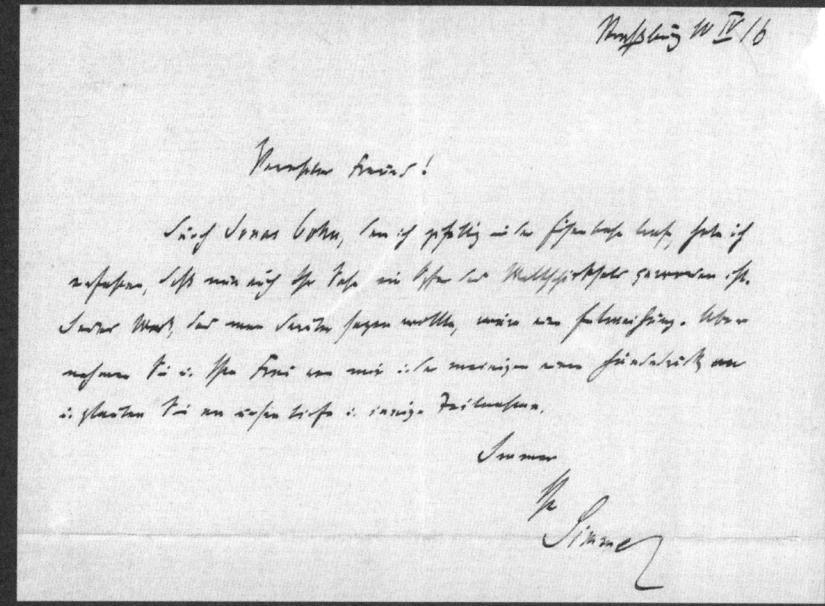

Brief von Georg Simmel an Husserl, 10. IV. 1916

Letter from Georg Simmel to Husserl, 10 April 1916

Letter of condolence from Georg Simmel

Georg Simmel (1858-1918)

Strasbourg, 10 April 1916
Dear Friend!
From Jonas Cohn, whom I by chance met on the train, I learned that now even your son has become a victim of the destiny of the world. Any word, which one would want to say, would amount to profanation. Please accept on behalf of myself and my wife the embrace of our hands to you and your wife, and please believe in our deepest and innermost sympathy.

Always,
Your,
Simmel

Philosophen im Krieg
Philosophers in War

- Winthrop P. Bell (1884-1965)
- Rudolf Clemens (1890-1914)
- Hedwig Conrad-Martius (1888-1966)
- Theodor Conrad (1881-1969)
- Waldemar Conrad (1878-1915)
- Johannes Daubert (1877-1947)
- Fritz Frankfurther (1889-1914)
- Moritz Geiger (1880-1937)
- Erich von Gündell (1854-1924)
- Martin Heidegger (1889-1976)
- Gustav Hübener (1889-1941)
- Fritz Kaufmann (1891-1958)
- Emil Lask (1875-1915)
- Kurt Lewin (1890-1947)
- Hans Lipps (1889-1941)
- Karl Löwith (1897-1973)
- Dietrich Mahnke (1884-1939)
- Arnold Metzger (1892-1974)
- Friedrich Neumann (1889-1978)
- Adolf Reinach (1883-1917)
- Heinrich Rickert jr. (1891-1917)
- Hermann Ritzel (1880-1915)
- Max Scheler (1874-1928)
- Edith Stein (1891-1942)

Der Münchener Phänomenologe Johannes Daubert (1877-1947) als Motorradfahrer bei der Bayerischen Kraftradfahrer-Abteilung (ca. 1914)

The Munich phenomenologist Johannes Daubert (1877 – 1947) as motorcyclist with the Bavarian division of motorized drivers (around 1914)

Die „Göttinger Philosophische Gesellschaft", ca. 1912
The "Göttingen Philosophical Society", around 1912

Von links nach rechts: Jean Hering, Friedrich Neumann, Adolf Reinach, Hans Lipps, Theodor Conrad, Max Scheler, Alexandre Koyré, Siegfried Hamburger, Hedwig Conrad-Martius, Rudolf Clemens, Gustav Hübener, Alfred von Sybel

From left to right: Jean Hering, Friedrich Neumann, Adolf Reinach, Hans Lipps, Theodor Conrad, Max Scheler, Alexandre Koyré, Siegfried Hamburger, Hedwig Conrad-Martius, Rudolf Clemens, Gustav Hübener, Alfred von Sybel

Mitglieder der „Göttinger Philosophischen Gesellschaft"
Members of the "Göttingen Philosophical Society"

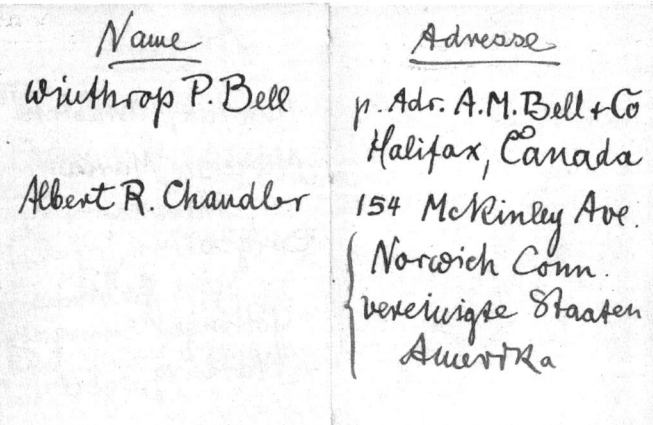

Mitgliederliste (erstellt 1913 von Jean Hering): Alexander Koyré, Dr. Hedwig Martius-Conrad, Gustav Hübener, Rudolf Clemens, Friedrich Neumann, Siegfried Hamburger, Hans Lipps, Herbert Leyendecker, Fritz Frankfurther, Jean Hering, Heinrich W. Rickert, Dr. Max Scheler, Dietrich Hildebrand, Dr. H. Th. Conrad, Dr. Adolf Reinach, Dr. Alfred v. Sybel, Winthrop P. Bell, Albert R. Chandler

Membership list (from Jean Hering, 1913): Alexander Koyré, Dr. Hedwig Martius-Conrad, Gustav Hübener, Rudolf Clemens, Friedrich Neumann, Siegfried Hamburger, Hans Lipps, Herbert Leyendecker, Fritz Frankfurther, Jean Hering, Heinrich W. Rickert, Dr. Max Scheler, Dietrich Hildebrand, Dr. H. Th. Conrad, Dr. Adolf Reinach, Dr. Alfred v. Sybel, Winthrop P. Bell, Albert R. Chandler

Winthrop P. Bell (1884-1965)

Winthrop Pickard Bell: geb. am 12. 5. 1884 in Halifax (Kanada), gest. 4. 4. 1965 Chester (Kanada). – 1909 Abschluss des Studiums der Philosophie („Master of Philosophy") an der Harvard University in Cambridge/Mass. Ab Herbst 1910 Studium in Deutschland, zunächst in Leipzig, dann ab Frühjahr 1911 in Göttingen bei Husserl. Mitglied der Göttinger Philosophischen Gesellschaft, der Vereinigung der Schüler Husserls. Im August 1914 kurz vor Abschluss der Promotion („Eine kritische Untersuchung der Erkenntnistheorie Josiah Royce's") wird der Kanadier Bell wegen angeblich deutschfeindlicher Äußerungen inhaftiert, das Promotionsverfahren für ungültig erklärt. Anfang 1915 Internierung für die Dauer des Kriegs in einem Lager in Ruhleben bei Berlin. Nach dem Krieg arbeitet Bell offiziell als Korrespondent für die Nachrichtenagentur Reuters in Deutschland, höchstwahrscheinlich aber als Spion für den britischen Geheimdienst. Anfang 1920 Rückkkehr nach Kanada. Bell hält den Kontakt mit Husserl und den anderen Phänomenologen aufrecht. 1922 Abschluss des Promotionsverfahrens. Im Herbst 1922 nach kurzer Lehrtätigkeit an der Universität von Toronto Wechsel an die Harvard University, wo er mit Unterbrechungen bis etwa 1927 lehrt. Danach verschiedene Reisen und Tätigkeiten, u.a. Mitarbeit im Unternehmen seines Bruders, Ralph P. Bell. 1961 Veröffentlichung eines Standardwerkes zur Geschichte seines Heimatlandes („The ‚Foreign Protestants' and the Settlement of Nova Scotia"). – Der Nachlass von W. P. Bell befindet sich im Mount Allison University Archives, Winthrop Pickard Bell fonds (Sackville, New Brunswick, Canada).

Winthrop Pickard Bell: born on May 12, 1884 in Halifax (Canada), died on April 4, 1965 in Chester (Canada). Completed his studies in philosophy (Master's degree) in 1909 at Harvard University. Studied philosophy in Germany: 1910 in Leipzig and then with Husserl in Göttingen in 1911. Member of the Göttingen Philosophical Society. Shortly before the completion of his PhD with Husserl in 1914 (*A Critical Investigation of the Theory of Knowledge in Josiah Royce*), Bell was detained on presumed charges of anti-German statements; his PhD thesis was declared disqualified. Beginning in 1915, Bell was interned for the duration of the war at an internment camp near Berlin. After the war, Bell worked as a correspondent for Reuters in Germany, and, most likely, was also employed by the British secret service. Bell returned to Canada in 1920 and maintained his contacts with Husserl and other phenomenologists. He finally completed his PhD in 1922. After a brief engagement at the University of Toronto, Bell taught at Harvard University until 1927. After leaving Harvard, Bell traveled extensively and published in 1961 a standard work on the history of Nova Scotia – *The 'Foreign Protestants' and the Settlement of Nova Scotia*. Bell's papers are housed at Mount Allison University Archives in Sackville, New Brunswick.

Bell, J.: On Four Originators of Transatlantic Phenomenology: Josiah Royce, Edmund Husserl, William Hocking, Winthrop Bell. In: Parker, K. A./Bell, J.: The Relevance of Royce. Oxford 2014, 47-68. – Bell, J.: The German Translation of Royce's Epistemology by Husserl's Student Winthrop Bell: A Neglected Bridge of Pragmatic-Phenomenological Interpretation? In: The Pluralist, Vol. 6, No. 1 (Spring 2011), 46-62. – Winthrop Pickard Bell, "The Idea of a Nation". Ed., and with an Introduction, by I. Angus. In: Symposium: Canadian Journal of Continental Philosophy 16, no. 2 (Fall 2012), 34-63. – Winthrop Pickard Bell, "The Work of Philosophy". Ed. by I. Angus. In: New Yearbook for Phenomenology and Phenomenological Philosophy, 12 (2012), 286-315. – Einleitung in: Bell, J./Vongehr, T. (Hg.): Eine kritische Untersuchung der Erkenntnistheorie Josiah Royces. Mit Kommentaren und Änderungsvorschlägen von Edmund Husserl. Texte aus dem Nachlass von Winthrop P. Bell (1914/22). In: Husserliana-Materialien, Bd. X. Dordrecht 2018, IX-XX. – Punch, T. M.: "Even If I Cannot Finish...:" Winthrop Bell and His Register. In: Journal of the Royal Nova Scotia Historical Society, vol. 7 (2004), 112-139.

„Wegen deutschfeindlicher Äußerungen in Schutzhaft"

Bei Ausbruch des Krieges wird Husserls Schüler, der Kanadier Winthrop P. Bell, der kurz vor Abschluss seiner Promotion steht, wegen angeblich deutschfeindlicher Äußerungen verhaftet. Die Umstände, die zur Inhaftierung führten, beschreibt seine Kommilitonin Edith Stein wie folgt:

„Dieses konservative Blatt <die ‚Schlesische Zeitung'> brachte eine abfällige Notiz über die ‚vaterlandslose Gesinnung' einiger Göttinger Professoren. Sie hätten sich zu einem Engländer, der wegen deutschfeindlicher Äußerungen in Schutzhaft war, begeben, um ihm die mündliche Doktorprüfung abzunehmen. Der ‚deutschfeindliche Engländer' war unser Freund Bell, die ‚vaterlandslosen Professoren' unser alter Meister Husserl und die beiden Kollegen, die Bell in den Nebenfächern zu prüfen hatten. Ihre Namen waren alle angeführt. <...> Bell war als Kanadier zunächst in Freiheit geblieben. (Die Kolonialengländer wurden erst Anfang 1915 interniert.) Eines Tages kam ein Bekannter (ein Deutscher) an seiner Wohnung vorbei und fragte ihn zum Fenster hinauf – das war echt Göttinger Stil, aber bei der Gemütsverfassung des Volkes in den ersten Kriegsmonaten höchst unvorsichtig –: ‚Was sagen Sie zur japanischen Kriegserklärung?' Bell antwortete ebenso unüberlegt zum Fenster hinaus: ‚Für uns ist sie natürlich sehr vorteilhaft.' Eine vorübergehende Dame hörte das, geriet in die größte Erregung, erstattete sofort Anzeige. Dabei wurde die Äußerung erheblich entstellt, so daß sie als deutschfeindliche Kundgebung erschien. Bell wurde in Schutzhaft genommen, durfte aber in seiner Wohnung bleiben. Da er sie nicht verlassen durfte, konnte er sich auch nicht an dem festgesetzten Prüfungstage in die Universität begeben, und seine wohlwollenden und teilnahmsvollen Lehrer beschlossen, die Prüfung in seiner Wohnung vorzunehmen. Damit erregten sie heftigen Anstoß bei ihren nationalistischen Kollegen; es wurde eine Fakultätssitzung einberufen, die Prüfung wurde für ungültig erklärt und sogar auch die Annahme der Arbeit, die schon vor Kriegsausbruch abgeliefert war. Als ich nach Göttingen kam, erzählte mir Husserl, daß Bell jetzt im ‚Karzer' in Haft gehalten werde. <...> Dieses Lokal hatte ich bisher noch nicht gesehen. Es lag im obersten Stock der ‚Aula', die ich bisher nur bei festlichen Anlässen betreten hatte und zu Beginn jedes Semesters, um meine Kolleggelder zu zahlen. Denn in diesem Gebäude waren die Geschäftsräume der Universität."

(Edith Stein: „Aus dem Leben einer jüdischen Familie", ESGA 1, S. 246-247)

"In detention due to anti-German statements"

With the outbreak of the war, Husserl's student, the Canadian Winthrop P. Bell, who was just about to finish his PhD, was arrested due to alleged anti-German statements. The circumstances which led to his interment were described by fellow-student Edith Stein:

"This conservative newspaper [the 'Schlesische Zeitung' ('The Silesian News')] carried a reference criticizing the 'unpatriotic attitude' of some professors at Göttingen. It was reported that these professors had visited an Englishman to administer the oral examination for his doctorate while he was in custody because of some anti-German statements he had made. The 'anti-German Englishman' was our friend Bell; the 'unpatriotic' professor, our old Master, Husserl, and his two colleagues who examined Bell in his minor subjects. Their names were all reported. […] Bell, as a Canadian, had at first remained at liberty. (Citizens of British colonies were not interned until the beginning of 1915.) One day an acquaintance of his (a German) while passing Bell's lodging had called up to him at the window: This, though so typical a practice in Göttingen, was a highly imprudent one in this case, considering the feelings of the people in those early months of the war. He [the German] had asked, 'What do you think of the Japanese declaration of war?' Just as unthinkingly, Bell answered from the open window, 'For us, it's obviously an advantage.' A woman passing by at that moment heard him and, greatly agitated, went at once to report him. In that report his comment was grossly exaggerated so that it appeared to have been an anti-German proclamation. Bell was taken into protective custody but was allowed to live at home. As he was not permitted to leave the house, he was unable to present himself at the university on the day that had been set for the examinations: So his benevolent and sympathetic teachers had decided to give him the examination at his apartment. By doing so they aroused violent protest from their nationalist colleagues. A faculty meeting was called and the examination was declared invalid, as was the acceptance of the thesis he had submitted, even though that had been done before the war began. Upon my return to Gottingen, Husserl told me Bell was now incarcerated in the university's 'lock-up'. […] I had never before seen this particular place. It was located in the upper story of the Auditorium which, so far, I had entered only on important festive occasions or when paying my course fees at the beginning of each semester. The university's administrative offices were in this building."

(Edith Stein "Life in a Jewish Family: An autobiography, 1891-1916". Translated by J. Koeppel. In: The Collected Works of Edith Stein, vol. I, ed. L. Gelber and Romaeus Leuven OCD, Washington 1986, p. 301-302)

Der (ehemalige) „Karzer" in der Universität Göttingen; eine Gefängniszelle, in der der kanadische Student Winthrop P. Bell kurz nach Kriegsbeginn für einige Zeit festgehalten wurde. In die Innenseite der Holztür hat er seinen Namen geritzt. Später kam Bell für die Dauer des Krieges in ein Internierungslager in Ruhleben bei Berlin.

The (former) "Karzer" in the University of Göttingen; a prison cell, in which the Canadian student Winthrop P. Bell shortly after the beginning of the war was detained for a period of time. On the inside of the wooden door, he inscribed his name. Bell later spent the duration of the war in an internal detention camp near Berlin.

„Wir aber müssen hier ausharren"

Freiburg 8. XI. 1918.
Lieber Freund!

Mit herzlichster Theilnahme höre ich von dem Kummer, der über Sie durch das Hinscheiden Ihres Vaters verhängt worden ist. So hatte also die Hoffnung nicht mehr die Kraft den seit vielen Jahren schwer Leidenden aufrecht zu erhalten: ganz nahe vor der Erfüllung musste er dahingehen. Aber er ist im Frieden der Seligen, die dieser irdischen Hölle der Selbstsucht, des wahnwitzigen Hasses, der Verwirrung aller ethischen Begriffe, der Verdunklung reiner Menschheitsziele entrückt sind. Wohl ihm. Wir aber müssen hier ausharren und fast verzweifelnd u. gelähmt unter der Last furchtbarster Eindrücke um die göttliche Gnade der Kraft bitten, der unabweislichen Forderung in thätigen Leistungen genug thun zu können, die uns auferlegt ist: der Forderung eine neue, bessere, selbstlose Menschenwelt aufzubauen, in der man leben u. in reinem Wirken sich erhöhen kann und lieben, statt im giftigen Anhauch des Hasses zu erstarren.

Mit innigen Wünschen weilen meine Gedanken oft bei Ihnen u. herzlichst wünschte ich Sie vor Ihrer Heimkehr zu sehen. Das wird wohl kaum möglich sein. Ich bin jetzt etwas danieder, erhole mich langsam von einer schweren Grippe. Daß mein Sohn zum 2ten Mal, schwer verwundet, in Jena liegt u. in Rekonvalescenz ist, haben Sie wohl gehört.
Mit den wärmsten Grüßen
Ihr
E Husserl

Freiburg in Baden Lorettostr. 40

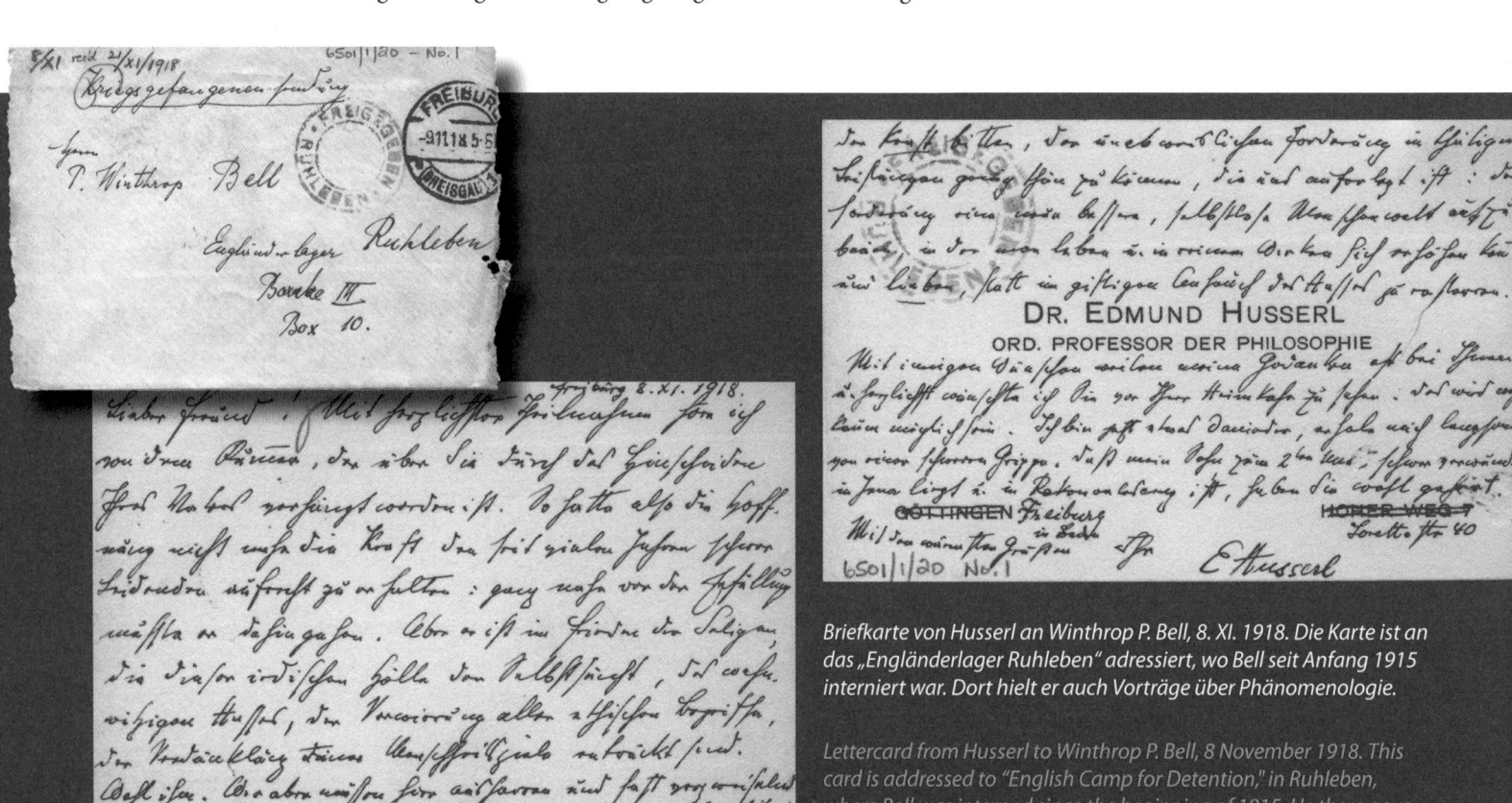

Briefkarte von Husserl an Winthrop P. Bell, 8. XI. 1918. Die Karte ist an das „Engländerlager Ruhleben" adressiert, wo Bell seit Anfang 1915 interniert war. Dort hielt er auch Vorträge über Phänomenologie.

Lettercard from Husserl to Winthrop P. Bell, 8 November 1918. This card is addressed to "English Camp for Detention," in Ruhleben, where Bell was interned since the beginning of 1915. He there gave lectures on pheneomenology.

"We, however, must here endure"

Freiburg, 8 November 1918.
Dear Friend!

It is with heartfelt sympathy that I hear of the grief that has befallen you with the passing away of your father. It seems that hope no longer possessed the force to sustain those who have been suffering gravely for so many years; so very close to fulfillment did he have to pass-away. But, he is among the peace of the blessed-ones, who are liberated from this earthly hell of selfishness, the madness of hatred, the confusion of all ethical concepts, and the darkness of all genuine human ends. Good for him. We, however, must here endure and, confused and paralyzed under the weight of most terrible experiences, we must ask divine grace for the force required to transform the ineluctable demand, which is placed upon us, into effective achievements, namely, the demand for a new, better, and altruistic world of humanity, in which one can live and love, and so elevate ourselves to pure actuality, rather than become petrified in the poisonous breath of hatred.

With heartfelt wishes my thoughts are often with you and I truly hope that I can see you before your return home. That will be hardly possible. I'm somewhat under the weather these days, and am slowly recovering from a severe flu. That my son is convalescing in Jena for the second time, gravely wounded, you have heard.
With warmest of greetings,
Your,
E. Husserl

Freiburg in Baden Lorettostr. 40

Häftlinge im Engländerlager Ruhleben (von links nach rechts): Winthrop Bell, I.J. Warkentin und Grant Lochhead (zwischen 1915 und 1918)

English internment camp inmates in Ruhleben (left to right): Winthrop Bell, I.J. Warkentin, and Grant Lochhead (between 1915 and 1918)

„Wer rettet das deutsche Volk nach seinem wahrhaftigen Sein?"

Hinterzarten 19. 4. 19
Lieber Freund.

Ich hatte nicht früher die Möglichkeit, Ihnen für Ihr Glückwunschtelegramm zu danken. Es war mir eine große, ganz große Freude, daß auch Sie an dem Tage nicht fehlten, den viele Zeichen der Liebe – zu meiner nicht geringen Überraschung – zum Feste gestaltet hatten. Obwol von den alten Schülern u. Freunden unter den gegebenen Verhältnissen niemand persönlich kommen konnte, so war ich doch im Geiste bei ihnen u. sie bei mir. Sie vor allem, lieber Herr Bell, hätte ich gerne wiedergesehen, ich habe mir es schon seit Jahren brennend gewünscht. Wie hätte ich Sie bei mir gehegt und gepflegt – was natürlich in philosophischem Sinne zu verstehen ist, denn wie es mit den Ernährungsverhältnissen auch hier im Süden steht, wissen Sie selbst nur zu gut.

Nun haben Sie Wichtigeres zu thun, als bei mir u. mit mir Phänomenologie zu treiben u. an der philos<ophischen> Reinigung der Menschheit mitzuhelfen. Sie treiben das edlere Geschäft, feurige Kohlen auf den Häuptern Ihrer „Feinde" zu sammeln u. als Seelenarzt bei Ihren Freunden zu wirken. Ich wußte es gleich, als Sie mir Ihren ersten unvergeßlichen Brief aus dem Fürstenhof schrieben, daß Ihnen eine große Mission von oben her zuteil geworden sei, Ihnen, dem Würdigsten u. nicht nur Berufenen, sondern Auserwählten, wie die innere Stimme mir sofort in leuchtender Evidenz sagte. Und wie herrlich hat sich dieser Glaube bestätigt. Ich erkannte sofort, als ich vor Monaten in der Frankf<urter> Zeit<un>g eine Anzeige über eine völlig neue u. gerechte Beurtheilung der deutschen Innenlage von englischer Seite, von Seite<n> des Berliner Reuter-Korrespondenten las, daß diese Stimme der Wahrheit aus Ihrem Munde kam. Und vor kurzer Zeit hörte ich mit tiefer Bewegung von Ihnen u. Ihrem Wirken Näheres durch meinen Freib<urger> Kollegen, Prof. Brinkmann, der im auswärtigen Amt beschäftigt ist.

Es handelt sich jetzt nicht um Rettung von Deutschl<ands> polit<ischer> Zukunft, um seine Rettung als einer in noch so bescheidenem Sinne gedachten politischen Macht – das ist vorüber, u. niemand hofft da das Mindeste –, sondern um eine Rettung der deutschen Nation vor völliger physischer u. ineins damit moralischer Verelendung. Und da sind Sie ein großer u. Hoffnung erweckender Helfer u. vielleicht Retter. Vielleicht ist da doch noch ein wenig zu hoffen. Nicht viel. Die täglichen Berichte, die grauenvoll fortschreitende Krankheit der deutschen Seele u. das physische Siechthum der kaum noch erträglichen Hungersnot erregten immer neue Anfälle der Verzweiflung. Wir sind so weit, daß uns der Bolschewismus nicht mehr ernstlich schreckt. Wir haben kaum noch etwas ernstlich zu verlieren. Am Ende, so sagt man sich, ist es gut so, daß die so viel gepriesene materielle Kultur zu Ende geht. Und wenn bei uns, dann auch bei den „Feinden".

Wo aber ist, fragt man sich dann, der allein Heil bringende Gegenstrom moralischer u. religiöser Erneuerung? Es ist, als ob der Hunger: der Hunger nach kräftigender u. nicht blos <den> Magen füllender Speise, nicht minder der Hunger nach durch Jahre hindurch entbehrten Reizmitteln, der Hunger nach dem natürlichen freien Dahinleben mit seinen täglich neu anregenden Hoffnungen, seinen Freuden versprechenden Zielen – als ob der Hunger in jeder Gestalt mit thierisch blinder Gier die Seelen ausgefüllt u. in ihnen alles höhere Menschentum ausgelöscht hätte. Die Masse, ein trüber Wirbel wahnsinniger Gier „regiert". Oder vielmehr, es gibt keine Regierung, es gibt kein Befehlen u. kein Gehorchen mehr. Alle staatliche Ordnung ruht doch schließlich darauf, daß die Menschen in ihren Seelen selbst der Idee der Pflicht sich beugen, also willentlich Pflichten auf sich nehmen in der Gesinnung darnach zu handeln. In den Seelen der Massen ist aber diese furchtbarste aller Revolutionen eingetreten: Die Idee der Pflicht ist von ihrem T<h>ron gestoßen, es gibt keine Pflichtwilligkeit mehr.

Ich weiß nicht, ob je in der Geschichte ein Volk so schwer krank darniederlag, ob es je eine solche Summe des Elends auf Erden gab. Gewiß „Blo<c>kaden" gab es genug u.

man hat genug Städte u. Staaten zerstört, Menschen dem Hungerwahnsinn preisgegeben u. die Übriggebliebenen zu Sklaven gemacht. Aber geschah dies je bei Völkern von einer hohen Stufe der Geistigkeit, bei Völkern, die zu höchstem Selbstbewußtsein nationaler Personalität emporgestiegen u. ihrer selbst als Träger hoher kultureller, wissenschaftlicher, technischer, künstlerischer, moralischer Missionen bewußt geworden waren? Schließlich sind ein Luther, Lessing, Leibnitz, Kant, Herder, Goethe, Schiller u.s.w. nicht bloß Reklamen frecher Berliner Handlungsreisender. Es gibt eine Seele des deutschen Volkes, in der diese Namen eingegraben sind, in der sie erworbene Kräfte u. unendliche Aufgaben bedeuten. Und diese Seele morden – giebt es einen grauenvolleren Mord in der ganzen Weltgeschichte? Doch nein, es heißt ja nicht Mord, es gibt dafür so viele schöne Worte aus dem Lexikon hoher Moral u. Religion – u. man soll nicht an der Menschheit verzweifeln, die ohne Ehrfurcht Himmelswerte ausspricht u. mit ihnen die grauenvollen Unthaten „rechtfertigt"?

Wer rettet das deutsche Volk nach seinem wahrhaftigen Sein, seinem geistigen Eros, wer die Kontinuität der deutschen Geistesentwicklung? Nach ihr langen wie Gift- u. Riesenschlangen die Mächte eines bald glühenden, bald kalten Hasses, dieses Hasses, der im Kriege (von flüchtigen u. schnell verfliegenden leidenschaftlichen Aufwallungen abgesehen) nie existiert hatte u. erst in diesen letzten Monaten des offen gewordenen Sinnes der „Völkerversöhnung" erwachsen ist und der unheimlich um sich greift wie ein fressendes Feuer. Frankreich – wie ganz anders wird dieses Wort jetzt ausgesprochen! Ohne Verwünschung, ohne leidenschaftliche Gebärden, ohne jedes Epitheton. Und doch, wie ganz anders klingt es. In all diesen Jahren war es ein Wort der Theilnahme, der Trauer: man mußte nur einen beliebigen einfachen Menschen hören. Und jetzt! Ich weiß, wie ich selbst mich innerlich wehren muß u. wie ich nur eine wirksame Rettung habe in dem Namen

Brief von Husserl an Winthrop P. Bell, 19. IV. 1919

Letter from Husserl to Winthrop P. Bell, 19 April 1919

Romain Rolland. Inmitten dieser Feuerfluten des Hasses eine grünende Insel, ein Garten edelster Menschlichkeit. So wirkt er gewiß bei Tausenden. Der „Johann Christoph" ist (trotz des sehr hohen Preises der deutschen Übersetzung) in gewaltigen Auflagen ausgegeben u. gekauft u. gelesen worden.

Ein wenig besser steht es mit England, weil von dort mehr Stimmen der Menschlichkeit bekannt wurden. Wie oft denke ich in Verehrung Bertrand Russel<l>'s, Macdonald's u. des Lord Cartwright, um nur einige Namen zu nennen. Ich wollte, daß Sie, nach England zurückgekehrt, B. Russel<l> aufsuchten u. ihm sagten, daß es hier in Deutschland noch redliche Männer gibt u. solche, die seiner in größter Verehrung gedenken. – Im Übrigen, ich habe auch meinen Bell u. ihm ist sogar die Kraft der großen Wirkung verliehen. Also dürfen wir noch hoffen. Doch ich will nicht zu einseitig sein.

Grund zu hoffen, habe ich auch insofern, als ich in der letzten Vorlesung des Kriegssemesters (Februar bis Mitte April) bei der hartgeprüften Jugend offene Herzen u. langende Sehnsucht nach dem Reich reiner Ideen beobachten konnte, u. nicht wenig Zuschriften aus der Ferne zum 8. April dafür sprechen, daß es auch noch einen Hunger nach Philosophie u. sogar nach „Ph<ilosophie> als strenger Wissenschaft" giebt, dessen Stillung die Blo<c>kade nicht wird hemmen können.

Ich selbst weiche den Basiliskenblicken der Zeit möglichst aus u. umgebe meine Seele, so gut ich es vermag, mit der Philosophie als wie mit einem Panzer: Ich konzentriere mich leidenschaftlich auf meine alten u. neuen Probleme. Ich arbeite mit so viel Erfolg, als es die unzureichende Ernährung zuläßt. Dazwischen fliehe ich in den Schwarzwald, da u. dort giebt es ein ländliches Wirtshaus mit relativ kräftigem Essen, u. die Höhenluft thut das ihre, mich wieder auf den Damm zu bringen.

Wenn Sie doch einmal wieder zu mir kommen können, werden Sie den Schwarzwald lieben u. das Philosophiren auf den grünen Matten in der anregenden Höhenluft schätzen lernen. Auch der süddeutsche Menschenschlag, so viel weniger verwandt er Ihrer Art ist als der norddeutsche, würde Ihnen seine wertvollen Seiten zeigen. Viel hätte ich Ihnen zu erzählen, viel mehr noch Sie mir. Daß sich doch dies schöne Symbol in uns bald verkörperte: die Feindesliebe, der Seelenbund der „Feinde", gestiftet durch die Liebe zu dem Eros.

Ich sorge mich um Ihre Gesundheit, die unter Ihrer Aufopferung für die große u. gute Sache dahinzuschmelzen droht. Mein einziger Trost ist, daß Ihnen das Bewußtsein des Segens nicht fehlen kann, der auf Ihrer Arbeit liegt, u. daß von ihm wieder eine Heilwirkung ausgehen muß.

Meine Frau, die für diesen Brief als vermittelnde Sekretärin fungierte, grüßt Sie herzlichst. Ich muß Morgen schon nach Freiburg zurück, das Dekanat d<er> philos<ophischen> Fakultät zu übernehmen. Leider wird diese unphilosophische Thätigkeit mich in meinen eigenen Arbeiten sehr hemmen. Im Sommersem<ester> lese ich 4stündig über Natur u. Geist, halte Übungen über ethische Grundprobleme u. vielleicht noch intime Übungen.

Vom Herzen grüße ich Sie als
Ihr freundschaftlich ergebener
EHusserl

"Who will save the German people in its genuine existence?"

Hinterzarten 19 April 1919
Dear friend,

I did not earlier have the opportunity to thank you for your congratulatory telegram. It was a great, very great joy for me that you, too, were not missing on this day, that many signs of love, and much to my surprise, were molded into this celebration. Even though no one from the old students and friends could personally come on account of the present circumstances, I was nonetheless with them all in spirit, as you were with me. Above all, dear Mr. Bell, I would have liked to see you again, I have been yearning to see you for years. How I would have cherished and taken care of you here with me – which, of course, is to be understood in a philosophical sense, since with regard to the condition of the food supply here in the South, you yourself know all too well.

You now have more important things to do than to pursue phenomenology with me and to assist me in the philos[ophical] purification of humanity. You are pursuing the noble business of heaping burning coals on your "enemies' " head and acting as a doctor of the soul with your friends.* I knew it right away, when you wrote to me your first unforgettable letter from Fürstenhof** that you had been given a great mission from above, to you, the most worthy and noble one, and not just called-upon, but specially chosen, as the inner voice immediately told me in glowing evidence. And how gloriously this conviction has been confirmed. I recognized at once, months ago, in a Frankfurter newspaper an announcement concerning an entirely new and just evaluation of the internal situation in Germany from the English perspective, and read from the pag[es] of a Berlin Reuter's correspondent, that this voice of the truth came from your mouth. And just recently, I was very moved in hearing about you and your effectiveness from my Frei[burg] colleague, Prof. Brinkmann, who is employed in the Foreign Office.

It is now not only a matter of salvaging Ger[many's] poli[tical] future as a political force conceived in a modest sense of that term – that is over now, and nobody here hopes for the least –, but for a salvation of the German nation from complete physical and therewith moral misery. And here you are of tremendous assistance in awakening hope and perhaps even being a saviour. Perhaps there's here still a little to hope for. Not much. The daily newsreports, the terribly progressing sickness of the German soul and the physical lingering infirmity of the scarcely tolerable famine provokes ever new bouts of despair. We are so far that Bolshevism no longer scares us seriously. We hardly have anything seriously to lose. In the end, it is said, it is a good thing that the much celebrated material culture comes to an end. And if with us, then also with the "enemies."

But, one asks oneself, where is the redeeming counter-current that would bring moral and religious renewal? It is, as if with hunger: a hunger for fortifying food and not just to fill the stomach, and last but not least, after all the years of suffering during the war, there is a hunger for everyday stimulants, and a hunger for a natural and effortless living day to day with its daily renewed hopes, the joy of promised goals – as if hunger in every form with animal blind greed filled the souls and wiped out in these souls any sense of higher humanity. The mass, a murky vortex of insane greed "rules." Or rather, there is no government, there are no orders and no more obeying. After all, all order of the state rests on the fact that men in their souls themselves bow to the idea of duty, that is, to voluntarily undertaken duties in the spirit of acting upon them. In the souls of the masses, however, this most terrible of all revolutions has occurred: the idea of duty has been dethroned, for there is no longer any willingness for duties.

I do not know whether there ever was in history a people who suffered so seriously such illness, whether there ever was such a total sum of misery on earth. Certainly, "blockades," there have been many, and one had destroyed enough cities and states, and people exposed the madness of hunger, with the remaining populations made into slaves. But, did this ever happen to a people of such elevated level of spirituality, amongst a people who have attained the highest self-confidence of national personality, and who had become aware of themselves as carriers of an elevated cultural, scientific, technical, artistic, and moral mission? After all, Luther, Lessing, Leibniz, Kant, Herder, Goethe, Schiller and so on, these names are not just advertisements from cheeky

Berlin traveling salesmen. There is a soul of the German people in which these names are buried, names which signify acquired powers and infinite tasks. And to murder this soul – is there in the entire history of the world, a more gruesome murder? But no, it's not called murder, for there are so many beautiful words in the lexicon of high morality and religion, and one should not despair of humanity, which fearlessly expresses heavenly values, and with such expressions, "justifies" these gruesome acts?

Who will save the German people in its genuine existence, in its spiritual eros, and who will save the continuity of German intellectual development? The powers of a glowing, at times cold-blooded hatred reach out towards the German people like giant, poisonious snakes; this hatred, which had never existed in the war (despite occassional and fleeting surges of passion), and only emerged in these past few months of the "reconciliation of peoples," whose meaning now becomes visible, has now sinisterly engulfed [everything] like an all-consuming fire. France – how differently this name is now spoken! Without curses, without passionate gestures, without any epithet. And yet, how different this name now sounds. In all these years it was a name of sympathy and grief: one only had to hear the common person. And now! I know how to defend myself within myself and how I have a true saviour in the name of Romain Rolland. In the midst of these flames of hatred, a green island, a garden of the noblest humanity. It certainly affects thousands of people. The "Johann Christoph" is published in huge editions, bought and is read (despite the very high price of the German translation).***

Things are a little better with England, because there are there more voices of humanity that have become known. How often do I think in admiration of the names of Bertrand Russell, Macdonald, and Lord Cartwright, to name but a few. I would like it, if you, when returned to England, could seek out B. Russell and tell him that here in Germany there are still honest men, those who hold him in the highest admiration. – By the way, I also have my Bell and even he has the power of great effectiveness. So we can still hope. But, I do not want to be too one-sided.

I still have reason to hope insofar that in the last lecture of the war semester (February to mid-April) I could observe the open hearts of hard-tested youth and their longing for the realm of pure ideas, and not a few letters from abroad on the 8th of April**** speak for it, that it is also a hunger for philosophy and even for "philosophy as a rigorous science," the nursing of which the blockades will not be able to inhibit.

I avoid the basilisk gaze of time as much as possible and surround my soul, as well as I can, with philosophy as armour: I concentrate passionately on my old and new problems. I work with as much success, as the inadequate nutrition allows. In between, I flee to the Black Forest, where a rural tavern with relatively robust food can be found now and again, and high-altitude air does its part in helping me to get back into good form.

When you shall once again be able to come back to visit me, you will love the Black Forest and learn how to appreciate doing philosophy on green carpets in stimulating mountain air. Even the southern German people, however much less related to your manners than North Germans, could show you their valuable sides. I would have much more to tell you, but you must have much more to tell me. That this beautiful symbol soon comes to embody in us: the love of the enemy, the confederation of souls of the "enemies," founded by the love for Eros.

I am concerned about your health, which given your sacrifice for great and good things, risks of melting away. My only consolation is that you shall not lack in the awareness of the blessings that comes from your work, and that from this work an effective of healing must issue forth.

My wife, who acted as the faciliting secretary for this letter, greets you sincerely. I have to go back to Freiburg tomorrow to take over the Dean's Office of the Faculty of Philosophy. Unfortunately, this unphilosophical activity will hinder me greatly in my own work. In the summer semester, I shall lecture 4 hours on nature and spirit, hold tutorials on basic ethical issues and maybe even smaller discussion groups.

I send you heartfelt wishes, and in friendship,
EHusserl

* Translator's note: allusion to Solomon, Proverb 25, lines 21-22: If your enemy is hungry, give him food to eat; if he is thirsty, give him water to drink. / In doing this, you will heap burning coals on his head, and the Lord will reward you.
** Translator's note: most likely the name of a hotel in Berlin or Leipzig.
*** Translator's note: A ten-volume "River Novel" (roman-fleuve), Jean-Christophe, earned Romain Rolland the Nobel Prize for Literature in 1915, and was originally published in France over 8 years (1904 – 1912).
**** Translator's note: Husserl's birthday

Hedwig Conrad-Martius (1888-1966), Theodor Conrad (1881-1969)

Hedwig Conrad-Martius: geb. 27. 2. 1888 in Berlin, gest. 15. 2. 1966 in München. – Vom WS 1907/08 bis SS 1909 Studium der Geschichte und Literatur an den Universitäten in Rostock und Freiburg, danach bis SS 1911 Studium der Philosophie, Psychologie und Kunstgeschichte in München (bei Alexander Pfänder). Ab WS 1911/12 für vier Semester Studium der Philosophie bei Husserl und Adolf Reinach in Göttingen. 1912 erhält sie für ihre Arbeit „Die erkenntnistheoretischen Grundlagen des Positivismus" den Preis der philosophischen Fakultät Göttingen. 1911/12 leitet sie die Göttinger Philosophische Gesellschaft. Juli 1912 Promotion bei Pfänder in München (mit ihrer umgearbeiteten Preisschrift). Sie heiratet wenig später Theodor Conrad, mit dem sie nach Bergzabern (Pfalz) zieht, wo das Ehepaar Conrad bis 1937 eine Obstplantage bewirtschaftet. In den Nachkriegsjahren treffen sie sich dort mit befreundeten Phänomenologen (J. Hering, A. Koyré, H. Lipps, E. Stein, A. von Sybel). Es entsteht der sogenannte „Bergzaberner Kreis". Ab 1930 Entfaltung einer regen Vortrags- und Publikationstätigkeit. Ab 1949 Lehraufträge für Naturphilosophie, seit 1955 Honorarprofessur an der Universität München. – Der Nachlass von Hedwig Conrad-Martius befindet sich in der Bayerischen Staatsbibliothek München.

Hedwig Conrad-Martius: born on February 27, 1888 in Berlin; died on February 15, 1966 in Munich. Studied history and literature at the Universities of Rostock and Freiburg from 1907 – 1909, and continued her studies in philosophy, psychology and art-history in Munich with Alexander Pfänder. Studied philosophy for four semesters with Husserl and Reinach in Göttingen. Received a prize in 1912 from the philosophy faculty at Göttingen for her work "The Epistemological-Theoretical Foundations of Positivism." Leader of the Göttingen Philosophical Society in 1911 – 1912. Awarded her PhD in 1912 in Munich with Pfänder on the basis of a reworked version of her awared-winning work in Göttingen. Married to Theodor Conrad in 1912, and directed together a fruit plantation in Bergzabern in the Pfalz until 1937. Frequent meetings

Theodor Conrad und Hedwig Martius heiraten 1912 und entschließen sich, in Bergzabern (Pfalz) eine Obstplantage zu bewirtschaften. Das Ehepaar steht weiterhin in engem Kontakt mit der Phänomenologen-Gruppe der Göttinger Jahre (Alexander Koyré, Alfred von Sybel, Jean Hering, Edith Stein). In den Nachkriegsjahren kommen die Phänomenologen öfters zu philosophischen Gesprächen in Bergzabern zusammen. Edith Stein, die sich im Haus der Conrads mehrfach und über längere Zeit aufhält, nennt es das „Phänomenologenheim" (die Aufnahme des Ehepaars stammt aus dem Winter 1918).

Theodor Conrad and Hedwig Martius were married in 1912 and decided to plant a fruit garden in Bergzabern (in the Pfalz). The couple remained in close contact with the phenomenological group from the Göttingen years (Alexander Koyré, Alfred von Sybel, Jean Hering, Edith Stein). In the years after the war, phenomenologists often came together for philosophical discussions in Bergzabern. Edith Stein, who stayed in the house of the Conrads often and for extended periods of time, called it "the home of phenomenologists" (photograph of the couple from the winter of 1918).

with phenomenologists after the Second World War (J. Hering, A. Koyré, H. Lipps, E. Stein, A. von Sybel), from which emerged the "Bergzabern Circle." In 1949, teaching position in philosophy of nature, followed by an honorary professorship at the University of Munich in 1955. – Her writings are housed in the Bavarian State Library in Munich.

Ales Bello, A./Alfieri, F./Shahid, M. (Hg.): Edith Stein, Hedwig Conrad-Martius. Fenomenologica, Metafisica, Scienze. Bari 2010. – Avé-Lallemant, E.: Hedwig Conrad-Martius (1888-1966) – Bibliographie. In: ZphF 31 (1977), 301-309. – Pfeiffer, A.: Hedwig Conrad-Martius. Eine phänomenologische Sicht auf Natur und Welt. Würzburg 2005. – Schmücker, Franz Georg: Das Geheimnis der Philosophie von Hedwig Conrad-Martius, in: Gottstein, D./Sepp, H. R. (Hg.): Polis und Kosmos. Perspektiven einer Philosophie des Politischen und einer philosophischen Kosmologie. Eberhard Avé-Lallemant zum 80. Geburtstag. Würzburg 2008, 330-337.

Theodor Conrad: geb. 22. 12. 1881 in Beurig bei Trier, gest. 23. 3. 1969 in Starnberg bei München. – Ab WS 1900/01 Studium der Mathematik, Physik, Philosophie und Psychologie zunächst in München, dann in Heidelberg, ab WS 1903/04 wieder in München (Studium der Philosophie und Psychologie u.a. bei seinem Onkel Theodor Lipps). SS 1907 Studium bei Husserl in Göttingen; dort Gründung der Göttinger Philosophischen Gesellschaft. Ende 1908 Promotion bei Lipps mit der Arbeit „Definition und Forschungsgehalt der Ästhetik". Danach Weiterführung des Studiums in Göttingen, München, Strassburg und Heidelberg zwecks Vorbereitung seiner Habilitation. 1911 In Straßburg hält Conrad Einführungskurse in die Phänomenologie in Straßburg. 1912 Heirat mit Hedwig Martius. Kurz danach entschließt sich das Ehepaar Conrad, zur Sicherstellung ihres weiteren Lebensunterhaltes eine Obstplantage in Bergzabern/Pfalz zu bewirtschaften. Theodor Conrad wird etwa Mitte 1915 zum Kriegsdienst eingezogen, aber wohl schon bald wieder entlassen. Während des Krieges wohnt er mit seiner Frau Hedwig Conrad-Martius, deren philosophische Tätigkeit er auch in den folgenden Jahren zu unterstützen versucht, abwechselnd in München und in Bergzabern. Nach Verkauf der Münchener Wohnung (etwa Mitte 1919) ziehen die Conrads ganz nach Bergzabern und leben (bis 1937) von den Erlösen der Obstplantage. – Der Nachlass von Theodor Conrad befindet sich in der Bayerischen Staatsbibliothek München.

Theodor Conrad: born on December 22, 1881 in Beurig near Trier; died on March 23, 1969 in Starnberg near Munich. Studied mathematics, physics, philosophy, and philospy in 1900 – 1901 in Munich and Heidelberg until 1904. Studied with Husserl in 1907 and founded the Göttinger Philosophische Gesellschaft. Awarded PhD in 1908 for his work "Definition and Research Content in Aesthetics" under the supervision of his uncle Theodor Lipps. Continued studies in Göttingen, München, Strasbourg, and Heidelberg for his habilitation, which he didn't complete. Gave introduction to phenomenology courses in Strasbourg, in 1911. Married Hedwig Martius in 1912. Briefly drafted into the military in 1915. Spent the remaining war-years in Munich and Bergzabern, and dedicated himself to their fruit plantation from 1919 to 1937. – Conrad's writings are housed in the Bavarian State Library in Munich.

Avé-Lallemant, E./Schuhmann, K.: Ein Zeitzeuge über die Anfänge der phänomenologischen Bewegung: Theodor Conrads Bericht aus dem Jahre 1954. In: Husserl Studies 9 (1992), 77-90. – Feldes, J.: Das Phänomenologenheim. Der Bergzaberner Kreis im Kontext der frühen phänomenologischen Bewegung. Nordhausen 2016. – Habbel, W.: Theodor Conrad als Entdecker, Lehrer und Forscher. In: Gottstein, D./Sepp, H. R. (Hg.): Polis und Kosmos. Perspektiven einer Philosophie des politischen und einer philosophischen Kosmologie. Eberhard Avé-Lallemant zum 80. Geburtstag. Würzburg 2008, 325-330.

„Sehr ernste Lage. Das deutsche Reich im Kriegszustande, 31. Juli 1914. Bekanntmachung"

"A very serious situation. The German Empire in condition of war, 31 July 1914. Declaration"

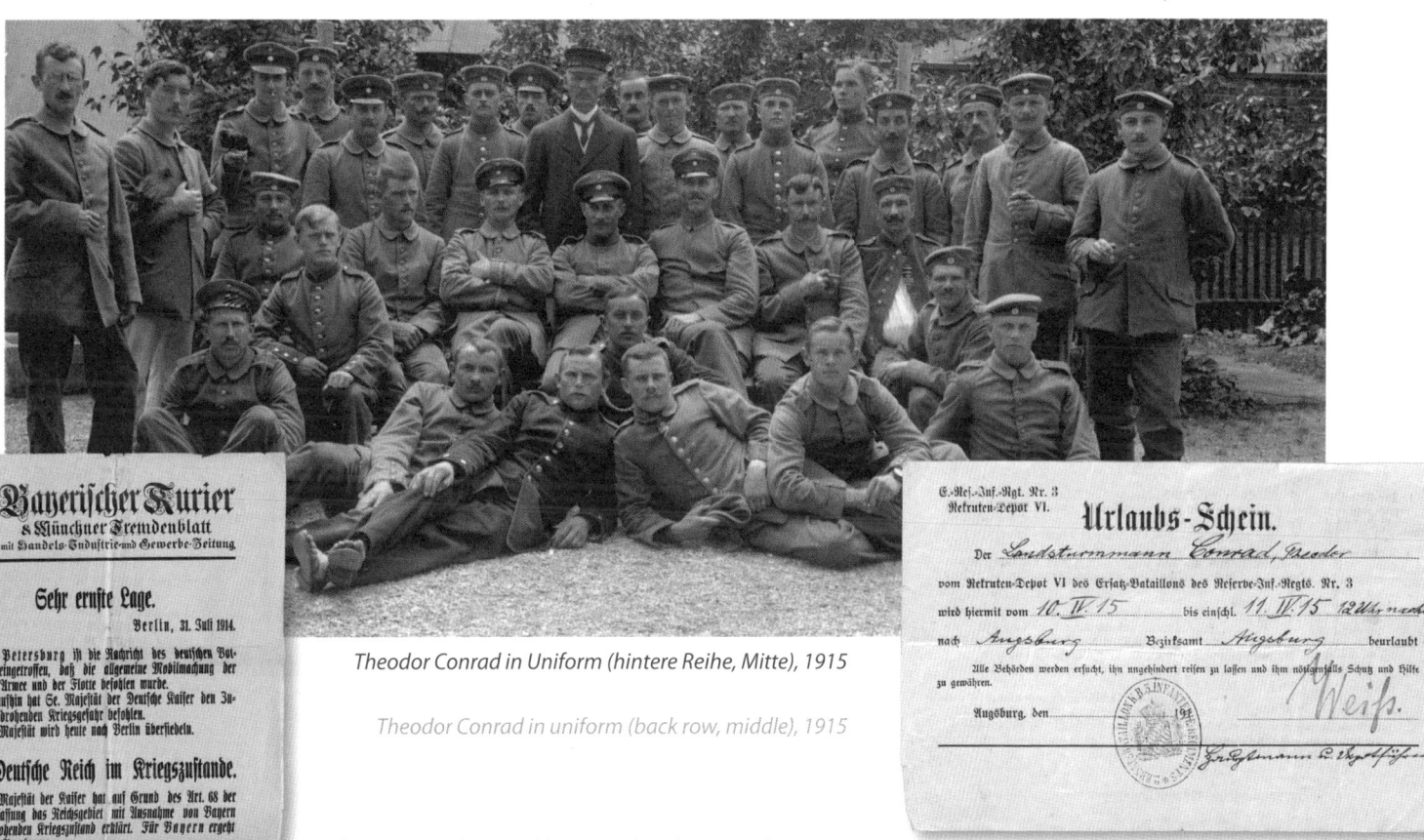

Theodor Conrad in Uniform (hintere Reihe, Mitte), 1915

Theodor Conrad in uniform (back row, middle), 1915

Dokument aus dem Nachlass von Theodor Conrad

Document from the Nachlass of Theodor Conrad

Auf den „Landsturmmann" Theodor Conrad ausgestellter „Urlaubs-Schein", gültig für den 10.-11. IV. 1915

From the "furlough-pass" for "Landsturmmann" Theodor Conrad, valid for 10 – 11 April 1915

„Allen Spendern von Liebesgaben sage ich meinen herzlichen Dank"
"I express my heartfelt gratitude for all contributions of gift parcels"

Hedwig Conrad-Martius bei der Arbeit in der Obstplantage (Aufnahme etwa Anfang der 1920er Jahre)

Hedwig Conrad-Martius working in the fruit plantation (photograph from around the beginning of the 1920s)

B e s t ä t i g u n g.

Den Empfang von zwei goldenen Eheringen sowie eines goldenen Armkettenbandes zur Unterstützung von Familienangehörigen von Kriegsteilnehmern bestätigt hiemit unter dem Ausdruck des wärmsten Dankes.

Am 7. August 1914.

Sekretariat des Oberbürgermeisters Dr. von Borscht.

Werbepostkarte der Conrad'schen Obstplantage (wohl aus der Zeit um 1920)

Advertisement post-card for the Conrads' fruit plantation.

Zu Beginn des Krieges spendet das Ehepaar Conrad ihre Eheringe und ein Armkettenband „zur Unterstützung von Familienangehörigen von Kriegsteilnehmern"

At the begining of the war, the Conrads donated their marriage ring and a bracelet "to support the families of soldiers in the war"

An Hedwig Conrad<-Martius> adressierte Dankeskarte für die an das Reserve-Infanterie-Regiment 222 geschickten Geschenke (sogenannte „Liebesgaben"), Januar 1915

A card expressing gratitude, addressed to Hedwig Conrad [-Martius] for the gifts sent to the Reserve Infantry Regiment 222 (so-called "gifts of love"), January 1915

Johannes Daubert (1877-1947)

Johannes Daubert: geb. 8. 6. 1877 in Braunschweig, gest. 11. 12. 1947 in Mainburg/Holledau. – Herbst 1896 bis Frühjahr 1898 Studium der Philosophie und Neueren Sprachen an der Universität Göttingen (u.a. bei G.E. Müller). Im Sommer 1898 Studium der Philosophie an der Universität Leipzig (u.a. bei J. Volkelt und W. Wundt). Ab WS 1898/99 Studium der Philosophie in München (u.a. bei Th. Lipps und ab 1901/02 auch bei A. Pfänder). Pfingsten 1902 erste Kontaktnahme mit Husserl; im SS 1905 Besuch von Husserls Lehrveranstaltungen in Göttingen und gemeinsamer Aufenthalt mit Husserl, Pfänder und anderen aus dem Phänomenologenkreis in Seefeld bei Innsbruck. Ab 1906 als Privatgelehrter in München. September 1914 Meldung als Kriegsfreiwilliger und Einsatz als Motorradfahrer an der Westfront. 1917 Ernennung zum Leutnant. Anfang 1919 aus dem Kriegsdienst entlassen. Danach ist Daubert als Landwirt in der Umgebung von München tätig und kommt nur periodisch zu philosophischer Arbeit. Er steht jedoch weiterhin mit Husserl, Pfänder und anderen Phänomenologen in Kontakt. Daubert hat nie etwas veröffentlicht (auch seine Dissertation nicht zum Abschluss gebracht), spielte jedoch eine wichtige Rolle bei der Bildung des Münchener Phänomenologenkreises. – Der Nachlass von Johannes Daubert befindet sich in der Bayerischen Staatsbibliothek München.

Johannes Daubert: born on June 8, 1877 in Braunschweig; died on December 11, 1947 in Mainburg/Holledau. Daubert studied philosophy and modern languages at the University of Göttingen from 1896 to 1898 (with G. E. Müller). He studied philosophy in Leipzig in 1898 with Johannes Volkelt and Wilhelm Wundt and in Munich, in 1898 – 1899, with Theodor Lipps; and in 1901-1902 with Alexander Pfänder. Makes first contact with Husserl in 1902. Together with Husserl, Pfänder, and others, Daubert frequents in 1905 the phenomenological circle in Seefeld near Innsbruck. Works as a private teacher in Munich, beginning in 1906. Volunteers for military in September 1914 and serves as a motorcycle rider on the Western Front. Promoted to Lieutenant in 1917. Ends his military service in 1919. After the war, Daubert remains in contact with Husserl, Pfänder, and other phenomenologists, and works in argiculture in the vicinity of Munich. Daubert never finished his PhD and never published any of this writings; his importance, however, for the Munich phenomenological circle was significant. – Daubert's papers are housed in the Bavarian State Library in Munich.

Fréchette, G.: Daubert et les limites de la phénoménologie: Étude sur le donné et l'évidence. In: Philosophiques, vol. 28, n° 2 (2001), 303-326. – Schuhmann, K./Smith, B.: Against Idealism: Johannes Daubert vs. Husserl's Ideas I. In: Review of Metaphysics 38 (1985), 763-793. – Schuhmann, K./Smith, B.: Questions: An Essay in Daubertian Phenomenology. In: Philosophy and Phenomenological Research 47 (1987), 353-384. – Schuhmann, K.: Daubert-Chronik. In: C. Leijenhorst/P. Steenbakkers (eds.): Karl Schuhmann: Selected Papers on Phenomenology. Dordrecht 2004, 279-354. – Smid, R. N.: An Early Interpretation of Husserl's Phenomenology: Johannes Daubert and the Logical Investigations. In: Husserl Studies 2 (1985), 267-290.

„Ich hätt auch gern mitgethan"

Göttingen 22. XI. 14.
Lieber Herr D<aubert>!
Dacht' ichs doch, daß Sie in dieser schweren Zeit nicht würden daheim bleiben wollen. Ich hätt auch gern mitgethan u. bin leider zu nichts mehr nütze; auch nicht zum Philosophieren, wozu ich eine innere Stille u. Sammlung brauche, die die jetzigen Lebensverhältnisse nicht ermöglichen. Sie mit Ihrem gestählten Körper, Ihren geübten Sinnen, Ihrem festen Willen werden draußen große Dienste leisten können. Ich wünsche Ihnen, daß Sie, an die rechte Stelle gebracht, die glücklichen Umstände finden, u. ich wünsche Ihnen dazu noch Manches Gute, was unter sothanen Verhältnissen ein alter guter Freund wünscht! Meine beiden Jungens kämpfen seit d 20. X. in Belgien, sie erstürmten mit Roulers u. Langemark, in der Nähe von L<angemark> liegen sie seitdem im Schützengraben. Ihre Comp<anie> hatte furchtbare Verluste, zuletzt wieder am 10. XI., die beiden blieben, sie selbst schreiben „wie durch ein Wunder", heil u. sind gutes Muts. Reinach ist auch in Nordfrankr<eich> freiwill<iger> Artillerist. Ich lese Logik u. halte Übungen, habe sogar Hörer. Meine Frau u. Tochter grüßen Sie herzl<ich>. – Erhalten Sie sich Ihren Freunden. Die mögen Sie nicht missen!
Ihr
EH

Feldpostkarte von Husserl an Johannes Daubert, 22. XI. 1914

Field post-card form Husserl to Johannes Daubert, 22 November 1914

Bitte schreiben Sie mir ab und zu!
H. Ritzel schickte mir vor Abgang in die Front seine Dissertation im Msc.

"I would have also gladly wanted to participate"

Göttingen 22 November 1914
Dear Mr. D[aubert]!
I thought it so, that you would not want to stay at home during this difficult time. I would have also gladly wanted to participate and am unfortunately no longer good for anything; not even for doing philosophy, for which I need to possess inner silence and composure, [but] which the present life-circumstances do not make possible. You with your armored body, your trained senses, your firm will, [you] will be able to do a great service out there. I wish that, brought to the right place, you find fortunate circumstances, and I wish you a lot of good things, what an old good friend desires under such circumstances! Both of my boys have been fighting in Belgium since the 20th of October, they stormed Roulers and Langemark; they have since been in the trenches in the vicinity of Langemark. Their com[pany] suffered terrible losses, most recently on the 10th of November, and both remain, in their own words, "by some miracle," safe and in good spirits. Reinach is also in Northern Fra[nce] as a volunteer artilleryman. I am lecturing on logic and give tutorials, and even have listeners. My wife and daughter greet you warmly. – Please take care of yourself, so that your friends will not have to miss you!
Your,
EH
Please write me now and then!
H. Ritzel sent me before leaving for the front his dissertation manuscript.

„Hurrah!"
"Hurray!"

München 30. XII. 14
Giselastr. 27
Lieber Herr Daubert!
Meine besten Glückwünsche zum neuen Jahre! Hoffentlich sind Sie bis jetzt und bleiben Sie auch weiter wohl und von Ihrer Aufgabe befriedigt. Mir selbst wird, hoffe ich, auch noch ein tätiger Anteil am Kriege zu teil werden. Wir hatten kürzlich schon eine 16 stündige Übungtour mit 3 Gefechten. Schreiben Sie bitte wieder.
Mit herzlichem Gruß
Ihr Brunswig

Munich 30 December 1914
Giselastr. 27
Dear Mr. Daubert!
My best wishes for the New Year! Hopefully you are doing well up to now and will remain well and satisfied with your task. For my part, I hope that I can still take an active part in the war. We recently had a 16-hour exercise in fighting 3 mock battles. Please write again.
With kind regards,
Your Brunswig

Feldpostkarte von Alfred Brunswig an Daubert, 30. XII. 1914. – Der Münchener Theodor Lipps-Schüler Alfred Brunswig (1877-1927), seit WS 1916/17 Professor für Philosophie in Münster, studierte im WS 1905/06 zusammen mit Johannes Daubert bei Husserl in Göttingen.

Field post-card from Alfred Brunswig to Daubert, 30 December 1914. A student of the Munich philosopher Theodor Lipps, Brunswig (1877 – 1927) studied along with Daubert in Göttingen with Husserl. He became Professor of Philosophy in Münster in 1916 – 1917.

„Sie Glückspilz haben die bessere Möglichkeit erwählen können, diese Zeit zu erleben: draußen; ich gönne es Ihnen"

München, Ismaningerstr. 102/3
Den 23. I. 1915

Lieber Herr Daubert!

Von Prof. Pfänder habe ich Ihre Adresse erfahren; erlauben Sie mir, Ihnen einige Cigarren zu schicken mit herzlichen Grüßen u. Wünschen. Den Widerspruch der Formate bitte ich daraus zu erklären, daß ich – der weise Mann tut das immer – das von der Feldpost zugelassene Gewicht ausnutzen wollte. Wenn Ihnen die kleinen Dinger zu nah an die Nase brennen, so werden Sie gewiß Soldaten genug kennen, die sie mögen. Sie sollen sich nicht geniert fühlen u. verleitet, Cigarillos zu rauchen, wenn das noch gegen Ihre festen Grundsätze verstößt.

Sie Glückspilz haben die bessere Möglichkeit erwählen können, diese Zeit zu erleben: draußen; ich gönne es Ihnen. Aber glauben Sie nicht, daß nicht auch hier das Leben neue Perspektiven auftut. Ich meine es nicht patriotisch, im Gegenteil; da könnte einem Angst vor der Zukunft werden. Sie spüren draußen nicht, wie sehr das – noch nicht überwundene, aber doch dick verschüttete – Mittelalter auflebt; der Papst bringt seine Firma in Schwung, Gott wird entdeckt als Faktotum der Weltgeschichte mit der ausdrücklichen u. einzigen Bestimmung, durch den deutschen Sieg die Überlegenheit des „Guten" über das „Böse" zu managieren (wobei es gleichgiltig, ob das Böse als „Barbarei" – siehe Rußland! – oder als Krämergeist – siehe Sombart-Scheler über England! – spezialisiert wird). Und deutlich heben sich plumpe u. feine Stiefel, Pfaffenpantoffel u. ganzalter Kommiß, um denen, die nicht dieses Glaubens sind (oder ihn wenigstens nicht „bekennend" herbeten) ihr Schicksal im „kommenden" Deutschland, im Reich der Zukunft, der Gnade u. Erwählung in praktischer, aber verständlicher Symbolik anzudeuten. Das greifbare „Deutschland der Zukunft" – siehe Rohrbach auf allen Wassern u. Kontinenten! Mit neuer Weltmission belastet, ohne die Kontinuität des Festlands mit dieser Welt – schon wie wir der Türkei im Falle eines Krieges helfen sollen, ist ziemlich zweifelhaft, ohne die innere Reife u. Stärke zum rechten Befehlen (vielleicht kommt sie später) – <…>

Es ist beengend, zu sehen wie ein ungeheurer Utilitarismus daheim die Größe in Frage stellt, die man sich so gern an den Menschen u. Ereignissen imponieren lassen möchte, wie die – nach kaiserlichem Wort ja nicht mehr citieren dürfenden – Parteien jetzt schon die Fettaugen der künftigen Siegesuppen sich sichern, indem sie für entsprechenden Quirl sorgen.

Und trotzdem: auch daheim haben sich Thore aufgethan, vielen, feinen Köpfen. „Methode" u. „Continuität" sind in ihrer Schätzung gesunken; die neue Krise hat das Erlebnis entschieden – u. für Sie zum Höherbauen.

Nun, ich schließe. Wahrscheinlich werde ich Sie auch noch draußen sehen, wenns lang genug dauert u. <als> „felddiensttauglicher Landsturm", wenn ich noch ausgebildet werden kann. Mit allen guten Wünschen

Ihr sehr ergebener
A. Fischer

Aloys Fischer (1880-1937); seit 1915 Professor in München, Begründer der modernen Pädagogik

Aloys Fischer (1880 – 1937); since 1915 Professor in Munich and founder of modern pedagogic studies

"You lucky devils have been able to choose the better way to experience this time: out there - I resent you all"

Munich, Ismaningerstr. 102/3
23 January 1915

Dear Mr. Daubert!

I learned of your address from Prof. Pfänder. Allow me to send you some cigars with warm regards and wishes. I would like to explain the confusing differences in sizes and sorts [of cigars] from the fact that I – the wise person always does this – wanted to fully use the weight approved by the field post. If the little things [i.e., cigarillos] burn you too close to your nose, then you will certainly know soldiers well enough who like them. You should not feel embarrassed and tempted to smoke cigarillos if that still violates your established principles.

Brief von Aloys Fischer an Johannes Daubert, 23. I. 1915

Letter from Aloys Fischer to Johannes Daubert, 23 January 1915

You lucky devils have been able to choose the better way to experience this time: out there - I resent you all. But, do not believe that life does not open up new perspectives. I do not mean patriotic ones, on the contrary; there could be developed an anxiety in the face of the future. They don't feel out there how much the not yet conquered, but densely buried Middle Ages comes again to be revived. The pope brings his company into full swing, God is discovered as a factotum of world history with the explicit and sole purpose of arranging the superiority of "good" over "evil" by a German victory (indifferent whether the evil becomes "barbarism" – see Russia! – or the mentality of a shop-keeper – see Sombart-Scheler on England!). And clearly, clumsy and fine boots are lifted up, parson's slippers and a very ancient army type, to those who are not of this faith (or at least not "confessing"), their destiny in "the coming" Germany, in the kingdom of the future, grace, and the like, to indicate the election in a practical but understandable symbolism. The tangible "Germany of the future" – see Rohrbach on all waters and continents! Burdened with a new world mission, without the continuity of the mainland with this world – even how we should help Turkey in the event of war, is quite doubtful, without the inner maturity and strength to the right command (maybe it will come later) – [...]

It is suffocating to see how a tremendous utilitarianism at home questions the greatness that one likes to associate with man and others. Events, as the parties – which according to the Imperial word are no longer able to quote – are already securing the fat eyes of the future soup of victory by providing the appropriate whisk.

And yet: even at home, doors have opened up, for many fine heads. "Method" and "continuity" has dropped in their estimate; the new crisis has decided the experience – and for you to build up.

Well, I finish. I'll probably see you outside, too, if it takes long enough and [as] "field service-ready Landsturm soldier", if I can still be trained. With all the best wishes,

Your very devoted
A. Fischer

„Sowie der Krieg zu Ende ist (!), sind Sie bei mir Gast u. da wollen wir philosophieren!"

Brügge 16. 3. 1905 <recte 1915>.
Lieber Freund!
Diesen Posten würde ich Ihnen wünsche<n>, hier im alten Brügge stationiert zu sein. Auf dem großen Markt u. der Hauptstraße viel militär<isches> Treiben; aber so wie man in die Seitenstraßen geht, welch friedliche, verträumte Stille! Ich bin so 2 Stunden lang umhergestreift u. habe mich fast in ein sagenhaftes Traumland verloren. Wie ich herkomme? Ich hole meinen jüngeren Sohn (Lungenschuß, 20. II., gut verheilend, Kugel operativ entfernt, fast schon in Reconvalescenz) aus Oostnieuwkerke, wo ich auch den anderen meiner Jungens treffen soll, der noch, u. hoff<entlich> weiter, wohlauf ist. Habe mich über Ihre Karte herzlich gefreut. Schreiben Sie doch nicht in so gr<oßen> Zwischenräumen. Sie fürchten die Tinte weit mehr als das Feuer. Meine „Ideen" bei Ihnen im Felde? Sie bringen es zu Stande diese Wirklichkeit „einzuklammern"? Sowie der Krieg zu Ende ist (!), sind Sie bei mir Gast u. da wollen wir philosophieren!
Herzlichste Grüße und Wünsche von
Ihrem
E Husserl

Feldpostkarte von Husserl an Johannes Daubert, 16. III. 1915

Field post-card from Husserl to Johannes Daubert, 16 March 1915

"As soon as the war is over (!), you will be my guest, and then we want to philosophize!"

Bruges 16 March 1905 [correction: 1915]
Dear friend!
I would wish this posting for you, to be stationed here in old Bruges. In the big market and on the main street, there is much military activity; but as soon as you walk into the side streets, what peaceful, dreamt silence! I was thus wandering around for about 2 hours and almost lost myself in an idyllic dreamland. How did I get here? I'm bringing my youngest son (shot through the lung, 20th of February, healing well, bullet removed surgically, almost convalescing) from Oostnieuwkerke, where I will also meet my other boy, who remains well, and hopefully will continue to be well. I was happy about your card. Do not write with such large intervals. You fear the ink far more than the gun-fire. My "Ideas" with you in the field?* You are able to "suspend" this reality? As soon as the war is over (!), you will be my guest, and then we want to philosophize!
Kindest regards and wishes from
Your,
E Husserl

* Translator's note: Ideen I, published in 1913.

„Wolfgang (der jüngere unsrer Söhne) ist am 20. Februar schwer verwundet worden"

Göttingen 21. 3. 15
Lieber Herr Daubert.
Den Tag vor der Abreise meines Mannes kam Ihre Karte, die uns außerordentlich freute. Wir waren schon in Sorge um Sie gewesen! Mein Mann konnte nicht mehr selbst antworten, beauftragte mich damit, Ihnen die letzten 7 Cigarren von seiner besten Sorte, die er sich u. andern nicht gegönnt u. für Sie aufgespart hatte, zu senden, u. ich hoffe, dieselben sind unbeschädigt in Ihren Besitz gelangt. – Wolfgang (der jüngere unsrer Söhne) ist am 20. Febr<uar> schwer verwundet worden – ein linksseitiger Lungenschuß – u. liegt seither im Feldlazareth 87 in Oostnieuwkerke. Mein Mann hat nach manchen Schwierigkeiten die Erlaubnis zur persönlichen Abholung erhalten u. ist am 14. d<ieses> nach O<ostnieuwkerke> abgereist, dort aber erst am 17. angelangt. Eben erhalte ich ein Telegramm aus Hertogenbusch, daß Wolf im Lazarethzug nach Dortmund transportiert sei u. er selbst auf dem Wege dahin. So hoffe ich morgen meinen armen guten Jungen in die Arme schließen zu können. Die Heilung ist übrigens auf bestem Wege. Die Kugel (Querschläger) wurde am 2. Tage entfernt, Fieber nach 3 Tagen weg, Blutauswurf auch schon vorbei. Es war noch viel Glück bei der Sache. Gerhart u. 2 tapfere Kameraden brachten den Verwundeten trotz argen Feuers hinter die Barrikade, wo ihn gleich Krankenträger, resp. Krankenwagen ins Lazareth brachten. 4 Stunden nach der Verwundung war er bereits da untergebracht – bei einer Lungenverletzung eine entscheidende Schnelligkeit. Da das Regiment in der abgelaufenen Woche in O<ostnieuwkerke> seine 8tägige Reservestellung hatte, so konnte mein Mann auch Gerhart wiedersehen, was wir als besonderen Glücksfall empfinden. Könnten wir nicht mehr von Ihnen hören? Sie wissen, wie lieb Sie uns sind.
Herzlichst
Ihre
Malv. Husserl
Auch viele Grüsse von Elli Husserl

"Wolfgang (the youngest of our sons) was badly wounded on the 20th of February"

Göttingen 21 March 1915
Dear Mr. Daubert.
Your card arrived the day before my husband's departure, which made us extremely happy. We had already been worried about you! My husband could not answer for himself and instructed me to give you the last 7 cigars of his best brand, which he and others are not allowed, and which he had saved to send you, and I hope they have come into your possession undamaged. Wolfgang (the youngest of our sons) was badly wounded on the 20th of February – a gunshot in the left lung – and remains since then in field-hospital 87 in Oostnieuwkerke. My husband received permission for a personal visit to fetch him after some difficulties, and left on the 14th for Oostnieuwkerke, but only arrived there on the 17th. I have just received a telegram from Hertogenbusch informing [me] that Wolf is to be transported to Dortmund on the hospital train, and he [Husserl] himself is making his way there. So, I hope to be able to embrace my poor good boy tomorrow. Incidentally, healing is well on its way. The bullet (ricochet) was removed on the 2nd day, fever after 3 days away, bleeding already stopped. It was still a matter of good luck. Gerhart and two brave comrades brought the wounded man behind a barricade despite intense gun-fire, where he was immediately brought to a clearing-station by a stretcher-bearer and an ambulance. 4 hours after the injury, he was already there – with a lung injury, that [proved to be] decisively speedy. Since the regiment received its 8-day period of rest in O[ostnieuwkerke] last week, my husband was also able to see Gerhart again, which we consider a special stroke of good luck. We'd wish to hear more from you. You know how dear you are to us.
Warmly,
Your
Malv. Husserl
Also many greetings from Elli Husserl

„Was der Krieg unmittelbar an künstlerischer und literarischer Produktion auslöst, ist wertlos"

München, Ismaningerstr. 102/3
Den 19. April 1915.

Lieber Herr Daubert!

Das war nett von Ihnen, daß Sie mich in Ihrem letzten Brief einen Blick in <die> Situation des Kriegsfreiwilligen thun ließen; geahnt, daß sie so oder ähnlich sein könnte, habe ich wohl, nicht zuletzt nach den Erfahrungen, die ich jetzt seit Monaten in der Turner-Landsturmriege mache, die in ihrer Zusammensetzung fast homogen ist (zufällig) u. überdies nur im Annex des Militärs. Sehr vieles ist nicht einmal als entferntes Mittel zum Zweck sinnvoll. Alles in Allem strengt mich namentlich das Gewehrexerzieren unglaublich an (meine Handgelenke haben sich als wenig kräftig herausgestellt); die „militärische Erziehung" lasse ich an mir abgleiten, nur die Präzision geistiger und körperlicher Bewegung verstehe ich zu schätzen, obschon ich nur gutgeleitete philosophische Diskussion gleichbegabter Köpfe in dieser Hinsicht als ebenso erfolgreich kenne.

Die „innere Lage" klärt sich täglich mehr. Sein Einfluß auf das geistige Leben ist z.Z. nicht spürbar, auch nicht zu erhoffen; was der Krieg unmittelbar an künstlerischer und literarischer Produktion auslöst, ist wertlos; das Erlebnis ist noch zu dicht vor den Augen, noch zu sehr Aufgabe, um Muße sein zu können; die Hoffnung, daß es langsam in die Quellenschichten der Produktivität durchsickert, ist aber unerschütterlich.

Die Wirkung auf das Ethos ist genau so Oberfläche, noch Nottugend, die unverstanden u. ohne jede Dauerfolge verfliegt, wenn ein Ende (oder gar ein voller Sieg) die materialen Mittel zum Gegenteil schafft. Wieweit ein vielseitig schielendes Ressentiment (anders in den Kriegsteilnehmern, anders in den Hinausgebliebenen, noch anders in den Gebrechlichen) vergiftend nachdauern kann, ist unklar. Der Fehler der Fürsorge als solcher wird in grandiosem Stil gemacht.

Innen<u>politisch</u> wird immer klarer, daß Rechte u. Mitte nichts gelernt u. nichts vergessen haben; unbeirrbar, auf das fast allgemein gewordene Gefühl der Unsicherheit des Irdischen gestützt streben sie nach einer Kulturdirektion, die auf die Dauer sicher das ankränkelt, was jetzt noch unzweifelhaft gesund ist, das Wollen, das Wollen, auch wenn der Erfolg noch nicht klar erkennbar ist, das Streben auch auf die Gefahr des gigantischen Fehlens hin. Rechte u. Mitte werden dem rein europäischen Deutschland Bismarcks treuer bleiben als er es selbst heute könnte u. als es ihre Gegnerschaft zu ihm plausibel erscheinen läßt.

Bei dieser Sachlage kommt alles auf die Sozialdemokratie an. Wenn ihr nicht die innere Wandlung – ich sage nicht: weg von den großen, auf den Staatenbund zielenden ursprünglichen Gedanken, sondern zunächst hin zur reinen täglichen praktischen Regierungsarbeit – gelingt, dann ist die Regierung, die augenblicklich aufgeschlossener ist wie je, in einer äußerst gefährdeten Lage. Lehnt die Sozialdemokratie das Wehrbudget, Kolonialetat u. derlei Dinge konsequent weiter ab, bleibt sie die einseitig <u>sozial</u>politisch arbeitende Partei oder verwandelt sie sich gar in eine reine Arbeiterpartei nach englischem Muster, dann bleibt der Regierung nichts anderes übrig, als auf Rechte u. Zentrum gestützt einen Kulturkampf mit <u>anderer</u> Front zu beginnen, und der „Militarismus", den man bisher Deutschland höchstens mit halbem Rechte vorgeworfen hat, wird seine Macht u. Größe vollenden.

So ungefähr spitzen sich die Dinge zu – spruchreif sind sie nicht, weil die Sozialdemokratie offensichtlich mit sich selbst u. ihrer Umorientierung noch nicht einig ist, u. weil die weltpolitische Stellung des Reiches noch nicht so sichtbar ist, wie sie es am Ende des Krieges – so oder so – sein muß.

Über das Kriegsbuch, seinen Zeitpunkt u. seine Art mir noch Gedanken zu machen, habe ich aufgegeben; die Situation ist unüberblickbar verwickelt u. die leitenden Diplomaten nicht mehr durchsichtig; ich schüttele mit den Ereignissen mit, u. weiß nur sicher, daß <u>zwei</u> Länder die Rechnung dieses Krieges am teuersten zahlen werden: Frankreich u. Österreich-Ungarn.

Von München kann ich Ihnen nichts erzählen, was Interesse hätte; die Aussicht auf ein Reichstabakmonopol stimmt keinen froh, der weiß, daß Monopol Einförmigkeit bedeutet, u. daß das Rauchen nicht bloß Qualitität – die kann „in Regie" genommen werden, sondern auch Qualitätswechsel erfordert, wenn es dauernd bleiben soll.

Lassen Sie sichs so gut gehen als möglich, und wenn Sie einmal wieder Zeit und Lust haben, erzählen Sie von Ihren Erlebnissen. Mit herzlichen Grüßen von meiner Frau und mir

Ihr sehr ergebener
A. Fischer

"What the war triggers directly in artistic and literary production is worthless"

Munich, Ismaningerstr. 102/3
19 April 1915.

Dear Mr. Daubert!

It was nice of you to let me have a look at the situation of a war-volunteer in your last letter. I suspected that it might be something like this, not least because of the experiences I have been having for months in the Turner-Landsturm-group [a Bavarian paramilitary sport unit], which is almost as homogeneous in composition (accidental) and, moreover, only an auxiliary military unit. Much is not even useful as a distant means to an end. All in all, rifle exercises strike me as unbelievable (my wrists proved to be less powerful). I let the "military education" slide off of me, I appreciate only the precision of mental and physical exercise, although I know only well-directed philosophical discussion of equally gifted minds in this regard as equally successful.

The "inner situation" is clearing itself more every day. Its influence on the spiritual life is for the moment not noticeable, not to be hoped for. What the war triggers directly in artistic and literary production is worthless; the experience is still too close in front of the eyes, too much of a task to be open for leisure. But, the hope that it slowly drips into the source layers of productivity is unshakeable.

The effect on the ethos is just as surperficial, still making a virtue from an emergency, the misunderstood effects and those without permanent consequence vanish, when an end (or even a full victory) creates the material means to the opposite. To what extent a versatile cross-eyed resentment (unlike in the war veterans, otherwise in those that didn't come back, still different in the crippled) can persist as poisonous remains unclear. The error of care as such is done in grandiose style.

Domestically, it is becoming increasingly clear that the Right and the Center learned nothing and have forgotten nothing. Unflinching, based on the almost universal feeling of uncertainty about the earthly, they strive for a cultural directorate, which in the long run confidently infects what is undoubtedly still healthy, willing, willing, even if success is not yet clearly recognizable, the drive also [tends] towards the danger of a titanic failure. The Right and the Center will remain more faithful to the purely European Germany of Bismarck than he could even today and as it makes their opposition to him seem plausible.

In this situation, everything depends on social democracy. If it doesn't succeed in the inner transformation – I am not saying: away from the great original ideas aimed at the confederation, but first to the pure daily practical government work – then the government, which is currently more open-minded than ever, arrives in a very precarious situation. If [this] social democracy continues to reject the defense budget, the colonial states, and such things, it will remain a one-sided socio-political working party, or it would even turn into a worker's party of the English kind, then it there will be no other option for the government than to begin on another front a cultural conflict, as supported by the Right and the Center, and "militarism," which one with only partial legitimacy accused Germany, will fulfill its power and magnitude.

This is how roughly things are coming to a head - not yet entirely ripe for a decision, since social democracy is evidently not united with itself nor with its re-orientation, and since its world-political position of the Empire is not yet in view, as it must be, however which way, at the end of the war.

Concerning the war-book, the timing and style of which is still making me think, I have given up; the situation has become complicated, without any over-view, and the leading diplomats are no longer transparent; I tremble along with events and only know for certain that the two countries that will have to pay dearly for this war are France and Austria-Hungary.

I can not tell you anything about Munich that would interest you; the prospect of an empire tobacco-monopoly makes nobody happy, one knows that monopoly means monotony, and that smoking is not just quality – it can be "directed" but also requires quality change if it is to remain permanent.

Be well as much as it is possible, and once you have time and desire again, tell me about your experiences. With warm regards from my wife and myself,

Your very devoted,
A. Fischer

Brief von Aloys Fischer an Johannes Daubert, 19. IV. 1915

Letter from Aloys Fischer to Johannes Daubert, 19 April 1915

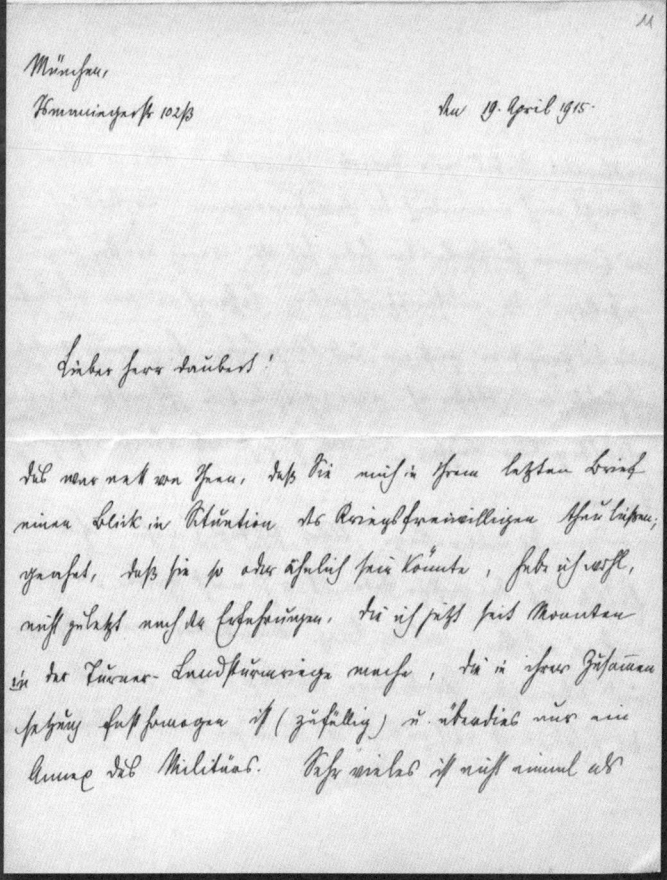

„Der Krieg – ich war von Oktober 14 bis zum Ende draußen – nahm mir die Ruhe zu philosophischer Sammlung"

Pasing 6. 4. 19.
Scharnhorststr. 24.
Hochverehrter Herr Professor!
Zu Ihrem 60. Geburtstage findet sich auch Einer ein, den Sie wohl schon für halb verschollen halten, der nun aber diesen Anlaß doch nicht vorüber gehen lassen kann, ohne Ihnen wiederum Dank zu sagen für das was Sie für ihn geworden sind und Ihnen von Herzen Glück für die Zukunft zu wünschen – Glück zur Vollendung Ihres Lebenswerkes u. Glück für Ihr u. Ihrer Familie persönliches Wohlergehen in dieser schlimmen Zeit.

Ich habe wohl oft das Bedürfnis gehabt, Ihnen zu schreiben, aber der Krieg – ich war von Oktober 14 bis zum Ende draußen – nahm mir die Ruhe zu philosophischer Sammlung. Er hat mich ziemlich ausgepumpt, und es ist beschämend, mit leeren Händen dazustehen. Ich bin auch jetzt noch nicht wieder zu geistiger Arbeit gekommen, obwohl der Druck u. die Unruhe der Zeit eine wahre Sehnsucht nach innerer Konzentration u. ernster philosophischer Arbeit erzeugen. Da ich mich verlobt habe, will ich meine äußere Existenz gern sichern. Ich suche nach einem kleinen Gute, um Landwirt zu werden. Nach einiger Zeit des Einarbeitens hoffe ich dann wieder Zeit und Ruhe zu wissenschaftlicher Tätigkeit zu finden. Ob mein Plan gelingt, hängt freilich von der Entwicklung der innerpolitischen Verhältnisse ab.

Verzeihen Sie bitte, wenn mein Brief nicht mehr pünktlich zu Ihrem Ehrentage eintreffen sollte. Die Krankheit und der Tod meiner Schwester hatten mich nach Braunschweig gerufen. Ich kam erst gestern von dort zurück.

Mit den Wünschen vieler arbeitsfroher u. -gesegneter Jahre und herzlichen Grüßen an Ihre Familie
Ihr stets getreuer
ergebener

Daubert.

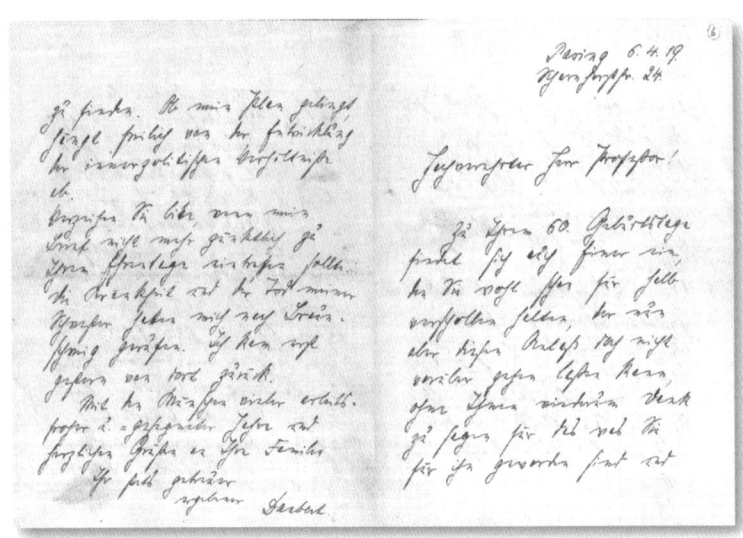
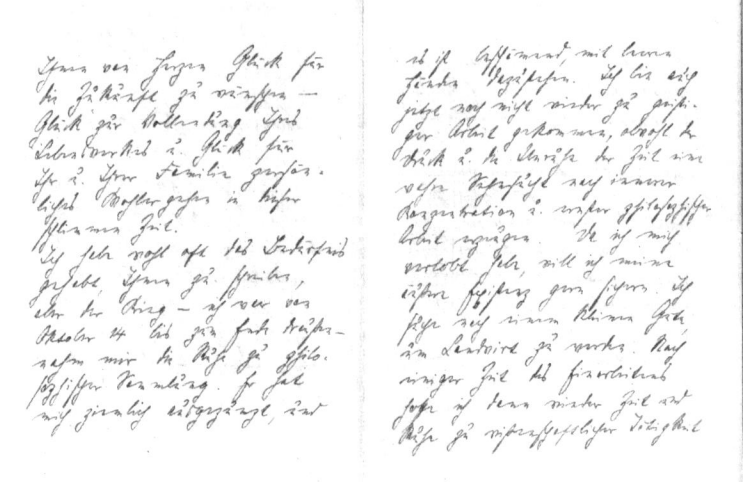

Brief von Johannes Daubert an Husserl, 6. IV. 1919

Letter from Johannes Daubert to Husserl, 6 April 1919

"The war – I was out in the field from October 14 until the end – took from me the tranquility of mind for philosophical concentration"

Pasing 6 April 1919.
Scharnhorststr. 24.

Dear Professor!
On the occasion of your 60th birthday, there is also one whom you thought half lost, but who can not let this occasion go by without thanking you for what you have become for him and to wish you from the heart good luck for the future – good luck for completion of your life's work and good luck for your family's personal well-being in this dire time.

I have often felt the need to write to you, but the war – I was out in the field from October 14 until the end – took from me the tranquility of mind for philosophical concentration. The war drained me pretty much completely, and it's shameful to stand there empty-handed. Even now I have not come back to spiritual work, even though the pressure and the restlessness of the times produces a genuine desire for inner concentration and serious philosophical work. Since I have become engaged, I want to secure my external existence. I'm looking for a little land to become a farmer. After some time of working, I hope to find time and peace to do scientific work again. Whether my plan succeeds, of course, depends on the development of internal political conditions.

Please forgive me if my letter does not arrive punctually in your honor. The illness and the death of my sister had called me to Brunswick. I came back from there only yesterday.

With wishes for many industrious and blessed years, and best wishes to your family
Your always faithful
devoted

Daubert

Auszug aus der „Kriegsstammrolle" von Johannes Daubert:
„… 8. 7. – 31. 12. 16 Stellungskampf in Flandern und Artois …"

Excerpt from the "roll call from the war" by Johannes Daubert:
"… 8.7. – 31.12.16, trench warfare in Flanders and Artois …"

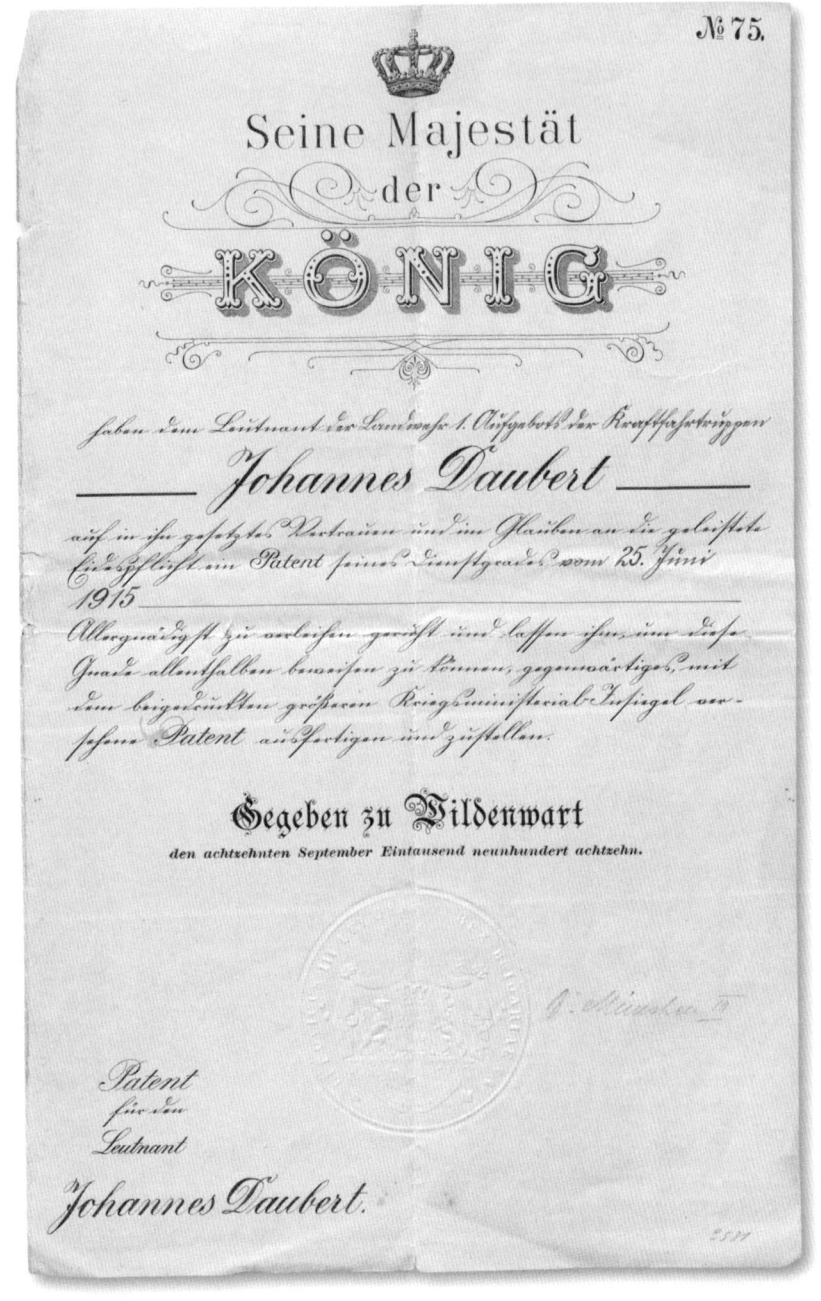

Johannes Dauberts „Patent für den Leutnant". – August Gallinger (1871-1959), Studienfreund von Daubert (später Professor für Philosophie in München), schreibt am 9. Oktober 1917 an Daubert:

„Auch, wenn Sie sich nicht in der Lage fühlen, wissenschaftlichen Meinungsaustausch <mit Husserl> zu pflegen, so fühlt er sich Ihnen doch persönlich so nahestehend, um jede Art von Lebensäußerung Ihrerseits mit Freude zu empfangen. Mit amüsiertem Kopfschütteln nahm er die Mitteilung Ihrer Offizierscharge auf. ‚Daubert ist Leutnant?' Ferner meinte er, sie hätten doch auf einer Urlaubsfahrt recht gut den Weg über Freiburg nehmen können. Er habe stets so viel Anregung von Ihnen gehabt, daß er sie wissenschaftlich u. persönlich schmerzlich vermisse. <…> Zufällig ist übrigens unser komm<andierender> General v. Gündell ein Schüler Husserls von Göttingen hier. – Die Tage vor Ypern waren saumäßig. 12 Tage nicht aus den Kleidern und so gut, wie gar keinen Schlaf. Dabei ein Feuer, wie ich es vorher nie, auch bei Aisne nicht, erlebt hatte. Mein Verbandsraum <…> zerstört, nachdem ich ihn, lediglich um einen Fliegerkampf zu betrachten, einige Sekunden vorher verlassen hatte. Das ganze Gepäck zerstört. Zu jeder Tages- u. Nachtstunde das ganze Gelände unter Feuer. In die Batterie-Stellungen gehen, war Hüpfen u. Kriechen von e<inem> Granatloch zum Andern."

Johannes Daubert's "application for Lieutenant." August Gallinger (1871 – 1959), a student friend, and later Professor for Philosophy in Munich, wrote on 9 October 1917 to Daubert:

"Even if you do not feel in the mood to exchange scientific views, he [Husserl] nonetheless feels very close to you, so that any sign of life from your side would be received with joy. With an amusing shaking of the head he received the communication of the officer promotion. 'Daubert is a Lieutenant?' He also said that you could very well make your way to Freiburg on a holiday trip. He always received from you such stimulation, that he painfully misses you, both scientifically and personally. […] By the way, our com[mander] General v. Gündell, a student of Husserl from Göttingen, happens to be here. The days before Ypres were lousy. 12 days in the same clothes and as good as no sleep. And a barrage, as I have never seen it, not even at the Aisne had I experienced such. My first-aid dressing station was destroyed […] after leaving it a few seconds before in order to look up at an airplane dogfight. All of the backpacks destroyed. Every day and night, for every hour, the entire area under fire. Going to the battery positions, hopping and creeping from one shell-hole to another."

Moritz Geiger (1880-1937)

Moritz Geiger: geb. 26. 6. 1880 in Frankfurt a.M., gest. 9. 9. 1937 in Seal Harbour (Maine, USA). – 1898 Beginn des Studiums der Rechtswissenschaften in München, im Sommer 1899 Literaturgeschichte, seit WS 1899/1900 Philosophie und Psychologie (bei Theodor Lipps). 1901-1902 Studium der Psychologie bei Wilhelm Wundt in Würzburg. 1904 Promotion bei Lipps („Bemerkungen zur Psychologie der Gefühlselemente und Gefühlsverbindungen"); danach Studium der Biologie und Psychiatrie. 1906 für ein Semester bei Husserl in Göttingen. 1907 Habilitation in München („Methodologische und experimentelle Beiträge zur Quantitätslehre"); ab Februar 1907 Privatdozent in München; Winter 1907/08 erster Aufenthalt in den USA (Arbeit bei Josiah Royce, Santayana und Hugo Münsterberg), seit 1915 a.o. Professor in München. Ende März 1915 Beginn des Militärdiensts (Ausbildung bei der Infanterie in Passau); 1916 halbjährige Tätigkeit bei der Polizei (Kurse über kriminalpsychologische Fragen), später bis Kriegsende 1918 im Kriegsministerium tätig. Herausgeber (mit Husserl, Pfänder, Reinach, Scheler; später Heidegger, Becker) des „Jahrbuchs für Philosophie und phänomenologische Forschung", 1913-1930. Ab 1919 Lehrtätigkeit an der Universität in München. November 1923 Berufung als ordentlicher Professor für Philosophie an die Universität Göttingen. 1933 Emigration in die USA; dort Lehrtätigkeit am Vassar-College in Poughkeepsie/New York und (wie schon 1926) als Gastprofessor an der Stanford University. – Der Nachlass von Moritz Geiger befindet sich in der Bayerischen Staatsbibliothek München.

Moritz Geiger: born on June 26, 1880 in Frankfurt; died on September 9, 1937 in Seal Habour (Maine, USA). Studied law in Munich in 1898; history of literature in 1899; and philosophy and psychology from 1899 – 1904 (with Theodor Lipps and Wilhelm Wundt). Obtained his PhD in 1904 with Lipps (*Remarks on the Psychology of the Elements of Feeling and the Connections of Feeling*). Studied biology and psychology. Studied one semester with Husserl in 1906 in Göttingen. Habilitation in Munich in 1907 (*Methodological and Experimental Contributions to a Theory of Quantity*). Privatdozent in Munich in 1907. First visits to the United States in 1907-1908 (with Josiah Royce, Santayana, and Hugo Münsterberg). Professor in Munich in 1915. Begins his military service in 1915 in the infantry and moves to the military police in 1916; he works in the Ministry of War until the end of the war. Along with Husserl and others, Geiger is the editor of the *Yearbook for Philosophy and Phenomenological Research* from 1913-1930. Moves from Munich to Göttingen as Professor in 1923. Geiger emigrates to the United States in 1933, where he teaches at Vassar College and as guest professor at Yale. – Moritz Geiger's papers are housed at the Bavarian State Library in Munich.

Moritz Geiger (1930)

Bellinger, G. J. und Regler-Bellinger, B.: Schwabings Ainmillerstraße und ihre bedeutendsten Anwohner: Ein repräsentatives Beispiel der Münchner Stadtgeschichte von 1888 bis heute. Norderstedt 2003, 475-482. – Berger, K.: Die Bedeutung der Kunst. In: K. Berger/W. Henckmann (Hg.): Moritz Geiger: Die Bedeutung der Kunst. Zugänge zu einer materialen Wertästhetik. München 1976, 8-16. – Fabiani, L.: Moritz Geiger (1880–1937). In: Sepp, H. R./Embree, L. (eds.): Handbook of Phenomenological Aesthetics. Dordrecht/Boston/London 2010, 127-130. – Henckmann, W.: Moritz Geigers Konzeption einer phänomenologischen Ästhetik. In: Moritz Geiger: Beiträge zur Phänomenologie des ästhetischen Genusses. Tübingen 1974, 549-590. – Métraux, A.: Edmund Husserl und Moritz Geiger. In: H. Kuhn/E. Avé-Lallemant/R. Gladiator (Hg.): Die Münchener Phänomenologie. Vorträge des Internationalen Kongresses in München 13.-18. April 1971. Den Haag 1975, 139-157. – Zeltner, H.: Moritz Geiger zum Gedächtnis. In: Zeitschrift für philosophische Forschung 14 (1960), 452-466.

„Wie man doch beim Militär nun wieder zum Schuljungen wird, zum ganz dummen Schuljungen"

Brief von Moritz Geiger an seine Schwester Fleur, 22. V. 1915

Pfingstsonntag Passau 22 Mai 1915

Liebe Fleur,

wie man doch beim Militär wieder zum Schuljungen wird, zum ganz dummen Schuljungen, der seinem Lehrer möglichst viel schlechte Streiche zu spielen sucht. Während ich dies schreibe, sollte ich eigentlich in der Kaserne sein und von 2 bis 6 Uhr Reinigungsdienst mitmachen, d.h. meist reinigen dann die andern und ich sitze dabei. Heute bin ich fortgeschlichen – wenn es herauskommt werde ich natürlich bestraft. Aber man muss eben alles tun, damit es nicht herauskommt. Man wird ganz abgebrüht darin. Als mir der Kammerunteroffizier im Anfang sagte: Es ist nicht wahr, dass der Herr Feldwebel Ihnen gesagt hat, Sie sollten sich eine neue Mütze geben lassen – war ich damals über diesen Zweifel an meinen Worten ganz empört. (Uebrigens stehe ich jetzt auf Grund klingender Beziehungen gerade mit diesem Herrn sehr gut.) Jetzt würde er mit seinem Zweifel an meinen Worten ganz recht haben. Es ist beinahe unerträglich beim Militär, wenn man alles ausführt, wie es befohlen ist. Jeder – oder fast jeder Vorgesetzte setzt voraus, dass ihn der Untergebene andauernd belügt & sich zu drücken versucht. Gerade dieser Zweifel wirkt so demoralisierend. Die meisten Unteroffiziere und Feldwebel haben garnicht erkannt, dass sie es bei uns in der grössten Zahl mit anständigen Leuten zu tun haben, die alles mögliche gut ausführen möchten. Dadurch dass sie immer Lügen voraussetzen und Drückebergerei vermuten, wird man zum „Verbrecher aus verlorener Ehre". Man wird gerade so wie es von Einem vorausgesetzt wird – es wird Einem ja doch nicht geglaubt. Aus der Pfingsterholung ist nichts geworden. Wegen Italiens ist aller Urlaub aufgehoben worden. Das ist eine selbstverständliche Notwendigkeit, die anerkannt werden muss. Dass mein Freund K. seine Leute versammelte und nur sagte: „Der Pfingsturlaub ist gestrichen worden, Ihr wisst ja schon deshalb – wegtreten" – ist weniger notwendig gewesen.

Ich bedauere, dass ich die ganze Entwicklung des Bruchs mit Italien kaum verfolgen konnte. Ich lese die kurzen angeschlagenen Telegramme der Passauer Zeitungen und lasse mir ausserdem die Münchner Neuesten schicken. Die Post erreicht mich aber ganz unregelmässig. Die Zeitungen sind meist zwei Tage alt, dann habe ich womöglich 2 Tage lang weder Zeit noch Lust zu lesen, höchstens die Telegramme und indessen sind die Zeitungen so alt geworden, dass sie kaum mehr Interesse haben.

Das Ereignis der Woche für mich war der Brief von Oberst P., den ich Dir schickte. Ich hatte ihm vor bald vier Wochen geschrieben, dass ich nicht felddienstfähig sei und ihn um Rat gebeten. Ich hatte die Hoffnung schon aufgegeben Antwort von ihm zu erhalten und mich damit abgefunden. Um so angenehmer war ich überrascht einen SOLCHEN Brief von ihm zu bekommen, der vielleicht der freundschaftlichste Brief ist, den ich je von einem älteren Mann erhalten habe.

Ich erzählte, wie ich Euch schon schrieb Leutnant D. davon, dass Oberst P. sich für mich Mühe geben wolle und dass er auch schon bei dem betreffenden Referenten im Kriegsministerium gewesen sei. Er sagte, dass das Regiment noch nicht über mich verfügt habe, dass es aber gut sei zu warten, bis nach meiner Versetzung nach München, die wahrscheinlich am 21. erfolgen würde. Sie ist nicht am 21. erfolgt aber es sind Anzeichen dafür vorhanden, dass sie am 26. verfügt wird. Ich schrieb den Umschwung Oberst P., der mir wieder einen sehr netten Brief umgehend schrieb und es billigte, dass ich bis nach meiner Versetzung warte und mir gleich eine Zeit angab, an der ich ihn aufsuchen soll. Ich hatte ihm angedeutet, dass ich gern in die Presseabteilung des Kriegsministeriums käme. Aber nach seinem Brief halte ich es für denkbar, dass er mich in der Feldzeugmeisterei – seinem eignen Arbeitsbereich unterbringt. Das wäre mir natürlich sehr angenehm. Leutnant D. erkundigte sich wieder sehr angelegentlich nach meiner Gesundheit; er fand, dass ich jetzt sehr gut aussehe und vielleicht körperlich eine Stärkung meiner Gesundheit vom Militär haben werde. Ich sagte ihm, dass ich es gesundheitlich nicht b<e>reue diese Militärzeit mitgemacht zu haben, was auch den Tatsachen entspricht. Wenn ich jetzt 14 Tage Nachkur mit vollkommener Ruhe haben könnte wäre ich sicher sehr erfrischt, NACHDEM ich es die 4 Wochen ausgehalten habe. Und noch etwas, sagte Leutnant D., was auch zum Kapitel der militärischen Unordnung gehört – eigentlich dem Ganzen die Krone aufsetzt: „Ihre Ausbildung war ja in der Tat eine sehr anstrengende. Sie sind ja nur aus Versehen in ein aktives Regiment gekommen" Es sollten nemlich die Leute über 30 Jahre in Landwehrregimenter kommen, die eine viel weniger anstrengende Ausbildung geniessen. Da die Ei<n>berufung Sache der Civilbehörden, der Bezirksämter ist, so hat diese nicht militärische Behörde Unordnung gemacht. Bei den Besichtigungen stellte es sich heraus und nun sucht man die Sache so gut wie möglich in Ordnung zu bringen. Wäre ich ein halbes Jahr älter, so wäre ich noch nicht einberufen – wäre ich in Preussen so wäre dies wohl offenbare bayerische Misverständnis spurlos an mir vorbeigegangen. Viele sind ausserdem zu Landwehrregimentern gekommen, die zufällig bei der Einteilung dorthin kamen. Mich hat das Pech getroffen. Aber ich habe es noch gut gegenüber dem armen F. Er macht unter Aufbietung seiner letzten Kräfte den regelmässigen Dienst mit. Seine Schmerzen werden immer stärker. Er wandte sich heute an Leutnant D., der erklärte nichts für ihn tun zu können. Der Arzt habe gesagt, seine Nierenschmerzen seien „nervöser" Natur (lies: eingebildet) – er müsse eben aushalten. Ich glaube er wird bald zusammenbrechen.

Ich hoffe es wird Dein Herz nicht weiter betrüben, dass ich mich von der Liste derjenigen, die den Reserveleutnant erstreben, habe streichen lassen. Die etwa 40 Leute mit Einjährigenberechtigung, die noch unter uns sind wurden gefragt, ob sie den Reserveleutnant erstreben. Ein gutes Drittel hatte keine Lust dazu. Ich gab natürlich an, dass ich mich körperlich nicht den Anstrengungen gewachsen fühle, was auch anerkannt wurde.

Vom Dienst habe ich gar nichts besonderes zu melden. Wir haben jetzt öfters Gefechtsübungen, die recht interessant sind – meist aber exerzieren wir, was masslos langweilig ist. Es lässt sich garnicht beschreiben, was für ein Gefühl es ist, wenn man entdeckt, dass es erst 7 Uhr ist – man schon 1 ½ Stunden Dienst hinter sich hat und noch weitere 4 Stunden bevorstehen.

Bald ist man beim Gefecht in Verteidigungsstellung. Dann liegt man stundenlang auf dem Bauch und ruht aus. Und dann kommen wieder Anstrengungen, die schwer ertragbar sind.

Vielleicht ist dies der letzte Sonntagsbrief aus Passau – vielleicht dauert es noch Wochen bis ich fortkomme. Beim Militär kann man nie wissen, was in der nächsten halben Stunde sein wird.

Herzlichst!

M.

"How one can still become in the military a schoolboy again, to become a very dumb schoolboy"

Letter from Moritz Geiger to his sister Fleur, 22 May 1915

Whitsunday Passau 22 May 1915

Dear Fleur,

How one can still become in the military a schoolboy again, to become a very dumb schoolboy, who tries to play on his teacher as many bad pranks as possible. As I write this, I should actually be in the barracks and be on cleaning routine from 2 to 6 o'clock, which means, that mostly the others clean while I am just sitting around. Today, I slipped away – if this comes out, I'll be reprimanded, of course. But, one has to do just about everything such that this doesn't come out. One becomes completely calloused and hard-nosed. When the non-commissioned officer for the quarters first said to me, "it is not true that Sergeant-Major has told you to get yourself a new cap" – I was at that time quite outraged in [his] doubting of my words. (Incidentally, I am now on very good terms with this gentleman, like two peas in a pod.) He would now be quite right with his doubt of my words. It is almost insufferable in the military to do everything as it is commanded. Every, or just about every supervisor, assumes that the subordinate is constantly lying to him and trying to evade his duties.

It is precisely this doubt that is so demoralizing. Most non-commissioned officers and sergeants have not realized that they are dealing with decent people who want to do everything well. The fact that they always assume lies and suspect the shirking of responsibilitys means that one becomes a "criminal from lost honor." One becomes exactly what one is presumed to be. Nothing has come from talk of Pentecost holidays. Because of Italy, all furloughs have been canceled. That this is a natural necessity must be recognized. That my friend K. gathered together his people and only said: "The Whitsun leave has been canceled, you know that already, therefore step away" – this was less than necessary.

I regret that I could hardly follow the whole development of the break with Italy. I read the short telegrams, pinned on a board, from the Passau newspapers and had the latest Munich news sent to me. The post reaches me quite irregularly. The newspapers are usually two days old, and then I mostly have neither time nor desire to read for 2 days, at the most [I read] the telegrams and meanwhile the newspapers have become so old that they are hardly interesting anymore.

The event of the week for me was the letter from Colonel P. that I sent you. I had written to him nearly four weeks ago that I was not field serviceable and asked for advice. I had already given up the hope to get an answer from him and resigned myself to it. All the more pleasant was I, to be surprised in receiving such a letter from him, which is perhaps the most friendly letter I have ever received from an older person.

I was telling you, as I wrote to you about Lieutenant D., that Colonel P. was trying to make an effort on my behalf, and that he had already been to the War Ministry with regard to the respective head of division. He said that the regiment did not yet have me at its disposal, but that it was good to wait until after my transfer to Munich, which would probably take place on the 21st. It did not happen on the 21st, but there are signs that it will be on the 26th. I wrote about this turn around in the situation to Colonel P., who immediately once again wrote for me a very nice letter and agreed that I wait until my transfer and immediately gave me a time when I should visit him. I had indicated to him that I would like to come to the Press Department of the War Department. But according to his letter, I think it possible that he will place me in a quartermaster's unit – his own work area. Of course, that would be very pleasant for me. Lieutenant D. inquired very carefully about my health; he thought that I now look very good and maybe physically will strengthen my health in the military. I told him that I did not regret my health to have participated in this military service, which is true. If I could have 14 days after the treatment with complete peace, I would be very refreshed, after having endured 4 weeks. And something else, said Lieutenant D., which also belongs to the chapter of military disorder – actually crowning the whole thing: "Your education was indeed a very strenuous one. After all, you came into an active regiment by mistake." People over 30 years of age should namely come to Landwehr regiments, who enjoy a much less strenuous education. Since the appointment is a matter for the civil authorities, the district offices, this non-military authority has made disorder. During the inspection, the issue became apparent, and now they are trying to get the thing as well as possible in order. If I were half a year older, I would not have been called-up – if I were in Prussia, this apparently Bavarian mis-understanding would have passed me by without a trace. Many have been, in any case, also called to Landwehr regiments, and came to these regiments accidently during the distribution. I was hit by a stroke of bad luck. But, my lot is still better than poor F. He did his regular duty with the last mobilization of his final strength. His suffering grew even more. He turned today to Lieutenant D., who told him that he could do nothing. The doctor has said, that his kidney pains are due to his "nervous" nature (read: imagined)—he'll have to tough-it out. I think that he'll soon fall apart.

I hope that your heart shall not be further darkened, that I can have my name removed from the list of those who are striving to become Lieutenants in the reserve. Around 40 people with an annual permission among us were asked if they aspired to attain the rank of a reserve Lieutenant. A good one-third didn't have any desire to do so. Naturally, I let it be known that I did not feel physically fit enough for such demanding efforts, which was duly acknowledged.

I have nothing special to report about [my] service. We now often have combat training, which is really interesting; but, mostly, we exercise, which is incredibly boring. It's something that can't at all be easily described, what a feeling it is, to discover that it is only 7 o'clock – one has already done 1 and half hours of service with still 4 hours to go.

Titelblatt eines unveröffentlichten Vortragsmanuskriptes von Moritz Geiger: „Erziehung nach dem Krieg", vom Februar 1918

Title page of an unpublished lecture manuscript of Moritz Geiger „Education after the War", February 1918

Soon is one in a defensive position [for] combat. One is then for hours laying on one's stomach and rests. And then comes more efforts, which are endured with great difficulty.

This is maybe the final Sunday letter from Passau – maybe it will be another [few] weeks before I get a chance to write again. One never knows in the military what the next half-an-hour might bring.

M.

Erich von Gündell (1854-1924)

Erich von Gündell: geb. 13. 4. 1854 in Goslar, gest. 23. 12. 1924 in Göttingen. – 1873 Beginn der militärischen Laufbahn als Fahnenjunker im Infanterie-Regiment 94. Nach verschiedenen Beförderungen und Tätigkeiten innerhalb des Miltärs wird Gündell im Juli 1900 für seine Verdienste als Chef des Generalstabs des Ostasiatischen Expeditionskorps in den Adelsstand erhoben. 1913 Direktor der Kriegsakademie und gleichzeitig Einreichung seines Abschiedsgesuches. Bei Kriegsbeginn als Führer des V. Reservekorps wiederverwendet. 1916 kommandierender General der Armeeeinheit, zu der auch Husserls Sohn Wolfgang gehört. August 1916 Auszeichnung mit dem Pour le Mérite in Anerkennung seiner Leistungen während der verlustreichen Kämpfe vor Verdun. 1917 Oberbefehlshaber der Heeresabteilung B im Elsass und 1918 Vorsitzender der Waffenstillstandskommission der Oberen Heeresleitung. Im SS 1914 Studium bei Husserl in Göttingen; persönlicher Kontakt zur Familie Husserl. 1922 Promotion zum Dr. phil. in Göttingen bei Georg Misch („Neuzeitliche Klassifikationen der philosophischen Systeme").

Erich von Gündell (1917)

Erich von Gündell: born on April 13, 1854 in Goslar; died on December 23, 1924 in Göttingen. Entered military service in 1873 as Officer Cadet in the 94th Infantry Regiment. After various postings and promotions, Gündell is ennobled for his service as Chief of the General Staff for the East Asian Expedition Corps. He serves as Director of the War Academy in 1913 and requests his retirement. Returns to service with the outbreak of the war as commander of the 5th Reserve Corps. In 1916, Commanding General of the Army Corps in which Husserl's son Wolfgang served. Receives the medal Pour le Mérite in 1916 for his efforts during the battle of Verdun. Commander of the Army Group B in Alsace in 1917. Chair of the Armistice Commission of the Army in 1918. Studied philosophy with Husserl in 1914 in Göttingen; maintains personal contact with Husserl's family. Obtained his PhD in 1922 with Georg Misch in Göttingen (*Modern Classifications of Philosophical Systems*).

v. Gündel, Erich: „Neuzeitliche Klassifikationen der philosophischen Systeme". Dissertationsauszug, in: Jahrbuch der Philosophischen Fakultät der Georg August-Universität zu Göttingen. Göttingen 1922 (zweite Hälfte), 44-48. – Obkircher, W. (Hg.): General Erich von Gündell. Aus seinen Tagebüchern: Deutsche Expedition nach China 1900-1901, 2. Haager Friedenskonferenz 1907, Weltkrieg 1914-1918 und Zwischenzeiten. Bearb. u. hg. von W. Obkircher. Hamburg 1939.

„Eine bedeutende Intelligenz, eine überlegene Persönlichkeit, eine Herrschernatur, wie man sofort merkt"

4. X. 14
Lieber Heinrich.

Ich habe Deinen Einschreibebrief richtig erhalten – leider zufällig das kleine Couvert mitaufgerissen, aber beim Lesen der ersten Zeile Deines Briefes sogleich in ein neues Couvert verschlossen, ohne das Verzeichnis entfaltet zu haben. Es ist gut aufgehoben. Vor 1 Woche war ich mit Malv<ine> in Arnstadt; die Jungens haben einen alle Kräfte ausschöpfenden Dienst u. sehen doch gut aus. Sie sind sehr gut einquartiert, obschon bei einfachen Fabriksarbeitern, u. haben gute Verpflegung. Heute ist Malv<ine> u. Elli zum letzten Abschiede u. zu ihrer letzten Ausrüstung mit Wäsche etc. dort. Sie ziehen in der 2. Hälfte d<er> Woche ins Feld, vermutlich nach Westen, obschon Göttinger auch im Osten stehen sollen. Man muß sich ordentlich zusammennehmen, um diese schwere Zeit zu ertragen. Der September war viel schwerer als der August. Die Sorgen wachsen u. man sieht auch so viele Trauer, u. täglich mehr. Die Siegeszuversicht ist darum doch unerschütterlich, aber die Opfer werden größer sein, als erhofft bzw. befürchtet.

Heute erhielt ich einen 4 Seiten langen Brief von meinem „Schüler", Exc<ellenz> v. Gündell, der im letzten Jahr sich hatte pension<i>er<e>n lassen u. jetzt als kommandierender General eines Armeekorps in Frankreich steht. Er war im letzten Jahr mein eifriger u. dankbarer Hörer u. wir verkehrten auch in der Familie. Eine bedeutende Intelligenz, eine überlegene Persönlichkeit, eine Herrschernatur, wie man sofort merkt. Auf solche Männer muß man Vertrauen haben u. es glauben, daß sie durchsetzen, was sie sich als Ziel gesetzt. Welch ungeheure Leistungen, welch todesmutigen Opfer, Tag für Tag. Ich bemühe mich zu arbeiten u. mich jetzt möglichst abzuschließen. Mein Befinden läßt noch viel zu wünschen übrig, ich bringe doch was zu Stande. Ich freute mich zu hören, daß Leo im Felde gesund geblieben ist u. wünsche weiter herzlich das Beste. Hier wird organisatorisch Gewaltiges

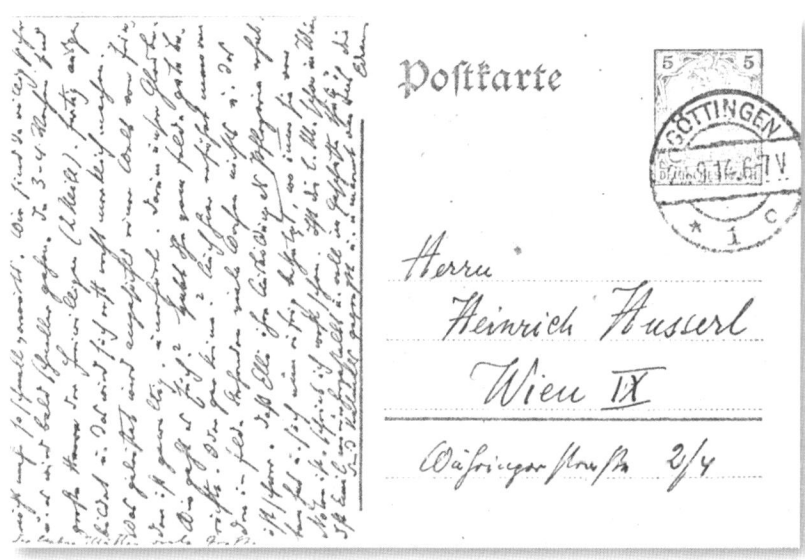

Postkarte von Husserl an seinen Bruder Heinrich, 4. X. 1914

Postcard from Husserl to his brother Heinrich, 4 October 1914

gethan, jeder miteingespannt, überall Freudigkeit im Opfern, Wirken für d<as> Ganze.

Wie geht es Dir l<iebe> Clotilde? Haltet Euch gut u. gesund. Euer treuer

Edmund.

Wie geht es der l<ieben> Mutter? Viele Grüße.

Erich von Gündell

"An heightened intelligence, a superior personality, a commanding nature, as one notices immediately"

4 October 1914
Dear Heinrich,

I have received your registered letter in good order – unfortunately, by chance, I tore open the little envelope, but at the time of reading the first line of your letter I immediately enclosed it in a new envelope, without having unfolded the list. It is in good hands. A week ago I was with Malv[ine] in Arnstadt; the boys are busy with an exhausting military training which pushes their strength to the limit and are looking very good. They are very well quartered, although with simple factory workers, and have good accommodations. Today, Malv[ine] and Elli [were there] for a final farewell with laundry etc. They'll move into the field in the second half of the week, presumably to the West, although Göttingen [troops] might also be [sent] in the East. One must put oneself together in a proper manner in order to endure this difficult time. September was much more difficult than August. The worries grow and one sees so much grief, and everyday, even more. Confidence in victory remains, nonetheless, unshakable, but the victims will be greater than expected or feared. Today, I received a 4-page letter from my "student," his Excellency v. Gündell, who had gone into retirement last year and who now serves as commanding general of an army corps in France. He was last year my eager and thankful auditor, and we were also regular visitors to his family. An heightened intelligence, a superior personality, a commanding nature, as one notices immediately. You have to have confidence in such men and believe that they see-through what they set themselves as their goal. What tremendous accomplishments, what courageous sacrifices, day in and day out. I strive to work and separate myself as much as possible from the world. My health leaves much to be desired, but I can do something. I was glad to hear that Leo stayed healthy in the field, and wish the best. Organizationally powerful things are done here, everyone involved, everywhere joy in sacrifice, work for the whole. How are you, Clotilde? Keep well and be healthy.
Your faithful,
Edmund

How are things with dear mother? Many regards.

Der 24 Meter hohe bei Damvillers am Ostufer der Maas errichtete sogenannte „Gündell-Turm", der einen Überblick über das Schlachtfeld geben sollte

A 24 meter high, so-called "Gündell-Tower" was built with an overview of the battlefield near Damvillers on the Eastern shore of the Maas River.

Liebe Eltern!

18. 8. <1915>

… Eben ging Exzellenz von Gündell die Stellung durch. Als er an meinem Unterstand vorbeikam, trat ich raus in feingewichsten Stiefeln und meldete mich zur Stelle. Er reichte mir die Hand und erkundigte sich in sehr freundlicher Weise nach meinem Befinden und fragte natürlich auch nach Papa, den er grüßen lässt und dem er nächstens selbst schreiben will. Dann ging er weiter. Exzellenz wurde von seinem Adjutanten, dem Major von Langsdorff und Hauptmann Henkel begleitet. Bitte schickt etwas gegen Flöhe, Läuse und Wanzen. …

Frau Besser schrieb mir, dass ihr Sohn sehr schwer verwundet sei und noch lebt (!).

W.

Dear parents!

18 August [1915]

… His Excellency von Gündell just inspected the positions. As he passed my dugout, I stepped out with my finely polished boots and reported at attention. He shook my hand and asked me in a very friendly way about my health and, of course, also asked about Papa, to whom he sends greetings and which he wants to write himself soon. Then he went on. His Excellency was accompanied by his adjutant, Major von Langsdorff, and Captain Henkel. Please send something against fleas, lice, and bedbugs. …

Mrs. Besser wrote to me that her son was very badly wounded and still alive (!).

W.

Aus den Kriegsbriefen der Husserl-Söhne: Wolfgang Husserl an seine Eltern, 18. VIII. 1915

From the war-letters of Husserl's sons: Wolfgang Husserl to his parents, 18 August 1915

Martin Heidegger (1889-1976)

Martin Heidegger: geb. 26. 9. 1889 in Meßkirch, gest. 26. 5. 1976 in Freiburg i. Br. – Von 1909 bis 1911 Studium der katholischen Theologie, anschließend bis 1913 Studium der Philosophie, Geistes- und Naturwissenschaften in Freiburg. 1913 Promotion bei Arthur Schneider („Die Lehre vom Urteil im Psychologismus"). Bei Ausbruch des Krieges Meldung als Kriegsfreiwilliger zum Militärdienst beim Ersatzbataillon 113. Mitte Oktober 1914 Entlassung aus gesundheitlichen Gründen (Herzbeschwerden). Ab Mitte August 1915 erneute Einberufung und Ausbildung im Ersatzbataillon 142. Ab November 1915 wegen seiner Herzerkrankung Versetzung zur militärischen Postüberwachungsstelle in Freiburg. WS 1915/16 Beginn der Lehrtätigkeit an der Universität Freiburg. 1916 Habilitation („Die Kategorien- und Bedeutungslehre des Duns Scotus") bei Heinrich Finke (Zweitgutachter ist Heinrich Rickert). März 1916 Ausbildung als Landsturmmann beim Ersatzbataillon 113 (4. Kompanie). Im Juli 1916 Ausbildung in Berlin zum Meteorologen. Ende August bis Anfang November 1918 Einsatz bei der Frontwetterwarte 414 (3. Armee) in Nouillon-Pont (etwa 40 Kilometer von Verdun entfernt). Dort beschäftigt er sich mit der mittelalterlichen Mystik und wohl auch mit den religionsphänomenologischen Aufzeichnungen von Adof Reinach, der 1917 gefallen war. November 1918 Beförderung zum Gefreiten. Von 1919 bis 1922 Assistent bei Husserl in Freiburg. 1923 bis 1928 Extraordinarius in Marburg, 1928 Nachfolger auf den Lehrstuhl von Husserl in Freiburg. Ab 1927 Mitherausgeber des von Husserl zu diesem Zeitpunkt gemeinsam mit Geiger, Pfänder und Scheler herausgegebenen "Jahrbuchs für Philosophie und phänomenologische Forschung" (1913-1930). 1933 lehnt Heidegger einen Ruf nach Berlin ab. 1933/1934 Rektor der Freiburger Universität. Von 1933 bis 1945 Mitglied der NSDAP. Nach dem Krieg bis zu seiner Emiritierung 1951 Lehrverbot. – Der Nachlass von Martin Heidegger befindet sich im Deutschen Literaturarchiv Marbach.

Martin Heidegger: born September 26, 1889 in Meßkirch, died May 26, 1976 in Freiburg. Studied from 1909 to 1911 Catholic Theology, then philosophy, humanities, and natural sciences until 1913 in Freiburg. Obtained his PhD under the supervision of Arthur Schneider ("The Doctrine of Judgment in Psychologism"). At the outbreak of the war, Heidegger reported as a volunteer for military service with the 113th Replacement Battalion; released from duty October 1914 due to a heart condition. From mid-August 1915, returned to military service with the 142nd Replacement Battalion. Re-assignment to the Postal Censorship Bureau in Freiburg in November 1915 due to heart disease. Began teaching at the University of Freiburg in 1915 – 1916. Habilitation ("The Theory of Categories and Meaning in Duns Scotus") in 1916 under the supervision of Heinrich Finke (second supervisor: Heinrich Rickert). March 1916, training as Landsturmmann in the 113th Replacement Battalion (4th Company). In July 1916, training in Berlin with a military unit of meteorologists. End of August to beginning of November 1918, service at the front with the 414th Weather Station (3rd Army) in Nouillon-Pont (about 40 kilometers from Verdun). He reads medieval mysticism and most likely was able to read the religious-phenomenological notes of Adolf Reinach, who died at the front in 1917. November 1918, promotion to corporal. From 1919 to 1922, Husserl's assistant in Freiburg. 1923-1928, extraordinarius in Marburg; 1928, successor to Husserl's Chair in Freiburg. From 1927, co-editor of the "Yearbook for Philosophy and Phenomenological Research" (1913-1930) published by Husserl together with Geiger, Pfänder, and Scheler. In 1933 Heidegger rejects a call to Berlin. 1933/1934, Rector of the University of Freiburg. From 1933 to 1945, member of the NSDAP. From 1945 to 1951, prohibited from teaching. – Martin Heidegger's papers are housed in the German Literature Archive Marbach.

Denker, A.: Heideggers Lebens- und Denkweg 1909-1919. In: Denker, A./Gander, H.-H./Zaborowski, H. (Hg.): Heidegger und die Anfänge seines Denkens. Heidegger-Jahrbuch I. Freiburg 2004, 97-122. – Holger Zaborowski: „Eine Frage von Irre und Schuld?" Martin Heidegger und der Nationalsozialismus. Frankfurt am Main 2010. – Fischer, M.: Religiöse Erfahrung in der Phänomenologie des frühen Heidegger. Göttingen 2013. – Kisiel, Th.: The Genesis of Heidegger's Being and Time. Berkeley/Los Angeles/London 1993. – Ott, H.: Martin Heidegger. Unterwegs zu seiner Biographie. Frankfurt a. M./New York 1988. – Safranski, R.: Ein Meister aus Deutschland. Heidegger und seine Zeit. München 1994. – Thomä, D. (Hg.): Heidegger-Handbuch. Leben – Werk – Wirkung. Stuttgart/Weimar 2003.

„Gleich im August meldete ich mich nochmals zum Militärdienst, obwohl ich frei war"

Hochgeehrtester Herr Geheimrat!

Beiliegend gestatte ich mir Ihnen, hochgeehrtester Herr Geheimrat, meine Doktorarbeit zu überreichen. Kurz vor Kriegsausbruch bekam ich die Exemplare; nachher hielt ich es für unpassend und unbedeutend, Doktorarbeiten zu versenden, wie man denn überhaupt mit aller Wissenschaft plötzlich auf die Seite gestellt war. Gleich im August meldete ich mich nochmals zum Militärdienst, obwohl ich frei war. Vor einer Woche mußte ich aber wieder entlassen werden, da mein Herzklappenfehler zu stark sich bemerkbar machte und ich den Märschen nicht mehr gewachsen war.

Zwar waren das gewiß noch keine eigentlichen Strapazen, aber ich bin doch stark mitgenommen, daß ich mich erholen muß. Aus dem Hegelstudium ist's mit einem Schlag zu Ende gewesen.

Sie müssen mich also, hochgeehrtester Herr Geheimrat, gütigst entschuldigen, daß ich mit meinem Referat nicht zur Stelle bin. Zwar hoffe ich, nach einiger Zeit wieder arbeiten zu können, aber ob dann noch mein Referat in dem

Martin Heidegger als Soldat (vorderste Reihe rechts)

Martin Heidegger as a soldier (front row, right)

Zusammenhang paßt, möchte ich nicht entscheiden. Und am Ende fallen noch mehr Referate aus, so daß Herr Geheimrat einen neuen Arbeitsplan für das Kriegsseminar aufstellen müßte.

So sehr man sich bei Kriegsausbruch mit aller Philosophie unnütz vorkam, so tiefbedeutsam wird sie in der Zukunft werden müssen, eine Kulturphilosophie und das System der Werte zuallererst. Ich denke mir deshalb, daß das Kriegsseminar, mag es sich inhaltlich gestalten wie immer, an Bedeutsamkeit hinter den früheren nicht zurückstehen wird, und es liegt mir daran, möglichst bald wieder nach Freiburg kommen zu können.

So wäre ich Ihnen, hochgeehrtester Herr Geheimrat, zu großem Dank verpflichtet, wenn Sie die Güte haben wollten, bezüglich des Seminars mir kurz Nachricht zu geben.

Ende Juli konnte ich noch drei Kapitel meiner Arbeit über die Kategorien- und Bedeutungslehre des Duns Scotus ausarbeiten, die ich Ihnen demnächst wohl vorlegen kann.
In aufrichtigster Verehrung und Dankbarkeit,
Ihr ergebenster
Martin Heidegger

Martin Heidegger an Heinrich Rickert, 3. XI. 1914 (Martin Heidegger/ Heinrich Rickert. Briefe 1912 bis 1933 und andere Dokumente. Aus den Nachlässen herausgegeben von Alfred Denker. Frankfurt am Main 2002, S. 20 f.)

Martin Heidegger to Heinrich Rickert, 3 November 1914

"Immediately in August, I reported once again for military service, even though I was free"

Most esteemed Mr. Privy Councilor!

Enclosed, I allow myself, most esteemed Mr. Privy Councilor, to submit my doctoral thesis. Shortly before the outbreak of the war, I received the copies. I subsequently thought it inappropriate and meaningless to send doctoral theses, when everything with science was suddenly put to the side. Immediately in August, I reported once again for military service, even though I was free. One week ago, however, I had to be released again, since my heart valve problem was too noticeable, and I was no longer up to the task of doing any marching.

Although there was certainly no true hardships, I'm still very much taken out, such that I must recover. With one blow, my Hegel studies have thus come to an end.

So, you have to kindly excuse me, most esteemed Mr. Privy Councilor, that I am not there with my presentation. But, I hope to be able to return to work some time soon, yet whether my presentation might then still be in context I don't yet want to decide. And in the end, more presentations will be canceled, so that Mr. Privy Councilor would have to draw up a new work plan for the war seminar.

Even as everything about philosophy became useless with the outbreak of the war, it will have to become in the future something profound, above all, philosophy of culture and a system of values. I, therefore, think that the war seminar, however it might be shaped, will not be less significant than the previous ones, and it is thus important for me, as soon as possible, to return to Freiburg.

I would, therefore, be very grateful to you, most esteemed Mr. Privy Councilor, if you would be so kind enough to send me a brief note about the seminar.

At the end of July, I was able to work through three more chapters in my work on the theory of categories and meaning in Duns Scotus, which I can probably present to you soon.
In the most sincere respect and gratitude,
Your most devoted,
Martin Heidegger

„Nun bin ich glücklich bei der Überwachungsstelle hier"

Hochgeehrtester Herr Geheimrat!
Nun bin ich glücklich bei der Überwachungsstelle hier. Da ich gleich Mittagsdienst habe und morgens noch Instruktionen empfange, war es mir bis heute nicht möglich, Sie zu besuchen. Hoffe aber sicher morgen, Freitag, Zeit zu bekommen.

Da ich abwechselnd eine Woche Morgen- und eine Woche Nachmittagsdienst habe und nachmittags von 3—4 lesen möchte (Grundlinien der antiken und scholastischen Philosophie) zweistündig, kann ich das nur so durchführen, daß ich alle 14 Tage vierstündig lese.

Ich glaube, daß sich das mit den wenigen Hörern sehr wohl vereinbaren läßt.

Näheres hoffe ich mit Herrn Geheimrat morgen besprechen zu dürfen.
In aufrichtigster Verehrung und Dankbarkeit
Ihr ergebenster
Martin Heidegger

Martin Heidegger an Heinrich Rickert, 4. XI. 1915 (Martin Heidegger/Heinrich Rickert. Briefe 1912 bis 1933 und andere Dokumente. Aus den Nachlässen herausgegeben von Alfred Denker. Frankfurt am Main 2002, S. 24)

Martin Heidegger to Heinrich Rickert, 4 November 1915

Martin Heidegger bei der Postüberwachungsstelle Freiburg

Martin Heidegger at the Postal Censorship Bureau in Freiburg

"I'm now happy here at the surveillance position"

Most esteemed Mr. Privy Councilor!
I'm now happy here at the surveillance position. Since I immediately have to go on duty and must undergo training tomorrow, it has proved impossible up to now to visit you. I do hope to certainly find some time tomorrow, on Friday.

Since I alternately have duty one week in the morning and one week in the afternoon, and would like to lecture for two hours from 3-4 in the afternoons (basic thoughts of ancient and scholastic philosophy), I can only do this by lecturing every fourteen days for four hours.

I believe that this can be reasonably done with few auditors.

I hope to be able to discuss matters with Mr. Privy Councilor tomorrow.
In the most sincere respect and gratitude,
Your most devoted,
Martin Heidegger

„Möge Ihnen diese militärische Zeit, wie ich auch fest hoffe, zum Segen gereichen"

Bernau (Baden) (bis etwa 25. Apr<il>)
28. 3. 1918.
Lieber Herr College.
Ich habe mich über Ihren Gruß vom Truppenübungsplatze außerordentlich gefreut. So brauche ich mich also nicht zu sorgen, wie Sie die Anstrengungen des Dienstes gesundheitlich ertragen. Die frische Stimmung, die aus Ihren fr<eundlichen> Zeilen spricht, giebt das beste Zeugnis für Ihr Wohlergehen. Daß Sie nun einmal die Philosophie ganz bei Seite thun mußten, ist ganz gut. Sie werden später – hoffentlich dauert ja der Krieg nach den herrlichen Siegen im Westen nicht mehr allzulang – mit desto größerer Spannkraft zu ihren schweren Problemen zurückkehren u. ich will herzlich gern das Meine thun, um Sie in medias res zu versetzen und Ihnen im συμφιλοσοφεῖν diese res nahe<zu>bringen. Möge Ihnen diese milit<ärische> Zeit, wie ich auch fest hoffe, zum Segen gereichen. Erfreuen Sie mich wieder gelegentlich mit Nachrichten. Mir wächst hier in dem stillen Hochthal ein großes Werk heran – Zeit u. Individuation, eine Erneuerung einer rationalen Metaph<ysik> nach den Principien.
Herzlichst grüßt Sie, wie auch meine Frau,
Ihr
EHusserl

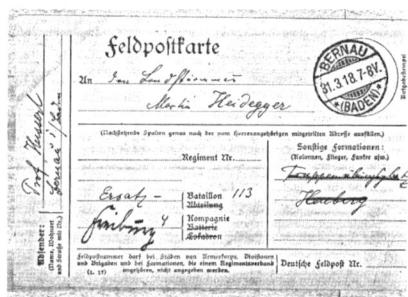

Feldpostkarte von Husserl an Martin Heidegger, 28.III.1918, adressiert „An den Landsturmmann Martin Heidegger, Ersatz-Bataillon 113, 4. Kompanie, Truppenübungsplatz Heuberg"

"May this time during this military service, as I firmly hope, be a blessing for you"

Bernau (Baden) (until about April 25th)
28 March 1918.
Dear colleague,
I was extremely happy to receive your greeting from the military training grounds. So, I need not worry about how you are enduring healthwise the demands of service. The vibrant mood that issues from your friendly lines delivers the best testimony as to your well-being. That you now must place philosophy completely aside is very good. Hopefully, the war will not continue for much longer after the glorious victories in the West. You can later return to your difficult problems with even more vigor, and I will gladly do everything on my part, to bring you back in medias res, and to make you better understand these matters by doing philosophy together. May this time during this military service, as I firmly hope, be a blessing for you. Do give me the pleasure occasionally of sending me some news. In the stillness of an elevated valley, a great work is growing here [on] time and individuation, [and on] a renewal of rational metaphysics on the basis of principles.
Sincere greetings, and also from my wife,
Your,
EHusserl

Field post-card from Husserl to Martin Heidegger, 28 March 1918, addressed to "the Landsturmmann Martin Heidegger, 113th Ersatz-Battaillion, 4th Company, Training Grounds Heuberg"

„Sie sind wie eine durch die Zimmerluft zartgewordene Topfpflanze"

Freiburg 11. V. 18.
Lieber Herr Kollege.
Ihr prächtiger Brief war mir eine wahre Freude u. wenn ich in Bernau nicht mehr antwortete, so lag es daran, daß ich inmitten wirklich produktiver Arbeit jede Stunde nützen mußte. Produktivität ist ja eine schwer errungene Kraftfülle, wie lange dauert es, wie große Mühen der vorbereitenden Arbeit, bis die corporea moles in Bewegung kommt u. das geistige Feuer hervorglühen lässt. Hier in Fr<eiburg> hatte ich aber gleich zu Anfang doch mehr zu thun als ich erwartet – ich fand meine Einl<eitung> in die Philos<ophie> hinsichtlich der ideengeschichtlichen Entwicklung des Ideals strenger Wissenschaft aus den methodolog<ischen> Conceptionen Platons nicht klar genug u. musste eine Vorlesungsreihe neu ausarbeiten. (Es handelt sich dabei auch um die Urmotive der Vernunftkritik bezogen auf Gorgias' 2. Argument, dann auf Descartes' Feld der reinen cogitatio – im Contrast zur antiken Entwicklung, die logisch-wissenschaftstheoretisch u. ontologisch lief, für die Neuzeit aber die bleibende Frucht der exacten Wissenschaften brachte.) Inzwischen kam Ihre neue, herzlich erfreuende Karte. Hätte ich doch gewußt, daß Sie bei meiner Ankunft 26. V. noch hier seien, ich hätte Sie gleich herangeholt! Zur Pfingstwoche gedenke ich, wenn möglich mit den Kindern (falls sie Urlaub bekommen), wieder nach Bernau <zu gehen>; die schwülen Frühlingswochen lasten auf mir zu hemmend in dieser Niederung u. vielleicht spanne ich etwas aus, nach der allzulangen Arbeitsperiode. Ich freue mich, daß Sie, wie ich gehofft, die Ausbildungszeit so gut überstehen, Sie sind wie eine durch die Zimmerluft zartgewordene Topfpflanze, die ins freie Feld, ins freie Licht u. unter den freien Himmel gesetzt kraftvoll emporwächst. Schön, daß Sie auch etwas lesen können, u. Sie haben trefflich gewählt. Jetzt ist nicht für Sie die Zeit für abstrakte Grübeleien. Lassen Sie sichs auch weiter gut ergehen u. bleiben Sie immer guten Muts. Wachsen Sie weiter in Gesundheit u. Kraft. Was frei, von innenher wächst u. nach oben, erreicht von selbst sein Telos.
Herzlich grüßt
Ihr EHusserl

"You are like a potted plant that has become delicate because of the air in the room"

Freiburg, 11 May 1918
Dear colleague,
Your splendid letter was a real pleasure for me, and if I could not answer it in Bernau, it was because I am in the midst of extremely productive work, [and] had to make use of every hour. Productivity is indeed a hard-earned vigor, how long might it continue, how much effort is needed for preparatory work, until the coporea moles begin to move and the spiritual fire begins to glow forth? Here in Freiburg, I immediately had more to do than expected at the beginning. I did not consider my introduction to philosophy to be clear enough in view of the historical development of the Ideal of rigorous science from Plato's methodological conception, and thus had to rework the lecture series. (These are also the basic motifs of rational criticism in relation to Gorgias' second argument, [and] then Descartes' field of pure cogitatio, in contrast to the development among the Ancients, which unfolded logically, scientifically, and ontologically, but which brought for the modern age the enduring fruit of the exact sciences). In the meantime, your new, very pleasant card arrived. If only I had known that you would still have been here, when I arrived on the 26th of May, I would have immediately picked you up! For Pentecost, I intend to go back to Bernau, if possible with the children (if they receive vacation). The sultry spring weeks are weighing down on me in this lowland and maybe I'll be able to relax after too-long a period of work. I am glad that, as I hoped, you fared well the training period. You are like a potted plant that has become delicate because of the air in the room, which grows strongly in open fields, in open light, and under the open sky. Wonderful, that you can also manage to read a bit, and you've chosen well. Now is not the time for you for abstract musings. Keep on being well and always remain in good spirits. Continue to grow in health and energy. Whatever grows freely from inside upwards will reach on its own its telos.
Warm greetings,
your,
EHusserl

„Ich in der Phänomenologie u. Sie als Wettermacher u. im Nebenamt als Religionsphänomenologe"

<…> Doch nun muß ich schließen u. füge noch Grüße, u. sehr herzl<iche>, von meiner Frau u. von Reesens, die zu unserer Freude hier sind (f<ür> 3 Wochen), bei. Zudem noch unsere freundschaftlichen guten Wünsche. Daß die Kriegsereignisse der letzten Zeit auf unseren Gemütern schwer lasten, brauche ich nicht zu sagen. Doch es wird gewiß zum Guten sein, u. wenn wir dagegen standhalten wollen, u. wir wollen es u. werden es natürlich, so geschieht es in der rechten Re-action, in der wir den Glauben an das Gute in der einzig möglichen Weise bekunden – thätig: indem wir an unserem Platze u. nach unseren kleinen (u. doch in der allgem<einen> Rechnung mitgezählten) Kräften zum Guten beitragen. Jeder also das seine, als ob die Erlösung der Welt davon grade abhienge, u. so ich in der Ph<änomenologie> u. Sie als Wettermacher u. im Nebenamt als Religionsphänomenologe. <…> ich vergaß das schöne, herzerfrischende Doppel-Kriegsbuch von Natorp zu erwähnen, das ich auch im Sommer las: Weltalter des Geistes u. Seele des Deutschen. Wir haben es auch hier u. jetzt liest es Frau Rees.

Schlussteil eines Briefes von Husserl an Martin Heidegger, 10. IX. 1918

Closing paragraph of a letter from Husserl to Martin Heidegger, 10 September 1918

"I, in phenomenology, and you as a weather-shaman and with the additional office of phenomenology of religion"

[...] I must now come to a close and add a few greetings, and very heart[felt], from my wife and from Reesens, who are here with us (for 3 weeks) much to our delight. In addition, our friendly good wishes. That the recent events of the war weighs heavily on our minds, this I don't need to say. But, it will be certainly for the good, and, if we want to resist against [these events], and if we want to do so and, of course, will do so, so it will happen in the correct response, in that we can manifest our conviction in the Good as the only possible way active [thing]: in that we can contribute in our position and through our own small efforts to the Good and thus be taken into account in the general reckoning. To each therefore his own, as if the redemption of the world hung in the balance, and so I, in phenomenology, and you as a weather-shaman and with the additional office of phenomenology of religion. [...] I forgot to mention the beautiful, refreshing double-war-book by Natorp, which I also read over the summer: Age of the Spirit and Soul of the German. We also have them here and Frau Rees is reading them now.

„Seit Frühjahr 1917 <…> war ich durch den Militärdienst an der Arbeit gehindert"

Hochverehrter Herr Geheimrat!
<…> Seit Frühjahr 1917, wo ich Sie kurz besuchte, war ich durch den Militärdienst an der Arbeit gehindert — was mir an Zeit blieb, verwandte ich zum Studium der Phänomenologie. Husserl hat mir das sehr erleichtert — und ich habe die Erfahrung gemacht, daß man nur im lebendigen Verkehr hineinkommt. Seit Januar 1918 tat ich wieder Außendienst und kam ins Feld bis zum Waffenstillstand. Diesmal ist mir der Dienst sehr gut bekommen — ich bin kräftiger und leistungsfähiger geworden. Nervosität und Schlaflosigkeit sind seitdem wie weggeblasen.

Bei der Rückkehr aus dem Felde begann gleich die Vorbereitung für das Zwischensemester (ich las über den Begriff der Philosophie). Nach kurzen Ferien, in denen ich kaum zu Atem kam, nahmen mich die Arbeiten für das Sommerkolleg in Anspruch: „Transzendentale Wertphilosophie und Phänomenologie".

Martin Heidegger an Heinrich Rickert, 27. I. 1920 (Martin Heidegger/ Heinrich Rickert. Briefe 1912 bis 1933 und andere Dokumente. Aus den Nachlässen herausgegeben von Alfred Denker. Frankfurt am Main 2002, S. 47)

Martin Heidegger to Heinrich Rickert, 27 January 1920

"Since the spring of 1917, [...] I was hindered in work due to military service"

Dear Mr. Privy Councilor!
[...] Since the spring of 1917, when I briefly visited you, I was hindered in work due to military service – and what remained free of my time, I used to study phenomenology. Husserl had made this much easier for me – and I learned that one can only enter into it through vibrant contact. Since January 1918, I did field service once again and entered into the front until the ceasefire. This time, I got along very well with my duties – I've become stronger and more efficient. Nervousness and insomnia have since evaporated.

When I returned from the front, the preparation for the intermediate semester began immediately (I lectured on the concept of philosophy). After a short vacation, during which I could hardly keep my breath, the demanding work for the summer seminar challenged me: "Transcendental Philosophy of Value and Phenomenology."

Martin Heidegger

Gustav Hübener (1889-1941)

Gustav Hübener: geb. 4. 7. 1889 in Hamburg, gest. 30. 9. 1940 in Kanada. – 1909-1913 Studium der deutschen Philologie, Anglistik, Volkswirtschaft, Geschichte, Philosophie und Psychologie in München, Berlin, Edinburgh, London, Paris und Göttingen. In Göttingen Studium der Philosophie bei Husserl und Reinach; Mitglied der Göttinger Philosophischen Gesellschaft. 1913 Promotion in Anglistik („Die stilistische Spannung in Miltons ‚Paradise lost'"). Etwa von 1916-1918 Militärdienst. 1920 Habilitation in Göttingen, dort für ein Semester Lehrstuhlvertretung. Seit 1921/22 Privatdozent im Fach Anglistik in Marburg, ab Oktober 1922 o. Professor für englische Sprache und Literatur an der Universität in Königsberg, ab 1925 in Basel, von 1930 bis 1937 an der Bonner Universität. 1937 Auswanderung nach Kanada; Übernahme einer Gastprofessur für Germanistik an der Mount Allison University in Sackville (New Brunswick). – Der Nachlass von Gustav Hübener befindet sich an der University of New Brunswick (Kanada).

Gustav Hübener: born on July 4, 1889 in Hamburg, died on September 30, 1940 in Canada. From 1909 to 1913, studied German philology, English, economics, history, philosophy, and psychology in Munich, Berlin, Edinburgh, London, Paris and Göttingen. In Göttingen, study of philosophy with Husserl and Reinach; member of the Göttingen Philosophical Society. 1913, PhD in English ("Stylistic Tension in Milton's Paradise Lost"). From 1916 to 1918, military service. 1920, Habilitation in Göttingen, and then there as a one-year replacement. Beginning in 1921-1922, Privatdozent in English in Marburg, from October 1922 Professor of English Language and Literature at the University of Königsberg, from 1925 in Basel, from 1930 to 1937 at the University of Bonn. 1937, emigration to Canada as a visiting professor for German studies at Mount Allison University in Sackville (New Brunswick). – The papers of Gustav Hübener are housed at the University of New Brunswick (Canada).

Hübener, G.: Die stilistische Spannung in Miltons "Paradise Lost". Göttingen 1913. – Hübener, G.: Scholastik und Neuenglische Hochsprache. In: Germanisch-Romanische Monatsschrift X (1922), 88-101. – Hübener, G.: Zur Erklärung der Wortstellungsentwicklung im Ags. In: Anglia. Zeitschrift für englische Philologie 39/3 (1916), 277-302. – Hübener, G.: Beowulf and Germanic Exorcism. In: The Review of English Studies, Vol. 11, No. 42 (Apr., 1935), 163-181.

Gustav Hübener (Photo aus späteren Jahren)

Gustav Hübener (photo from his later years)

„Dieser Krieg ist für mich persönlich eine sehr milde Prüfung"

<...> Ich hoffe von Herzen, daß es Ihnen gut geht. Dieser Krieg ist für mich persönlich eine sehr milde Prüfung. Aber wenn man gerade alle die fortgehen sieht, die man als lebendigste Hoffnung für das neue Europa betrachtete, so erscheint einem die Allgemeinheit schwer bestraft. Und doch liegt es nur an den verwirrten Herzen, daß sie den Frieden noch nicht gefunden haben.
Herzlich grüßt Sie Ihr
ergebener
Gustav Hübener.

Schlussteil eines Briefes von Gustav Hübener an Max Scheler, 25. XII. 1915

Concluding section of a letter from Gustav Hübener to Max Scheler, 25 December 1915

"This war is for me personally a very mild test"

[...] I sincerely hope that you are well. This war is for me personally a very mild test. But if one looks at all those who are going away, who can be seen as the most vibrant hope for a new Europe, so it would appear that the general public is severely punished. And yet it is only with those confused hearts, who have not yet found peace.
With heartfelt wishes,
Your devoted,
Gustav Hübener.

„Wie sichtbar hat das gütige Geschick gewaltet als es Sie nach kurzem Einblick in das harte kriegerische Leben wieder ungebrochen in Ihr ‚stilles Tal' entließ"

Am Rondeel 19
Hamburg.
Sehr verehrter, lieber Herr Doktor,
Seit Sie uns besuchten sind nun schon mehrere Wochen verstrichen und es drängt mich Ihnen zu schreiben. Zunächst möchte ich Ihnen meine herzlichste Freude aussprechen über den günstigen Befund des dortigen Arztes. Wie sichtbar hat das gütige Geschick gewaltet als es Sie nach kurzem Einblick in das harte kriegerische Leben wieder ungebrochen in Ihr ‚stilles Tal' entließ. – Sie sprachen von zwei Möglichkeiten des Lebens, unter denen sich die Zukunft Ihnen darstellt – einem contemplativen, philosophischen Dasein und einem dem öffentlichen Leben bestimmten. Wenn ich für Sie wünsche, so wünsche ich Ihnen ein Leben, das seinen Sitz und Schwerpunkt in einem ‚stillen Tal' behält, so weit es auch seine geistigen Fäden mit einem weiten Umkreis des Wirkens verwebt.

Seit Sie Hamburg verließen machte die Kieferentzündung bei mir eine rasche Besserung durch. Ich bin zwar noch nicht wieder ganz genesen darf aber jetzt zu Hause schlafen und hoffe in vierzehn Tagen etwa so weit zu sein, daß ich ins Feld kommen kann.

Nun schon fast zwei Jahr Schreibstuben- und Lazarettatmosphäre lassen den Gedanken, in die größere Freiheit des Frontlebens zu kommen, schön und befreiend erscheinen.

Und der Krieg entwickelt sich ja in immer neue Phasen, wird fast für gedankenlose Stunden ein selbstverständlicher Teil unseres Lebens. Wie ist es da notwendig wenigstens soviel Luft und Bewegungsfreiheit sich zu verschaffen für die persönliche Entwicklung wie die Verhältnisse es gestatten.

Ich hoffe draußen jedenfalls die Unteroffizierswürde zu erreichen und eine erhöhte körperliche Leistungsfähigkeit. Besonders auf das Reiten freue ich mich. –

In einer(?) Nummer der „Weißen Blätter", die mir zufällig in die Hände geriet, las ich eine anonyme, rüpelhafte Bemerkung über Ihren „Genius d. Krieges". Ist dieser sonderbare Schickele deren Urheber? Abgesehen von dem törichten Inhalt des Geschwätzes verstehe ich nicht wie er als Schriftsteller nicht einmal soviel Formgefühl besitzt, daß er die Tradition seiner eigenen Zeitschrift unangetastet läßt, deren Ruf Sie doch durch Einsetzung Ihres Namens und Ihrer Feder begründeten. –

Sehr erfreute mich die Entgegnung Försters auf die gegen ihn gerichteten Angriffe zu lesen. Jedes Wort, das er über die Notwendigkeit eines neuen Tons in den gegnerischen Ländern als erste Basis für eine Wendung zum Frieden sagt, kann man unterschreiben. Aber wie schwer ist es zu hoffen, daß diese Bereitwilligkeit zum gegenseitigen Verständnis schon Eingang in die Herzen der entscheidenden Männer gefunden hat.

Gebe Gott, daß Rumänien <die> letzte Phase, verspielter Trumpf in den Händen der Feinde ist und Erziehungsinstrument jener Alldeutschen, die jede Wand einrennen wollen. Aber – Gottes Wege sind nicht unsere Wege und wer weiß wie viel Furchen er noch in den Acker Europas pflügen will, damit eine Saat aufgehe, wie er sie braucht. – Meine Mutter schrieb Ihnen von einem Wiedersehen nach dem Kriege. Das ist auch meine herzlichste Hoffnung, lieber Herr Doktor! Ich dachte noch viel an Ihre Worte bei Ihrem Besuch und sprach viel mit Frl. Möhring von Ihnen.

Mit den herzlichsten Grüßen von meiner Angehörigen, auch an ihre Frau
Ihr ergebener Gustav Hübener.

> *"How manifest did benevolent fate [gütiges Geschick] hold sway when,*
> *after a brief glimpse into the tough life of a soldier,*
> *you again found yourself without distraction in your 'peaceful valley'"*

At the Rondeel 19
Hamburg.
Honored and dear Herr Doctor,

Several weeks have passed since you visited us and I am eager to write you. First of all, I would like to express to you my most cordial joy about the favorable findings of the doctor there. How manifest did benevolent fate [*gütiges Geschick*] hold sway when, after a brief glimpse into the tough life of a soldier, you again found yourself without distraction in your "peaceful valley". You spoke of two possibilities of life for which the future presents itself to you – a contemplative, philosophical existence and a public life. If I can make a wish for you, it would be to wish you a life which enjoys its place and center of gravity in a "peaceful valley," as much as it can interweave with the spiritual threads of an encompassing circle of action.

Since you left Hamburg, I've made a quick recovery from my jaw inflammation. Although I am not yet fully recovered, I can now sleep at home and hope in fourteen days to be so far that I can come to the front.

After almost two years of being in a writing cabinet and hospital atmosphere, many thoughts come to mind, in which the great freedom of life at the front appears as beautiful and liberating.

And the war still develops in ever new phases, becoming for absent-minded hours an obvious part of our lives. How necessary it now becomes, that at least as much air and freedom of movement for personal development, as with personal relations, can be afforded.

In any case, I hope to attain the rank of a non-commissioned officer as well as achieve an higher level of physical performance. I am especially looking forward to riding.

In an Issue of the "White Leaves," which just happened to land into my hands, I read an anonymous and boorish remark about your "Genius of War." Is this peculiar Schickele its author? Apart from its foolish content of gossip, I do not understand how he, as a writer, does not even have so much a sense of form as to leave untouched the tradition of his own journal, whose reputation you established by giving your name and your pen.

I was very pleased to read Förster's reply in view of the attacks directed against him. Every word, which he utters about the need for a new tone in the enemy countries as the first basis for a turn to peace can be counter signed. But how difficult is it to hope that this willingness for mutual understanding has already found its way into the hearts of those men who decide.

Let God grant that Romania, in this last phase, plays the role of the misplayed hand of the enemies and [thus become] an object lesson for those Pan-Germans who want to smash every barrier. But – God's ways are not our ways and who knows how many furrows he still wants to plow in the field of Europe, so as to sow seeds as he needs them. My mother wrote to you about a reunion after the war. That is also my heartfelt hope, dear Doctor! I have often thought about your words during your visit and talked a lot with Fräulein Möhring about you.

With warmest regards from my family, also to your wife,
Your devoted Gustav Hübener

Brief von Gustav Hübener an Max Scheler, etwa 1916

Letter from Gustav Hübener to Max Scheler, around 1916

Fritz Kaufmann (1891-1958)

Fritz Kaufmann: geb. 3. 7. 1891 in Leipzig, gest. 9. 8. 1958 in Zürich. – Von 1910 bis 1914 Studium der Rechtwisssenschaft, Literaturwissenschaft und Philosophie in Genf, Berlin (bei Carl Stumpf), Leipzig (bei Wilhelm Wundt) und Göttingen (bei Husserl). 1914-1918 Teilnahme am Ersten Weltkrieg. 1918 kommt die geplante Promotion an der Universität Leipzig mit der im Feld verfassten Arbeit („Der Konflikt") nicht zustande. Anfang 1919 Fortsetzung des Studiums in Freiburg. 1924 Promotion bei Husserl („Das Bildwerk als ästhetisches Phänomen"), anschließend Tätigkeit als dessen Assistent. 1926 Habilitation bei Husserl („Die Philosophie des Grafen Paul Yorck von Wartenburg"). Danach Lehrtätigkeit als Privatdozent in Freiburg bis etwa 1935, ab 1936 Gastprofessor an der Hochschule für die Wissenschaft des Judentums in Berlin. Dort Zusammenarbeit mit Martin Buber und Leo Baeck. 1938 Emigration über England in die USA. 1938-1946 Lehrtätigkeit an der Northwestern University in Evanston und 1946-1954 an der University of Buffalo. Mitherausgeber der Zeitschrift *Philosophy and Phenomenological Research* und der *Library of Living Philosophers* sowie der Zeitschrift *Judaism*. 1954 für ein Jahr als Gastdozent an der Hebrew University in Jerusalem. Nach seiner Emeritierung 1958 lässt sich Kaufmann in der Schweiz nieder. – Der Nachlass von Fritz Kaufmann befindet sich im Husserl-Archiv Leuven und im Leo Baeck Institute.

Fritz Kaufmann: born on July 3, 1891 in Leipzig, died on August 9, 1958 in Zurich. From 1910 to 1914, studied law, literature, and philosophy in Geneva, Berlin (with Carl Stumpf), Leipzig (with Wilhelm Wundt) and Göttingen (with Husserl). 1914-1918, served in the First World War. In 1918, his anticipated PhD at the University of Leipzig with a dissertation written at the front ("Conflict") did not come to fruition. Continuation of studies in Freiburg in 1919. 1924, PhD with Husserl ("The Picture as an Aesthetic Phenomenon"), followed by an appointment as Husserl's assistant. 1926 habilitation with Husserl ("The Philosophy of Count Paul Yorck von Wartenburg"). Teaching as a private lecturer in Freiburg until 1935, from 1936 guest professor at the University for the Science of Judaism in Berlin. Collaborates with Martin Buber and Leo Baeck. 1938 Emigration via England to the United States. 1938-1946 teaching at Northwestern University in Evanston and 1946-1954 at the University of Buffalo. Co-editor of the journal *Philosophy and Phenomenological Research*, the *Library of Living Philosophers*, and the journal *Judaism*. In 1954, as a visiting lecturer at the Hebrew University in Jerusalem. After his retirement in 1958 Kaufmann settled in Switzerland. – The papers of Fritz Kaufmann are housed at the Husserl Archive Leuven and at the Leo Baeck Institute.

Fritz Kaufmann (ca. 1915)

Fritz Kaufmann (around 1915)

Gadamer, H.-G.: Nachwort. In: Kaufmann, F.: Das Reich des Schönen. Stuttgart 1960, 397–403. – Landgrebe, L.: Fritz Kaufmann in Memoriam. In: Zeitschrift für philosophische Forschung, Jg. 12 (1958), 612-615. – Lotz, C.: Fritz Kaufmann (1891-1958). In: Sepp, H. R./Embree, L. (eds.): Handbook of Phenomenological Aesthetics. Dordrecht/Boston/London 2010, 177-180. – Oppenheim, L.: Fritz Kaufmann's Literary Aesthetics as Defined by His Study of Thomas Mann. In: Kaelin. E. F./Schrag, C. O. (eds.): American Phenomenology: Origins and Developments. Dordrecht 1989, 31-42. – Rahner, K.: Protokoll aus einem Husserl Seminar bei Fritz Kaufmann. In: Ders.: Sämtliche Werke Bd. 2, Freiburg i. Br. 1996, 427-430. – Skarda, C./Kersten, F.: Fritz Leopold Kaufmann. In: Encyclopedia of Phenomenology. Ed. Lester Embree et al. Dordrecht 1997, 385–387.

„Ich liebte ihn vor allen anderen"

Am 24. Dec<ember> 1914.
Göttingen.
Lieber Herr Kaufmann!

Es kommt der Weihnachtsabend heran, ich bin dabei den Schreibtisch etwas in Ordnung zu bringen, vor der stillen Feier, die wir diesmal mit nahen Freunden begehen; da finde ich Ihren warmherzigen, lieben Brief, lese ihn von Neuem und fühle mich gedrängt, Ihnen nochmals zu schreiben. Sie erinnern sich, das große Thema war der Tod unseres lieben Fritz Frankfurt<h>er, der Ihnen als naher Freund und mir als einer der treuesten Schüler entrissen wurde. Dieser Verlust hat mich sehr niedergedrückt; ich liebte ihn vor allen anderen. – Viel edles Blut ist geflossen! Mit tiefer Trauer gedenke ich besonders unserer Göttinger Bataillone bei den 233ern und 234ern, wo ein Haupttheil unserer Studentenschaft kämpft oder vielmehr kämpfte! Denn was ist davon noch übrig! Ich kann es leicht berechnen, wenn ich mir sage, daß um Mitte d. M. von der kriegsstarken 11. Comp<anie>, wo meine Jungens stehen, nur noch 70 Gewehre übrig waren. Wie wird Deutschland nach dem erhofften, aber so schwer erkämpften Siege den Verlust des größten Theils dieser akadem<ischen> Jugend ertragen? Ist ein solcher Verlust überhaupt zu ersetzen? Doch ich will nicht Klagen wiederholen, die ich Ihnen sicherlich schon ausgesprochen habe. Ich hoffe, daß die bewegte Thätigkeit, in der sie nicht viel Zeit haben werden, traurigen Gedanken nachzuhängen, Sie weiter befriedigt u. Ihnen Gelegenheit giebt mit Erfolg, seis auch nur im Kleinen, an dem gewaltigen Ziele mitzuarbeiten, das den Namen trägt: Deutschlands Zukunft!

Ich sende Ihnen also meine herzlichsten Weihnachtswünsche. Halten Sie sich weiter so tapfer und möge Ihre körperliche Kraft inmitten dieser großen Anspannungen wachsen und ev<tl>. immer größeren Genüge thun. Mir geht es im Leiden leidlich. Es wird mir sehr schwer den Zugang zu den inneren Intuitionen zu finden, denen meine Lebensarbeit gilt; ich komme also wenig vorwärts u. darunter leiden meine Nerven, wie auch u. vor Allem unter den großen Aufregungen der Zeit. Allmälig wird es, wenn auch langsam besser, die Horizonte werden hie u. da freier.

Meine Jungens sind, dem Himmel sei Dank, noch gesund, immerfort in der schlammigen Umgebung Yperns und im Feuer.

Brief von Husserl an Fritz Kaufmann, 24. XII. 1914

Letter from Husserl to Fritz Kaufmann, 24 December 1914

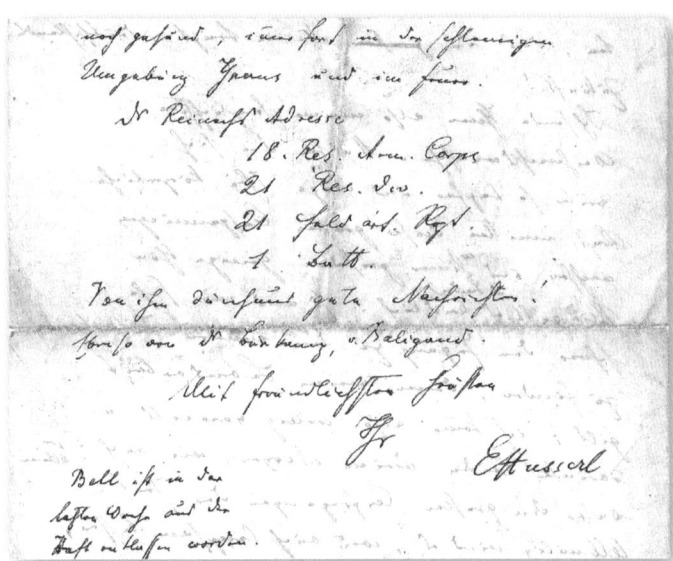

Dr Reinachs Adresse
18. Res<erve>-Arm<ee>Corps
21. Res<erve>Div<ision>
21. Feldart<illerie>-Reg<imen>t
1. Batt<erie>.
Von ihm durchaus gute Nachrichten!
Ebenso von Dr Burkamp, v. Baligand.
Mit freundlichsten Grüßen
Ihr
EHusserl
Bell ist in der letzten Woche aus der Haft entlassen worden.

"I loved him above all others"

On the 24th of December 1914
Göttingen
Dear Mr. Kaufmann!

Christmas Eve is approaching, I am in the process of putting the desk in order before the quiet celebration we are celebrating this time with close friends. I find here your warm-hearted, precious letter, read it anew and feel compelled to write to you again. You remember, the major issue was the death of our dear Fritz Frankfurt[h]er, who was snatched from you as a close friend and from me as one of the most loyal disciples. This loss has depressed me a lot. I loved him above all others. – A lot of noble blood has flowed! With deep sadness I especially remember our Göttingen battalions of the 233rd and 234th, where a major part of our student body fights or rather fought! What now remains of it! I can easily calculate it, if I tell myself that by the middle of the month of the war-strong 11th Company, my boys remain with only 70 rifles left. How will Germany, after the hoped-for, but so hard-won victory, endure the loss of the greater part of this academic youth? Is such a loss to be replaced at all? But I do not want to repeat complaints that I have certainly already pronounced. I hope that the eventful activity, in which you will not have much time to dwell on sad thoughts, will continue to satisfy you. You have the opportunity to succeed, even if only on a small scale, to collaborate with the enormous aims that carries the name: Germany's future!

So, I send you my heartfelt Christmas wishes. Keep up your bravery and may your physical strength grow and evolve in the midst of these great tensions to do more and more. I am suffering tolerably. It will be very difficult for me to gain access to the inner intuitions that my life's work is about. So, I'm moving a little forward and my nerves suffer as well, and especially among the great disturbances of the time. Gradually, albeit slowly improving, the horizons will become here and there more free.

My boys, thank Heaven, are still healthy in the muddy surroundings of Ypres and in combat.

Dr Reinach's address
18th Reserve Army Corps
21st Reserve Division
21st Field-Artillery Regiment
1st Battery
Good news from him!
Also by Dr Burkamp, v. Baligand.
With kindest regards,
Your
EHusserl
Bell was released from prison last week.

„Der Krieg mit seinen tiefbewegenden Ereignissen hat mich verschlossen gemacht"

Göttingen 20. 9. 15.

Lieber Herr Kaufmann!
Mit herzlichster Antheilnahme empfieng ich Ihre Mittheilung von dem unerwarteten Tode Ihres Vaters, der Ihrem Herzen so nahe gestanden. In Ihrem Alter verlor auch ich den meinen. Fast schämte ich mich wie leicht ich den Verlust, nach den ersten großen Erschütterungen, ertrug – aber eine stille, wehmütige, unerfüllbare Sehnsucht begleitet mich in Gedanken an ihn durch mein ganzes Leben. Die sterben eigentlich nicht, die wir liebend verehrt; sie streben und thun nicht mehr, sprechen nicht mehr zu uns, fordern nichts von uns; und doch, ihrer gedenkend fühlen wir sie uns gegenüber, uns in die Seelen blickend, mit uns fühlend, uns verstehend, billigend oder misbilligend.–

Ihre beiden letzten Briefe liegen seit Langem vor mir, ich habe sie wiederholt gelesen – um so öfter, da ich nicht so bald antworten konnte. Das hat z. Th. seelische Gründe. Der Krieg mit seinen tiefbewegenden Ereignissen hat mich verschlossen gemacht; es wird mir unglaublich schwer aus mir herauszugehen u. mich auszusprechen – auch da, wo ich lebendigsten Antheil nehme; ja gerade da wird mirs am Schwersten. Ich habe durch den Tod Monat für Monat viele mir nahe stehende Menschen verloren, jüngere u. ältere Freunde, in rascher Folge. Dazu kamen gesundheitliche Störungen, die aber fast alle ihre psychischen Ursachen haben. Dadurch verlor ich immer wieder die Continuität meines wissenschaftlichen Lebensfadens; wenn ich nicht fruchtbar arbeiten kann, mich nicht mehr selbst verstehe, meine Msc. lesen, aber ihnen nicht Intuitionen unterlegen kann, bin ich in übelster Situation. Zuletzt vertrug ich plötzlich nicht mehr das Rauchen, worin ich vielleicht gesündigt habe, u. hatte Anzeichen einer Nikotinvergiftung; mußte daher in ärztliche Behandlung gehen. Ähnliche nervöse Störungen hatte ich in Halle Jahre lang, und en masse; Göttingen hatte mich davon völlig kuriert – bis in dem letzten Jahr kannte ich dergl. nicht mehr. Ich muß in dieser Labilität des Befindens, die längere Perioden guten Befindens nicht ausschließt (wie hätte ich sonst in Halle die Log<ischen> U<ntersuchungen> geschrieben!) unendliche Geduld üben u. will ich nicht auf wissenschaftliche Leistungen, also auf die Fortführung meiner Lebensarbeit verzichten, so muß ich die guten Stunden nützen u. darf nicht Allotria treiben, wie z. B. Briefe an liebe junge Freunde schreiben! Und nun ist eben eine bessere Zeit, ich habe zudem für Ende Oktober eine Arbeit zugesagt zu Eucken's 70. Geburtstag – also bis auf Weiteres bin ich für jede Minute gebunden u. hoffe es allen dunklen Mächten zu trotz durchzusetzen u. mich damit auch wieder dauernd gesund zu arbeiten. Käme nur der Frieden, ein schöner Friede, dann würden auch meine Nerven Frieden geben.

Dies zur Erklärung! Bedauern müssen Sie mich nicht, momentan bin ich „oben" u. habe freundlich gehegte Gedanken, die ich nicht mehr loslasse. – Und nun, wo ich noch nichts auf Ihre schönen Probleme u. Meditationen Eingehendes gesagt habe, muß ich schließen! Mitgedacht habe ich u. wenn Sie wieder da sind, sprechen wir u. tauschen aus. Jedenfalls wissen Sie, daß Ihre Worte herzlich aufgenommen u. verstanden sind. Schreiben Sie also wieder!

Leben Sie wohl, treu allem Guten und unserem Vaterlande.
Ihr
EHusserl.

Von Frl. Stein hatte ich wiederholte Briefe aus Weisskirchen (Lazarett), zuletzt aus Breslau. Sie hat tüchtig mitgeschafft, als Schwester.

Diese Woche haben wir Prof. Wendland begraben. Dr Burkamp soll das eis<erne> † I. Klasse in den Argonnen erworben haben. Meine Söhne wohlauf.

"The war with its deeply moving events has closed me up"

Göttingen 20 September 1915
Dear Mr. Kaufmann!
With heartfelt sympathy I received your communication of the unexpected death of your father, who was so close to your heart. At your age, I had also lost my father. I was almost ashamed of how easily I endured the loss after the first great shock – but a quiet, wistful, [and] unfulfillable longing accompanies me in my thoughts of him throughout my life. They do not actually die, those whom we adored with love; they no longer strive and do anything, they no longer speak to us, they demand nothing from us; and yet, in remembring them, we feel that they are looking at us, gazing into our souls, feeling with us, understanding us, with approval or disapproval.

Your last two letters have been lying in front of me for a long time, I have read them repeatedly, and so often that I could not answer sooner. This has, in part, to do with spiritual circumstances. The war with its deeply moving events has closed me up; it will be incredibly difficult to extricate myself from myself and express myself – even for those things in which I take a most lively interest; indeed, it is precisely with these things that it proves to be the hardest for me. Month after month, I have lost many people who were close to me, younger and older friends, in quick succession. In addition, there were health problems, but almost all of them have psychological causes. I thereby always lost again the continuity of my scientific threads of life. I am unable to work productively, and no longer understand myself, [and am not able to] read my manuscripts, and fail to ground them in intuitions – I am in the most terrible of situations. Recently, my body suddenly didn't tolerate smoking anymore, where I have sinned, and had seen signs of nicotine poisoning. I had therefore to receive medical treatment. Comparable nervous irregularities I had experienced in Halle for many years, and massively. Göttingen had completely cured me – up until the last few years, I did not have any more of these. I must in this unstable condition not exclude longer periods of feeling well (how could I have otherwise written in Halle the Logical Investigations!) and exercise infinite patience, and if I don't want to renounce my scientific achievements, and thereby, the continuation of my life-work, so I need to make use of those good hours effectively, and should not pursue skylarking, for example, like writing letters to cherished young friends! And now the times have become better, I have committed to a work for Eucken's 70th birthday for the end of October, and until then, I am booked every minute and hope to finish everything, despite all these dark forces, and thereby that by working I shall be able to become healthy again in a lasting way. If only peace would come, a beautiful peace, then my nerves would give me peace.

All of this as an explanation! You must not worry about me, at the moment I am "above" and have amiable, precious thoughts, which do not let go of me. And now, when I have not yet said anything in detail about your wonderful problems and meditations, I must close! I have given them consideration and when you are here again, we'll talk and exchange our ideas. In any case, do know that your words were warmly received and understood. Please therefore write again!

Farewell, believe in what is good and in our Fatherland.
Your,
EHusserl.
From Fräulein Stein I have received frequent letters from Weisskirchen (military hospital), most recently from Breslau. She has been brilliant as a nurse.

This week we buried Prof. Wendland. Dr Burkamp is said to have acquired the Iron [Cross] First Class in the Argonne. My sons are doing well.

Brief von Husserl an Fritz Kaufmann, 20. IX. 1915

Letter from Husserl to Fritz Kaufmann, 20 September 1915

„Sie können sich denken, wie ich mit allen national Gesinnten unter dem entsetzlichen Zusammenbruch unserer großen u. stolzen Nation litt u. noch leide"

Lieber Herr Kaufmann!

Die neue Bekundung Ihrer treuen Anhänglichkeit hat mich herzlich gefreut. Als Ihr Brief kam, war ich von einer sehr schweren Grippe, in der sich Frl. Stein als Mitpflegerin rührend betheiligt hat, noch ganz parterre. Allmälig kam ich in die Höhe, soweit es die seelischen Erschütterungen zuließen. Sie können sich denken, wie ich mit allen national Gesinnten unter dem entsetzlichen Zusammenbruch unserer großen u. stolzen Nation litt u. noch leide. Ich suchte mich durch Vertiefung in die philos<ophische> Arbeit zu retten – wie ich denn in all den Kriegsjahren diesen Kampf um die geistige Selbsterhaltung kämpfe. Ich habe periodenweise, u. in der Folge der Kriegsjahre immer mehr, sehr fruchtbar gearbeitet. Aber wie schwer war's mir gemacht. Wie viel war innerlich zu überwinden, wie lastete auf der Seele, daß sie nicht als thätige nationale Kraft sich in Reih u. Glied stellen konnte. Aber Ph<änomenologie> ist auch ein necessarium u. ein nationaler, obschon übernationaler Wert. – Die Lehre war auch nicht ohne Erfolg, so klein unser Fr<eiburger> Kreis war. Wir wollen hoffen, glauben! Vor allem wir wollen arbeiten, nach schönsten, dereinst auch praktisch höchst bedeutsamen Zielen <streben>. Sursum corda. So Gott will, wird trotz so schwerer Verluste, der ph<änomenologische> Nachwuchs die schönen Anfänge fortführen. Und auch auf Sie l<ieber> H<err> K<aufmann> rechne ich. Seien Sie meiner Theilnahme, jeder mögl<ichen> Förderung sicher. Vielleicht können Sie noch einmal hieher kommen.

Herzlichst
Ihr
EHusserl

Feldpostkarte von Husserl an Fritz Kaufmann, 17. I. 1919

"You can imagine how I am suffering and still suffering along with other patriotically minded people given the terrible collapse of our great and proud Nation"

Dear Mr. Kaufmann!

The recent display of your loyal attachment made me very happy. When your letter arrived, I was still completely under the weather from a very severe flu; Fräulein Stein was lovingly engaged as care-taker. Gradually, I got myself back on my feet as much as possible given the emotional shocks. You can imagine how I am suffering and still suffering along with other patriotically minded people given the terrible collapse of our great and proud Nation. I tried to save myself by deepening myself into philosophical work as I had done during all these years of war in struggling for spiritual self-preservation. I periodically was able to work very productively, and in the course of the war-years, ever more so. Yet, how hard it was all made for me. How much had to be over-come inwardly, how the soul was burdened, that it [the soul] could not come into line as an active national force. Yet, phenomenology has also a necessity and a national, although trans-national value. The teaching was not without success, however, our Freiburg circle was small. We want to hope, and believe! Above all, we want to work towards the most beautiful, and at the same time, most practically important and significant aims. Lift up your hearts [*Sursum corda*]. God willing, the phenomenological progeny will continue from these wonderful beginnings, despite such heavy losses. And I count on you as well, dear Herr Kaufmann. Be assured of my sympathy and of any possible support. Maybe you could come here once again.

Sincerely,
Your,
EHusserl

Field post-card from Husserl to Fritz Kaufmann, 17 January 1919

Fritz Kaufmann

"Der Konflikt"

DER KONFLIKT

(E i n e   S t u d i e).

I n a u g u r a l - D i s s e r t a t i o n

zur Erlangung der Doktorwürde

bei der Philosophischen Fakultät der Universität Leipzig

eingereicht von

F r i t z   K a u f m a n n

aus Leipzig.

V o r w o r t.

    Diese Arbeit ist auf kurzem Urlaube in der Heimat niedergeschrieben worden. Sie ist aber in allem Wesentlichen im Felde und aus dem Bestreben entstanden, bedrängende Eindrücke und Fragen der Zeit dadurch zu bewältigen, dass sie in systematischem Zusammenhange zur Begreifung, Klärung und persönlichen Entscheidung gelangten. Die Kühle der Begrifflichkeit sollte nur die Hitze des Tages, nicht die Wärme lebendiger Teilnahme tilgen. – Graben und Zelt verboten die Nutzung von Literatur. Daher konnte und musste auf Zitate und Auseinandersetzungen verzichtet werden. Dennoch erhebt die Studie in keiner Weise den Anspruch reiner Originalität. Vielmehr bekennt der Verfasser dankbar den starken und entscheidenden Einfluss, den auf sein ganzes Denken sein verehrter und bewunderter Lehrer Husserl und in zweiter Linie Dilthey durch Vermittlung Eduard Sprangers ausgeübt haben.

D i s p o s i t i o n.

	Seite
Die Absicht der Arbeit.	1
I. Ueber das Wesen der geschichtlichen Person	4
II. Die Struktur des Konfliktes	29
1. Die Träger des Konfliktes	29
2. Die Modi der Konfliktgegebenheit	37
3. Die Bedingungen der Konfliktgegebenheit	43
Nachbemerkung	55
III. Der Verlauf des Konfliktes	58
Vorbemerkung	58
1. Das Vorstadium des Konfliktes (die Krisis)	61
2. a) Die Seinsfrage	61
b) Die Unruhe der Erwartung	66
c) Die dissoziierenden Kräfte	67
d) Die Möglichkeiten der Konfliktvermeidung	77
e) Die Vorbereitung für den Konflikt	85
2. Die Zeit des Konfliktes	87
a) Die Auslösung des Konfliktes	88
b) Die beherrschenden Tendenzen des Konfliktverlaufes	94
c) Konfliktaustrag und Konfliktbeendigung	108
C_1. Latenz und Apparenz	108
C_2. Austrag und Beendigung des inneren Konfliktes	112
C_3. Austrag und Beendigung des äußeren Konfliktes	130

"Conflict"

Foreword

This work was written during a short vacation in our native country. However, the essentials of this work developed at the front and from the need to gain mastery over overwhelming experiences and questions by way of placing them in systematic contexts of understanding, clarification, and personal decision. The coldness of concepts is only meant to extinguish the heat of the day, not the warmth of participation. The trenches and time prohibited the use of literature. Citations and critical engagements had therefore to be abandoned. Nevertheless, the study in no way claims to any pure originality. Rather, the author gratefully acknowledges the strong and decisive influence exercised on his whole thinking by his esteemed and admired teacher Husserl, and secondly, by Dilthey through the intermediary of Eduard Spranger.

The Aim of the Work

I. On the essence of the historical person

II. The structure of conflict
    1. The bearers of conflict
    2. Modes of conflict
    3. Conditions for conflict
    Postscript

III. The progress of conflict
    Introduction
    1. Preliminary stage of conflict (crisis)
        a) The question of being
        b) The restlessness of expectation
        c) Diss-associating forces
        d) Possibilities for the avoidance of conflict
        e) Preparations for conflict
    2. The time of conflict
        a) The triggering of conflict
        b) The dominating tendencies of conflict's progress
        c) The discharge of conflict and the end of conflict
            C1. Latence and appearance
            C2. The discharge of conflict and the end of internal conflict
            C3. The discharge of conflict and the end of external conflict

Typoskript der von Fritz Kaufmann etwa 1918 verfassten Dissertation mit dem Titel „Der Konflikt" (die Promotion in Leipzig kam aber nicht zustande)

Typed manuscript of Fritz Kaufmann's PhD thesis "Conflict" from around 1918 (the defense in Leipzig never occured)

Kurt Lewin (1890-1947)

Kurt Lewin: born on September 9, 1890 in Mogilno (Poland), died on February 12, 1947 in Newtonville (Massachusetts, USA). Studied medicine and biology in 1909, followed by philosophy and psychology in Freiburg, Munich, and Berlin (among others, with Carl Stumpf). In August 1914, reported as a volunteer for the war. In October 1914, assigned to the artillery at the front (deployment in France and Russia). September 1914, oral doctoral examination. 1916, graduation ("Mental Activity in the Inhibition of Volitional Processes and the Basic Law of Association"). In July 1916, assigned to the Artillery Inspection Commission in Berlin, and most likely worked on sound measuring devices developed by Erich von Hornbostel and Max Wertheimer at the Physical Institute of the University of Berlin ("direction listener for artillery education"). Lewin also developed a method for qualifying examiners as radio operators. July 1917, back at the front. 1917, publication of the essay "Kriegslandschaft" as well as various reviews of war publications in the "Zeitschrift für angewandte Psychologie." April 1918, promotion to Lieutenant. On August 9, 1918, his youngest brother Fritz is killed in combat. On August 26, 1918, Lewin is severely wounded, followed by several months of hospitalization while working on his habilitation ("The Concept of Genesis in Physics, Biology and History of Development," 1922). April 1919, released from military service. From 1920 to 1933, teaching and research at the Friedrich Wilhelm University in Berlin (along with Wolfgang Köhler, Kurt Koffka and Max Wertheimer, Lewin belongs to the Berlin School of Gestalt Psychology). After emigrating to the United States in 1933, Lewin initially teaches at Cornell University in Ithaca for two years, then at the University of Iowa. 1944 teaching at the Massachusetts Institute of Technology (MIT) and established the Research Center of Group Dynamics. – The papers of Kurt Lewin are housed in the Psychological History Research Archive of the Fernuniversität Hagen.

Geuter, U.: Polemos panton pater - Militär und Psychologie im Deutschen Reich 1914-1945. In: M. G. Ash/U. Geuter (Hg.): Geschichte der deutschen Psychologie im 20. Jahrhundert. Opladen 1985, 146-171. – Hoffmann, C.: Wissenschaft und Militär. Das Berliner Psychologische Institut und der I. Weltkrieg. In: Psychologie und Geschichte 5, 3/4 (1994), 261-285. – Lück, H. E.: Kurt Lewin. Eine Einführung in sein Werk. Weinheim/Basel 2001. – Marrow, A. J.: The Practical Theorist. The Life and the Work of Kurt Lewin. New York 1969. – Patnoe, S.: A Narrative History of Experimental Social Psychology: The Lewin Tradition. New York (1988). – Schönpflug, W. (Hg.): Kurt Lewin – Person, Werk, Umfeld. Historische Rekonstruktionen und aktuelle Wertungen. Frankfurt am Main 2007.

„Dr. Maria Landsberg <und> Dr. Kurt Lewin, z. Zt. im Felde. Verlobte. Charlottenburg. Im September 1917"

"Dr. Maria Landsberg [and] Dr. Kurt Lewin, currently serving at the front. Engaged. Charlottenburg. In September 1917"

Dr. Maria Landsberg
Dr. Kurt Lewin
z. Zt. im Felde
Verlobte
Charlottenburg
Im September 1917

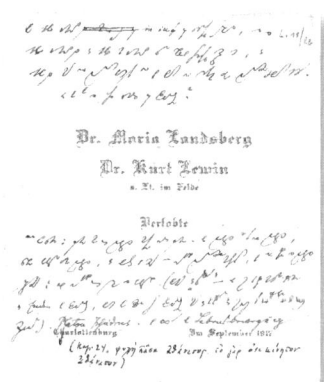

Von Kurt Lewin 1917 versandte Verlobungsanzeige, die Husserl für seine Notizen benutzte

An engagement notice sent by Kurt Lewin in 1917, which Husserl used for his notes

23382 Deutsche Verlustliste. (Nr. 1129.) 8. Mai 1918.

Lewin, Fritz, Ltn. d. R. — 12. 8. Körlin, Kolberg — l. verw.
Lewin, Kurt — 25. 9. Posen — gefallen
Leyk, Paul, Gefr. — 12. 10. Thal, Weltershausen — l. verw.
Lichtenthäler, Reinhold — 17. 4. Roßbach, Oberwesterwald — gefallen.
Lichter, Stephan — 8. 12. Rimshuscheid, Prüm — leicht verw.
Liebe, Franz — 17. 10. Taplaken, Wehlau — leicht verw.

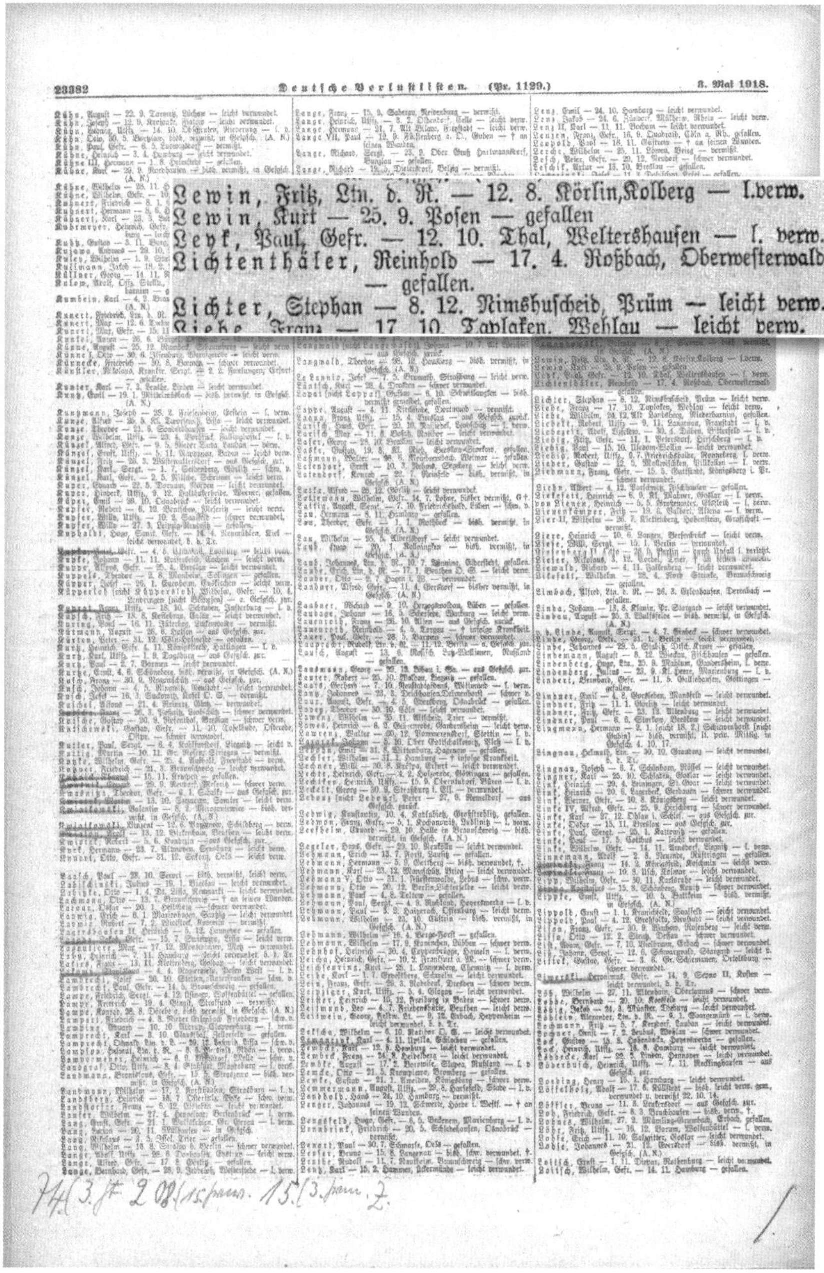

Kurt Lewin wird nach einer schweren Verwundung im August 1918 aus der Armee entlassen. Sein jüngerer Bruder Fritz fällt am 9. August 1918. In der „Deutschen Verlustliste" (siehe den Ausschnitt oben rechts) wird Kurt Lewin mit seinem Bruder Fritz verwechselt und als gefallen gemeldet: „Lewin, Fritz. Lt. d. R. – 12.8. Körlin, Kolberg – l<eicht> verw. Lewin, Kurt – 25.9. Posen – gefallen."

Kurt Lewin was released from the army after a severe injury in August 1918. His younger brother Fritz died in combat on August 9, 1918. In the "German list of causalities" (see the section top right) Kurt Lewin is confused with his brother Fritz and reported as killed: "Lewin, Fritz. Lt. d. R. - 12.8. Körlin, Kolberg - slightly wounded Lewin, Kurt - 25.9. Poznan – killed."

„*Da den Infanteristen in manchen Fällen andere Landschaftsgebilde begegnen mögen, sei erwähnt, daß ich Feldartillerist bin*"

Mitteilungen.

Kriegslandschaft.

Von

Kurt Lewin.

Die folgenden Ausführungen betreffen ein Kapitel der Phänomenologie der Landschaft.

Allgemein sei dies vorausgeschickt: Wenn man etwa einen einzelnen Hügel vor sich hat, der als „Raumgestalt" in der Ebene steht, mit seinem Fuſs unter ihre Oberfläche reichend, so kann man sich auch vorstellen, daſs es sich nur um eine Krümmung der Ebene, um eine Bodenwelle handelt: man kann den Hügel auch als „Flächengestalt" sehen. Oder wenn der Spaziergänger Äcker und Wiesen als Natur im ästhetischen Sinne vor sich sieht, so kann er sich sehr wohl auch die ganz andere Landschaft vorstellen, die der Ackerbauer hier antreffen würde. Auf eine solche Vorstellung hin kann dann zweierlei eintreten. Entweder ändert sich tatsächlich die phänomenologisch wirkliche Landschaft: an Stelle des Raumgestalthügels steht nun wirklich ein Flächengebilde da. In der Regel jedoch behält die neue Landschaft den Charakter als etwas nur Vorgestelltes gegenüber der phänomenologisch wirklichen Landschaft. Diese Position als Vorstellung gegenüber der Wirklichkeit wird auch dadurch nicht beeinträchtigt, daſs man die vorgestellte Landschaft „sieht": Die Tatsache des Wahrgenommenwerdens macht den Flächenhügel noch nicht zu einem wirklichen Flächenhügel, sondern läſst ihm die Stellung eines vorgestellten Gebildes.[1] Auch gegenüber den im folgenden beschriebenen Landschaftsgebilden war ein solches Ersetzen durch andere, vorgestellte Gebilde in der Regel möglich.[2]

---

[1] Legt man den Gebrauch des Wortes Wahrnehmung für die Phänomenologie durch eine Beziehung auf die Wirklichkeit fest, so wäre dieser Sachverhalt so auszudrücken: Das Sehen des Flächenhügels ist kein Wahrnehmen, sondern ein Vorstellen.

[2] Die angegebenen Unterscheidungen mögen zugleich dem Einwand vorbeugen, es handle sich im folgenden um phänomenologische Verdinglichungen psychologischer Prozesse.

Kurt Lewin „Kriegslandschaft", in: Zeitschrift für angewandte Psychologie, Bd. 12, Leipzig 1917, S. 440-447 (Exemplar aus Husserls Privatbibliothek / copy from Husserl's private library)

"Since members of the infantry may in some cases meet with other landscape formations, I ought to mention that I am a field artilleryman"

The following observations form a contribution to the phenomenology of landscape.

To begin with some general remarks: if, for instance, one is confronted by a single hill, which is set into the plain as a "spatial form" with its base below the surface, one can also imagine that it is merely a curvature in the plain, a bump in the ground; one can also see the hill as a "planar form." Or if the pedestrian sees the fields and meadows before him as nature in the aesthetic sense, he can also well imagine the quite different landscape that the farmer would encounter here. Two things can happen after the occurrence of such an idea. Either the phenomenologically real landscape actually changes: instead of the hill as a spatial form, there now really is a planar form. As a rule, though, the new landscape retains the character of something merely imagined as opposed to the phenomenologically real landscape. And this status of idea as opposed to reality is not affected by one's "seeing" of the imagined landscape: the fact that the planar hill is perceived is not enough to make it into a real planar hill, but grants it the status of an imagined formation.* Such substitution of other, imagined formations was also possible, as a rule, for the landscape formations described in the following.**

While a formation's phenomenological properties are not significantly altered by its status as phenomenological reality or unreality, it ought to be noted that I will only give an account of those formations that I have at some stage encountered as real landscape formations.

Since members of the infantry may in some cases meet with other landscape formations, I ought to mention that I am a field artilleryman.

* If the use of the word "perception" in phenomenology is defined by a relationship to reality, then this situation could be expressed as follows: the seeing of the planar mound is not a perception, but an ideation.

** The given differentiations may also serve to repudiate the objection that the following considerations represent phenomenological reifications of psychological processes.

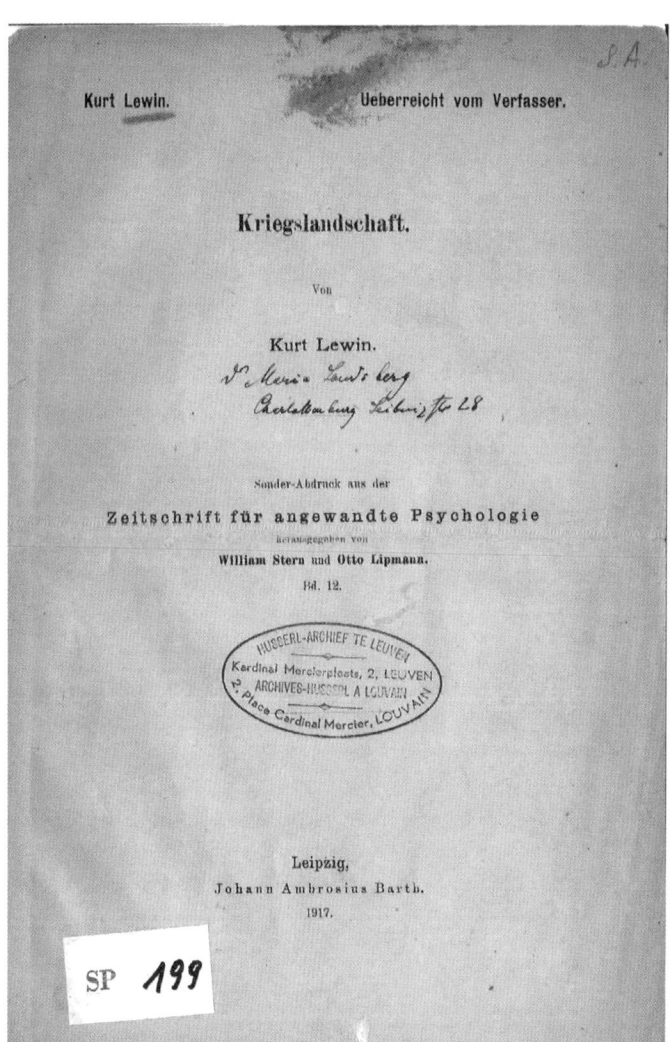

(Kurt Lewin: The Landscape of War. Translated by Jonathan Blower, Art in Translation (2009), 1:2, 199-209)

Hans Lipps (1889-1941)

Hans Lipps: geb. 22. 11. 1889 in Pirna bei Dresden, gef. 10. 9. 1941 bei Dudino (Russland). – 1909 Beginn eines Studiums der Kunstgeschichte, Ästhetik, Architektur und Philosophie in München. 1910-1911 freiwilliges Militärdienstjahr in Dresden. Zwischen SS 1911 und WS 1913/14 Studium der Biologie, Medizin und Philosophie (bei Husserl und Reinach) in Göttingen. 1912 Promotion in Biologie („Über Strukturänderungen von Pflanzen in geändertem Medium"); im Juni 1913 absolviert Lipps die ärztliche Vorprüfung im Fach Medizin. Mitglied der Göttinger Philosophischen Gesellschaft. SS 1914 Fortsetzung des Studiums in Straßburg. 1914-1918 Teilnahme am Krieg, zunächst als Feldhilfsarzt, später als Bataillonsarzt. Kriegseinsätze an der Westfront und vom Oktober 1917 bis Januar 1918 in Russland. Verwundung im Frühjahr 1918. Im November 1918 Entlassung aus dem Kriegsdienst. Fortsetzung des Studiums in Göttingen und Freiburg. 1921 Promotion in Medizin („Über die Wirkung einiger Colchicinderivate"); kurz darauf Habilitation in Philosophie in Göttingen unter der Leitung des Mathematikers Richard Courant („Untersuchungen zur Philosophie der Mathematik"). Zwischenzeitlich immer wieder als Schiffsarzt tätig. 1928 Vertretung des Ordinarius für Philosophie in Marburg, ab 1936 Lehrstuhl in Philosophie in Frankfurt a. M. Im September 1939 wurde Lipps als Arzt zur Wehrmacht eingezogen. – Der Nachlass von Hans Lipps befindet sich in der Bayerischen Staatsbibliothek München.

Hans Lipps als Einjährig-Freiwilliger (ca. 1910/11)

Hans Lipps: born November 22, 1889 in Pirna near Dresden, killed in action on September 10, 1941 in Dudino (Russia). Began study of art history, aesthetics, architecture, and philosophy in Munich in 1909. 1910-1911, voluntary military service year in Dresden. Between 1911 and 1914, studied biology, medicine, and philosophy (with Husserl and Reinach) in Göttingen. 1912, PhD in Biology ("On Structural Changes of Plants in Changed Medium"). June 1913, Lipps completed his preliminary examination in medicine. Member of the Göttingen Philosophical Society. 1914, continuation of studies in Strasbourg. 1914-1918, served in the war, first as a field medical officer, later as a battalion doctor. War operations on the Western Front and from October 1917 to January 1918 in Russia. Wounded, Spring 1918. In November 1918, released from military service. Continuation of studies in Göttingen and Freiburg. 1921 doctorate in medicine ("On the Effects of Some Colchicine Derivatives"). Shortly thereafter, habilitation in philosophy in Göttingen under the direction of the mathematician Richard Courant ("Studies on the Philosophy of Mathematics"). During this time also worked as a ship's doctor. 1928 replacement professor for philosophy in Marburg, starting from 1936, chair in philosophy in Frankfurt. In September 1939, Lipps was drafted into the Wehrmacht as a doctor. – The papers of Hans Lipps are housed in the Bavarian State Library Munich.

Rodi F. u.a. (Hg.): Zum 100. Geburtstag von Hans Lipps: Beiträge zu seiner Biographie. In: Dilthey-Jahrbuch 6 (1989). – Rogler, G.: Die hermeneutische Logik von Hans Lipps und die Begründbarkeit wissenschaftlicher Erkenntnis. Würzburg 1998. – Wewel, M.: Die Konstitution des transzendentalen Etwas im Vollzug des Sehens. Eine Untersuchung im Anschluß an die Philosophie von Hans Lipps und in Auseinandersetzung mit Edmund Husserls Lehre vom „intentionalen Bewußtseinskorrelat". Düsseldorf 1968.

Hans Lipps as a one-year volunteer (circa 1910/11)

„Sehr betrübliche Verluste in unserem phänomenologischen Kreise – Frankfurther u. Clemens"

Göttingen 11. 3. 15
Lieber Herr Dr!
Es freute mich sehr von Ihnen endlich ein Lebenszeichen zu erhalten u. mich nicht mehr um Sie sorgen zu müssen. Möge es Ihnen weiter wohlergehen und mögen Sie mit Ihrer in dieser Zeit so segenbringenden Kunst manchem Wackeren unserer Verwundeten, aber auch wackeren Feinden, hilfreich zur Seite stehen.

Von Dr Reinach haben wir fortgesetzt gute Nachrichten. Von den sehr betrüblichen Verlusten in unserem phänom<enologischen> Kreise – Frankfurt<h>er u. Clemens – haben sie wohl gehört. Von meinen beiden Jungens hat der Jüngere Ende Febr<uar> eine gut heilende Lungenverwundung erlitten, vorläufig liegt er noch in Oostnieuwkerke. Der Ältere ist brav in der Front.

Mit herzlichen Wünschen, auch von meiner Familie,
Ihr
EHusserl

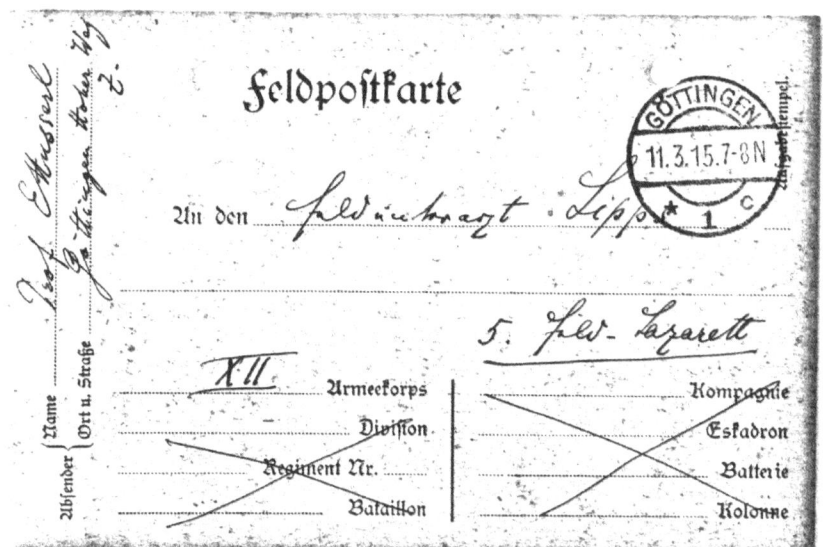

Feldpostkarte von Husserl an Hans Lipps, 11. III. 1915

Field post-card from Husserl to Hans Lipps, 11 March 1915

"Very terrible losses in our phenomenological circle – Frankfurther and Clemens"

Göttingen 11 March 1915
Dear Mr. Dr!
It was very nice to finally get a sign of life from you and to no longer have to worry about you anymore. May you continue to keep well and may you continue with your art which brings so many blessings, as you stand in assistance to these brave wounded soldiers of ours, and even to those valiant enemies.

From Dr. Reinach we continue to get good news. Of the very terrible losses in our phenomenological circle – Frankfurther and Clemens – you have heard. Of my two boys, the youngest suffered end of February a wound to the lungs (which healed well), and for the moment, he's still in Oostnieuwkerke. The older one is valiantly at the front.

With warm wishes, also from my family,
Your,
EHusserl

„Seine Tätigkeit kann als mustergültig bezeichnet werden"

Hamburg 15. 4. 31
Beurteilung für Herrn Dr. Lipps
Herr Dr. Lipps war 1918 Unterarzt im Leib-Grenadierregiment Nr. 100 in der Zeit des schwersten Ringens an der Westfront. Seine Tätigkeit kann als mustergültig bezeichnet werden. Sein aufopferndes sich Einsetzen für die vielen Verwundeten ohne Rücksicht auf eigene Gefahr verdient höchste Anerkennung. L. war auch ein sehr beliebter Kamerad.
Watzdorf
Oberstleutnant a.D.
früher Kommandeur des Leib Gren. Rgts 100.

"His service can be described as exemplary"

Hamburg 15 April 1931
Assessment for Dr. med. Lipps
Dr. Lipps was in 1918 a medical Sergeant in the 100th Leib-Grenadier Regiment during the time of the hardest combat on the Western Front. His service can be described as exemplary. His self-sacrificing commitment to the many wounded regardless of his own peril deserves the highest recognition. Lipps was also a very popular comrade.
Watzdorf
Lieutenant Colonel, retired
former commander in the 100th Leib-Grenadier Regiment.

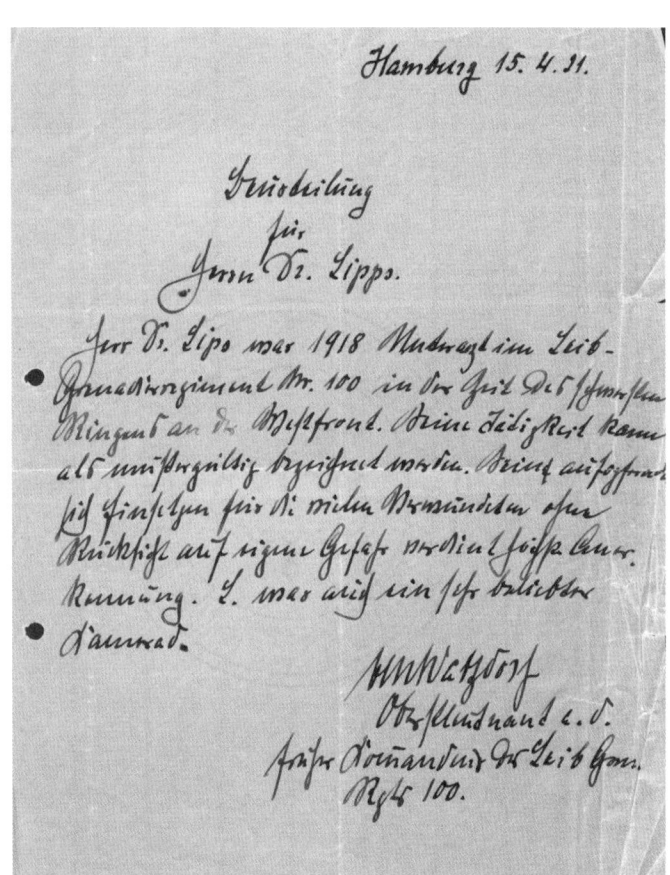

Zeugnis über Hans Lipps' Dienstzeit als Soldat (ausgestellt April 1931)

Certificate of Hans Lipps' service as a soldier (issued April 1931)

Hans Lipps in Uniform mit einer Eule in den Händen (ca. 1917)

Hans Lipps in uniform with an owl in his hands (around 1917)

I.

Man kann nicht schlechthin von „dem Soldaten" reden, sondern nur von dem Soldaten dieses oder jenes Krieges. Denn die soldatische Existenz bestimmt sich durch die Form eines Krieges. Es gibt eine Morphologie des Krieges. „Form" bzw. „Stil" meint dabei nicht das, was kritisch, militärfachwissenschaftlich als der je andere Stand von Taktik und Waffenwirkung zur Erscheinungsform eines Krieges gehört. Sie ist hier von sekundärer Bedeutung. Aber in diesem verschiedenen „Gesicht" eines Krieges drückt sich aus, was weltanschaulich die Zeit bewegt, aus deren Ordnung der Krieg geboren wird. Es wird nicht nur dasselbe verschieden abgehandelt, — es geht um anderes. Man kann die Taktik eines Krieges nicht herausschneiden aus dem, was in einer Zeit allgemein zur Gestaltung drängt.

Gerade der letzte Krieg bedeutet in den Mitteln seiner Durchführung, wie es hier nichts gab, was er sich nicht unterstellt hätte, eine Aufgipfelung dessen, was gewollt und gekonnt wurde in seiner Zeit. Zugleich bezeichnet er eine Wende. Denn dieser letzte Krieg, der kein Ziel hatte, wo kein Konflikt auf Entscheidung drängte, fand auch keine Entspannung: die eine Seite warf die Waffen hin, als sie müde geworden war. Er ist nicht eigentlich fertig geworden. Wir bleiben bezogen auf diesen Krieg. Er hat unsere Zeit bestimmt. 1914 ist ein Einschnitt. Was davor liegt, ist uns unwirklich geworden.

Schon äußerlich fällt der Unterschied auf dieses Krieges gegenüber denen Friedrichs des Großen, Napoleons, 1870/71. Denn wenn wir von der Schlacht bei Tannenberg absehen oder der Siegfriedbewegung 1917 — dieser Krieg war merkwürdig arm an genialen Lösungen. Es gab keine Manöver, die leicht zu übersehen, deren Berechnung man mitmachen kann. Es gibt keine Bilder in diesem Krieg. Das Erfindungsreiche der Taktik stand im

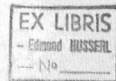

Hans Lipps, „Der Soldat des letzten Krieges", Frankfurt am Main 1935. – Titelblatt und Seite 5 des Exemplars aus Husserls Privatbibliothek mit handschriftlicher Widmung: „Mit verehrungsvollen Grüßen in Dankbarkeit, H. L."

Hans Lipps, "The Soldier of the Last War," title-page and page 5 from Husserl's copy in his private library with the hand-written dedication "Yours sincerely in gratitude"

„Es gibt eine Morphologie des Krieges"

Man kann nicht schlechthin von „dem Soldaten" reden, sondern nur von dem Soldaten dieses oder jenes Krieges. Denn die soldatische Existenz bestimmt sich durch die Form eines Krieges. Es gibt eine Morphologie des Krieges. „Form" bzw. „Stil" meint dabei nicht das, was kritisch, militärfachwissenschaftlich als der je andere Stand von Taktik und Waffenwirkung zur Erscheinungsform eines Krieges gehört. Sie ist hier von sekundärer Bedeutung. Aber in diesem verschiedenen „Gesicht" eines Kriegs drückt sich aus, was weltanschaulich die Zeit bewegt, aus deren Ordnung der Krieg geboren wird. Es wird nicht nur dasselbe verschieden abgehandelt, – es geht um anderes. Man kann die Taktik eines Krieges nicht herausschneiden aus dem, was in einer Zeit allgemein zur Gestaltung drängt.

Gerade der letzte Krieg bedeutet in den Mitteln seiner Durchführung, wie es hier nichts gab, was er sich nicht unterstellt hätte, eine Aufgipfelung dessen, was gewollt und gekonnt wurde in seiner Zeit. Zugleich bezeichnet er eine Wende. Denn dieser letzte Krieg, der kein Ziel hatte, wo kein Konflikt auf Entscheidung drängte, fand auch keine Entspannung: die eine Seite warf die Waffen hin, als sie müde geworden war. Er ist nicht eigentlich fertig geworden. Wir bleiben bezogen auf diesen Krieg. Er hat unsere Zeit bestimmt. 1914 ist ein Einschnitt. Was davor liegt, ist uns unwirklich geworden.

Schon äußerlich fällt der Unterschied auf dieses Kriegs gegenüber denen Friedrich des Großen, Napoleons, 1870/71. Denn wenn wir von der Schlacht bei Tannenberg absehen oder der Siegfriedbewegung 1917 – dieser Krieg war merkwürdig arm an genialen Lösungen. Es gab keine Manöver, die leicht zu übersehen, deren Berechnung man mitmachen kann. Es gibt keine Bilder in diesem Krieg. <…>

(Hans Lipps, Der Soldat des letztes Krieges, S. 5)

"There is a morphology of war"

One can not simply speak of "the soldier," but only of the soldier of this or that war. For the soldier's existence is determined by the form of a war. There is a morphology of war. "Form" as well as "style" do not mean what is understood, from a critical and military studies point of view, as each different in status from tactics and the effect of weapons that belong to the manifestation of war. This [the manifestation] is of secondary importance here. However, in these different "faces," war expresses itself, which moves the world-view of the epoch, from the order in which war emerges. It is not just the same thing that is dealt with differently – it is about something else. One can not cut out the tactics of war from what comes in an epoch generally into creation.

Precisely because the last war represented through its manner of execution, where nothing existed that was not subjugated to the war, a culmination of what could be willed and what could be achieved in its epoch. At the same time, the war represented a turning point. Because in this last war, which did not have a goal, where conflict did not lead to decision, it also could not find any relief: one side threw its weapons away, once it became tired. It didn't come to an end. We remained connected to this war. It determined our time. 1914 is a rupture. What came before has become for us unreal.

Even outwardly, differences of this war appear clearly in contrast to those of Frederick the Great, Napoleon, 1870/71. Because if we abstract from the Battle of Tannenberg or the Siegfried movement in 1917 – this war was strangely impoverished in ingenious solutions. There were no maneuvers that could be easily surveyed, for which calculations could be made. There are no images in this war. […]

Karl Löwith (1897-1973)

Karl Löwith: geb. 9. 1. 1897 in München, gest. 24. 5. 1973 in Heidelberg. – Nach dem Abitur meldet sich Löwith im Oktober 1914 als Kriegsfreiwilliger und kommt nach dreimonatiger Ausbildung zunächst an die französische Front (Peronne); im Mai 1915 wird sein Regiment zum bayerischen Alpenkorps an die österreichisch-italienische Grenze versetzt. 1915 schwere Verwundung bei einer nächtlichen Patrouille, danach zweijährige italienische Kriegsgefangenschaft. 1917 kehrt Löwith nach München zurück und beginnt dort ein Studium der Biologie und Philosophie (u.a. bei Alexander Pfänder und Moritz Geiger); im Frühjahr 1919 Studium an der Freiburger Universität bei Husserl und Heidegger sowie Fortsetzung seines Biologie-Studiums. 1923 Promotion in München bei Geiger („Auslegung von Nietzsches Selbst-Interpretation und Interpretationen"). 1928 Habilitation bei Heidegger („Das Individuum in der Rolle des Mitmenschen"), anschließend Privatdozent in Marburg. 1934 Emigration nach Italien, dort 1934-36 Rockefeller Scholar an der Universität Rom. Wegen seiner ehemals jüdischen Religionszugehörigkeit wird Löwith 1935 in Deutschland die Lehrbefugnis entzogen (bzw. Beurlaubung nach dem Auslaufen der „Frontsoldatregelung"). 1936 Emigration nach Japan, dort bis 1941 Gastprofessor an der Kaiserlichen Universität Sendai, danach Emigration in die USA, dort bis 1949 Professsor für Religionsgeschichte am Hartford Theological Seminary (Connecticut), dann bis 1952 an der New School for Social Research in New York. Danach Rückkehr nach Deutschland und von 1952 bis zu seiner Emeritierung 1964 Professor in Heidelberg.

Karl Löwith: born on January 9, 1897 in Munich, died on May 24, 1973 in Heidelberg. After graduating from high school, Löwith volunteers in October 1914 and after three months' training, arrived at the front in Peronne, France. In May 1915, his regiment is transferred to the Bavarian Alpine Corps on the Austrian-Italian border. In 1915, he was seriously wounded during a night patrol, taken prisoner, and spends two years in an Italian prisoner of war camp. In 1917, Löwith returns to Munich, where he begins to study biology and philosophy (inter alia with Alexander Pfänder and Moritz Geiger). In the spring of 1919, studies at the University of Freiburg under Husserl and Heidegger, and continues his studies in biology. 1923, PhD in Munich with Geiger ("Interpretation of Nietzsche's Self-interpretation and Interpretations"). 1928, habilitation with Heidegger ("The individual in the Role of Fellow Human Beings"). Private lecturer in Marburg until his 1934 emigration to Italy. 1934-1936, Rockefeller Scholar at the University of Rome. Due to his former Jewish religious affiliation, Löwith was deprived of a teaching permission in Germany in 1935 (released from teaching duty after the expiration of the "front-line soldier regulations"). In 1936, emigrated to Japan, there until 1941 visiting professor at the Imperial University of Sendai, then emigration to the United States, until 1949 Professor of Religious History at Hartford Theological Seminary (Connecticut), until 1952 at the New School for Social Research in New York. Returns to Germany and from 1952 until his retirement 1964, Professor in Heidelberg.

Liebsch, B.: Verzeitlichte Welt. Variationen über die Philosophie Karl Löwiths. Würzburg 1995. – Wiebrecht Ries: Karl Löwith. Stuttgart 1992. – Löwith, K.: Mein Leben in Deutschland vor und nach 1933. Ein Bericht. Neu herausgegeben von F.-R. Hausmann, mit einem Vorwort von R. Koselleck, 2. Auflage. Stuttgart 2007. – Wolin, R.: Heidegger's Children: Hannah Arendt, Karl Löwith, Hans Jonas, and Herbert Marcuse. Princeton/Oxford 2001.

„Den Krieg als eine Chance des Lebens und Sterbens willkommen zu heißen"

Als mich der Krieg während unsres Sommeraufenthalts am Starnbergersee in meinem 18. Lebensjahr überraschte, war ich ein Schüler der vorletzten Klasse des Münchner Realgymnasiums. Im Oktober 1914 meldete ich mich freiwillig zum Heer. Nach knapp drei Monaten war ich als Infanterist ausgebildet und kurz vor Weihnachten kam ich mit einem Ersatzbataillon an die französische Front, wo wir bei Peronne die Schützengräben bezogen. – Der Drang zur Emanzipation von der bürgerlichen Enge der Schule und des Zuhause, ein inneres Zerwürfnis mit mir selbst nach dem Bruch meiner ersten Freundschaft, der Reiz des „gefährlich Leben", für das uns Nietzsche begeistert hatte, die Lust sich ins Abenteuer zu stürzen und sich zu erproben, und nicht zuletzt die Erleichterung des eigenen, durch Schopenhauer bewusst gewordenen Daseins in der Teilnahme an einem es umfassenden Allgemeinen – solche und ähnliche Motive bestimmten mich, den Krieg als eine Chance des Lebens und Sterbens willkommen zu heissen. <…>

Wir schossen mit unsern neuen Zielfernrohrgewehren abwechselnd auf Gemsen und Italiener, die zu bestimmten Tageszeiten über eine Brücke des Travenanza-Bachs das Essen zu einer Feldwache trugen. Mein Hauptmann wünschte zur Feststellung des Feindes Gefangene zu machen, und ich meldete mich zur Führung einer 3 Mann starken Patrouille. Wir stiegen nachts das steile Tal hinab und überquerten den Bach. Gegen 4 Uhr morgens lösten sich die dichten Nebel des Waldes plötzlich auf und wir befanden uns unversehens direkt gegenüber einer etwa 20 Mann starken Abteilung Alpini. Ein unbemerktes Zurück über den Bach war nicht möglich, ich ging hinter einem Baum in Anschlag, verständigte durch Zeichen meine Leute, zielte und feuerte. Im nächsten Augenblick war ich wie von einem atemberaubenden Schlag auf die Brust getroffen. Der Anprall hatte mich mit dem Gesicht zur Erde platt auf den Boden geworfen. Ein leises Gefühl sickernden Blutes und die Unfähigkeit mich mit den Händen vom Erdboden zu erheben, liessen mich blitzschnell erkennen, dass ich nicht mehr zurück konnte und von nun ab in den Händen des Feindes war. Das Schicksal meiner 3 Kameraden erfuhr ich erst später durch Briefe: einer hatte auf der Flucht einen tödlichen Bauchschuss erhalten und die beiden andern fielen tags darauf bei einer zweiten Patrouille. Unter den von meinem Vater aufbewahrten Briefen fand ich einen Bericht des Soldaten F., worin dieser meinen Eltern den „Heldentod" ihres Sohnes beschreibt. Sein höchst phantasievoll ausgeschmückter und sentimentaler Bericht enthält nicht ein wahres Wort, aber sämtliche Zeitungsphrasen, und doch bin ich überzeugt, dass er das selber alles geglaubt hat. – Mir schoss im Augenblick der Verwundung und der Erkenntnis der Situation der triviale Gedanke durch den Kopf: „wie schade um das schöne Paket!", das ich tags zuvor von zu Hause bekommen hatte und welches ausgezeichnete Zigaretten enthielt, die nun für immer dahin waren. Dann verlor ich das Bewusstsein und fand mich wieder auf einer Tragbahre in dem gespenstisch flackernden Licht eines düstern Unterstandes, wo sich ein Arzt freundlich um mich bemühte, während ein junger Dolmetscher meine Habseligkeiten an sich nahm. <…>

Im 2. Monat unterbrach ein heller Tag die Einsamkeit meines nur durch Schmerzen unterschiedenen Daliegens: die väterliche Liebe und Energie hatte das Wunder vollbracht, den einzigen Sohn (meine Schwester war schon 1908 im Alter von 16 Jahren gestorben) im Feindesland für einige Stunden besuchen zu dürfen. <…> Nach 8 Monaten Krankenlager wurde ich in ein österreichisches Kriegsgefangenenlager verbracht, ein kleines Kastell am Meeresstrand von Finalmarina, wo ich mich allmählich erholte, obschon die verletzte Lunge so schlecht verheilt war, dass sie für immer untätig blieb.

(Aus: Karl Löwith, „Mein Leben in Deutschland vor und nach 1933. Ein Bericht". Neu hg. von Frank-Rutger Hausmann, Stuttgart/Weimar 2007, S. 3 ff.)

"To welcome the war as a chance of life and death"

When the war caught me by surprise during my summer holidays on Lake Starnberg in my 18th year, I was a student in the next to last year at the Munich Realgymnasium. In October 1914, I reported as a volunteer to the army. After less than three months, I was trained as an infantryman and shortly before Christmas I arrived at the front in France with a replacement battalion, where we entered into the trenches in Peronne. The urge for emancipation from the bourgeois confines of school and home, an inner quarrel with myself after the break of my first friendship, the charm of the "dangerous life" for which Nietzsche had inspired us, the desire to throw oneself into adventure, and, not least of all, the release of one's own existence, to which [we] were awoken by Schopenhauer, by participating in something encompassing and universal – these and comparable motivations determined me to welcome the war as a chance of life and death. [...]

We used our new riflescopes to shoot alternately at mountain goats and Italians, who at certain times of the day carried food over a bridge over the Travenanza stream to a guard post. My Captain wished to capture the enemy, and I volunteered to lead a 3-man patrol. We descended the steep valley at night and crossed the stream. Around 4 o'clock in the morning, the dense fog of the forest suddenly dissolved and we found ourselves suddenly opposite a 20-man strong group of Alpini.[1] As it was impossible to return back over the stream unnoticed, I went behind a tree and leveled my rifle and communicated with my people through signs, aimed and fired. The next moment I was struck by a stunning blow to the chest. The impact had knocked me down face first to the ground. A faint feeling of seeping blood and the inability to lift my hands from the ground made me realize in a flash that I could not go back and from now on was in the hands of the enemy. The fate of my three comrades I learned only later through letters: one had received a mortal shot in the stomach while retreating and the other two fell in combat while on a second patrol the following day. Among the letters kept by my father, I found a report by a soldier F., who describing to my parents the "heroic death" of their son. His highly imaginative, embroidered, and sentimental account does not contain one word that is true, but contains a host of news-paper phrases, and yet I am convinced, that he believed everything himself. In the moment of being shot and awareness of the situation, the trivial thought flashed through my mind: "what a pity for the beautiful package!", which I had received the day before from home, and which contained excellent cigarettes, which were now gone forever. I then lost consciousness and found myself lying on a stretcher in the ghostly flickering light of a gloomy shelter, where a doctor gently cared for me, while a young interpreter took my belongings. [...]

In the second month, one bright day the loneliness of my painful laying-there was interrupted: fatherly love and energy had accomplished a miracle: to receive permission to visit his only son (my sister had died in 1908 at the age of 16) in the enemy country for a few hours' visit. [...] After 8 months in the hospital, I was taken to an Austrian POW camp in a small fort on the sea at the beach of Finalmarina, where I gradually recovered, although the injured lung healed so poorly that it remained forever inactive.

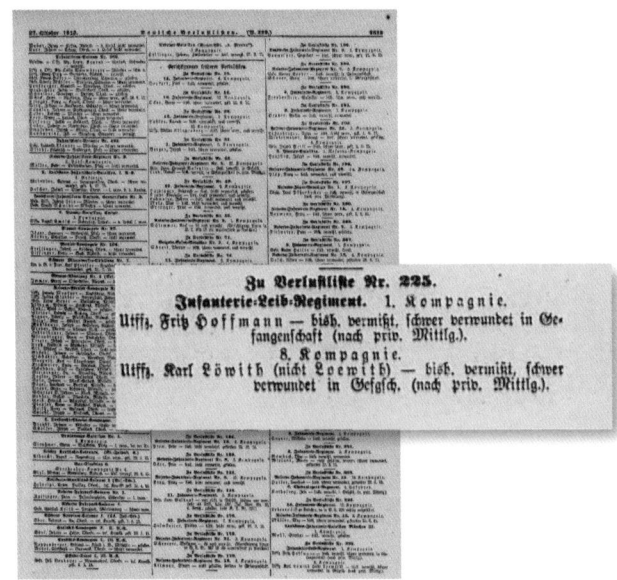

Ausschnitt aus den „Deutschen Verlustlisten", 27. Oktober 1915: „8. Kompagnie, Unteroffizier Karl Löwith (nicht Loewith) – bisher vermißt, schwer verwundet in Gefangenschaft (nach privater Mitteilung)"

Extract from "German casuality lists," 27 October 1915: "8th Company, Sergeant Karl Löwith (not Loewith) – considered up to now missing, gravely wounded in prisoner of war camp (according to private communication)"

---

1 Translator's note: an Italian mountain troop.

„Dabei hatte er dem Tod schon ins Auge geschaut"

Im Winter <…> war ich öfters mit dem etwa gleichaltrigen Karl Löwith zusammen, mit dem ich Erinnerungen an München austauschen konnte, obwohl er Pfänder nicht sehr schätzte. Überhaupt brachte er mich oft fast zur Verzweiflung durch seine Kritik an allem und jedem, seine ständigen Zweifel. Dabei hatte er dem Tod schon ins Auge geschaut: er war an der italienischen Front mit einer Patrouille im Frühnebel geradewegs in die feindlichen Stellungen geraten und im Geschützfeuer der Italiener als einziger mit dem Leben davon gekommen, wenn auch schwer verwundet. Es sei seltsam, was man in so einem Augenblick denke, bemerkte er manchmal, er habe nur nach seinen Zigaretten getastet! Er war dann lange in italienischer Gefangenschaft und lernte dadurch das Land und die Sprache lieben. Plötzlich wurde er eines Tages ausgetauscht und kam als Totgesagter zu seinen beglückten Eltern zurück: in einer Schublade fand er die Beileids- und Trauerbriefe, die diesen auf die Todesanzeige hin geschickt worden waren, „Es ist irgendwie verpflichtend, wenn man da liest, welch' gute Meinung die Menschen von einem hatten, was sie alles von einem erwarteten!" pflegte er gedankenvoll zu sagen. Eine jüngere Schwester war ebenfalls gestorben, und die Mutter hing nun mit abgöttischer Liebe an dem wiedergeschenkten Sohn.

(Aus: Gerda Walther: „Zum anderen Ufer. - Vom Marxismus und Atheismus zum Christentum", Remagen 1960, S. 212 f.)

"He had already looked death in the eye"

In the winter, I was often with Karl Löwith (we were nearly the same age), with whom I could exchange memories about Munich, even though he did not appreciate Pfänder very much.

In general, he often brought me close to despair with criticism of everything and everyone, his constant doubts. He had already looked death in the eye: on the Italian front, he was underway with a patrol in the early morning fog and arrived at an enemy position and was the only one who survived the Italians' fire, even though he was badly wounded. It's strange what one thinks of in such a moment, he would often remark, [as] he had [then] only reached for his cigarettes! He was then in Italian captivity for a long time and thus learned to love the country and the language. Suddenly, he was exchanged one day and came back to his fortunate parents as a man back from the dead: in a drawer he found the condolences and mourning letters which had been sent in response to [his] obituary, "it is somehow compulsory, when you read these, what such a good opinion people had of you, what they all expected of you!" he used to say thoughtfully. A younger sister had also died, and the mother was now hanging on in doting love for the returned son.

Gerda Walther (1897-1977; Schülerin von Alexander Pfänder und Edmund Husserl) berichtet in ihrer Autobiographie von den Kriegserlebnissen ihres Kommilitonen

A report by Gerda Walther (1897 – 1977) in her autobiography about Karl Löwith's war-experiences. Walther studied with Alexander Pfänder und Edmund Husserl.

Dietrich Mahnke (1884-1939)

Dietrich Mahnke: geb. 17. 10. 1884 in Verden an der Aller, gest. 25. 7. 1939 bei Fürth. – SS 1902-WS 1905/06 Studium der Mathematik, Physik und Philosophie (u.a. bei Husserl) in Göttingen. 1911-14 als Oberlehrer an einem Gymnasium in Stade. Teilnahme am Krieg als Leutnant beim Reserve-Infanterie-Regiment 75 zuerst als Zugführer der 9. Kompanie, dann von März 1915 bis Oktober 1916 als Führer der 11. Kompanie an der Westfront. September 1916 Verwundung. Mahnke setzt sich in mehreren Veröffentlichungen mit dem Krieg auseinander (z.B. 1917: „Der Wille zur Ewigkeit. Gedanken eines deutschen Kriegers über den Sinn des Geisteslebens"; 1932/35 verfasst er die Geschichte seines Regiments: „Kriegstaten und Schicksale des Res.-Inf.-Regiments 75. 1914/18"). Mit Husserl führt er einen auch philosophisch bedeutenden Briefwechsel. 1918-1922 Studienrat in Stade; ab 1923 Oberstudienrat in Greifswald. 1922 Promotion bei Husserl („Leibnizens Synthese von Universalmathematik und Individualmetaphysik"), 1926 Habilitation in Greifswald („Neue Einblicke in die Entdeckungsgeschichte der höheren Analysis"), 1927 Lehrstuhl in Marburg. – Der Nachlass von Dietrich Mahnke befindet sich in der Universitätsbibliothek Marburg.

Dietrich Mahnke: born on October 17, 1884 in Verden on the Aller, died on July 25, 1939 in Fürth. From 1902 to 1906, studied mathematics, physics, and philosophy (among others, with Husserl) in Göttingen. 1911-1914, senior teacher at a high school in Stade. Served in the war as a Lieutenant in the 75th Reserve Infantry Regiment and as platoon leader of the 9th Company; from March 1915 to October 1916, Commander of the 11th Company on the Western Front. Wounded in September 1916. During the war, Mahnke writes several publications: "The Will to Eternity. Thoughts of a German Warrior on the Meaning of Intellectual life" (1917); "The Acts of War and Destinies of the 75th Reserve Infantry Regiment 75. 1914/18" (1932-1935). With Husserl, he exchanges philosophically important letters. 1918-1922, lecturer in Stade; from 1923, senior teacher in Greifswald. 1922, PhD with Husserl ("Leibniz's Synthesis of Universal Mathematics and Individual Metaphysics"), 1926, habilitation in Greifswald ("New Insights into the History of the Discovery of Higher Analysis"), 1927, chair in Marburg. – The papers of Dietrich Mahnke are housed in the University Library Marburg.

Tilitzki, C.: Die deutsche Universitätsphilosophie in der Weimarer Republik und im Dritten Reich. 2 Bände. Berlin 2002, 256-260. – Wohltmann, H.: Dietrich Mahnke (1884-1939). In: Niedersächsische Lebensbilder 3 (1957), 157-166. – Zaunick, R.: Zum Gedächtnis von Dietrich Mahnke (1884-1939). In: Mitteilungen zur Geschichte der Medizin, der Naturwissenschaften und der Technik 38 (1939), 353-356.

Dietrich Mahnke (ca. 1930)

Dietrich Mahnke (around 1930)

„Unbesiegbar durch Reinheit der Gesinnung und Festigkeit des Willens"

Göttingen 3. VIII. 14.
Werter Freund!
Vom Herzen danke ich Ihnen für die Karte, die Sie mir von Hannover-Bahnhof aus schrieben. Diese Zeilen warmen Gedenkens, so ganz erfüllt von der großen Gesinnung, die diese große Zeit fordert, haben mir sehr wohlgethan. Auch wir sind hier bemüht in Wollen u. Thun die nötige Hingabe zu üben. Meine beiden Jungens, obschon noch nicht so ganz über die Jahre des Wachsens hinaus, haben sich als Kriegsfreiwillige gemeldet u. werden soeben in der Kaserne untersucht, auch meine Tochter will sich zu Diensten melden. Überall ist hier Begeisterung, tiefer Ernst, feste Entschlossenheit, und so ist Gott in und mit uns. Ich wollte Ihnen seit Wochen schreiben und für Ihre schöne Zusendung danken. Mit großem Interesse habe ich das so liebevoll gezeichnete Bild des trefflichen Rector Cassmann aufgenommen; die Schrift gefiel mir so gut, u. dieser Beitrag zur Gesch<ichte> des Schulwesens erschien mir so lehrreich, daß ich sie bei Gelegenheit Herr Geh. Rat Reinhart (vom Unterr<ichts>-Ministerium) geben wollte, mit dem ich ab u. zu fr<eundlichen> Verkehr habe. Doch nun gilt es die Blicke der Gegenwart zu<zu>wenden u. in ihr zu handeln. Meine wärmsten Segenswünsche begleiten Sie. Es thut mir wohl einen Mann wie Sie an der Vorderfront zu wissen u. glauben zu dürfen, daß Tausende u. Tausende deutsche Männer unbesiegbar durch Reinheit der Gesinnung und Festigkeit des Willens für unser Volk einstehen, ihm die Führer sind u. es unbesiegbar machen.
Vom Herzen
Ihr alter Lehrer u. Freund
EHusserl

"Invincible through purity of mind and firmness of will"

Göttingen 3 August 1914
Dear friend!
I thank you from the heart for the card you wrote to me from the Hannover train station. These lines of warm remembrance, so full of the magnificient attitude demanded by these great times, have been very good for me. We are also determined in will and deed to do the necessary sacrifices. Both of my boys, even though not very much beyond the years of growth, have reported as war-volunteers and were immediately taken to the barracks for examination, and even my daughter wants to report for duty. Everywhere there is here enthusiasm, profound earnestness, firm determination, and so God is in and with us. I wanted to write to you for weeks now, and thank you for your nice mail. With great interest I have taken the very instructive sketched image of the excellent Rector Cassmann. I liked his writing so well and his contribution to the history of the school system seemed so instructive to me that, on occasion, I would take it to Mr. Privy Councilor Reinhart (from the Ministry of Education), with whom I have friendly interaction. But now, we must turn our eyes to the present and to act on the present. My warmest blessings accompany you. It does me well to know that a man like you is at the front and to believe that thousands and thousands of German men remain invincible through their purity of mind and firmness of will to fight for our nation, that they are leaders of the nation and make the nation invincible.
From the heart,
Your old teacher and friend,
EHusserl

Postkarte von Husserl an Dietrich Mahnke, 3. VIII. 1914

Postcard from Husserl to Dietrich Mahnke, 3 August 1914

„Wir neiden den Kämpfern die Hingabe mit Leib u. Leben"

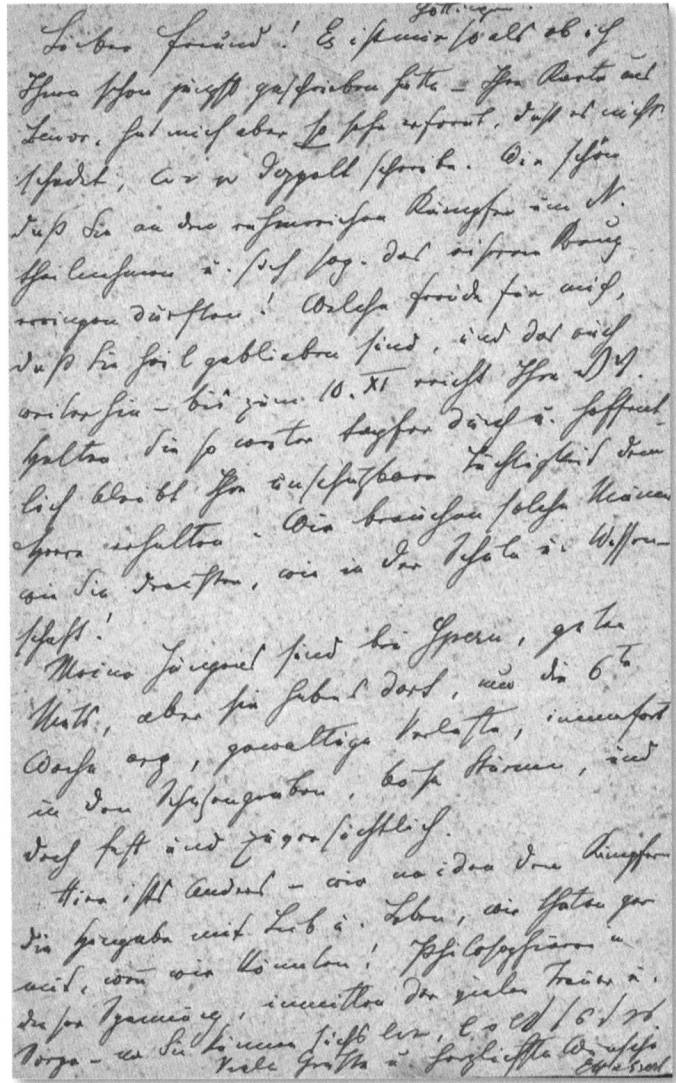

Feldpostkarte von Husserl an Dietrich Mahnke, 27. XI. 1914

Field post-card from Husserl to Dietrich Mahnke, 27 November 1914

Göttingen
Lieber Freund!
Es ist mir so als ob ich Ihnen schon jüngst geschrieben hätte – Ihre Karte aus Beuvr<y> hat mich aber so sehr erfreut, daß es nicht schadet, wenn ich Ihnen doppelt schreibe. Wie schön, daß Sie an den ruhmreichen Kämpfen um N<amur> theilnehmen u. sich sog<ar> das eiserne Kreuz erringen durften! Welche Freude für mich, daß Sie heil geblieben sind, und das auch weiterhin – bis zum 10. XI. reicht Ihre Nachricht. Halten Sie so weiter tapfer durch u. hoffentlich bleibt Ihre unschätzbare Tüchtigkeit dem Heere erhalten. Wir brauchen solche Männer wie Sie draußen, wie in der Schule u. Wissenschaft!

Meine Jungens sind bei Ypern, guten Muts, aber sie habens dort, nun die 6te Woche, arg, gewaltige Verluste, immerfort in den Schützengräben, böse Stürme, und doch fest und zuversichtlich.

Hier ists Anders – wir neiden den Kämpfern die Hingabe mit Leib u. Leben, wir thäten gar mit, wenn wir könnten! Philosophieren in dieser Spannung, inmitten der vielen Trauer u. Sorge – na Sie können sichs denken, daß es damit nicht so gut geht.
Viele Grüße u. herzlichste Wünsche

EHusserl

"We envy the fighters' devotion with body and life"

Göttingen
Dear friend!
It seems to me that I have written to you recently. Your card from Beuvry gave me great joy, so that it doesn't matter that I write to you twice. How nice that you take part in the glorious battles around Namur and have even won the Iron Cross! What a joy for me that you have remained healthy, and continue to do so. Your messages reached me until the 10th of November. Remain steadfast and firm, and hopefully your invaluable efficiency will remain with the army. We need such men as you out there, as we do for school and science!

My boys are in Ypres, they are of good cheer, but they have there, now in their 6th week, terrible, grave losses, always in the trenches, bad storms, and yet are firm and confident.

Here, things are different – we envy the fighters' devotion with body and life, we would join in, if we could! To do philosophy in these tense times, in the midst of so much mourning and concern – well, you can imagine how things are here not faring so well.

Greetings and warmest wishes,

EHusserl

„Wir sind wahrhaftig zum Siege berufen"

<…> Wenn Sie wieder ins Feld gehen, tun Sie es nur in Zuversicht auf Deutschland und Ihren eigenen guten Stern. Wenn man die niedrig verleumderische Antwort auf unser würdig-ernstes Friedensanerbieten liest, steigt einem die Schamröte ins Gesicht. Wir sind wahrhaftig zum Siege berufen und werden hoffe ich seiner gewürdigt werden.
Vom Herzen
Ihr alter Lehrer
EHusserl

"We are truly called to victory"

[...] When you go back again to the front, do so only with confidence in Germany and your own lucky star. When one reads the base and slanderous response to our dignified and serious peace offerings, a blush of shame rushes to one's face. We are truly called to victory and I hope that it shall be honored.
From the heart,
Your old teacher,
EHusserl

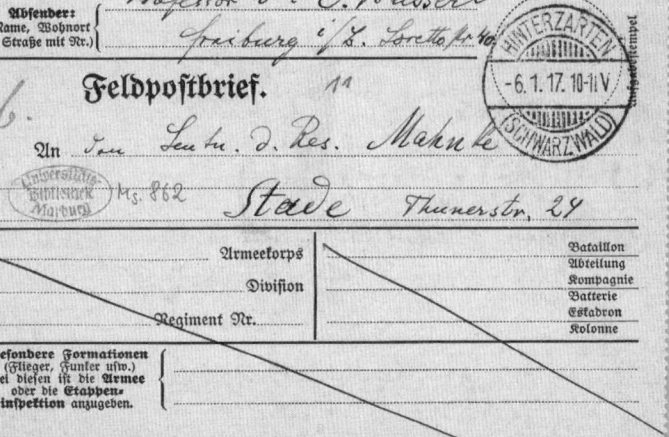

Schlussteil eines Feldpostbriefes von Husserl an Dietrich Mahnke, 5. I. 1917

Concluding section from a field post-letter from Husserl to Dietrich Mahnke, 5 January 1917

„Im Kriege, sagt man wohl, verstummt die Philosophie"

Einführung

Der Krieger und die Ewigkeit.
Im Kriege, sagt man wohl, verstummt die Philosophie. Die Unrast des Lebens im Felde, die endlosen Märsche von Ort zu Ort, das Gewühl des Kriegslagers und das Toben der Feldschlacht lassen keine Ruhe zu stillem Grübeln und Zusammenfassen der Gedanken, wie es dem Wahrheitsforscher Lebensbedürfnis ist. Ist nicht das rastlose Vorwärtsstürmen siegreicher Heere gerade entgegengesetzt dem Ideal des friedlichen Gelehrten, der es liebt, stehen zu bleiben und nach dem ruhenden Pol in der Erscheinungen Flucht zu suchen, nach den ewigen Ideen, die bestehen im Wechsel des Geschehens? Ja, ist nicht das Leben der Gedanken ein entbehrlicher, vielleicht gar schädlicher Luxus für den Soldaten, der täglich und stündlich seiner ganzen Aufmerksamkeit bedarf, um nur sein physisches Dasein, sein leibliches Leben zu schützen und zu erhalten?

Und doch ist, anders angesehen, gerade dem Krieger geistige Vertiefung, sei es Religion, sei es Philosophie, besonders nötig. Niemandem ist ja das handgreifliche, unmittelbare Erleben der Vergänglichkeit aller irdischen Güter so beständig nahe wie ihm, niemand bedarf daher auch des zuversichtlichen Ausblicks zum Reiche der ewigen Wahrheiten und Werte dringlicher als er für sein tägliches Leben. Eine einzige schwere Granate, und ein schönes Haus hier in Lens stürzt zusammen und begräbt unter seinen Trümmern das ganze Hab und Gut einer Familie, den Erwerb eines arbeitsvollen Lebens. Eine einzige Mine im Schützengraben, und tot oder verwundet liegen auf dem Boden alle Posten, die zwischen den beiden benachbarten Schulterwehren nach dem Feinde ausschauten. Und solches Erlebnis hat der Krieger nicht einmal, sondern es wird ihm zur Gewohnheit wie das tägliche Brot. Er steht mit dem „Gevatter Tod" auf du und du und weiß nur vom eignen kleinen Lebenslichtlein nicht, wie bald es ausgebrannt sein wird – gleich dem Paten des Todes, von dem das Märchen erzählt.

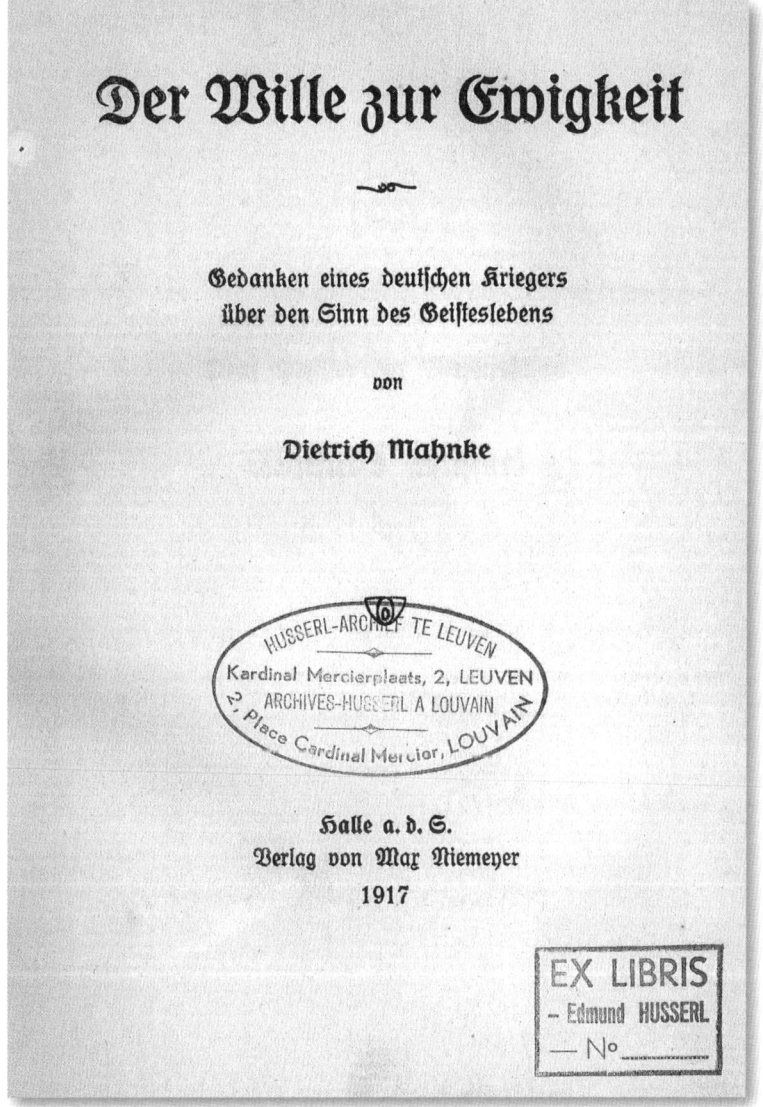

Dietrich Mahnke: „Der Wille zur Ewigkeit. Gedanken eines deutschen Kriegers über den Sinn des Geisteslebens". Halle a.d.S. 1917. – Exemplar aus Husserls Privatbibliothek mit der Widmung: „Dem Meister der Wesensschau Edmund Husserl in treuer Ergebenheit sein dankbarer Schüler Dietrich Mahnke. La Louvière (Belgien), 1. Juli 1917."

Dietrich Mahnke, "The Will to Eternity. Reflections of a German Warrior on the Meaning of Spiritual Life." This example from Husserl's private library, with the dedication: "To the Master of the Intuition of Essences, Edmund Husserl, in loyal devotion from his grateful student Dietrich Mahnke. La Louvière (Belgium), 1 July 1917."

Wenn die feindliche Artillerie sich auf unsern Schützengraben einschießt, erst zwar zu weit, dann zu kurz, jetzt aber gerade recht, wenn nun Schuß auf Schuß genau „sitzt" und Lücke auf Lücke in die Reihe der Kameraden reißt, wenn man dann unaufhörlich neue Eisenballen voller Zerstörungsenergie anheulen hört und der instinktive Lebenswille mit angstvollem Sträuben sich fragt: ist dies nun deine Granate, erfüllt sich jetzt dein Lebensschicksal? – ja, dann braucht man einen festen Halt, um sich in der Brandung der Grauensgefühle aufrecht halten zu können. Man bedarf eines Ewigkeitswertes, der alles zeitlich Vergängliche überdauert, um dem lauernden Tode gelassen ins Angesicht schauen zu können. Man würde der blassen Verzweiflung erliegen, wenn man nicht sein flüchtiges Dasein tief unter den Meereswellen des Lebens verankert wüßte im Felsengrund einer Ideenwelt, die durch alle Stürme des irdischen Ringes in ihrer erhabenen, göttlichen Ruhe nicht gestört werden kann.

Ein dauernd angespanntes elastisches Band wird schlaff; soll unser Geist in der unaufhörlichen Anspannung der Todeserwartung seine Elastizität bewahren, so muß er die Fähigkeit haben, sich mitten im Heulen der Granaten in ein geistiges Land des Friedens zu erheben. Will man stundenlang neben einem bergestiefen Abgrund herschreiten, ohne vom Schwindel hinabgerissen zu werden, so muß man vorwärts und aufwärts schauen, dahin, wo, unerreicht vom Hauch der Grüfte, der Bergesgipfel in die reinen Himmelslüfte ragt.

Der Krieger braucht Ewigkeitsglauben im Dräuen der Vergänglichkeit. Er braucht Religion – denn Religion ist Ewigkeitshoffnung – er braucht Philosophie – denn Philosophie ist Ewigkeitsdenken, ist Welt- und Lebensbetrachtung sub specie aeterni. Mit einem Worte, er bedarf des inneren, geistigen Lebens, denn der Sinn alles Geisteslebens ist der Wille zur Ewigkeit. Das ist die tiefste Erfahrung, die manche Kampftage voller Angst und Todesgefahr mir fester und fester eingeprägt haben und die dann in den langen Monaten geduldigen Ausharrens im Stellungskriege mit ihren häufigen Anlässen zur Selbstbesinnung aus der Ahnung drangvoller Stunden zu klarer, dauernder Überzeugung geworden ist. <…>

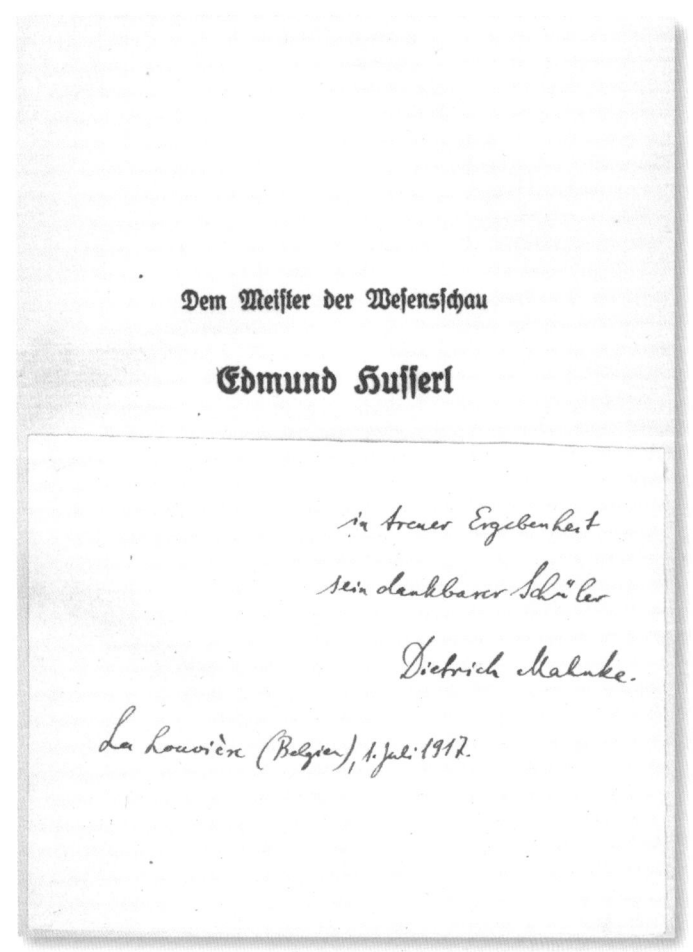

Auszug aus: Dietrich Mahnke, Der Wille zur Ewigkeit, S. 1-4.

Extract from Dietrich Mahnke, Der Wille zur Ewigkeit, *1-4.*

"In war, it is well said, philosophy goes silent"

Introduction

The warrior and eternity.
In war, it is well said, philosophy goes silent. The restlessness of life in the field, the endless marches from place to place, the bustle of the war camp, and the raging battle of the field leave no peace for quiet pondering and summarizing of thinking, as the truth-seeker's need for life is. Is not the restless storming of victorious armies just counterposed to the ideal of the peaceful scholar who loves to stand still and seek refuge in the phenomenon of a calming orientation within appearances, aligned according to eternal ideas, existing within the change of events? Yes, is not the life of thought a dispensable, perhaps even detrimental luxury for the soldier, who needs every day and hour all his attention to protect and preserve only his physical existence, his physical life?

And yet, in other words, the warrior's spiritual deepening, be it in religion or philosophy, is especially necessary. Nobody is ever so close to the tangible, immediate experience of the transience of all earthly goods as he is; no one therefore needs the confident outlook to the realm of eternal truths and values more urgently than he does for his daily life. A single heavy grenade, and a beautiful house here in Lens crashes and is buried under its rubble, with all the belongings of a family and the acquisition of a busy life. A single mine in the trench, and those in the listening posts, who are looking out for the enemy between the neighboring traverse, are lying dead and wounded on the ground. And the warrior doesn't have this experience just once, but it becomes an habit for him just like daily bread. He stands next to "Father Death" in an intimate relation and knows nothing of his own tiny light of life, how soon it might burn out, just as with the godparents of death in the fairy tale.

When the enemy artillery launches itself against our trenches, first too far, then too short, but now just right, if now a shot "sits precisely" and tears a gap in a row of comrades, then you will incessantly [hear] how new iron balls full of destructive energy scream, and the instinctive will to live with fearful hesitancy asks: is this now your grenade, is your fate now to be fulfilled? Yes, then you need a firm hold in order to be able to hold up in a surge of horrors. One needs an everlasting value that outlasts everything transient in time in order to be able to calmly face a death lurking around the corner. One would succumb to pale desperation, if one did not know that one's fleeting existence is deeply anchored under the ocean waves of life in the rock bottom of a world of ideas, which can not be disturbed by all the storms of earthly struggle in its sublime, divine calm.

A permanently strained elastic band becomes limp. If our mind is to maintain its elasticity in the constant tension of the expectation of death, it must have the capacity to rise to a spiritual land of peace in the midst of the scream of grenades. If one wants to walk for hours alongside an overburdened abyss without being torn down by vertigo, one must look forward and upward to where, unmatched by the breath of the tombs, the summit of the mountain rises into the pure air of the heavens.

The warrior needs faith in eternity in the thrill of transience. He needs religion, because religion is the eternity of hope; he needs philosophy, because philosophy is the eternity of thinking; it is the world and life as considered sub specie aeterni. In a word, he needs the inner, spiritual life, for the purpose of all spiritual life is the will to eternity. This is the deepest experience which many days of battle, full of fear and danger of death, have impressed on me firmly and even more firmly, and which, over long months of patient endurance in the war of the trenches with its frequent occasions for self-reflection, has become clear and enduring during the foreboding of long hours. [...]

Dietrich Mahnke

„Ich liebe dieses Büchlein und möchte es in vieler Hände sehen und auf vieler Herzen wirken lassen"

Freiburg i/B. 19. VII. 17.
Lieber Freund!
<…> Sehr erstaunt bin ich von Niemeyer kein Exemplar Ihres „Willens zur Ewigkeit" erhalten zu haben. Ich hatte noch ein Beiblatt zur Empfehlung des Buchs für die phänomenologisch Interessierten entworfen, das auch gedruckt worden ist (als ein von mir an den Verlag geschriebener Brief). Ist denn das Buch noch nicht zur Versendung gelangt? Den Text habe ich mir nach Ihrer letzten Korrektur zusenden lassen und ich brauche nicht zu sagen, wie sehr mich Ihr warmer Widmungsbrief freut – der es aber natürlich unmöglich gemacht hat, daß ich selbst dem Buch ein empfehlendes Vorwort schrieb. Ich liebe dieses Büchlein und möchte es in vieler Hände sehen und auf vieler Herzen wirken lassen. Im ganzen entspricht es, im Stile der Gedankenführung, meinen Überzeugungen, aber es fehlt auch nicht an Differenzen, über die ich mich zur Zeit nicht aussprechen kann. <…>

Ich möchte Sie bitten Ihre Schriften, besonders das kleine Büchlein an Philosophen zu versenden, die irgendwie sich für die neue Richtung interessieren. So an Natorp - Marburg, Stumpf - Berlin, Volkelt - Leipzig, Eucken - Jena, Misch in Göttingen (mein Nachfolger), Pfänder und Geiger (München), Reinach - Göttingen, Hensel - Erlangen, Frischeisen-Köhler - Halle a/S. (Die Kantstudien sind eigentlich in aller Händen, die zugehörigen Schriften werden nicht leicht übersehen, aber hier besteht die Gefahr für das kleine Kriegsbuch.) Schreiben Sie doch auch eine Selbstanzeige desselben für die Kantstudien.
In einer Woche schließe ich die Vorlesungen und gehe etwa d<en> 28. d<ieses> in den Schwarzwald (Bernau). Wie haben die aufregenden politischen Vorgänge der letzten Zeit auf Sie gewirkt?
Ich grüße Sie vom Herzen
Ihr
EHusserl

"I love this little book and would like to see it in many hands and see its impact on many hearts"

Dear friend!
[...] I am very surprised that Niemeyer did not send me a copy of your "Will to Eternity." I had also written a supplement to the recommendation for the book for the phenomenologically interested, which was also printed (as was a letter written by me to the publisher). Has the book not yet been shipped? I have had the text sent to you after your last correction, and I need not say how pleasant your warm dedication letter is for me – but, of course, it made it impossible for me to write a favorable foreword for the book. I love this little book and would like to see it in many hands and see its impact on many hearts. On the whole, in the spirit of its thinking, it is very much my belief, but there are no lack of differences about which I cannot talk at the moment. [...]

I would like to ask you to send your writings, especially the little book, to philosophers who are somehow interested in a new direction. So, to Natorp - Marburg, Stumpf - Berlin, Volkelt - Leipzig, Eucken - Jena, Misch in Göttingen (my successor), Pfänder und Geiger (Munich), Reinach - Göttingen, Hensel - Erlangen, Frischeisen-Köhler - Halle. (The Kantstudien are actually in everybody's hands, the accompanying texts are not easily overlooked, but here is the danger for the small war book.) Please write an announcement for your book for Kantstudien.
In one week I will finish lecturing and go around the 28th of this month to the Black Forest (Bernau). How have the exciting political events of recent times affected you?
I greet you from the heart,
Your,
EHusserl

Auszug aus einem Brief von Husserl an Dietrich Mahnke, 19. VII. 1917

Extract from a letter of Husserl to Dietrich Mahnke, 19 July 1917

Arnold Metzger (1892-1974)

Arnold Metzger im Jahr 1915

Arnold Metzger in 1915

Arnold Metzger: geb. 24. 2. 1892 in Landau/Pfalz, gest. 16. 8. 1974 in Badgastein/Österreich. – 1910-1914 Studium der Philosophie, Nationalökonomie und Geschichte in Berlin, Heidelberg und Jena. Juli 1914 Promotion bei Rudolf Eucken in Jena („Untersuchungen zur Frage der Differenz der Phänomenologie und des Kantianismus"). Bei Kriegsbeginn Meldung als Kriegsfreiwilliger bei den Chevaulegers (leichte Kavallerie) in Landau. April 1915 Einrücken ins Feld (zunächst Grabendienst in Flandern und im Artois). September/Oktober 1915 Lazarett und anschließende Rückversetzung nach Landau. Juni 1916 Beförderung zum Unteroffizier. September 1916 Versetzung an die Ostfront. Dort bis April 1917 Tätigkeit als Dolmetscher beim deutschen Nachrichtenoffizier in der bulgarischen Armee in der Umgebung von Sofia. April 1917 gerät Metzger in Kriegsgefangenschaft und kommt in ein Lager in Sibirien (dort hält er Vorträge über Phänomenologie); im Mai 1918 Flucht und Rückkehr zur Armee. November 1918 Vorsitzender des Soldatenrats Brest-Litowsk und von Dezember 1918 bis März 1919 Leiter des Kulturdezernats der Reichszentrale für Heimatdienst in Berlin. 1920-1924 Assistent von Husserl in Freiburg. 1933 Abbruch des Habilitationsverfahrens bei Eduard Spranger in Berlin (als Habilitationsschrift war die 1933 unter dem Titel „Phänomenologie und Metaphysik" veröffentlichte Arbeit vorgesehen). 1934-1937 Lehrtätigkeit an der Hochschule für die Wissenschaft des Judentums in Berlin. 1938 Emigration zunächst nach Paris, 1940 nach England und schließlich 1941 in die USA. Vorträge an den Universitäten Harvard, Columbia und Yale. 1946 bis 1948 Dozent am Simmons College in Boston (Mass.). Auf Einladung des Bremer Kongresses kehrt Metzger 1950 nach Deutschland zurück. Ab 1952 Honorarprofessor für Philosophie an der Universität München. – Der Nachlass von Arnold Metzger befindet sich in der Bayerischen Staatsbibliothek (ein ausgewählter Kopienbestand befindet sich im Institut für Zeitgeschichte in München).

Arnold Metzger: born on February 24, 1892 in Landau / Pfalz, died on August 16, 1974 in Badgastein / Austria. 1910-1914, studied philosophy, economics, and history in Berlin, Heidelberg, and Jena. 1914, PhD thesis with Rudolf Eucken in Jena ("Investigations on the Question of the Difference between Phenomenology and Kantianism"). At the beginning of the war, reported as a volunteer with the Chevaulegers (light cavalry) in Landau. April 1915, arrival at the front (served in the trenches in Flanders and Artois). September – October 1915, military hospital and subsequent return to Landau. June 1916, promotion to corporal. September 1916, transfer to the Eastern Front. Until April 1917, worked as an interpreter for a German intelligence officer in the Bulgarian army in the area of Sofia. In April 1917, Metzger entered into captivity and lectures on phenomenology in a prisoner of war camp in Siberia. May 1918, escaped and returned to the army. November 1918, Chairman of the Soldiers' Council Brest-Litovsk. From December 1918 to March 1919, Head of the Cultural Department of the Reich Center for Homeland Service in Berlin. 1920-1924, Assistant to Husserl in Freiburg. 1933, Metzger stopped his habilitation with Eduard Spranger in Berlin (the intended Habilitationsschrift was published 1933 under the title "Phenomenology and Metaphysics"). 1934-1937, taught at the University for the Science of Judaism in Berlin. 1938, emigrated to Paris, and in 1940 to England and in 1941 to the USA. Lectures at Harvard, Columbia, and Yale Universities. 1946-1948, lecturer at Simmons College in Boston. Metzger returned to Germany in 1950 at the invitation of the Bremen Congress. From 1952, Honorary Professor of Philosophy at the University of Munich. – The papers of Arnold Metzger are housed in the Bayerische Staatsbibliothek (a selected copy collection is in the Institute of Contemporary History in Munich).

Böckelmann, F.: Annäherungen an Arnold Metzgers Phänomenologie der revolutionären Selbstreflexion. In: Zeitschrift für philosophische Forschung 24 (1970), 372-388. – Günther, G.: Ideen zu einer Metaphysik des Todes. In: Archiv für Philosophie 7, H 3/4 (1957), 335-347. – Henckmann, W.: Metzger, Arnold. In: Neue Deutsche Biographie 17 (1994), 254 f. – Sonnemann, U.: Nachwort. In: Arnold Metzger: Phänomenologie der Revolution. Frühe Schriften. Frankfurt am Main 1979, 235-246. – Tilitzki, C.: Die deutsche Universitätsphilosophie in der Weimarer Republik und im Dritten Reich. 2 Bände. Berlin 2002, bes. 648-650.

„Der Krieg und der Intellektuelle"

Nordwestlicher Kriegsschauplatz, 15. Oktober 1915
Der Krieg und der Intellektuelle
Es scheint mir, daß in der bisherigen Feldpostbriefliteratur zugunsten von Schilderungen der kriegerischen Ereignisse oder von Erlebnissen die unmittelbar mit dem Felde zusammenhängen, jene mehr problematischen Geschehnisse zurückgedrängt wurden, die den einzelnen Menschen als solchen angehen; ich meine jene Tatsachen, wo es sich um das Schicksal des hinter dem Soldaten verborgenen Menschen handelt: um seine Sehnsucht, sein Glück und seine Not und alle die Regungen, welche in der Abgeschlossenheit der Seele vor sich gehen und die Ereignisse unsichtbar begleiten. Diese subjektiven Begleiterscheinungen des Krieges, jenseits von jedem Worte, sind von ungemeiner Bedeutung: vielleicht ist in ihnen der irrationale Ursprung einer in und durch den Krieg geborenen „neuen" Kultur zu sehen.

Ich spreche vor allem von dem Schicksal des geistigen Menschen, der, ein Soldat neben den anderen, draußen den vaterländischen Pflichten genügt. Man hat sich, soviel ich sehe, die eigentümliche Lage dieses Menschen bisher noch nicht zum Bewußtsein gebracht. Man sah das Einfache: den Soldaten, der sein Leben zur Verfügung stellt; man sah weniger die Einstellungen und Umstellungen, die inneren Opfer und Überwindungen: das innere Heldentum, von dem aus erst das soldatische Schicksal dieser Menschen seine Farbe und Atmosphäre bekommt.

Was heißt für den intellektuellen Menschen „Soldat" sein? Wie vermag er sich dem ungeheuren, alle Menschlichkeitsunterschiede nivellierenden militärischen Apparat einzugliedern? Das Soldatenleben hat seine ihm zugehörigen Stilgesetze, die sein Wesen ausmachen und die notwendig erfüllt werden müssen – wie jedes gegenständliche Ganze seine Ordnung und Form hat, die es zu diesem und keinen anderen machen. „Soldat" sein heißt im Besitz eines unmittelbaren Lebens sein. Der Soldat ist seinem Wesen nach – nur davon spreche ich – von aller Intellektualität frei; das heißt aber: er ist frei von allen Hemmungen, welche notwendig die Geistigkeit eines Menschen mit sich bringt. Er ist von diesem Pathos erfüllt, welches das Draufgängertum liebt, welches bereit ist, mit der naiven Selbstverständlichkeit des Helden in den Tod zu gehen, seine „Pflicht" erfüllend. Er bedarf nicht der Reflexion, jenes intellektuellen, seine Hemmungslosigkeit beeinträchtigenden Apparates: fragend nach dem „Sinn" seines Opfers, des Kampfes, in dem er steht. Seine Sorgen sind auf das Nächste gerichtet: auf alle vitalen und militärischen Maßnahmen, die geeignet erscheinen, seine augenblickliche Lage zu verbessern, dem Feinde Schaden zuzufügen, eine Position auszunützen etc. Und er tut es mit der Gewandtheit des Menschen, der frei ist von aller Problematik und Zweifel.

Dieser Krieg fällt geschichtlich in eine Zeit, die von jener romantischen Personalkultur erfüllt war, welche in der Heranbildung von Menschlichkeiten das „Endziel" sah. Das wertvolle Menschentum war das Problem: es ist gleichgültig, ob die Lösung im „Objektiven" gesucht wurde, in Werten der Gesellschaft und des Staates, oder in jener Liebe zu den aller Personalität beraubten „transzendenten" Werten der Philosophie. Alle Strebungen, so verschieden sie waren, lebten in der Sehnsucht nach „Menschen" schlechthin, einer Sehnsucht, die nicht die Geister einte, sondern einsam machte, da keine übergreifende, beheimatende Größe da war, worin sie sich alle hätten finden können. Eine wundervolle Generation war gekommen, die von einer herrlichen Echtheit des Strebens beseelt war, die mit der Heiligkeit des gläubigen Herzens an sich arbeitete. Wir erinnern uns der Richtungen des jungen Deutschland, der Sezessionen und Bünde, der jungen Dichter, der philosophischen Generation und ihrer Diskussionen, die sie führten. Wir wissen, daß die Irrwege, die sie taten und über die ein Philistertum spöttelte, wahrhaftig keine Blasphemien waren.

Diese Generation hatte Nerven, sie war in den Einzelnen ihrer Vertreter ungemein differenziert. Ihr Leben selbst hatte die Naivität verloren, in dem Sinne wie der problematische Mensch sie verliert. Denn sie waren problematisch, sie waren noch nicht fertig geworden, sie hatten noch nicht die Sicherheit des die innere Problematik überwunden habenden, neugeborenen Menschen erreicht. So ist diese Jugend zu verstehen: sie war suchend und hatte die Sehnsucht nach dem Ziel.

Mitten in diese Entwicklung fällt der Krieg. Ich sprach oben von den seelischen Voraussetzungen des soldatischen Lebens, gewissermaßen von der Form, unter der das Leben eine soldatische Haltung gewinnt, und sagte, wie durchaus unintellektuell dieses Leben orientiert ist. Würden wir nicht durch die Erfahrung belehrt werden, würden es nicht die Briefe vom Felde erzählen, a priori wären wir von den Opfern, die nicht körperlicher Art sind, überzeugt, die das Kriegs- und Soldatenleben als solches stellt und die bedeutender sind als der Einsatz des Lebens.

Es ist offenbar klar, daß die Unintellektualität des militärischen Lebens die rücksichtslose Anpassung von seiten des geistigen Menschen verlangt; er ist aber andererseits vor die unendliche Aufgabe gestellt, sich irgendwie mit dem „Sinn" des Krieges, in dem er das Leben als Opfer bringt, mit dem „Sinne" seines Opfers in seiner Weise abzufinden, daß er aus der Lösung den Glauben an den „gerechten" Zweck schöpft. Er ist gezwungen, alle ideologische Problematik, die ihm der Krieg aufgibt, zu überwinden, jene Unentschlossenheit der geistigen Haltung, die ihn an der soldatischen Tat und Hemmungslosigkeit behindert beziehungsweise sie ihm unmöglich macht. Er ist gezwungen, gewissermaßen seine Ideologie mit den soldatischen Anforderungen in Einklang zu bringen. Das ist eine vitale Notwendigkeit: es wirkt stilwidrig, ungemein komisch, wenn eine geistige Attitüde in die militärische Haltung hineinragt. „Man" wird das „Unsoldatische" auf Schritt und Tritt gewahr: dieser Mensch ist vor der Front als Vorgesetzter nicht brauchbar. Ich sage: es tritt an den geistigen Menchen die vitale Notwendigkeit, über alle Problematik hinweg zu dem bejahenden „Glauben" zu kommen, der seine Menschlichkeit zusammenhält und ihm die ethische Möglichkeit verleiht, „soldatisch" zu leben.

An diesem Glauben hängt aber sein soldatisches Schicksal. Besteht für den „Mann" im Gewöhnlichen durchaus kein Problem, ihn in das militärische Leben einzugliedern – so ist die glückliche Vollendung des Weges, den der differenzierte Mensch dahin zurückzulegen hat, die sehr bedeutsame Frage, weil in diesem Wege jene ungeheure Ideologie, die Krieg und verändertes Dasein aufgeben, an ihn herantritt, zugleich mit der rücksichtslosen Forderung, die Souveränität über sie zu gewinnen. Ich sagte, daß Naivität und über jede Hemmung erhabene Ungebrochenheit wesentliche Merkmale soldatischer Psychologie sind. Wie dieses Menschentum der geistige Mensch gewönne, war unsere Frage, die wir dahin beantworteten, daß eine resolute, von dem Glauben an den

„gerechten" Zweck unseres Krieges getragene Bezwingung der Probleme ihn dazu disponiere. Wir wissen, welch ungemeine Schwierigkeiten ethischer und intellektueller Natur diese Forderung in sich schließt – welch heldenhaftes Draufgängertum, um dieses Wort für ethische Dinge anzuwenden, notwendig ist, um zu jenem „Kinde" zu werden, wo die Kindheit zu neuer Offenbarung wird und in der gläubigen Hingebung an die Sache besteht.

"War and the Intellectual"

Northwest from the theater of operations, October 15, 1915
The war and the intellectual
It seems to me that hitherto in the literature of letters from the front, descriptions of war-time events or the experiences which are intimately connected to the front have been favored, whereas more problematic occurences have been repressed that concern the individual person as such. I have in mind those facts where the fate of the person hidden behind the soldier is concerned: his yearning for his happiness and his distress and all the violent impressions which occur in the seclusion of the soul and accompany invisibly [the] experiences. These subjective accompanying manifestations of war, beyond any words, are of immense significance: perhaps therein one might discern the irrational origin of a "new" culture born in and through the war.

Above all, I speak of the fate of the spiritual man who, each soldier next to the other, fulfills his patriotic duties out-there at the front. As far as I can see, the unique situation of this person has not yet been brought to awareness. One saw what was simple: the soldier who makes his own life available; one saw less those attitudes and changes, the inner sacrifices and overcomings: the inner heroism, only from which the soldier's destiny of such individuals receives its color and atmosphere.

What does it mean for an intellecual person to be "a soldier?" How can he integrate himself into the tremendous military apparatus, which levels out all differences among humanity? The soldier's life possesses its own rules of style which form its essence, and which must necessarily be fulfilled, just as every objective whole possesses its order and form, which makes it this order and not another. To be a soldier means being in the immediate possession of life. By his very nature, the soldier is (and I am only speaking of this) free from any quality of being an intellectual, but this means: he is free from all the inhibitions which necessarily come along with the spirituality [*Geistigkeit*] of being a human. He is filled with this passion, which loves bravado, and which remains prepared to die with the hero's naive unquestioned acceptance, and fulfill his "duty." He does not require the reflection of such intellectuals which minimizes his self-abandon to the apparatus: asking for the "meaning" of his sacrifice, for the "meaning" of the combat for which he fights. His concerns are directed towards what comes next: towards the vital and military measures which are liable to improve his momentary situation and bring harm against the enemy, to exploit a position, etc. And he does so with the agility of the person who is free from doubt and everything problematic.

This war occurs historically at a time that was filled with a romantic culture of personality, and which saw therein the "ultimate goal" for the formation of humanities. Valuable humanity was the problem: it does not matter whether the solution was sought in the "objective," in the values of society and the state, or in that love for the anonymous "transcendent" values of philosophy. All aspirations, however different they were, lived in the desire for "humanity" as such; it was a desire that did not unite all spirits, but made them lonely, since there lacked an overarching and sheltering greatness in which each could all have found the other. A wonderful generation had arrived, animated by a glorious genuineness of endeavor, and to form oneself with the sanctity of a devout heart. We remember the tendencies of the young Germany, the secessions and communities, the young poets, the philosophical generation and the discussions which they pursued. We know that the erroneous ways that they followed and which became the object of scorn among philistines, were not true blasphemies.

This generation possessed nerves and was immensely differentiated among its individual representatives. The life of this generation had lost its naivety much as a person who becomes problematic losses it. [This generation] became problematic, they were not finished, they still had not arrived at a new-born humanity that possessed the certainty of having overcome the internal problematic. This youth is thus to be understood: they were searching and yearning for the goal.

In the middle of this development occured the war. I spoke above about the spiritual conditions of a soldier's life, as well as, to a certain extent, the form in which they achieve a soldier's attitude, and I said how this life is not all oriented towards an intellectual life. If we had not been instructed by experience, had it not been recounted through letters from the front, a priori we would have not been convinced about sacrifice, and not of the physical kind, but as that kind which the life of the soldier and war as such gives and which are more meaningful than the employment of life.

It is clearly evident that the unintellecutal military life demands a heedless adaptation on the part of the spiritual individual. He is, on the other hand, placed before an infinite task of something coming to terms with the "meaning" of war, to which he gives his life, with the "meaning" of his sacrifice in such a manner that from this solution he can draw forth a conviction in the "just" purpose. He is forced to overcome all ideological problems which the war delivers to him as well as any indecisiveness in his mental attitude which hinders or renders impossible his soldier's deed and abandonment. He is forced to reconcile his ideology with the soldier's exigencies. This is a vital necessity: it becomes stylistic adverse and extremely funny when a mental attitude stands out from military posture. "One" becomes aware of what is unbecoming of a soldier at every turn: this person is not useful at the front as superior officer. Let me state: there is a vital need for spiritual individuals to reach beyond all problems towards an affirmative "conviction," which can hold together his humanity and give him the ethical possibility to a "soldier's" life.

A soldier's destiny depends on this conviction. If the "man" in ordinary life has no problem integrating himself into military life, then the happy completion of the path which the differentiated person takes poses the very important problem [which must be solved], because from this path comes a tremendous ideology, assigned by the war and a transformed existence, as well as at the same time, a heedless demand to gain sovereignty over them. I claimed that naiveté and sublime robustness above all inhibitions are essential features of the soldier psychology. How this kind of humanity was acquired by the spiritual man was our question, which we answered by deciding that a resolute conquest of the problems, based on the conviction in the "just" purpose of our war, would avail the soldier to this dispostion. We know what extreme difficulty of ethical and intellectual nature is implied with this demand, and what heroic recklessness is necessary – to apply this word to ethical things – to become that "child," where childhood becomes a new revelation and consists in a religious devotion to the cause.

Arnold Metzgers Aufzeichnungen vom 15. Oktober 1915, die er in der „Vossischen Zeitung" veröffentlichte

Arnold Metzger's notes from 15 October 1915 (published in the "Vossische Newspaper")

„Ich bin überzeugt, daß nach dem Kriege eine starke antisemitische Bewegung durch Deutschland geht"

Malgidia, 26. November 1916

<...> Die „jüdische Frage" beschäftigt mich innerlich Tag und Nacht. Es scheint, daß sie sich mir zur persönlichen Angelegenheit herauswächst. – Der Erlaß des Kriegsministeriums bedeutet die offene Absage an das Judentum. Wir werden uns in Zukunft danach zu richten und vor irgendwelchen optimistischen Illusionen zu hüten haben. Wir, die deutschen Juden, müssen es begreifen und unsere ethische Haltung der Gesellschaft gegenüber dementsprechend einstellen, daß Europa nichts mit uns zu tun haben will, daß wir niemals europäische Bürger, politisch-gesellschaftlich verstanden, zu werden die Aussicht haben.

Wir müssen weiter begreifen, daß die Schuld nicht an der europäischen führenden Gesellschaft liegt. Meines Erachtens ist der Versuch, das Judentum innerlich zu gewinnen, von dieser Gesellschaft schon des öfteren, aber ohne durchgreifenden Erfolg, unternommen worden. Alle Versuche der Europäisierung scheiterten an der Konstitution des Judentums.

Für viele bedeutet diese Konstitution einen Mangel, „die ewige Krankheit". Ich sehe in ihr etwas unendlich Verheißungsvolles, voll von Zukunft und Positivität. Diese Positivität des Judentums muß uns allen zur Überzeugung werden, daß wir endlich diese peinlichen Versuche, uns, unter Preisgabe unseres Stolzes und unserer Mission, Europa zu Füßen zu werfen, aufgeben.

Ich sage: das Judentum, das in Europa nichts zu gewinnen hat für sich und seine innere Entwicklung (wohl aber hat Europa und vor allem Deutschland noch sehr in diese jüdische Schule zu gehen), muß innerlich frei werden. In einer Theorie des Judentums wird ersichtlich, daß die vielen mit Recht „übel" genannten Eigenschaften der Juden, die keiner mehr haßt als ich, ein Produkt dieser falschen, untauglichen Assimilationsbestrebungen sind, daß sie aber durchaus nicht das zentrale Wesen angehen.

Das Problem lautet: Worin liegt die merkwürdig abweisende Reaktion Europas, speziell Deutschlands, auf alles, was jüdisch heißt? Daraus die zweite Frage: worin liegt die Europa unverständliche Eigenart jüdischen Seins? Daraus die dritte gesellschaftspolitische Frage: welche Konsequenzen zieht das Judentum aus seiner „Fremdheit" und welche Aufgaben fallen ihm kraft seiner Eigenart zu?

In der Behandlung dieser Fragen, die ein Begreifen der jüdischen Geschichte und Tradition, jüdischen Gehabens in der Gesellschaft überhaupt voraussetzen, wird sich herausstellen, daß die Seele des Judentums seine alles andere überragende Sehnsucht zu Gott und göttlichen Dingen ausmacht, daß das Religiöse alle seine sonstigen Betätigungen in sich einsaugt, und daß von hier aus sein gesellschaftliches Gebaren zu würdigen ist. Wie stellt sich jüdische Religiosität dar, und was ist damit gemeint, wenn ich sage, daß das Leben der Juden nur unter dieser Kategorie zu verstehen ist? –

Für heute noch ein Wort über die Internationalität des Judentums! Es ist zweifellos richtig: der Jude ist international, und ursprünglich hat er zu nationalen Dingen keine Fühlung. Warum sollten wir nicht offen von unserer Stärke reden dürfen? Warum sollten wir nicht offen zugestehen, daß wir durchaus keinen Sinn für die Blutopfer haben, die für die Größe der Nation, gleichgültig welcher, dargebracht werden? Wir haben die Pflicht, davon zu sprechen, daß die Aufgabe der Menschheit, insbesondere der jüdischen Menschheit, in der Arbeit für eine – nennen wir das Kind bei seinem Namen – messianische Zukunft besteht. – Von der Internationalität des Judentums wird noch viel zu sprechen sein.

Um es noch zu vereinfachen: Ich bin überzeugt, daß nach dem Kriege eine starke antisemitische Bewegung durch Deutschland geht, vielleicht vergleichbar mit osteuropäischen Allüren. Wir werden uns nicht fürchten, sondern die Aufgabe haben, die Einzigartigkeit jüdischer Ideologie zu realisieren.

Die erste Arbeit, die mich nach dem Kriege ganz beschäftigen wird, soll eine eingehende Bearbeitung jüdischer Geschichte und Kulturarbeit sein. So sehr ich wünsche, meine vor dem Kriege liegenden philosophischen Arbeiten zum Abschluß zu bringen, ich werde mich zu ersterem entschließen, weil ich zu der jüdischen Zukunft vielleicht in irgendeiner Weise etwas beitragen kann <...>

"I am convinced that a strong anti-Semitic movement will pass through Germany after the war"

Malgidia, November 26, 1916

[...] The "Jewish question" preoccupies me day and night. It seems that it is growing into a matter of personal concern for me. The decree of the Ministry of War means the open rejection of Judaism. In the future, we will have to look back towards it and protect ourselves from what-ever optimistic illusions. We, the German Jews, must understand it and change accordingly our ethical attitude towards society, that Europe does not want anything to do with us, that we will never have the prospect of becoming European citizens, politically and socially understood.

We must further understand that guilt does not reside with the leading European society. In my view, the attempt to win Judaism internally has been undertaken by this society many times, but without any major success. All attempts at Europeanization failed due to the constitution of Judaism.

For many, this constitution means a lack, "the eternal sickness." I see in this sickness something infinitely promising, full of future and positivity. This positivism of Judaism must convince us all that we must finally give up these embarrassing attempts to throw ourselves at the feet of Europe at the price of our pride and our mission.

I say: Judaism, which has nothing to gain for itself and its inner development in Europe (but Europe and especially Germany have still a lot to learn in this Jewish school), has to become internally free. In a theory of Judaism it becomes evident that the many rightly "evil" qualities of the Jews, which no one hates more than I, are a product of these false and unsuitable assimilation efforts, but that they certainly do not address the essential existence.

The problem is: Where does the strange and rejecting reaction of Europe reside, and in particular, Germany, to everything that is called Jewish? Hence the second question: what is the incomprehensible distinctiveness of being Jewish? From this, the third sociopolitical question: what consequences does Judaism draw from its "foreignness" and which tasks fall to it by virtue of its distinctiveness?

In the treatment of these questions, which presuppose a comprehension of Jewish history and tradition, of Jewish behavior in society as a whole, it will turn out that the soul of Judaism constitutes its all-pervading desire for God and divine things, that the religious absorbs all other activities, and that in these terms its social comportment is to be dignified. What is Jewish religiousness, and what does it mean when I say that the life of the Jews is to be understood only under this category?

Just another word today about the internationalism of Judaism! It is undoubtedly correct: the Jew is international, and originally he has no contact with national things. Why should we not openly talk about our strengths? Why should we not openly admit that we have absolutely no sense for the blood sacrifices offered for the greatness of the nation, no matter what? It is our duty to say that the task of humanity, especially of Jewish humanity, is to work for a – let's call the child by its name – messianic future. There is still much to talk about the internationalism of Judaism.

To make it even simpler: I am convinced that a strong anti-Semitic movement will pass through Germany after the war, perhaps comparable with the atmosphere in Eastern Europe. We will not be afraid, but have the task of realizing the uniqueness of Jewish ideology.

The first work that will occupy me entirely after the war will be a thorough study of Jewish history and cultural work. As much as I wish to finish my pre-war philosophical work, I will choose the former because perhaps I can contribute in some manner to the Jewish future [...]

Auszug aus einem Brief von Arnold Metzger an seine Mutter, 26. XI. 1916

Excerpt from a letter from Arnold Metzger to his mother, 26 November 1916

„Ich bin nicht zum Führer der nach ‚seligem Leben' ringenden Menschheit berufen – im leidensvollen Drange der Kriegsjahre habe ich das anerkennen müssen, mein Daimonion hat mich gewarnt"

Erste Seite des Typoskripts „Phänomenologie der Revolution. Eine politische Schrift über den Marxismus und die liebende Gemeinschaft", das Arnold Metzger in einer handschriftlichen Fassung im August 1919 an Husserl schickte. Im Oktober 1919 nahm der S. Fischer Verlag das Manuskript zwar zur Publikation an, Metzger zog es jedoch auf Drängen Husserls wieder zurück. Spätere Überarbeitungsversuche scheiterten (vgl. Arnold Metzger: „Phänomenologie der Revolution. Frühe Schriften". Mit einem Nachwort von U. Sonnemann, Frankfurt am Main 1979).

First page from the typed manuscript "Phenomenology of Revolution. A Political Text about Marxism and a Loving Community," which Arnold Metzger sent to Husserl in an hand-written version in August 1919. In October 1919, Fischer Verlag accepted the manuscript for publication, but Metzger asked for the manuscript back at Husserl's urging. Future attempts at revision did not materialize.

Bernau i/Baden 4. Sept\<ember\> 1919.
Lieber Herr Metzger!
Ich habe Ihre Schrift \<„Phänomenologie der Revolution"\> auf mich wirken lassen, ich habe mich in der letzten Woche so gut es mir in der Unruhe des Schwarzwaldgasthofes möglich war in Ihre Gedanken vertieft u. mir rechte Mühe gegeben.

Das sagt viel für die Stärke der Resonanz, die schon die ersten Sätze, auf die der vorfühlende Blick bei dem Empfang des Msc. traf, in meiner Seele weckten, u. für die Stärke fortwirkender Theilnahme in Mitdenken und Selbstdenken, in die ich hineingezogen und in der ich festgehalten wurde. Es sagt das so viel bei dem Zustande meiner Augen, denen das Lesen an sich schon eine harte Sache, aber das Lesen so blasser u. undeutlicher Schriften eine Qual ist. Zum Glück konnte ich mir das Msc auch einmal von meiner Tochter vorlesen lassen u. dabei zugleich den Eindruck beobachten, den es auf eine jener jungen Seelen von, fast möchte ich sagen, harter Gradheit u. Wahrhaftigkeit übt, die sich den grauenvollen Kriegserlebnissen zu Trotze zum reinen Licht hinaufgereckt haben. – Der Ton macht die Musik. Wir hörten – wir Mistrauischen, durch so viele böse Erfahrung an Anderen u. an uns selbst so skeptisch, so feinhörig gewordenen – wir hörten einen reinen, ja wirklich einen ganz reinen Ton: den Ton einer wahrhaft selbstlosen Hingabe an „die Ideen". Wir verstanden diese radikale Gesinnung, die fest entschlossen ist das Leben nicht als Handelsgeschäft führen und ansehen zu wollen mit den 2 fortlaufenden Rubriken Soll und Haben (in denen das Sollen nichts weiter ausdrückt als Forderungen auf Haben), und die todfeind ist allem „Kapitalismus", aller Endwertung u. daher sinnlosen Aufhäufung von Haben und korrelativ allen egoistischen Personwertungen – darin beschlossen Ehren, Ruhm, Stolz –, sogar auch Stolz auf reformatorische Einsichten, Ziele, Missionen.

In dem unsichtbaren Bunde der „Gottesfreunde", der „Brüder vom wahrhaftigen Leben" dürfen wir uns, und wie ich hoffe für allezeit, vereint wissen. Denn diese selbe Gesinnung darf ich wohl als den letzten Ertrag eigener persönlicher Entwicklung meines nicht eben leichten Lebens bezeichnen. Daß Sie mir übrigens Ihre Schrift zugeschickt haben – diese Schrift –, das erweist ein großes und diese selbe Gesinnung bei mir schon voraussetzendes Vertrauen, für das ich Ihnen herzlich danken darf. Es kann nur so sein, daß Sie durch die phrasenlose Nüchternheit und radikale Sachlichkeit meiner Schriften hindurch das sie tragende persönliche Ethos fühlten. Und in der That, das musste wohl echt sein, denn sie sind (wie die Ihre) aus der Not geboren, aus unsäglicher seelischer Not, aus einem völligen „Zusammenbruch", in dem es nur die eine u. einzige Rettung gab: ein völlig neues Leben in der verzweifelten u. verbissenen Entschlossenheit, es in radikaler Ehrlichkeit von vorn anzufangen und fortzuführen und schlechthin vor keiner Consequenz zurückzuschrecken. Nicht als ob ich damals schon, also schon im letzten Jahrzehnt des vor<igen> Jahrhunderts, die innere Hohlheit der die gesammte europäische Kultur beherrschenden Willensrichtungen erschaut und insbesondere ihren vornehmsten Exponenten, den beispiellosen Aufschwung des neuen deutschen Reiches, einer tieferen Kritik unterzogen hätte – und somit auch mein Eigenleben allseitig neu orientirt hätte. <…>

Sie sehen, meine Anfänge, meine ursprünglichen Motive u. Nöte, die mir zugewachsenen absoluten Forderungen, vielleicht darf ich sagen (wie es sich in mir selbst unweigerlich giebt u. nennt) meine Mission – sind andere als die Ihren. Und doch treffen wir zusammen und meine theoretische Lebensarbeit ist mit für Sie gethan, für Sie, der von Beruf u. Willen Praktiker ist. Das von mir, wie ich sagen darf, in leidenschaftlichstem Redlichkeitswillen u. in zweifelsüchtigster Selbstkritik theoretisch Erarbeitete fordert Ihr nachverstehendes Studium u. dann kommt die Ihnen originär zugedachte gewaltige Aufgabe, das Studium der Menschheitsrealitäten u. deren philos<ophische> Durchleuchtung und Leitung. Meine Aufgabe ist das nicht, ich bin nicht zum Führer der nach „seligem Leben" ringenden Menschheit berufen – im leidensvollen Drange der Kriegsjahre habe ich das anerkennen müssen, mein Daimonion hat mich gewarnt. Vollbewußt u. entschieden lebe ich rein als wiss<enschaftlicher> Philosoph (ich habe daher keine Kriegsschrift geschrieben, ich hätte das als ein prätentiöses Philosophengethue angesehen). Nicht weil mir die Wahrheit u. Wissenschaft als der höchste Werth gilt. Im Gegentheil: „der Intell<e>ct ist Diener des Willens", also auch ich Diener des praktischen Lebensgestalters, des Menschheitsführers. <…> Freilich ist es da die Tragik meiner Lebenslage, daß ich, zunächst durch die Erschütterungen des Kriegs u. durch zeitweise Überanspannungen, dann aber auch durch die von Jahr zu Jahr übermächtig auf mich eindringenden Massen immer neuer Fundamentalprobleme, in der Leidenschaft des Vorwärtsstrebens und in der Not der geistigen Selbsterhaltung – zu keinen abschließenden Veröffentlichungen gekommen bin. <…>

"I am not called to lead humanity in striving towards a 'blessed life.' I had to acknowledge this during the painful course of the war years: my daimonion had warned me"

Bernau i. Baden
September 4th, 1919
Dear Mr. Metzger:
I have been letting your manuscript ["Phenomenology of Revolution"] work on me during the past week, and have endeavoured to submerge myself in your thoughts as much as the lack of quiet in a Schwarzwald Inn would permit.

That is a testimony to the power of the response evoked in me by the very first sentences I glanced at, as well as to the power of the ongoing community of thinking along with you as well as by myself into which I have been drawn and in which I am firmly held. This means a lot in view of the condition of my eyes which makes even ordinary reading difficult and reading such faint and indistinct handwriting a torture. I was fortunate that I could also have my daughter read the manuscript to me, and so could witness the impact which your almost harsh, direct truthfulness that defied grim war experience and raised itself to a pure light, has on her young soul. – The tone makes the music, and we have heard – we who have learned to mistrust, we whom many evil experiences have made so sceptical, so sensitive to ourselves and others – have heard a clear tone, yes, truly, a completely pure tone, the tone of genuine dedication to the ideal. And we understood the radical determination to keep life from degenerating into a commercial enterprise viewed in terms of "Debit" and "Credit" sides of a ledger in which the debit is never more than a demand on credit. We understood the determination which is radically opposed to all "capitalism" which values possession – and thus its senseless accumulation – above all else, a dedication which corrects even all egotistic personal values, whether honor, fame, or pride – yes, even the pride of reforming insights, goals, and tasks.

I hope we shall always feel joined to one another in the fellowship of the "friends of God" and the "brotherhood of true life." For I, too, can point to such determination as the final fruition of the unfolding of my own, often not easy, life. That you should have sent me your manuscript – especially this manuscript – shows a great faith which anticipates such determination on my part: and for this I should like to thank you sincerely. I can only think that you have sensed some of the sustaining ethos through the laconic sobriety and strict concentration on the matters at hand in my writings. You must have sensed that this ethos is genuine, because my writings, just as yours, are born out of need, out of an immense psychological need, out of a complete collapse in which the only hope is an entirely new life, a desperate, unyielding resolution to begin from the beginning and to go forth in radical honesty, come what may. I cannot claim to have recognized already then, that is, in the closing decade of last century, the inner emptiness of the guiding aims which dominated the entire European culture, or specifically, to have subjected their outstanding example, the rise of the new German empire, to a deeper critique, thereby reorienting my entire personal life as well. […]

As you can see, my beginnings, my most basic motives and difficulties, the absolute demands which have accrued to me, perhaps I can call it my mission – for as such it in fact presents itself and confronts me within – are other than yours. And yet we have encountered each other, and the theoretical work of my life is carried out also for you, for you who are a man of action by vocation and preference. The theoretical gains which I have achieved, I can say, in a passionate striving for honesty and in most detailed self-criticism, demand a study which you have yet to undertake; then comes the demanding task originally attributed to you, the study of human realities and their philosophical clarification and guidance. That is not my task; I am not called to lead humanity in striving towards a "blessed life". I had to acknowledge this during the painful course of the war years: my *daimonion* had warned me. I live consciously and by choice purely as a scientific philosopher (I have written no books concerning the war, since I regarded that as a pretentious philosophical ostentation). Not that I consider truth and science the highest values. Quite the contrary, "Intellect is the servant of the will," and so also I am the servant of those who shape our practical life, of the leaders of humanity. […] Of course the tragic element in my situation is that I have produced no definitive publication, at first because of the shocks of the war and occasional overwork, but also because of the mass of ever new fundamental problems which, between the desire to strive forward and the need for spiritual self-preservation, press themselves on me overwhelmingly from year to year. […]

(See the entire letter, translated by Erazim Kohák, in: Husserl: Shorter Works. McCormick, P. and Elliston, F. A. eds. University of Notre Dame Press, 1981, 360-64)

Auszüge aus einem insgesamt 14-seitigen Brief von Husserl an Arnold Metzger, 4. IX. 1919 (geschrieben im Anschluss an die Lektüre von Metzgers Manuskript „Phänomenologie der Revolution")

Excerpts from a 14-page letter from Husserl to Arnold Metzger (4 September 1919), written after reading Metzger's manuscript "Phenomenology of Revolution"

Friedrich Neumann (1889-1978)

Friedrich Neumann: geb. 2. 3. 1889 in Wilhelmshöhe (Kassel), gest. 12. 12. 1978 in Göttingen. – Von 1907 bis 1914 Studium der klassischen Philologie, Germanistik und Philosophie in Marburg (SS 1907-WS 1908/09), München (SS 1909, u.a bei Theodor Lipps) und Göttingen (WS 1909/10-WS 1913/14, u.a. bei Adolf Reinach und Husserl). Mitglied der Göttinger Philosophischen Gesellschaft. Ende 1913 Staatsexamen für die Lehrbefähigung an Schulen. 1914 Promotion („Geschichte des neuhochdeutschen Reimes von Opitz bis Wieland") bei Edward Schröder im Fach deutsche Philologie. 1914 als Kriegsfreiwilliger Dienst an der Westfront, zeitweise in demselben Regiment (Nr. 234) wie Husserls Söhne, zuletzt als Leutnant und Kompanieführer. Nach Kriegsende zwei Jahre im Schuldienst in Kassel. 1921 Habilitation in Göttingen („Die religiösen Anschauungen Freidanks", ungedruckte Arbeit), danach zunächst als Privatdozent für Deutsche Philologie an der Universität in Göttingen, dann ab WS 1921/22 an der Universität Leipzig; dort von 1922 bis 1927 ordentlicher Professor für deutsche Philologie, von 1927 bis 1945 an der Universität in Göttingen. Von Mai 1933 bis März 1938 Rektor, anschließend bis 1943 Prorektor der Universität Göttingen. Nach dem 2. Weltkrieg wegen seines politischen Engagements in der NS-Zeit (ab 1933 Mitglied der NSDAP) zunächst seines Amtes enthoben, später als Mitläufer eingestuft und 1954 ordnungsgemäß emiritiert. – Der Nachlass von Friedrich Neumann befindet sich in der Universitätsbibliothek Göttingen.

Friedrich Neumann: born on March 2, 1889 in Wilhelmshöhe (Kassel), died on December 12, 1978 in Göttingen. 1907 to 1914, studied classical philology, German philology, and philosophy in Marburg (1907-1909), Munich (1909, including with Theodor Lipps) and Göttingen (1909-1914, including with Adolf Reinach and Husserl). Member of the Göttingen Philosophical Society. 1913, state examination for teaching qualification in schools. 1914, PhD ("History of the New High German Rhyme from Opitz to Wieland") with Edward Schröder in German philology. Served on the Western Front in 1914 as a war volunteer, at times with the same regiment (No. 234) as Husserl's sons; promoted to Lieutenant and Company Commander. After the war, two years in the school service in Kassel. 1921, habilitation in Göttingen ("The Religious Views of Freidank," unpublished), and Privatdozent for German Philology at the University of Göttingen; from 1921/22 at the University of Leipzig; from 1922 to 1927 Full Professor of German philology, from 1927 to 1945 at the University of Göttingen. From May 1933 to March 1938 Rector, then until 1943 Vice Rector of the University of Göttingen. After World War II, initially dismissed from his post due to his political involvement during the Nazi era (from 1933 onwards, member of the NSDAP), later classified as a follower, and retired in 1954. – The papers of Friedrich Neumann are housed in the University Library Göttingen.

Hunger, U.: Zufall oder Bestimmung? Der Weg des Germanisten Friedrich Neumann zum politischen Rektorat 1933-38. In: Heizmann, W./van Nahl, A.: Runica – Germanica – Mediaevalia. RGA-Bd. 37. Berlin/New York 2003, 309-347. – Neumann, F.: Reserve-Infanterie-Regiment Nr. 234. In: Thüringen im und nach dem Weltkrieg. Geschichtliches Erinnerungswerk an die Kriegsteilnahme, die politische Umwälzung und Erneuerung Thüringens. Bd. 2. Leipzig 1921, 209-217. – Neumann, F.: Langemarck. In: Zeitschrift für Deutsche Bildung 14 (1938), 413-424.

Friedrich Neumann (um 1930)

Friedrich Neuman (around 1930)

„Wir erleben diesen Krieg als etwas Übergewaltiges"

4. XI. 14
Lieber Herr Dr.!
Eine große Freude war mir Ihre Karte! Sie sind also bei demselben Regim\<ent\> wie meine beiden Jungens, die bei der 11. Komp\<anie\> fechten. Zufällig hatte ich von meinen Jungen vom selben Tag Nachricht (Wolfgang's Karte an Prof. Wellhausen); auch aus dem Schützengraben und mitten im Granatenfeuer, es war die erste Nachricht seit dem 18ten X u. wir waren schon in größter Sorge. Vielleicht finden Sie Gelegenheit bei der 11. Comp\<anie\> vorzusprechen, sie finden dort auch sonst Bekannte. Sie können sich denken, wie uns Zurückgebliebenen, und insbes\<ondere\> die da Kinder, Geschwister, nahe Menschen, draußen wissen, jedes Lebenszeichen, jede Nachricht aus der Front bewegt u. beglückt. Wir erleben diesen Krieg als etwas Übergewaltiges, und in solcher Zeit reine Phänomenologie treiben, ist schwer. Immer wieder werden die Gedanken aus den reinen Höhen der Idealität zurückgerissen in die harte Welt der Realitäten. Die Zuversicht auf einen endlichen Sieg ist die alte, ungebrochen, so sehr wir von all den Verlusten ergriffen sind. Prof Schröder ist bei Lille, Brandi in Metz, Reinach in Nordfrankreich, u. so sind viele Doz\<enten\> im Felde. Die Universität hat ihren kleinen Betrieb; relativ viel Damen! Meine herzlichsten Wünsche geleiten Sie in den Kämpfen. Vielen Dank für Ihr treues Gedenken! Ihr
EHusserl

Feldpostkarte von Husserl an Friedrich Neumann, 4. XI. 1914

Field postcard from Husserl to Friedrich Neumann, 4 November 1914

"We're experiencing this war as something tremendous"

4 November 1914
Dear Dr.!
Your card was a great pleasure for me! So, you're in the same regiment as my two boys, who are figthing with the 11th Company. By chance, I received news from my boys on the very same day (Wolfgang's card to Prof. Wellhausen); also from the trenches and in the midst of artillery fire, it was the first news since the 18th of October and we were already very worried. Maybe you'll have the opportunity to speak with the 11th Company, you'll also find there some acquaintances. You can imagine how we who are left behind, and especially those, who have children, siblings, close acquaintances outside, are moved and heartened with every sign of life and every news from the front. We're experiencing this war as something tremendous and to pursue in such times pure phenomenology is difficult. Again and again, thoughts are torn away from the pure heights of ideality back to the harsh world of realities. Confidence in a definitive victory remains unbroken and assured, even as we are shaken by all these losses. Prof. Schröder is in Lille, Brandi is in Metz, Reinach is in northern France, and there are so many professors out in the field. The university has its small undertaking; there are relatively many ladies! Let my heartfelt wishes accompany you during the fighting. Thank you for your devoted thoughts!
Your,
EHusserl

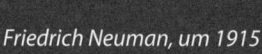

Friedrich Neuman, um 1915

Friedrich Neuman, around 1915

„Es ist unsagbar, wie viele abgerufen wurden, ehe sie das Gesäte ernten konnten"

Hamburg, Rondeel 19
Ostern 1915.

Lieber Herr Neumann, ich freute mich herzlich durch Ihre freundlichen Karten zu hören, daß Sie auf so ehrenvolle Weise für einige Zeit die Heimat genießen können. Und Ihre nett gedachte Übersendung der diss<ertation> trifft mit dem Umstand zusammen, daß ich gerade den Osterurlaub zur Verfügung habe um Ihnen ausführlicher über mein Ergehen zu schreiben. – Es läßt sich auch jetzt Klareres darüber angeben. Nach häufigen Untersuchungen wurde ich schließlich nur für garnisondienstfähig befunden und war so ziemlich Herr meiner selbst. Da ich aber für andere Arbeit keine Muße und Gelegenheit sah, laße ich mich hier beim Generalkommando verwenden. Oder vielmehr zunächst bei einem Artillerieregiment in der Nähe militärisch schleifen. Ich werde dann bei der Sondierung von Zeitungsnachrichten in historischen Zwecken als „wissenschaftlicher Hilfsarbeiter" helfen. Vielleicht komme ich im Sommer auf irgend einen Posten noch hinaus. Es ist eine Tätigkeit, die meinen Kräften entspricht und zugleich mich mit den Zeitereignissen, wenn auch in eine entferntere Verbindung setzt.

Doch genug von mir. Ihre Arbeit erweckte durch die feste Stringenz ihrer Sprache und Führung die selben schlummernden Erinnerungen an das liebe versunkene Göttingen. An das Beste, was wir damals wollten. Gebe Gott, daß seine fragmentarische Gestalt nicht allzu lange mehr, wie alles was der Krieg nicht vollenden ließ, auf ihr völliges Erscheinen zu warten braucht. Es ist unsagbar wie viele abgerufen wurden, ehe sie das Gesäte ernten konnten. Das tritt wohl uns hier hinten deutlicher vor Augen als Ihnen es draußen tat, wo jetzt das Stärkste, ja alles Leben fest sich zusammenschweißt und blutend weiterführt. Ich denke da vor allem an <Rudolf> Clemens. Denn wenn er nicht, wie <Günther> Müller-Rastatt sagte aus Zorn in die Gefangenschaft geraten zu sein noch immer schweigt, so bleibt keine Hoffnung mehr. Er soll, wie jetzt das Gerücht geht, sich nicht mit einem Frl. Zweig, wie ich aus seiner Andeutung schloß, kriegsmäßig verheiratet haben, sondern mit einer Witwe aus Leipzig, der er von früher verpflichtet war.

"It is unspeakable how many were taken away before they could reap the harvest"

Hamburg, Rondeel 19
Easter 1915.

Dear Mr. Neumann, I was delighted to hear from your friendly cards that you can enjoy your home in such an honorable way for some time. And your kind and thoughtful sending of your dissertation coincides with the circumstances that I currently have the Easter vacation at my disposal to write to you in more detail about how I am doing. Much is now clear about my condition. After frequent examinations, I was finally declared to be only capable of garrison duty and was thus pretty much in command of myself. But since I saw no leisure and opportunity for other work, I allowed myself to be employed at General Headquarters. Or, rather, at first with a regiment of artillery here nearby for drill, I will then assist in reviewing newspaper articles for historical purposes as a "scientific assistant." Maybe in the summer I'll go to another post. It is an activity that corresponds to my powers and at the same time sets me in relation to the events of the times, albeit in a more remote connection.

But enough about me. Your work awakened through the firm stringency of your language and guidance the same dormant memories of dear sunken Göttingen. For the best of what we back then wanted. God grant that its fragmentary shape does not have to wait too long, like everything the war did not finish, for its complete appearance. It is unspeakable how many were taken away

Von den übrig gebliebenen Göttingern übt <Dietrich von> Hildebrand, wie ich nach seiner letzten Nachricht vermute noch weiter den Sanitätsdienst aus. <Siegfried> Hamburger ist in Straßburg. <Jean> Hering ist dort als Lehrer tätig. Ich hörte jedoch von beiden seit mehr als einem Monat nichts. Der einzige, mit dem ich persönlich zusammen war ist Müller-Rastatt. Er studiert in Göttingen weiter. Jetzt gerade schloß er eine religionsphilosophische Arbeit für Husserl ab. –

So verstreute uns Phänomenologen die rasche Zeit. Doch ich hoffe in diesen Frühlingstagen – meine intensivste Beschäftigung – daß die heraufziehende Entscheidung mit dem Frieden auch uns einmal ein Wiedersehen bringen wird.

Über jedes Wort, das Sie von sich weiter hören laßen freue ich mich herzlichst.
Stets Ihr
Gustav Hübener.

Brief von Gustav Hübener an Friedrich Neumann, Ostern 1915

Letter from Gustav Hübener to Friedrich Neumann, Easter 1915

before they could reap the harvest. Well, that seems to be more obvious to us here than to you outside, where now the strongest, indeed, all life is solidly welded together and continues bleeding. I'm thinking of [Rudolf] Clemens. For if he does not remain silent, as [Günther] Müller-Rastatt has said, out of anger, there is no hope left. He is rumored not to have married a Fräulein Zweig, as I concluded from his war-time suggestion, but to a widow from Leipzig to whom he was formerly bound.

Of the surviving Göttingen people, [Dietrich von] Hildebrand serves, as I infer from his last report, in the medical service. [Siegfried] Hamburger is in Strasbourg. [Jean] Hering works as a teacher there. However, I have not heard from either one for more than one month. The only person with whom I was personally in contact is Müller-Rastatt. He continues to study in Göttingen. Right now he is completing a religious-philosophical work for Husserl. –

So this is how the rapid times has scattered us phenomenologists. But I hope in these spring days – my most intense occupation – that the approaching decision with peace will also bring us once again a reunion.

I look forward to every word that you wish to hear from yourself.
Always Yours,
Gustav Hübener.

Brief von Husserl an Friedrich Neumann, 11. XI. 1916

Letter from Husserl to Friedrich Neumann, 11 November 1916

„Die Vermutung liegt übrigens nahe, daß sein Widersacher kein anderer ist als sein früherer Kompanieführer Leutnant Ebbinghaus"

Freiburg 11. XI. 16
Sehr geehrter und lieber Herr Doktor!
Ich komme heute mit einer herzlichen Bitte. Zu meiner peinlichsten Überraschung theilt mir mein Sohn mit, es sei aus einer Andeutung eines ihm bekannten Officiers zu entnehmen, daß bei der Officierswahl sich im III. Batl. ein Widerspruch gegen ihn erhoben habe, während in seinem, dem II. Batl. die Wahl glatt verlaufen sei. Ich brauche Ihnen nicht zu sagen, was eine Ablehnung bei der Off<iziers>wahl – und eine solche ist ja nun zu befürchten – für einen jungen Mann bedeutet, und ich bin voll Besorgnis, wie auf meinen Sohn, bei seinem stark entwickelten Ehrgefühl ein derartiger Schlag wirken würde. Ich würde es Ihnen sehr danken, lieber Herr Doktor, wenn Sie die Güte hätten, sich zu erkundigen, was eigentlich gegen meinen Sohn geltend gemacht worden ist. Daß es einen ernstlich berechtigten Grund haben könnte ist doch bei Charakter u. Gesinnungen meines Sohnes gänzlich ausgeschlossen. Die Vermutung liegt übrigens nahe, daß sein Widersacher kein anderer ist als sein früherer Komp<anie>führer Lt. Ebbinghaus, mit dem mein Sohn zu Anfang in nahezu freundschaftlichem Verkehr stand, über dessen merkwürdig ungleiches und nicht selten verletzendes Benehmen er sich aber nachher oft beklagt hat.

Selbstverständlich würde ich Ihre aufklärenden Mitteilungen absolut discret behandeln – auch meinem Sohn gegenüber, der von dieser Anfrage an Sie nichts erfahren soll.

Wenn Sie bei Gelegenheit über sich selbst und Ihr Wohlergehen einige Zeilen beifügen wollten würden Sie mich sehr erfreuen.
Im Voraus bestens dankend
herzlichst
Ihr alter Lehrer
Prof. EHusserl

"The assumption is obvious that his adversary is none other than his former company commander Lieutenant Ebbinghaus"

Freiburg 11 November 1916
My dear, dear Herr doctor!
I come today with a heartfelt request. To my most embarrassing surprise, my son informs me that it can be inferred from a suggestion from an officer known to him that in the election of the officers in the 3rd Battalion an objection was raised against him while in his own, the 2nd Battalion, the election went smoothly. I do not need to tell you what a rejection in the officers' election – and one that is now to be feared – means for a young man, and I am full of concern regarding my son for his highly developed sense of honor that such an impact might have. I would very much like to thank you, dear Doctor, if you could kindly inquire about what actually has been asserted against my son. That it could have a seriously legitimate reason with respect to character and intentions of my son can be completely excluded. Incidentally, the assumption is obvious that his adversary is none other than his former company commander, Lieutenant Ebbinghaus, with whom my son initially stood in almost amicable communication, but whose strangely uneven and often injurious behavior he has often complained about afterwards.

Of course, I would treat your enlightening communications with absolute discretion – even to my son, who should learn nothing of this request to you.

If you would add a few lines concerning yourself and your well-being on occasion, this would greatly please me.
Best thanks in advance,
Sincerely,
Your old teacher,
Prof. EHusserl

Friedrich Neumann

„<Ich> hoffe sogar, noch manchmal aus der Form, in der ich den Krieg erlebte, inneren Gewinn zu ziehen"

Cassel-Wilhelmshöhe, 20. 5. 1919.
Sehr geehrter Herr Professor!
All das, was sie mir vor einigen Wochen schrieben, drängt mich zu einer Antwort. Ich wollte freilich meinen Brief auf freundlicheren Tage hinausschieben. Aber das dunkele Tal, durch das wir hindurch müssen, wird uns noch lange umfassen. Und so nehme ich Einiges wenigstens mir heute von Herzen. Das Meiste von dem, was mich bewegt, mag ich in diesen erregten Wochen nicht aussprechen.

Daß Sie in diesem Frühjahr das 60. Lebensjahr vollendeten, war mir entgangen, zumal mein Briefwechsel mit Freunden, die mich erinnern konnten, im letzten Revolutionsquartal an Regelmäßigkeit eingebüßt hat.

Ich komme nicht mit der Wendung des „Glückwünschens". Aber aus tiefstem Herzen möchte ich Ihnen danken für das, was sie in mir erweckt haben. Ich möchte den ersten Tag segnen, der mich zu Ihnen in den Hörsaal führte. Ich kann vielleicht später einmal davon sprechen, wie mir die Phänomenologie ein Erretter aus philosophischer Not wurde, wie sie mich aus engen Gassen auf freies, lichtes Feld führte.

Sie haben gegeben und werden noch so viel geben! Mögen auch die nächsten Jahre in steigendem Maße für unsere Mitmenschen eine Zeit des Nehmens werden! Sie gehn fast zeitlos Ihren Weg. Und darum gerade kann und muß die Phänomenologie noch so viel für Wissen und Leben bedeuten. Denn immer mehr, glaube ich, kann man erkennen, wie viele Philosophien unserer Zeit doch nur eine Scholastik der bestehenden mechanistischen Weltbilder waren.

Sie nehmen viel Anteil an meinen Zukunftsplänen! Natürlich will ich weiter arbeiten an den geistigen Problemen, die uns umstehen. Es ist für mich ja Zwang. Die langen Kriegsjahre haben mir freilich den Weg etwas verlängert, so daß ich immer noch der Außenwelt ein Fremdling bin. Ich hadere nicht mit dem Geschick; hoffe sogar, noch manchmal aus der Form, in der ich den Krieg erlebte, inneren Gewinn zu ziehen. Aber eine stille Arbeitszeit muß ich nun noch durchmachen, ohne bei den schwierigen Verhältnissen sagen zu können, wie sich für mich die Verhältnisse gestalten werden. Ich schrieb Ihnen wohl schon, dass ich im Herbst meine Studien zur neuhochdeutschen Schriftsprache herauszubringen gedenke. Fast die Hälfte ist bereits gedruckt. Professor E. Schröder liest wieder liebenswürdiger Weise die Korrektur mit. Nach außen hin werde ich zunächst einmal als Germanist erscheinen. Im Laufe der Jahre wird aber wohl der Philosoph sich dabei immer mehr kundgeben können. Plane ich doch, mich immer mehr syntaktischen Studien hinzugeben. Daß dort in Freiburg eine Arbeit über Humboldt entsteht, interessiert mich daher kernhaft.

Da ich nach dem Kriege nicht mehr in der Lage bin, beruflos auf unbestimmte Zeit zu bleiben, habe ich zunächst einmal den Schuldienst bejaht. Zudem hatte ich das Staatsexamen gemacht und 1914 das Seminarjahr begonnen. Wenn man zu etwas angesetzt hat, muß man es auch zu Ende führen. In etwa vier Wochen denke ich diesen Vorbereitungs- <der Text bricht ab>

Briefentwurf von Friedrich Neumann an Husserl, 20. V. 1919

Draft of a letter from Friedrich Neumann to Husserl, 20 May 1919

Friedrich Neumann, um 1915

Friedrich Neumann, around 1915

"[I] even hope to profit internally from the war in the form in which I experienced it"

Cassel-Wilhelmshöhe, 20 May 1919.
Dear Herr Professor!
Everything that you wrote me a few weeks ago compels me to write in response. I wanted, of course, to postpone my letter for more felicitous days. But, the dark valley through which we must now pass will embrace us for still much time to come. And so let me at least take some things from the heart today. Most of what moves me remains impossible for me to express in these agitated weeks.

It had escaped me that you were celebrating your 60th birthday this spring, especially since my correspondence with friends who could recall this for me has lost its regularity during the last quarter revolution.

I do not come with the phrase "congratulations." Yet, from the bottom of my heart I want to thank you for what you have awakened in me. I want to bless that first day which led me to you in the lecture hall. Maybe later I can talk about how phenomenology became a savior from philosophical distress, how it led me out of the narrow streets into an open and bright field.

Your have given and will continue to give so much! May the coming years also be in increasing measure a time of taking for our fellow human beings! You are going about your timeless ways. And that is precisely why phenomenology can and must mean so much for knowledge and life. More and more, I believe that one can see how many philosophies of our time were only a Scholasticism of the presently mechanistic worldview.

You are participating a great deal in my future plans! Of course, I want to keep working on the spiritual problems which surround us. It's a compulsion for me. The long war-years have, of course, extended my path, so that I am still a stranger to the outside world. I do not quarrel with destiny. [I] even hope to profit internally from the war in the form in which I experienced it. But, I still must endure a quiet working time, without being able to say how the relations will be shaped for me. I already wrote to you that I intend to publish my studies on the new High German written language in the autumn. Almost half of it is already printed. Professor E. Schröder kindly reads the corrections again. From

Friedrich Neumann als Leutnant der Reserve in in der Champagne, Januar 1917

Friedrich Neumann as Lieutenant in the Reserves, in Champagne, January 1917

outward appearances, I will at first appear as a Germanist. Over the years, however, the philosopher will most likely become more and more manifest. I am planning to indulge more and more with studies of syntax. I am, therefore, very interested in the fact that a work on Humboldt is emerging here in Freiburg.

Since I am no longer in a position to remain without employment after the war for an indefinite amount of time, I have accepted after all service in the teaching profession. In addition, I had passed the state examination and in 1914 started the seminar that year. When one has started something, one must see it through. In about four weeks, I think that this preparation- [the text breaks off]

Max Scheler (1874-1928)

Max Scheler (ca. 1912)

Max Scheler (around 1912)

Max Scheler: geb. 22. 8. 1874 in München, gest. 19. 5. 1928 in Frankfurt am Main. – 1894 Studium der Philosophie (Psychologie) in München, ab 1895 Medizin, dann Wechsel nach Berlin. 1896 Philosophiestudium in Jena, dort 1897 Promotion bei Rudolf Eucken („Beiträge zur Feststellung der Beziehungen zwischen den logischen und ethischen Prinzipien"). 1899 Habilitation bei Eucken („Die transzendentale und die psychologische Methode"), danach ab 1900/01 Privatdozent in Jena, wo er 1902 zum ersten Mal Husserl begegnete. 1906 bis 1910 Privatdozent in München. Dort schließt er sich dem Schülerkreis von Theodor Lipps an, die sich ab etwa 1902 mit Husserls Phänomenologie auseinandersetzen. Wegen privater Verwicklungen (öffentlich ausgetragene Ehestreitigkeiten) wird Scheler 1910 von der Universität München entlassen. Er hält daraufhin in kleinem Kreis außerhalb der Universität Vorlesungen (u.a. in der Göttinger Philosophischen Gesellschaft, deren Mitglied er war, vor Schülern Husserls) und lebt von 1912 bis 1918 als freier Schriftsteller zumeist in Berlin. Herausgeber (mit Husserl, Geiger, Pfänder, Reinach; später für kurze Zeit mit Heidegger) des „Jahrbuchs für Philosophie und phänomenologische Forschung" (1913-1930). Im September 1914 meldet sich Scheler als Kriegsfreiwilliger beim Luftschiff-Ersatzbataillon in Köln (dort wird er wegen eines Augenastigmatismus abgelehnt). Im August 1916 Einberufung zum Kriegsdienst bei der Feldartillerie in Schwerin, aber wiederum wegen seines Augenleidens nach kurzer Zeit als dienstuntauglich entlassen. Von 1917 bis 1918 als Referent im Auftrag des deutschen Generalkommandos und des auswärtigen Amtes in den Niederlanden und der Schweiz tätig. Während des Krieges entfaltet Scheler eine rege Publikationstätigkeit (1915: „Der Genius des Krieges und der Deutsche Krieg"; 1915/16: „Soziologische Neuorientierung und die Aufgabe der deutschen Katholiken nach dem Krieg"; 1916: „Krieg und Aufbau"; 1917: „Die Ursachen des Deutschenhasses"). 1919 wird Scheler zum Direktor des Instituts für Sozialwissenschaften in Köln ernannt, danach Professor für Philosophie und Soziologie an der Universität Köln. – Der Nachlass von Max Scheler befindet sich in der Bayerischen Staatsbibliothek München.

Max Scheler: born on August 22, 1874 in Munich, died on May 19, 1928 in Frankfurt am Main. 1894, study of philosophy (psychology) in Munich, from 1895, medicine in Berlin; 1896, study of philosophy in Jena. 1897, PhD with Rudolf Eucken ("Contributions to the Determination of the Relations between Logical and Ethical Principles"). 1899, Habilitation with Eucken ("The Transcendental and the Psychological Method"). 1900-1901, Privatdozent in Jena. Meets Husserl in 1902. 1906-1910, Privatdozent in Munich. Joins the circle of students around Theodor Lipps, who are engaged with Husserl's phenomenology since 1902. Due to personal difficulties and disputes, Scheler is released in 1910 by the University of Munich. Gives lectures to a small circle outside the university (among others, the Göttingen Philosophical Society, of which he was a member); lives from 1912 to 1918 mostly as a freelance writer in Berlin. Editor (with Husserl, Geiger, Pfänder, Reinach, later for a short time with Heidegger) of the "Yearbook for Philosophy and Phenomenological Research" (1913-1930). In September 1914 Scheler reports as a war volunteer at an airship replacement battalion in Cologne (where he is rejected due to an eye stigmatism). In August 1916, conscription to military service with the field artillery in Schwerin, again dismissed as unfit for service due to eye ailment. From 1917 to 1918, active as a speaker on behalf of the German General Command and the Foreign Office in the Netherlands and Switzerland. During the war, Scheler publishes briskly: 1915, "The Genius of War and the German war"; 1915/16, "Sociological Reorientation and the Task of German Catholics after the war"; 1916, "War and Construction"; 1917, "The Causes of German Hatred". In 1919, Scheler was appointed director of the Institute for Social Sciences in Cologne, and subsequently Professor of philosophy and sociology at the University of Cologne. – The papers of Max Scheler are housed at the Bavarian State Library in Munich.

Bermes, Ch./Henckmann, W./Leonardy, H. (Hg.): Person und Wert. Schelers „Formalismus": Perspektiven und Wirkungen. Freiburg/München 2000. – Good, P. (Hg.): Max Scheler im Gegenwartsgeschehen der Philosophie. Bern/München 1975. – Henckmann, W.: Max Scheler. München 1998. – Kelly, E.: Structure and Diversity. Studies in the Phenomenological Philosophy of Max Scheler. Dordrecht 1997. – Mader, W.: Max Scheler in Selbstzeugnissen und Bilddokumenten. Reinbek bei Hamburg 1980. – Orth, E. W./Pfafferott, G. (Hg.): Studien zur Philosophie von Max Scheler. Internationales Max Scheler - Colloquium „Der Mensch im Weltalter des Ausgleichs". Freiburg 1994.

„Hat er sich auch als Freiwilliger gemeldet?"

"Did he volunteer as well?"

1/XI 14 Göttingen
Lieber Herr College.
Ich habe seit Beginn der Kriegszeit keine weiteren Correcturbogen d<es> Jahrb<uchs> bekommen. Ich vermuthe, daß Sie keine Msc. zum Druck gesendet haben, in der Meinung, daß wir damit bis zu Ende d<es> Kriegs pausieren wollen. Es ist aber richtiger, das Jahrb<uch> fortzudrucken, so daß es bei Ende d<es> Feldzugs sofort ausgegeben werden kann. Das entspricht auch dem Wunsche des Verlegers (der in Frankreich steht), mit dem ich mich in Verbindung gesetzt habe. Ich bitte Sie daher den Rest Ihres Msc. (den Text aufs äußerste zusammengedrängt u. unter Ausschaltung aller Excurse) an die Druckerei zu senden. Bitte auch genau durchzusehen u. insbesondere sorgsam zu corrigieren, da Coll. Reinach nicht mehr behilflich sein kann. Erfreulicherweise haben wir von ihm fortdauernd gute Nachrichten. Wie geht es Ihnen, l<ieber> H<err> C<ollege>, u. Ihrer Gemahlin? Haben Sie von Dr Hildebr<and> Nachricht? Hat er sich auch als Freiwilliger gemeldet? Meine beiden Söhne sind 12./X. ausgerückt und stehen seit d 20. X. mitten in den schweren Kämpfen in Belgi<e>n; um Dixmuiden etc. Seit 2 Wochen sind wir ohne Nachricht u. daher in ernster Sorge. – Das Semester hat angefangen, wir lesen, wenn auch vor kleinen Collegien. Bei mir gehts eigentlich noch.
Mit fr<eundlichen> Grüßen
Ihr
EHusserl
Herrn Niemeyer geht es auch gut.

1 November 1914 Göttingen
Dear colleague,
Since the beginning of the war, I have not received any further proofs for the Yearbook. I suppose you did not send a manuscript to the printer, in the view that we will take a pause until the end of the war. It is, however, more correct to continue printing the Yearbook, so that it could be issued immediately at the end of the campaign. This also corresponds to the wish of the publisher (who is in France), with whom I am in contact. I therefore ask if you could send the remainder of your manuscript to the printer (the texts should be compressed and exclude all tangents). Please also look carefully and especially make the corrections carefully, since colleague Reinach is no longer helpful anymore. Fortunately, we have continued good news from him. How are you, dear colleague and your wife? Do you have any news from Dr Hildebr[and]? Did he volunteer as well? My two sons have since October 12 moved out and find themselves since October 20th in hard fighting in Belgium around Dixmuiden. We are without any news since 2 weeks and therefore are very much concerned. The semester has begun, we are giving lectures, albeit for small seminars. Things are still ok for me.
With kind regards,
Your,
EHusserl
Mr. Niemeyer is also doing well.

Postkarte von Husserl an Max Scheler, 1. XI. 1914

Postcard from Husserl to Max Scheler, 1 November 1914

„Lange hatte ich mit meinem Militärverhältnis zu tun"

Seebad Heringsdorf, Villa Krüger,
9. Juli 15.
Sehr verehrter Herr Professor!
Vor allem – ich habe keinerlei Anfragen in puncto Jahrbuch von Ihrer Seite erhalten. Da ich viele Wochen in Österreich (Meran) war, ist es ja möglich, daß ich Ihre Briefe nicht erhielt. Alles, was ohne Absenderangabe, blieb liegen, was geschlossen war, ging (wenn möglich) zurück; eine ganze Reihe Sachen erhielt aber weder ich selbst noch der Absender. Auf diese Weise gingen mir eine ganze Anzahl Postsachen verloren.

Sie sind in einer völligen Täuschung befangen, wenn Sie annehmen, daß mir an der Erhaltung meines Verhältnisses zu Ihnen und zum Jahrbuchunternehmen weniger wie früher gelegen sei. Es ist mir ganz unfaßlich, wie Sie auf diese sonderbare Idee geraten können: Nach so langer Zeit treuer Zusammenarbeit! Wenn ich den Jahrbuchaufsatz bisher nicht fertig gestellt habe, so lag dies an mehreren Umständen. Lange hatte ich mit meinem Militärverhältnis zu tun. Ich hatte mich freiwillig zum Luftschiffersatzbataillon Köln gemeldet und auf den Eintritt (Mitte Juni) vorbereitet. Dann wurde ich wegen meines rechtsseitigen, durch Glas ununterstützbaren Augenastigmatismus nicht genommen; jetzt bin ich zur Feldartillerie gestellt und erwarte hier immer noch meine Einberufung. Zweitens wurde ich durch mein Kriegsbuch, zu dem ich täglich eine Menge Briefe, Recensionen, Polemiken u.sw. erhalte, sehr wider meinen Willen ziemlich stark in diese größte unser Aller Sorgen hineingezogen; was ja wohl auch begreiflich ist. Ich hatte dabei manche günstige Gelegenheit, bes<onders> dem Ausland gegenüber unserer Sache zu nützen und durfte solche nicht vorübergehen lassen. Vor allem aber nahm ich nicht an, daß der Verleger jetzt – wo fast alle Verlage ruhen und die gelehrte Jugend zum größten Teil draußen ist, das Jahrbuch herausbringen will. Wenn Sie schreiben, daß mir meine sonstige litter<arische> Tätigkeit so viel wichtiger erscheine als die Förderu<n>g des Jahrbuches, so beachten Sie nicht, daß Alles, was ich (außer dem Kriegsbuch) in letzter Zeit veröffentliche, lange vor dem Kriege geschrieben war. Die Aufs<ätze> sollten März 1914 erscheinen und es lag nur am Verleger, daß sie erst jetzt kommen.

Übrigens bin ich schon seit 2 Monaten wieder mit rein philosophischen Sachen beschäftigt; Sie geben sich einer grundirrigen Vorstellung hin, wenn sie meinten, ich sei in der Richtung, meine rein philosophischen Interessen etwas zugunsten einer publicistischen Tätigkeit dauernd zurückzustellen.-

<...>

Ich hätte Sie gerne noch Manches Persönliche gefragt. Aber die Piquirtheit und Fremdheit des Tones Ihres Briefes macht dies leider unmöglich.
Ergebenst
Max Scheler.

Auszug aus einem Brief von Max Scheler an Husserl, 9. VII. 1915

Excerpt from a letter from Max Scheler to Husserl, 9 July 1915

"For a long time I had to deal with my military relationship"

Seebad Heringsdorf, Villa Krüger,
9 July 15.
Dear Professor!
Above all, I have not received any Yearbook requests from your side. Since I spent many weeks in Austria (Meran), it is possible that I did not receive your letters. Everything that was left without a return address remained there, and what was unopened was (when possible) sent back. Many things were received neither by myself or the sender. In this manner, a great many pieces of mail were lost for me.

You are entirely deluded in assuming that I have less interest in maintaining my relationship as earlier times with you and the Yearbook. It is quite incomprehensible to me how you can come up with this strange idea: after so many years of faithful cooperation! If I have not completed the Yearbook essay thus far, this was due to several circumstances. For a long time I had to deal with my military relationship. I had volunteered for the airship replacement battalion in Cologne and prepared for the entrance (mid-June). I was then not accepted because of my eye astigmatism (right-sided), which cannot be corrected with glasses. I am currently assigned to field artillery and am still waiting for my orders. Second, I became through my war book, for which I daily receive a mass of letters, reviews, and polemical writings, very much against my will drawn into this greatest of all cares, which is, of course, understandable. In doing so, I thereby had many good opportunity, especially abroad, to benefit our cause and not let them pass by. Above all, I did not suppose that the publisher now – where almost all publishers are resting and the learned youth is mostly out there – wants to publish the Yearbook. When you write that my other literary activity seems to be much more important to me than the promotion of the Yearbook, you don't give due to the fact at all that I have published lately (except the war book), long before the war was prescribed. The essays were to appear in March, 1914, and that they only now appear is due only to the publisher.

By the way, I've been busy with purely philosophical matters for two months now. You give yourself a basically erroneous idea, when you think that I am constantly putting to the side my purely philosophically interests in favor of more journalistic activities.

Das 1915 erschienene „Kriegsbuch" von Max Scheler („Der Genius des Krieges und der deutsche Krieg")

Max Scheler's "War-book," published in 1915 ("The Genius of War and the German War")

[...]
I would like to have inquired about more personal things. But the sharp and strangeness of the tone of your letter makes this regrettably impossible.
Humbly,
Max Scheler.

„Ich bin trotz Ihrer Darlegungen ‚Pazifist'"

Heidelberg, 14/2 15
Sehr verehrter Herr College!
Haben Sie vielen herzlichen Dank für die freundliche Uebersendung Ihres schönen Werkes <„Der Genius des Krieges">! Ich habe es mit grosser Spannung und mit freudiger Zustimmung zu sehr vielen Dingen durchgelesen und darf mir wol die Freiheit nehmen Ihnen zu sagen, daß es meiner Ansicht nach das einzige unter den vielen Kriegsbüchern und Kriegsschriften überhaupt ist, welches Wert habe, und zwar grossen Wert.

Ich sage das, obwol ich gerade in den grundlegenden Gedanken nicht Ihrer Meinung bin. Auch den Gegner Ihrer Grundgedanken muß es mit Freude und hoher Achtung erfüllen zu sehen, wie, im besten Sinne des Wortes, grosszügig Sie alles behandeln, so ganz ohne persönliche Schimpferei und Gehässigkeit.

Die grundlegenden Angelegenheiten, in denen ich nicht mit Ihnen gehen kann, sind aber diese:

1) Die Berechtigung des Krieges überhaupt. Ich bin trotz Ihrer Darlegungen „Pazifist". Nicht zwar aus eudämonistischen und öconomischen Gründen, sondern

a) wegen des „Du sollst nicht töten" im allgemeinen und zwar deshalb nicht, weil wir Wesen und Bedeutung des Todes u. zumal des gewaltsamen Todes doch eben nicht kennen. Wer weiss, was das eigentlich den gewaltsam Getöteten angehen wird? (Zu sagen, man „wolle" ja doch nur kampfunfähig machen scheint mir – (verzeihen Sie das herbe Wort) – eine gewisse Dosis „cant" zu enthalten.)

b) wegen der Möglichkeit, daß Intelligenzen höchster Art jung vernichtet werden. Stellen Sie sich vor, Goethe, Kant und Beethoven seien jung als „Kriegsfreiwillige" gefallen. Hätten Sie statt dessen nicht lieber die Kriege Friedrichs d. Gr. u. 1813 verloren gehen sehen?

"Despite your statements, I am a 'pacifist'"

Heidelberg, 14 February 1915
Dear Colleague,
Thank you very much for the friendly sending of your beautiful work "The Genius of War"! I have read it with great suspense and with the joyful approval of many things, and may take the liberty of telling you that, in my opinion, it is the only one among the many war books and war memoirs which has value, and indeed great value.

I say that although I disagree with the basic idea. The opponent of your basic ideas must also be able to see with joy and great respect how, in the best sense of the word, you treat everything with generosity, without personal words of abuse and malice.

The basic affairs in which I can not enter with you, however, are these:

1) The justification of the war. Despite your statements, I am a "pacifist." Not for eudaemonistic and economic reasons, but

a) because of the "Thou shalt not kill" in general, and that the "not" is there because we just do not understand the nature and significance of death, and, especially, violent death. Who knows what this will actually do to those violently killed? (To say that one only wants to "incapacitate" seems to me – I apologize for the harsh word – to contain a certain dose of "cant.")

b) because of the possibility that the highest level of intelligence will be destroyed young. Imagine that Goethe, Kant, and Beethoven fell young as "war volunteers." Would you not prefer instead that the wars of Frederick the Great and the War of 1813 had been lost?

2) In my opinion, all "warfare" concerns only civilization, not "culture." The history of actual cultural achievements (philosophy, science, art) remains perfectly understandable, without mentioning any war, or even anything political at all!

3) You overestimate, it seems to me, the French and underestimate the British as to their cultural significance. You do not know what I want to call the "secret" Great Britain. There is deep religiosity and metaphysics, even mysticism, especially among the Scots. And there one indeed appreciates the greatness of individuality (in contrast to what you say on page 423!) – more than unfortunately with us. And there you have an honest respect for the "opponent" that you miss so often with us. The circles that I

2) Aller „Krieg" geht meines Erachtens nur die Zivilisation, nicht die „Kultur" an. Die Geschichte der eigentlichen Kulturleistungen (Philos<ophie>, Wissenschaft, Kunst) bleibt durchaus verständlich, ohne daß irgend ein Krieg, ja überhaupt irgend etwas Politisches auch nur erwähnt wird!

3) Sie überschätzen, wie mir scheint, die Franzosen und unterschätzen die Briten ihrer Kulturbedeutung nach. Sie kennen nicht, was ich das „heimliche" Grossbritannien nennen möchte. Da steckt tiefe Religiosität und Metaphysik, ja Mystik, zumal bei den Schotten. Und da schätzt man gerade die grosse Individualität (im Gegensatz zu dem, was Sie Seite 423 sagen!) – mehr als leider bei uns. Und man hat die ehrliche Achtung vor dem „Gegner", die man bei uns so oft vermisst. Die Kreise, an die ich denke, sind alle nicht materialistisch = sensualistisch = chauvinistisch! Ich habe den Eindruck, daß bei uns gerade unter den Akademikern viel mehr von dieser Dreiheit zu finden ist als in Britannien.

Sie haben Recht, es naiv zu nennen, daß man sich über die brit<ische> Kriegserklärung bei uns gewundert hat. Ich habe mich nicht gewundert. Alle meine ehrlichen britischen Freunde haben mir immer wieder gesagt: „Der Krieg kommt sicher, die kleine Minderheit die, wie wir, dagegen ist, habe gar keine Macht." Aber „even the idea of a war between Germany and Great Britain would be frivolous" hat mir ein Aberdeener Freund auch gesagt! –

Noch einige Stellen, die mich besonders gefreut haben: Seite 165 ff., 307, 318!, 334!, 369/70 Anm. 96, 403/4 (die famose protestantische Theologie!). Aber das sind nur wenige Stellen unter vielen. –

Wenn ich Ihnen meine „Wirklichkeitslehre" senden werde, werden Sie des Näheren sehen können, wie ich über „Kultur", „Staat" und was damit zusammenhängt, denke. Für heute nur noch dieses, daß ich, wenn man es richtig versteht, wol sagen könnte „credo in unam sanctam, catholicam ecclesiam", als dem Staat, dass ich aber nicht an die Staaten als an eigentliche Wesentlichkeiten „glaube".

Nochmals vielen Dank u. beste Grüsse von meiner Frau und Ihrem aufrichtig ergebenen
Hans Driesch.
P.S. Sehr gespannt bin ich auf Ihre Schrift über den Tod.

---

think of are all not materialistic = sensualistic = chauvinistic! I have the impression that there is much more of this trinity among us academics than in Britain.

You are right to call it naive that you were wondering about the British declaration of war. I did not wonder. All my honest British friends kept telling me, "the war is coming, the small minority who, like us, oppose it, have no power at all." But "even the idea of a war between Germany and Great Britain would be frivolous," an Aberdeen friend also told me!

A few more passages that have particularly pleased me: page 165 ff., 307, 318 !, 334 !, 369/70 Note 96, 403/4 (the famous Protestant theology!). But these are just a few places among many.

If I send you my "Theory of Reality" you will be able to see in more detail how I think about "culture," "state," and what is related to it. For today only this more, that I, when correctly understood, can truly say 'credo in unam sanctam, catholicam ecclesiam' [I believe in one Catholic Church], as the state, and that I do not actually 'believe' in states as something essential.

Thanks again and best regards from my wife and your sincerely devoted
Hans Driesch.
P.S. I am very curious about your writing about death.

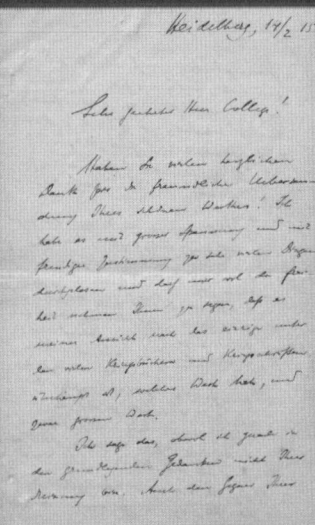

Brief von Hans Driesch an Max Scheler, 14. II. 1915

Letter from Hans Driesch to Max Scheler, 14 February 1915

Hans Driesch (1867-1941), Biologe und Philosoph

Hans Driesch (1867-1941), biologist and philosopher

„Dass in der grossen Weltfrage auch unsere tiefgrabenden Philosophen den Spaten einsetzen"

Speyer, den 17. August 1915

Hochgeehrter Herr!
Die letzten Monate beständig auf Reisen zwischen München und Messines, bitte ich tausendmal um Entschuldigung, dass ich erst heute für die überaus gütige Zusendung des Werkes „Der Genius des Krieges" innigst danke. Es ist freudig zu begrüssen, dass in der grossen Weltfrage auch unsere tiefgrabenden Philosophen den Spaten einsetzen, und wie ich unterwegs hörte, ist Ihr Werk bereits in weiten und hohen Kreisen beachtet worden. Ich möchte grollen, dass mir Gehetzten nicht jetzt schon ein paar ruhige Tage beschieden sind, um Ihren Gedanken zu folgen.

In vorzüglicher Hochachtung und unter Erneuerung meines Dankes

Euer Hochwohlgeboren
ergebenster
M. v. Faulhaber,
Bischof v. Speyer

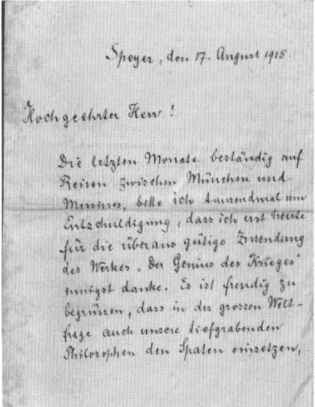
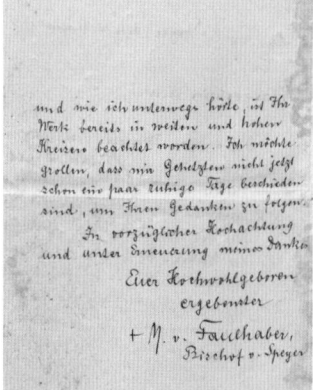

Brief von Bischof Michael v. Faulhaber an Max Scheler, 17. VIII. 1915

Letter from Bishop Michael von Faulhaber to Max Scheler, 17 August 1915

Michael v. Faulhaber (1869-1952) als Feldprobst im Jahr 1917

Michael von Faulhaber (1869-1952) as military chaplain in 1917

"That also our profoundly digging philosophers will use the spade for the great questions of the world"

Speyer, 17 August 1915

Dear Sir!
Constantly traveling between Munich and Messines these last months, I apologize a thousand times, that I am only today expressing my sincerest thanks for the very kind sending of your work "The Genius of War." It is such a joy to welcome that also our profoundly digging philosophers will use the spade for the great questions of the world, and heard on the road, that your work has already been noticed in wide and high circles. I want to complain, I, who am busy all the time, that I have not been given a few quiet days to follow your thoughts.
  With the greatest respect and renewal of my thanks,

Yours truly,
M. v. Faulhaber,
Bishop v. Speyer

Michael v. Faulhaber in einem Schützengraben an der Westfront

Michael von Faulhaber in a trench on the Western Front

Edith Stein (1891-1942)

Edith Stein, ca. 1918

Edith Stein, around 1918

Edith Stein: geb. 12. 10. 1891 in Breslau, 9. 8. 1942 im KZ Auschwitz-Birkenau ermordet. – Ab 1911 Lehramtsstudium an der Universität in Breslau; 1913 bis 1916 Studium an den Universitäten in Göttingen und Freiburg in den Fächern Psychologie, Philosophie (u.a. bei Husserl und Adolf Reinach), Geschichte und Germanistik. – Zu Kriegsbeginn freiwillige Ausbildung als Krankenschwester. Von April bis September 1915 im Typhuslazarett in Mährisch-Weißkirchen tätig. 1915 Staatsexamen in Göttingen, danach Referendarzeit in ihrer Heimatstadt Breslau und 1916 Promotion („Zum Problem der Einfühlung") bei Husserl in Freiburg. Von 1916 bis 1918 Assistentin von Husserl. Danach mehrere vergebliche Versuche zur Habilitation zugelassen zu werden (in Göttingen mit der Arbeit „Psychische Kausalität", in Breslau und Freiburg mit der Arbeit „Potenz und Akt"). Schlüsselerlebnis für ihre Konversion von der jüdischen zur katholischen Glaubenszugehörigkeit ist ihre Beschäftigung mit der Heiligen Teresa von Ávila, deren Schriften sie bei ihren Besuchen in dem Haus des Ehepaars Conrad in Bergzabern kennenlernt. Beeindruckt hat sie auch der Umgang der befreundeten Anna Reinach mit dem Kriegstod ihres Mannes Adolf Reinach. Im Januar 1922 Taufe in Bergzabern und Aufnahme in die römisch-katholische Kirche. Ab Ostern 1923 Tätigkeit als Lehrerin in Speyer. Ab 1932 Tätigkeit in der katholischen Einrichtung des deutschen Instituts für wissenschaftliche Pädagogik in Münster. Oktober 1933 Aufnahme in den Karmel Maria vom Frieden in Köln. 1938 zusammen mit ihrer Schwester Rosa Übersiedelung in den Karmel im niederländischen Echt. August 1942 Verhaftung und Ermordung der Schwestern im Vernichtungslager Auschwitz-Birkenau. Papst Johannes Paul II. spricht Edith Stein am 1. Mai 1987 selig. Heiligsprechung am 11. Oktober 1998. – Der Nachlass von Edith Stein befindet sich im Edith-Stein-Archiv des Karmels Maria vom Frieden in Köln.

Edith Stein: born on October 12, 1891 in Breslau, murdered on August 9, 1942 in Auschwitz-Birkenau. 1911, studied teaching at the University of Breslau; 1913-1916, studied psychology, philosophy (with Husserl and Reinach), history, and German at the Universities of Göttingen and Freiburg. With the outbreak of the war, volunteered for training as a nurse. From April to September 1915, served in the field hospital for typhoid in Mährisch-Weißkirchen. 1915, state examinations in Göttingen, followed by teacher training in Breslau; 1916, PhD ("On the Problem of Empathy") with Husserl in Freiburg. 1916-1918, Husserl's assistant. After repeated attempts (in Göttingen with the work "Psychological Causality," and in Breslau und Freiburg with the work "Potency and Act"), she was unable to complete her habilitation. Decisive experience for her conversion from Judaism to the Catholic faith after her study of Teresa of Ávila's writings, which she discovered during her visits at the Conrads in Bergzabern. Influence as well of Anna Reinach after the death of her husband, Adolf Reinach. January 1922, baptism in Bergzabern and entry into the Roman-Catholic church. 1923, teacher in Speyer and in the Catholic German Institute for Scientific Pedagogy in Münster. October 1933, enters to the Karmel Maria vom Frieden convent in Cologne. 1938, together with her sister Rosa, moves to the Carmelites in Holland (Echt). August 1942, arrested and then murdered at the Auschwitz-Birkenau concentration camp. Edith Stein canonized by Pope John Paul II on 11 October 1998. – Edith Stein's papers are housed at the Edith-Stein-Archiv des Karmel Maria vom Frieden in Cologne.

Posselt, T. R.: Edith Stein. The Life of a Philosopher and Carmelite. Washington D.C. 2005. – Beckmann, B.: Phänomenologie des religiösen Erlebnisses. Religionsphilosophische Überlegungen im Anschluß an Adolf Reinach und Edith Stein. Würzburg 2003. – Calcagno, A. (ed.): Edith Stein: Women, Social-Political Philosophy, Theology, Metaphysics and Public History. New Approaches and Applications. Heidelberg/New York/Dordrecht/London 2016. – Fetz, R. L./Rath, M./Schulz, P. (Hg.): Studien zur Philosophie von Edith Stein. Freiburg/München 1993. – Imhof, B. W.: Edith Steins philosophische Entwicklung. Leben und Werk. Basel/Boston 1987. – Müller, A. U.: Grundzüge der Religionsphilosophie Edith Steins. Freiburg 1993.

„Ich muss nicht, ich darf"

Mitten in unser friedliches Studentenleben hinein platzte die Bombe des serbischen Königsmordes. Der Juli war erfüllt von der Frage: Wird es zu einem europäischen Kriege kommen? Alles sah danach aus, als ob ein schweres Gewitter heraufzöge. Aber wir konnten es nicht fassen, daß es wirklich dazu kommen sollte. Wer im Krieg oder nach dem Krieg herangewachsen ist, der kann sich von der Sicherheit, in der wir bis 1914 zu leben glaubten, keine Vorstellung machen. Der Frieden, die Festigkeit des Besitzes, die Beständigkeit der gewohnten Verhältnisse waren uns wie eine unerschütterliche Lebensgrundlage. Als man schließlich merkte, daß der Sturm unaufhaltsam näherkam, suchte man sich den Verlauf klarzumachen. Das stand fest, daß er ganz anders würde als alle früheren Kriege. Eine so entsetzliche Vernichtung würde es sein, daß es nicht lange dauern könnte. In ein paar Monaten würde alles vorbei sein. <…>

Als ich zur letzten Seminarsitzung in Reinachs Arbeitszimmer trat, war noch niemand da. Auf seinem Schreibtisch lag ein großer, aufgeschlagener Atlas. Bald nach mir kam Kaufmann. Auch er bemerkte die aufgeschlagene Landkarte. „Reinach studiert auch den Atlas", sagte er. Es wurde an diesem Abend nicht mehr philosophiert. Man sprach nur noch von den kommenden Ereignissen. „Sie müssen auch mit, Herr Doktor?", fragte Kaufmann. „Ich muß nicht, ich darf", gab Reinach zurück. Ich freute mich herzlich über diese Antwort. Sie entsprach durchaus meinem eigenen Empfinden.

(Edith Stein: „Aus dem Leben einer jüdischen Familie", ESGA 1, S. 240-241)

"It's not that I must, it's that I'm allowed to go"

In the midst of our placid student life, the bombshell of the Serbian assassination of royalty exploded. July was dominated by the question: Will war break out in Europe? Everything seemed to indicate that a terrible storm was looming. Yet, we found it inconceivable that it could really come to this. No one growing up during or since the war can possibly imagine the security which we assumed for ourselves to be living before 1914. Our life was founded on an indestructible basis of peace, stable ownership of property, and the permanent circumstances to which we were accustomed. When one finally noticed that the storm was inevitably approaching, one attempted to get a clear idea of what was likely to happen. One thing was certain. It would be completely different from all other previous wars. The destruction would be so terrible that it could not possibly last long. In a few months, it would all be over. [...]

When I entered Reinach's study for the final session of his seminar, the room was empty. A very large map was spread out on his desk. Kaufmann arrived soon after I did. He also noticed the open map. "Reinach, too, is studying the map," he said. That evening there was no more philosophizing. We only talked about the coming events. "Must you also go, Herr Doctor?" Kaufmann asked. "It's not that I must, it's that I'm allowed to go," Reinach replied. His statement pleased me very much. It expressed so much my own feelings as well. (Edith Stein: "Life in a Jewish Family", CWES 1, 293-294; translation slightly modified)

Edith Stein hatte sich bei Kriegsbeginn als Krankenschwester ausbilden lassen. Vom April bis September 1915 war sie im Typhuslazarett in Mährisch-Weißkirchen tätig.

Edith Stein trained as a nurse at the beginning of the war. From April to September 1915, she worked in the typhoid field hospital in Moravian-Weisskirchen.

„Heute hat mein individuelles Leben aufgehört und alles, was ich bin, gehört dem Staat; wenn ich den Krieg überlebe, dann will ich es als neu geschenkt wieder aufnehmen"

Freiburg 9. II. 17.
Goethestr. 63.
Lieber Herr Ingarden,
herzlichen Dank für Ihren Brief. Es freut mich sehr, daß Sie Fortschritte im Verständnis des Deutschtums machen. Sie sind „verliebt in die polnische Seele" – gerade die Worte kamen mir auch, als ich mir neulich einmal den Grundunterschied unserer Stellung zu Staat und Volk klar zu machen suchte. Sehen Sie, ich kann so wenig in Deutschland verliebt sein wie in mich selbst, denn ich bin ja es selbst, d. h. ein Teil davon. Die Völker sind „Personen", die ihr Leben haben, ihr Werden und Wachsen und Vergehen. Es ist ein Leben jenseits des unsern, obwohl es das unsere mit in sich einbezieht. Darum kann man nicht sinnvoll fragen, ob sie groß oder klein sein „sollen", d. h. ob wir etwas dazu tun sollen, denn das liegt so wenig im Bereiche unserer Macht, wie die Zellen darüber zu beschließen haben, ob der Organismus, den sie aufbauen, wachsen oder abnehmen soll. Aber wir werden nicht bloß aufgebraucht wie Zellen, sondern wir können uns unseres Verhältnisses zu dem Ganzen, dem wir angehören, bewußt werden (ich glaube sogar, daß die wirksamen Entwicklungstendenzen erlebbar sind) und können uns freiwillig unterordnen. Je lebendiger und mächtiger dies Bewußtsein in einem Volke wird, desto mehr gestaltet es sich zum Staate, und diese Gestaltung ist seine Organisation. Staat ist selbstbewußtes Volk, das seine Funktionen discipliniert. Da mir nun das Erstarken des Selbstbewußtseins mit einer aufsteigenden Entwicklungstendenz verbunden zu sein scheint, so scheint mir die Organisation als ein Zeichen innerer Kraft und das Volk das vollkommenste (seiner Durchbildung als Volk, natürlich nicht seinen „Charakteranlagen" nach), das am meisten Staat ist. Und ich glaube bei ganz objektiver Betrachtung sagen zu können, daß es seit Sparta und Rom nirgends ein so mächtiges Staatsbewußtsein gegeben hat wie in Preußen und im neuen Deutschen Reich. Darum halte ich es für ausgeschlossen, daß wir jetzt unterliegen. Vielleicht erscheint Ihnen das alles als wüste Spekulation. Das ist es aber nicht. Reichlich unklar, das weiß ich, aber durchaus auf Phänomenen beruhend. Ein Erlebnis hat sich mir besonders eingeprägt: wie ich am Tage unserer Mobilmachung nach 24stündiger Fahrt heimkam und mich aus dem Familienkreise zurückzog, weil ich es nicht ertragen konnte, von gleichgültigen (d. h. persönlichen) Angelegenheiten reden zu hören; da stand es mir plötzlich ganz klar und deutlich vor Augen: heute hat mein individuelles Leben aufgehört und alles, was ich bin, gehört dem Staat; wenn ich den Krieg überlebe, dann will ich es als neu geschenkt wieder aufnehmen. Das war kein Produkt eines überreizten Nervenzustandes, sondern ist bis heute in mir lebendig geblieben, und ich leide die ganze Zeit darunter, daß ich nicht den rechten Platz gefunden habe, um ganz in diesem Sinne zu handeln. Und das ist der Geist, der bei uns lebendig ist, wenn auch die Mehrzahl anders denken mag und ganz gewiß viel dummes Zeug geschwätzt wird. Von Haß gegen „englischen Krämergeist", von Kulturprogramm gegen „östliche Barbarei" ist ja bei meiner Auffassung keine Spur. Mein Vertrauen auf unsere Regierung beruht darauf, daß wir Männer an der Spitze haben, die keine genialen Projekte machen, sondern ganz still und demütig zu erlauschen suchen, wohin der Lauf des Weltgeschehens gehen will. Und die Schwäche der Entente (+ Herrn Wilson) ist es, daß sie ein Programm hat zur Gestaltung Europas. Solche Pläne können immer nur gelingen, wenn sie zufällig mit der Tendenz der historischen Entwicklung zusammenfallen. Sonst kommt man unfehlbar unters Rad. Ja, nun also Amerika (das steht natürlich an der Nullgrenze der staatlichen Entwicklung)! Die Stimmung bei uns ist keineswegs gedrückt, vielmehr ein hellerer, heiterer Trotz: „und wenn die Welt voll Teufel wär" <…>
Recht herzliche Grüße
Edith Stein.

Brief von Edith Stein an Roman Ingarden, 9. II. 1917 (ESGA 4, S. 42 ff.)

"Today my individual life ceased, and everything who I am belongs to the state. Should I survive the war, I would then want to begin my life anew based on this conviction."

63 Goethestrasse
Freiburg
9 February 1917
Dear Herr Ingarden,

Thank you very much for your letter. I'm very happy that you are making progress in understanding Germanness. You are "in love with the Polish soul." Those are precisely the words that came to me recently as I attempted to become clear about the fundamental distinction between our positions regarding the state and the people. You see, I can no more be in love with Germany than I can with myself for, indeed, I am Germany, that is, I am a part of Germany. People are "persons" who have life: they are born, they grow, and they pass away. We have life beyond our own, though it includes our own. It thus makes no sense to ask whether it "should" be large or small, that is, whether we should do something for it, for we have as little control over that as cells which form an organism have in deciding whether or not they should grow. However, we are not just only consummed like cells, but we are able to become conscious of our relationship to the whole to which we belong (I even believe that we can experience effective developmental tendencies) and voluntarily can subordinate ourselves to it. The livelier and more powerful consciousness becomes in a people, the more the people develop into a state. This development is its organization. The state is a self-conscious people which disciplines its own functions. Since, for me, the strengthening of self-consciousness appears to be connected with an increasing tendency in development, it likewise appears that organization is a sign of inner strength; the people who are most organized (according to the complete formation of the people, certainly not according to their "character traits") is a people who can most become a state. And I believe I can say quite objectively that the self-consciousness of being a state is more powerful in Prussia and the new Germany than anywhere since Sparta and Rome. I therefore rule out the possibility of defeat.

Perhaps all of this appears to you as wild speculation. However, it is not. I know that this is not very clear, but phenomena supports this throughout. There is an experience in particular that especially made an impression on me: when I arrived home on the day of our mobilization after a twenty-four-hour trip, I withdrew from the family circle because I could not bear to hear the discussions of banal (personal) concerns. It, then, suddenly became quite clear to me: today my individual life ceased, and everything who I am belongs to the state. Should I survive the war, I would then want to begin my life anew based on this conviction. This was not the product of an overly excited nervous condition but has remained with me until this day. I suffer continually because I have not found the right place from which totally to live up to this conviction. And that is the spirit that lives among us even though the majority may think otherwise and most certainly values a lot of nonsensical gossip.

In my mind, there is no trace of hatred against the "English small-mindedness" of cultural programs or against "Eastern barbarians." My trust in our government rests on the fact that we have leaders who do not pursue any grandiose projects but rather seek quietly and humbly to discover the course of world events. And the weakness of the Entente (and Mr. Wilson) is that they have a plan for the structuring of Europe. Such plans could succeed only if they were accidentally to coincide with the tendency of historical development. Otherwise, without fail we would fall into bad times. Indeed, also America (which stands at the beginning of political development). The voice among us is in no way suppressed. Rather, it is enthusiastic with a bright and cheerful defiance: "and though his world, with devils filled,"* [...]

Kindest regards,
Edith Stein

* Translator's note: a line from Luther's hymn "A Mighty Fortress is our God."

Letter to Edith Stein from Roman Ingarden, February 9, 1917 (CWES 12, 43-46; translation slightly modified)

Roman Ingarden (1893-1970); polnischer Phänomenologe, der von 1912 an mit Unterbrechungen bei Husserl studierte und bei ihm 1918 in Freiburg mit einer Arbeit uber Bergson promovierte (Aufnahme 1916).

Roman Ingarden (1893-1970). Polish phenomenologist, who studied from 1912 with various interruptions with Husserl and earned his PhD in 1918 in Freiburg with a thesis on Bergson (photo from 1916).

„Gerhart Husserl ist wieder verwundet, und wieder am Kopf"

12. X. <1918>

Vor mir liegt ein Stoß Briefe und eine ganze Bibliothek: 4 Bände Schleiermacher-Predigten (Original-Ausgabe), die Brüder Karamasoff, die Christuslegenden von S. Lagerlöf und eine Sammlung deutscher religiöser Dichtungen in den Büchern der Rose. Dabei ist noch nicht alles da, was ich zu erwarten habe. Doch trotz aller Liebesbeweise, für die ich herzlich dankbar bin, liegt es mir heute gänzlich fern, in der üblichen Weise „Geburtstag zu feiern". Man ist doch jetzt innerlich ganz in Anspruch genommen durch die große Entscheidung, die in der nächsten Zeit fallen soll. Erst schien es mir so klar und unzweideutig, was man wünschen müßte. Aber nun fühle ich wieder, daß wir es ja nicht wissen können, was das wahrhaft Heilsame ist, und daß darum all unser Hoffen und Wünschen Torheit ist. Man muß hinnehmen, was auch kommen mag, und dann sehen, das Beste daraus zu gestalten. Ob wohl der Mann, in dessen Hände jetzt das Geschick der Welt gelegt ist, die ganze Last der Verantwortung fühlt, die auf ihm ruht? – Zu der allgemeinen Sorge kommt noch eine besondere: Gerhart H<usserl> ist wieder verwundet, und wieder am Kopf. Man weiß noch nichts Näheres. Ich sprach gestern nur Elli <Husserl>, die Eltern waren – von den Aufregungen abgespannt – schon zu Bett gegangen, als ich kam. Es kam vor einigen Tagen eine kurze Karte aus dem Kriegslazarett Sedan, nicht eigenhändig geschrieben, aber unverkennbar von ihm selbst diktiert, seitdem nichts mehr. Gestern gelang es mir noch, Elli durch Interpretation des Wortlauts zu beruhigen, aber heute fürchte ich mich fast davor, wieder hinzugehen. Es wäre zu schrecklich für die ganze Familie, wenn es schlimm ausginge.
Viele Grüße und nochmals von Herzen Dank!

Ihre
Edith Stein

"Gerhart Husserl has been wounded again in the head"

12 October [1918]

A mound of letters and an entire library stand before me: four volumes of Schleiermacher's sermons (original edition), the Brothers Karamazov, the legends of Christ by S. Lagerlöf, and a collection of German religious poems from the Books of the Rose. That is still not all that I expect to have. However, in spite of all of the proofs of love, for which I am very thankful, it is completely alien to me to "celebrate a birthday" in the usual manner because I am now completely preoccupied with the great decision that should soon happen. This decision appears to me as so clear and unambiguous, which is what one must wish for. And yet, I now feel again that we cannot truly know what is genuinely healing, and that therefore all of our hopes and wishes migth be foolish. One must accept whatever might come, and then try to make the best of it. I wonder if the person in whose hands the fate of the world rests feels the entire weight of the responsibility that rests on him?

In addition to these general concerns, there is a special one: Gerhart Husserl has been wounded again in the head. There is no additional information. Last evening, I only spoke with Elli, because when I arrived, the parents had already gone to bed, weary from the agitation. A few days ago, a brief card arrived from the field hospital at Sedan. It was not handwritten, yet unmistakably dictated by him. Since then, no more news. Yesterday, I succeeded in comforting Elli with an interpretation of the wording of the note. It would be horrible for the entire family if things do not go well.
Best regards and again, thanks from the heart.

Your,
Edith Stein

Brief von Edith Stein an Roman Ingarden, 12. X. 1918 (ESGA 4, S. 53)

*Letter from Edith Stein to Roman Ingarden,
12 October 1918 (CWES 12, 141-142 ; translation slightly modified)*

Die Gefallenen
The Fallen Ones

Der Grabstein von Adolf Reinach auf dem Stadtfriedhof in Göttingen (gefallen am 16. XI. 1917 bei Dixmuide in Belgien)

The tombstone of Adolf Reinach at the city cemetery in Göttingen (killed on November 16, 1917 at Dixmuide in Belgium)

Rudolf Clemens (1890-1914)

Rudolf Clemens: geb. 1890 in Görlitz, gef. 21. 10. 1914 in Langemarck (Belgien). – Als 19-jähriger gibt Clemens zusammen mit dem befreundeten Schriftsteller Arnold Zweig (1887-1968) die Literaturzeitschrift „Die Gäste" heraus, in der er selbst Gedichte und Novellen veröffentlicht (z.B. 1910 die Novelle „Der Abschied vom Leben", die autobiographische Züge trägt). Ab SS 1910 Studium u.a. der Theologie und Besuch der Lehrveranstaltungen Husserls in Göttingen; als Schwerpunkt Studium der Iranistik bei Friedrich Carl Andreas (1846-1930). August 1914 Meldung als Kriegsfreiwilliger. Am 21. Oktober 1914 fällt Clemens in der Schlacht bei Langemarck. Einen im Auftrag Husserls begonnenen Index für die zweite Auflage der „Logischen Untersuchungen" kann Clemens nicht mehr zum Abschluss bringen. Auch sein Promotionsverfahren scheint nicht abgeschlossen worden zu sein. Max Scheler, dem Clemens nahe stand, veröffentlicht 1917 in der Vierteljahreschrift „Summa" posthum seinen Aufsatz „Saulus" (unter dem Pseudonym „Dr. Clemens Ritter"). In den 1950er Jahren bemüht sich Arnold Zweig, der auf Anraten von Clemens im Wintersemester 1911/12 ebenfalls bei Husserl studierte, vergebens um die Herausgabe des literarischen Werkes von Clemens. – Dokumente aus dem Nachlass von Rudolf Clemens befinden sich in der Universitätsbibliothek Göttingen (u.a. im Nachlass von Friedrich Carl Andreas), in der Staatsbibliothek München (Nachlass Max Scheler) und im Arnold Zweig Archiv bei der Akademie der Künste in Berlin.

Rudolf Clemens: born in 1890 in Görlitz, killed in combat on October 21, 1914 in Langemarck (Belgium). As a 19-year-old, Clemens together with his friend, the writer Arnold Zweig (1887-1968), edited the literary journal "The Guests," in which he publishes poems and short stories (1910, he publishes his partly auto-biographical novella "Farewell to Life"). 1910, begins his studies in theology, attends Husserl's lectures in Göttingen, and studies Iranian Studies with Friedrich Carl Andreas (1846-1930). August 1914, volunteers for the war. Killed in combat on October 21, 1914 at the battle of Langemarck. His index for the second edition of the "Logical Investigations," commissioned by Husserl, left unfinished, probably as well as his PhD examinations. Max Scheler, with whom Clemens was close, publishes his essay "Saulus" in 1917 in the quarterly volume "Summa" (under the pseudonym "Dr. Clemens Ritter"). In the 1950s, Arnold Zweig, who also studied with Husserl on the advice of Clemens in the winter semester of 1911/12, tried in vain to publish the literary work of Clemens. – Documents from the estate of Rudolf Clemens can be found in the Göttingen University Library (inter alia in the estate of Friedrich Carl Andreas), in the Staatsbibliothek München (estate of Max Scheler) and in the Arnold Zweig Archive at the Akademie der Künste in Berlin.

Rudolf Clemens, ca. 1909-1912 (Ausschnitt aus einem Gruppenphoto). – Edith Stein schreibt über Clemens: „Eine führende Rolle <in der ‚Göttinger Philosophischen Gesellschaft'> spielte Rudolf Clemens. Er war Sprachwissenschaftler. Sein dunkelblonder Bart und seine Krawatten, seine weiche Stimme und seine zugleich gemütvollen und schelmischen Augen erinnerten an die Zeit der Romantiker. Sein Ton war freundlich, aber es war eine Freundlichkeit, die mir kein unbedingtes Vertrauen einflößte." (ESGA 1, S. 204)

Rudolf Clemens, between 1909 and 1912 (section from group-photo). – Edith Stein writes about Clemens: "Rudolf Clemens was one who had a leading role [in the 'Göttingen Philosophical Society']. He was a philologist. His dark blond beard, his neckties, his soft voice, and his eyes, which were both soulful and mischievous, all were reminiscent of the time of the Romantics. His tone was friendly, but it was a friendliness which failed to inspire me with unqualified confidence in him." (CWES 1, 253-254)

Clemens, R.: Der Abschied vom Leben. Novelle. In: Die Gäste, Nr. 6 (1910), 46-60. – Dr. Clemens Ritter (wohl Pseudonym von Rudolf Clemens): Saulus. In: Summa. Eine Vierteljahresschrift. Blei, F. (Hg.), Erstes Viertel (1917). – Bernhard, J./Schlör, J. (Hg.): Deutscher, Jude, Europäer im 20. Jahrhundert: Arnold Zweig und das Judentum. Bern/Berlin/Bruxelles 2004, 64 f. – Rduch, R.: Unbehaustheit und Heimat: das literarische Werk von Arnold Ulitz (1888-1971). Frankfurt am Main/Berlin/Bern 2009, 28 u. 175.

„Bei heutiger Durchsicht der amtlichen 84. Verlustliste finde ich leider meinen Sohn als ‚vermißt' aufgeführt"

Görlitz, Lutherstr. 28, II., den 28. 11. 1914

Sehr geehrter Herr Professor!

Für Ihre gütige Anteilnahme an dem Verbleib meines lieben Sohnes sprechen ich Ihnen, Herr Professor, meinen wärmsten Dank aus.

Bei heutiger Durchsicht der amtl<ichen> 84. Verlustliste finde ich leider meinen Sohn als „vermißt" aufgeführt.

Sonst habe ich weder von ihm, noch von amtlicher Seite, bis auf eine Nachricht vom 16. d<es> M<onats>, bald nach Ankunft in Belgien geschrieben, etwas erfahren.

Ein von anderer Seite an Rudolf gerichteter Brief war mit dem Vermerk „vermißt" zurückgekommen.

Ich bin nun in größter Besorgnis und Ungewißheit über das ihn betroffene Schicksal und kenne leider auch gar keine Namen von Kameraden, an die ich mich wenden, die mir etwas mitteilen könnten.

Sollten Sie, Herr Professor, vielleicht noch etwas über meinen lieben Sohn erfahren und mir dies mitteilen wollen, wäre ich Ihnen sehr dankbar.

Mit größter Hochachtung

Ihr

R. Clemens

"With today's inspection of the 84th official list of causalities, I unfortunately find my son listed as missing"

Görtlitz, Lutherstr. 28, II., November 28, 1914

Dear Herr Professor!

My warmest thanks go out to you, Herr Professor, for your sympathy regarding the whereabouts of my dear son.

With today's inspection of the 84th official list of causalities, I unfortunately find my son listed as missing.

Otherwise, I have not heard anything from him, nor from the official side, save for a message from the 16th of this month, written soon after his arrival in Belgium,

On the other hand, a letter addressed to Rudolf was returned with the note "missing."

I now find myself greatly concerned and uncertain about the fate that befell him and unfortunately, I do not know any names of comrades to whom I might turn, who could tell me something.

Should you, Herr Professor, perhaps learn something about my dear son, and which you would like to communicate to me, I would be very grateful.

With the greatest respect,

Your,

R. Clemens

Brief des Vaters von Rudolf Clemens an Friedrich Carl Andreas, 28. XI. 1914. Bei Prof. Andreas (1846-1930) hatte Rudolf Clemens in Göttingen Iranistik studiert. – Wohl als Antwort auf eine Nachfrage seiner Eltern schreibt Wolfgang Husserl in einem Brief, ebenfalls am 28. XI. 1914: „Nun wegen Dr. Clemens. In der Verlustliste wird er als vermisst geführt, von seinen Kameraden ist rein nichts über ihn herauszukriegen, da fast alle, die ihn kannten, tot sind (er gehörte nämlich dem 3. Zug an, der am 10. <November> mitgestürmt hat)."

Letter from Rudolf Clemens' father to Friedrich Carl Andreas, November 28, 1914. Rudolf Clemens studied Iranian Studies in Göttingen with Prof. Andreas (1846-1930). Most likely in response to a request from his parents, Wolfgang Husserl writes in a letter, also on November 28, 1914: "Well, with regard to Dr. Clemens. He's listed as missing in the list of losses, and nothing can be learned from his comrades about him, since almost all who knew him are dead (he belonged to the 3rd platoon, which took part in the attack on the 10th of November)."

Nach langer banger Ungewißheit erhielten wir nun die schmerzliche Nachricht, daß mein lieber, hoffnungsvoller, einziger Sohn, mein guter Bruder und Schwager,

Dr. phil. Rudolf Clemens
Kriegsfreiwilliger in einem Reserve-Infanterie-Regiment

am 21. Oktober 1914 im Alter von 24 Jahren im Kampfe fürs Vaterland gefallen ist.

Görlitz, den 14. Januar 1918.
Lutherstraße 28, Sechsstädteplatz 2.

Rudolf Clemens, Kgl. Lokomotivführer a. D.
Elsa Pohl, geb. Clemens
Hermann Pohl, Kaufmann, z. Z. im Felde.

„Nach langer banger Ungewißheit erhielten wir nun die schmerzliche Nachricht"
"After a long period of frightful uncertainty, we have now received the painful news"

Erst im Januar 1918 veröffentlichten die Angehörigen die Todesanzeige von Rudolf Clemens, der im Oktober 1914 in Flandern gefallen war.

The notification of Rudolf Clemen's death was only published in January 1918. He was killed in combat in Flanders in October 1914.

Husserl im Vorwort zur zweiten Auflage der „Logischen Untersuchungen", Zweiter Band, II. Teil (1921): „Das Desiderat eines Index zu dem Gesamtwerke konnte leider nicht erfüllt werden, da mein hoffnungsvoller Schüler, Dr. Rudolf Clemens, der die Bearbeitung übernommen hatte, für das Vaterland gefallen ist."

Husserl in the Forward to the Second Edition of the "Logical Investigations," Second Volume, Second Part (1921): "The desiderata for an index to the entire work would unfortunately not be completed, given that my promising student, Dr. Rudolf Clemens, who had taken on this work, died for the Fatherland."

Vorwort. VII

derten Methode gewonnen, die hier, ähnlich wie in anderen Wissenschaften, die Gemeinsamkeit begrifflich bestimmter Arbeitsprobleme und feste Entscheidungen nach Wahrheit und Falschheit ermöglicht. Ich muß noch ausdrücklich bemerken, daß es sich bei M. Schlick nicht bloß um irrelevante Entgleisungen handelt, sondern um sinnverkehrende Unterschiebungen, auf die seine ganze Kritik aufgebaut ist.

Nach diesen Worten der Abwehr muß ich zum III. Abschnitt noch bemerken, daß ich meine Stellung zum Problem der phänomenologischen Deutung der Frage- und Wunschsätze schon kurz nach der ersten Ausgabe des Werkes geändert habe, und daß hier mit kleinen Überarbeitungen, wie sie zurzeit allein vorgenommen werden konnten, nicht auszukommen war. Der Text blieb daher ungeändert. Weniger konservativ durfte ich hinsichtlich des vielbenutzten Anhanges über „äußere und innere Wahrnehmung" sein. Bei Erhaltung des wesentlichen Textgehaltes erscheint er jetzt in erheblich verbesserter Gestalt.

Das Desiderat eines Index zu dem Gesamtwerke konnte leider nicht erfüllt werden, da mein hoffnungsvoller Schüler, Dr. Rudolf Clemens, der die Bearbeitung übernommen hatte, für das Vaterland gefallen ist.

Freiburg i. Br., Oktober 1920.   E. Husserl.

Waldemar Conrad (1878-1915)

Waldemar Conrad: geb. 22. 5. 1878 in Halle a.d. Saale, dort gest. am 10. 7. 1915. – Conrad war ein Sohn des mit Husserl befreundeten Staatswissenschaftlers Johannes Conrad (1839-1915). 1903 Promotion in Göttingen im Fach Chemie („Das elektrochemische Verhalten einiger Bleiverbindungen"). WS 1903/04-WS 1904/05 Studium der Philosophie bei Husserl in Göttingen, das er dort nach Unterbrechung (wegen Krankheit und zeitweiligem Studium in München u.a. bei Theodor Lipps) im SS 1907 fortführt. Conrad ist einer der ersten Schüler Husserls. Unter dem Namen Conrad-Ritschl Veröffentlichung von Märchen und Dramen (z.B. „Die Teufelssonate", 1908). Vor dem Krieg zahlreiche Veröffentlichungen zur Ästhetik. Bei Kriegsbeginn Meldung als freiwilliger Krankenpfleger in Halle a. d. Saale, dort ist Conrad kurz nach dem Abschluss seiner Habilitation („Einstellung und Arbeitswechsel als pädagogische und allgemein-psychologische Probleme") an Lungenentzündung und Herzschwäche gestorben. Sein Hauptarbeitsgebiet war in den letzten Lebensjahren die Pädagogik. Tätigkeit als Privatdozent der Philosophie und Pädagogik an der Technischen Hochschule in Dresden.

Waldemar Conrad: born on May 22, 1878 in Halle a.d. Saale, died in Halle a.d. Saale on July 10, 1915. Conrad was a son of the political scientist Johannes Conrad (1839-1915), a friend of Husserl. 1903, PhD in Göttingen in chemistry ("The Electrochemical Behavior of Some Lead Compounds"). 1903-1905, studied philosophy with Husserl in Göttingen, which he continues in 1907 after an interruption due illness; and intermittent studies in Munich with Theodor Lipps. Conrad is one of Husserl's first students. Under the name Conrad-Ritschl, publication of fairy tales and dramas ("The Devil Sonata", 1908). Before the war, numerous publications on aesthetics. With the outbreak of the war, reported as a volunteer medical orderly in Halle a. d. Saale. Conrad died shortly after the conclusion of his Habilitation ("Attitude and Change of Work as Educational and General Psychological Problems") of pneumonia and heart failure. His main field of work was pedagogy during the final years of his life. Privatdozent of Philosophy and Education at the Technische Hochschule in Dresden.

Angelucci, D.: Waldemar Conrad (1878-1915). In: H. R. Sepp/L. Embree (eds.): Handbook of Phenomenological Aesthetics, Dordrecht/Heidelberg/London 2010, 53-56. – Conrad-Ritschl, W.: Die Teufelssonate. Drama in fünf Akten. Leipzig 1908. – Dessoir, M.: Zur Erinnerung an Waldemar Conrad. In: Zeitschrift für Ästhetik und allgemeine Kunstwissenschaft 11 (1916), 77. – Konstantinovic, Z.: Phänomenologie und Literaturwissenschaft. München 1973, 38-50. – Krenzlin, N.: Zur Kritik der phänomenologischen Methode in der Ästhetik: Eine Auseinandersetzung mit den literaturästhetischen Anschauungen Waldemar Conrads. Berlin 1968. – Wirth, W.: Waldemar Conrad. In: Archiv für die gesamte Psychologie 34, 3-4 (1915), 565-573.

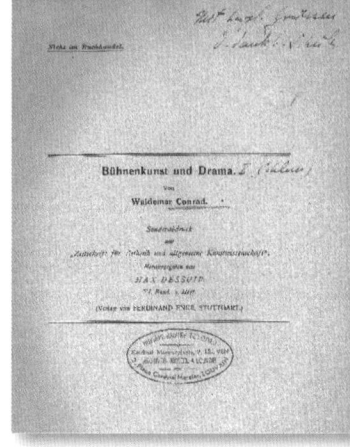

Ein Sonderdruck eines Aufsatzes von Waldemar Conrad befindet sich in Husserls Privatbibliothek mit der Widmung: „Mit herzl<ichen> Grüssen I<hr> dankb<arer> Schüler"

Off-print of an essay by Waldemar Conrad in Husserl's private library with the dedication: "With sincere greetings Your grateful student"

„Ich möchte glauben, daß wir bei seinem Ernste u. seinen Fähigkeiten tüchtige Leistungen, u. bei entsprechend fortgeschrittener Entwicklung sehr gute, von ihm erhoffen dürfen"

Wien 23. XII. 1908.
Hochgeehrter Herr College!
Dr W. Conrad kann ich Ihnen nur auf das Wärmste empfehlen. Von Charakter und Erziehung könnte ich viel Gutes sagen. Er verfügt auch über eine sehr solide wissenschaftliche Bildung: Naturwissenschaft hat er fachmäßig studirt und in der physikalischen Chemie das Doctorat gemacht. Erst nachher hat er sich ganz der Philosophie zugewendet, und daß er sich ihr mit großem Ernst u. Fleiß hingegeben hat, dafür zeugen seine, auch nach meinem Urtheil sehr tüchtigen Aufsätze, von denen ich den ersten und die 1te Hälfte des zweiten genau gelesen habe, während ich von der Existenz eines 3ten erst durch Ihren Brief erfahren habe. Es ist Dr C<onrad> hoch anzurechnen, daß er den Versuchungen, die eine starke literarische Begabung mit sich bringt (u. grade für den Aestheticker mit sich bringt), widerstanden und sich in den Linien strenger Wissenschaft gehalten hat. Das Problem der Constitution des ästhetischen Gegenstandes hat er sich selbst gestellt u. nur bei dem ersten Aufsatz habe ich ihn in der Einleitung beraten. Ich möchte glauben, daß wir bei seinem Ernste u. seinen Fähigkeiten tüchtige Leistungen, u. bei entsprechend fortgeschrittener Entwicklung sehr gute, von ihm erhoffen dürfen. Von seinen Absichten auf eine Habilitation sprach er zu mir vor etwa 2 Jahren, als er mir den Entwurf zu seinem 1ten Art<ikel> vorlegte. Daß ich ihn sowenig als irgend welche andere und schon fortgeschrittenere meiner Schüler zu einer Habilitation in Göttingen ermutigte, lag hauptsächlich daran, daß ich nicht sicher sein konnte gerade meine Schüler bei meinen Fachcollegen u. der Fakultät durchzusetzen. <…>

Auszug aus einem Brief von Husserl an Paul Natorp, 23. XII. 1908

Excerpt from a letter from Husserl to Paul Natorp, 23 December 1908

"I should like to believe that we may expect much that is good from him, given his seriousness and his abilities for efficient achievements, and with a correspondingly advanced development, [we can expect] very good things"

Vienna 23 December 1908
Very esteemed colleague!
I can only warmly recommend Dr W. Conrad to you. I could say much that is good about his character and education. He also possesses a very solid scientific formation: he studied science at the university and obtained a doctorate in physical chemistry. Only later did he turn entirely to philosophy, and that he devoted himself with tremendous seriousness and diligence is attested by his essays, which, according to my judgment, are very fine, of which I have read the first and the first half of the second carefully, and I have learned of the existence of a third only through your letter. It is to be credited to Dr. Conrad that he resisted temptations, which come forth from a strong literary talent (and this is precisely what he brings to aesthetics), and kept himself in the direction of rigorous science. He has set for himself the problem of the constitution of aesthetic objects. Only in the first essay did I advise him in the Introduction. I should like to believe that we may expect much that is good from him, given his seriousness and his abilities for efficient achievements, and with a correspondingly advanced development, [we can expect] very good things. He talked about his intentions for a habilitation about 2 years ago when he presented the draft of his first article. That I encouraged him as little as I do with other and more advanced students of mine for a habilitation in Göttingen was mainly because I could not be certain if I could push through immediately my students with my colleagues and with the faculty. […]

„Ein groß angelegter Lebensplan hat mit diesem Opfertode seinen vorzeitigen Abschluß gefunden"

"A grandly projected plan of life has come to premature end with this sacrified death"

Waldemar Conrad †.

Von

W. Wirth.

Der Verfasser der Abhandlung über »Einstellung und Arbeitswechsel«, die den größten Teil unseres Heftes bildet, weilt beim Erscheinen dieser seiner Habilitationsschrift leider schon nicht mehr unter den Lebenden. Am 10. Juli dieses Jahres ist Herr Dr. phil. Waldemar Conrad, Privatdozent der Philosophie und Pädagogik an der K. Technischen Hochschule zu Dresden, erst 37 Jahre alt in Halle an Lungenentzündung und Herzschwäche verschieden. Er hatte dem Vaterlande seit Beginn des Krieges mit nur kurzen Unterbrechungen als freiwilliger Krankenpfleger in Halle gedient und daneben nicht nur seine Habilitation vollendet, sondern auch noch eine einstündige Vorlesung an seiner Hochschule übernommen. Ein groß angelegter Lebensplan hat mit diesem Opfertode seinen vorzeitigen Abschluß gefunden, der in einer relativ langen Vorbereitungs- und Prüfungszeit herangereift, in letzter Zeit eine so reiche Fruchtbarkeit entfalten ließ, daß der vielseitig begabte Forscher wohl bald das allgemeine Interesse auf sein tiefernstes Streben gelenkt hätte, das durch ein inniges Verhältnis zur Kunst veredelt wurde, wie geschaffen für die Herrlichkeit der neuen Stätte seines Wirkens. War doch der Entschlafene, der am 22. Mai 1878 in Halle als Sohn des ihm erst jüngst in den Tod vorausgegangenen Professors der Nationalökonomie Johannes Conrad geboren wurde, ein Enkel des bekannten Leipziger Philologen Friedrich Ritschl, der uns Philosophen vor allem als Lehrer und Protektor Nietzsches unvergeßlich ist, und so lockte ihn, der sich unter dem Namen Conrad-Ritschl auch als Dramen- und Märchendichter versucht hat, wohl auch dieses Philosophenideal, Denker und Dichter zugleich zu sein. Er hält es geradezu für eine Hauptaufgabe des Dramas, die Zuschauer als eine einheitliche, möglichst homogene Gemeinde für eine Weltanschauung zu begeistern, bei der das Wollen und Handeln des Menschen im Mittelpunkt steht[1]). Sachlich verband ihn jedoch

1) Lit. 2, S. 386 ff.

Titelblatt und erste Seite des von Wilhelm Wirth verfassten Nachrufes auf Waldemar Conrad, der am 10. VII. 1915 infolge von Lungenentzündung und Herzschwäche gestorben war. Das in Husserls Bibliothek befindliche Exemplar des Nachrufes trägt die Widmung: „In vorzüglicher Hochachtung überreicht v. Verf." („Waldemar Conrad". In: Archiv für die gesamte Psychologie 34, 3-4, Leipzig: Engelmann, 1915, 565-573)

Title page and first page of the obituary written by Wilhelm Wirth for Waldemar Conrad, who died on July 10, 1915 due to pneumonia and heart failure. The copy of the obituary in Husserl's library bears the dedication: "With highest esteem from the author."

In den Kant-Studien 1915 veröffentlichte Todesanzeigen u.a. von Waldemar Conrad und vom Neukantianer Emil Lask

The notification of death for Waldemar Conrad and for the Neo-Kantian Emil Lask published in Kant-Studien, 1915

Von Max Dessoir verfasster Nachruf auf Waldemar Conrad ("Zur Erinnerung an Waldemar Conrad", in: Zeitschrift für Ästhetik und allgemeine Kunstwissenschaft 11, 1916, S. 77)

Max Dessoir's obituary for Waldemar Conrad

Fritz Frankfurther (1889-1914)

Fritz Frankfurther (Ausschnitt aus einem Gruppenphoto, ca. 1911)

Fritz Frankfurther (section from a group-photo, around 1911)

Fritz Frankfurther: geb. 27. 1. 1889 in Breslau, gef. 22. 11. 1914 bei Langemarck. – WS 1908/09 Studium der Mathematik in Breslau (u.a. bei Adolf Kneser); ab WS 1910/11 in Göttingen (u.a. bei Hermann Weyl). Besuch von Lehrveranstaltungen in Philosophie bei Husserl und Reinach. Mitglied der „Göttinger Philosophischen Gesellschaft". Bei Ausbruch des Krieges als Freiwilliger zum Reserve-Infanterie-Regiment 233. – Edith Stein beschreibt Fritz Frankfurther wie folgt: „Fritz Frankfurther stammte aus Breslau und studierte Mathematik. Aus seinen braunen Augen schaute kindliche Offenheit, Treuherzigkeit und Güte. Die helle Freude am Philosophieren, die den meisten von uns eigen war, trat bei ihm besonders liebenswürdig hervor. Als er mir einmal etwas aus Husserls Kant-Kolleg erzählte, das ich noch nicht gehört hatte, unterbrach er sich selbst plötzlich und sagte: ‚Nein, was jetzt kommt, ist zu schön, um es vorher zu verraten. Das müssen Sie selbst hören.' " (ESGA 1, S. 204). – Fritz Frankfurther fiel am 22. November 1914 in der Schlacht bei Langemarck.

Fritz Frankfurther, born on January 27, 1889 in Breslau, killed in combat on November 22, 1914 near Langemarck. 1908-1909, studied mathematics in Breslau (among others, with Adolf Kneser). 1910-1911, studied in Göttingen (among others, with Hermann Weyl). Attended the lectures in philosophy with Husserl and Reinach. Member of the Göttingen Philosophical Society. With the outbreak of the war, volunteered with the 233rd Reserve Infantry Regiment. In Edith Stein's description: "Fritz Frankfurther was from Breslau and studied mathematics. His brown eyes had a look of childlike candor, trust, and kindliness. The pure delight most of us experienced in philosophizing was most charmingly apparent in him. Once, while telling me something Husserl taught in his course on Kant, which I had not yet attended, Fritz interrupted himself suddenly, 'But, no! What comes next is too marvelous to be divulged ahead of time. You have to hear that for yourself.'" (CWES 1, 254) – Fritz Frankfurther was killed in combat at the battle of Langemarck on November 22, 1914.

„Gefr. Fritz Frankfurther (6. Komp.) … gest. an seinen Wunden, 22.11.14"

"Private Fritz Frankfurther (6th Company) … died from his wounds, November 22, 1914"

Ausschnitt aus „Deutsche Verlustlisten", Liste Preußen 169, S. 5179, 9. März 1915, Reserve-Infanterie-Regiment Nr. 233: „Berichtigung früherer Angaben: Gefr. Fritz Frankfurther (6. Komp.) – Breslau – bisher verwundet, gest. an seinen Wunden, 22.11.14". – Wolfgang Husserl schreibt in einem Brief vom 9. XII. 1914 an seine Eltern: „Zu unserem großen Bedauern ist Dr. Frankfurt<h>er gefallen. Wir haben ihn öfters gesprochen; als wir ihn das letzte Mal sahen, ging es ihm nicht gut. Er hatte was am Bein und hinkte."

Extract from "German causality lists," Prussia List 169, p. 5179, March 9, 1915, Reserve Infantry Regiment No. 233: "Correction of earlier information: Gefr. Fritz Frankfurther (6th comp.) – Breslau – wounded so far, died of his wounds, 22.11.14". – Wolfgang Husserl writes in a letter of December 9, 1914 to his parents: "To our great regret, Dr. Frankfurther has been killed. We often spoke with him; when we last saw him, he was not feeling well. He had something on his leg and limped."

Emil Lask (1875-1915)

Emil Lask: geb. 25. 9. 1875 in Wadowice bei Krakau, gef. 26. 5. 1915 bei Turza-Mala in Galizien. – Ab SS 1894 zunächst Studium der Rechtswissenschaft in Freiburg, dann der Philosophie (bei Heinrich Rickert) und Nationalökonomie (bei Max Weber). Oktober 1895 bis Oktober 1896 Militärdienstjahr als Einjährig-Freiwilliger. Ab WS 1896/97 Studium bei Wilhelm Windelband in Straßburg, von 1898 bis 1901 wieder in Freiburg, dort 1901 Promotion bei Heinrich Rickert („Fichtes Idealismus und die Geschichte", 1902 veröffentlicht). 1905 Habilitation bei Windelband in Heidelberg („Rechtsphilosophie"); danach zunächst als Privatdozent an der Universität Heidelberg, dort seit Februar 1910 als außerordentlicher Professor. Lask führt die Gedanken seiner Lehrer Rickert und Windelband, den Hauptvertretern des Südwestdeutschen Neukantianismus in kritischer Auseinandersetzung weiter, nimmt jedoch auch Anregungen von Husserls „Logischen Untersuchungen" auf. Große Wertschätzung Lasks unter den Phänomenologen. 1914 meldet er sich als Kriegsfreiwilliger an die Front zum Einsatz in Galizien, wo er im Mai 1915 fällt. – Der Nachlass von Emil Lask befindet sich in der Universitätsbibliothek Heidelberg.

Emil Lask: born on September 25, 1875 in Wadowice near Krakow, killed in combat on May 26, 1915 in Turza-Mala in Galicia. 1884, studied law in Freiburg, and then philosophy (with Heinrich Rickert) and economics (with Max Weber). 1895-1896, military service as a one-year volunteer. 1896-1897, studied with Wilhelm Windelband in Strasbourg, from 1898 to 1901 again in Freiburg; obtained PhD with Heinrich Rickert ("Fichte's Idealism and History", published in 1902). 1905, habilitation with Windelband in Heidelberg ("Philosophy of Right"); Privatdozent at the University of Heidelberg; 1910, Associate Professor. Continues his work in Neo-Kantianism along with receptive influence on his thinking from Husserl's "Logical Investigations." Gains reputation within phenomenological circles. With the outbreak of the war, volunteers for military service; serves at the front in Galicia, where he is killed in combat in May 1915. – The papers of Emil Lask are housed at the University Library Heidelberg.

Glatz, U. B.: Emil Lask. Philosophie im Verhältnis zu Weltanschauung, Leben und Erkenntnis. Würzburg 2001. – Lukàcs, Georg von: Emil Lask. Ein Nachruf. In: Kant-Studien 22 (1918), 349-370. – Nachtsheim, S.: Emil Lasks Grundlehre. Tübingen 1992. – Ollig, L.: Der Neukantianismus. Stuttgart 1979, 66-72. – Schuhmann, K./Smith, B.: Two Idealisms: Lask and Husserl. In: Kant-Studien 84 (1993), 448-466. – Sommerhäuser, H.: Emil Lask 1875-1915. Zum neunzigsten Geburtstag des Denkers. In: Zeitschrift für philosophische Forschung 21 (1967), 136-145.

„In den nächsten Tagen ein Brief"

Lieber Herr Professor! Es ist ekelhaft, daß ich nicht geschrieben habe. Herzl. Dank für Ihren Brief. Hier ein veraltetes ziemlich schlechtes Bild aus meiner damaligen Landsturm- und Landwirtschaftszeit. In den nächsten Tagen ein Brief.
Herzlich grüßt Ihr
Lask

"In the next few days, a letter"

Dear Professor! It's disgusting that I have not written. Sincere thanks for your letter. Here is a rather outdated and poor photo from my former Landsturm and agricultural time. In the next few days, a letter.
Yours sincerely,
Lask

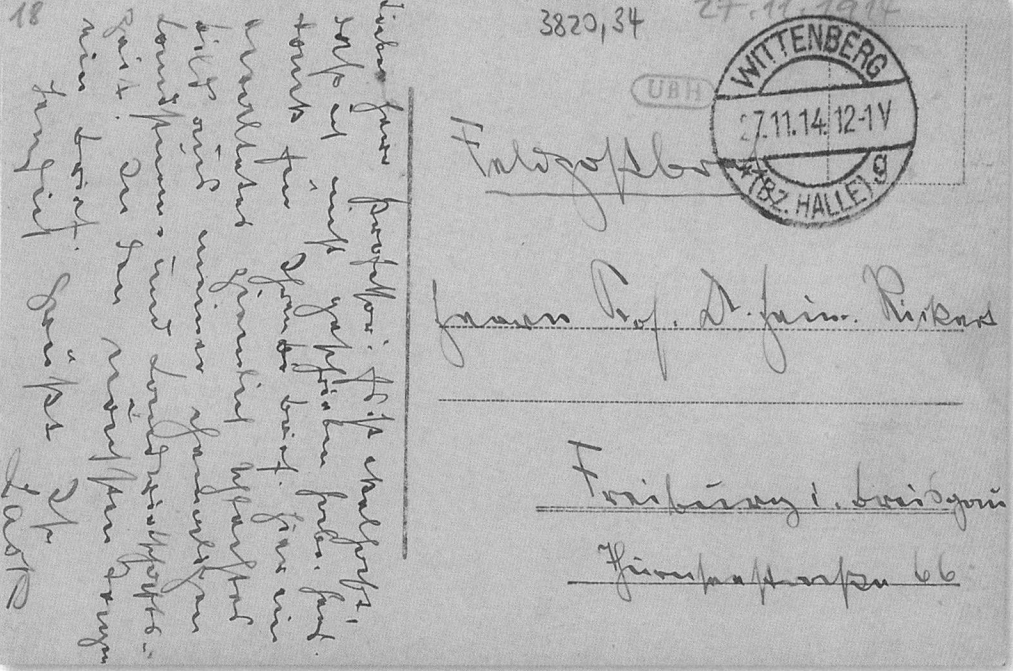

Feldpostkarte von Emil Lask an Heinrich Rickert, 27. XI. 1914. – Auf dem Photo Emil Lask in Uniform als Gefreiter bei einer Bauernfamilie.

Field postcard from Emil Lask to Heinrich Rickert, 27 November 1914. In the photo, Emil Lask is in uniform as a private with a peasant family.

„Ich bin nicht fürs Militär geboren"

den 19. März 1915.

Liebe Frau Professor! Haben Sie ~~kürzlichen~~ herzlichen Dank für Ihren lieben und frohstimmenden Brief. Ich wollte Ihnen jeden Tag wenigstens ein ganz kurzes Wort schreiben. Aber es war gradezu unmöglich. Auch heute komme ich nur zu ganz flüchtigen Zeilen, zu einer Postkarte auf einem Briefbogen geschrieben. Die Lage hat sich bei uns ein bischen zugespitzt. Wir sind in grösserer Gefechtsbereitschaft, es knallen mehr Schüsse als sonst. Und vor allem: die kleinen Pflichten des Dienstes, all die kleinen Sorgen um die Bekleidungsstücke u.s.w. durchdringen den ganzen Tag. Und wenn wir wirklich hier unten im Quartier sind wie jetzt, da ich diese Zeilen schreibe, so sitze ich hier in einer elenden Stube mit etwa 15-20 Menschen, 7 Schäfchen und 2 Zicklein zusammen- von allem andern lieber ganz zu schweigen. Ich kann einfach keine Musse finden auch nur zum kürzesten Brief. Wieviel weniger zur Besinnung über den Krieg und mein jetziges Leben oder gar zu sonstiger philosophischer Betrachtung. Damit ist Ihre Frage beantwortet, ob ein neuer Frühling gekommen ist. Zu allem kommt noch hinzu, dass ich körperlich müder geworden bin. Der Dienst war bisher noch garnicht anstrengend, aber dies ganze Leben hier muss doch irgendwie sehr angreifend und an der Gesundheit nagend sein. Vielleicht geht es aber auch wieder in die Höhe. Für die augenblicklichen Ansprüche reicht es aus. Aber wie mag es werden, wenn es einmal weitergeht? Denn wir liegen bisher die ganze Zeit an derselben Stelle, nordöstlich von Alexander Ypsilantis hohem Turm am Kamme der Karpathen. Im Schützengraben, im Unterstand, in der Ranzenhütte spielt sich das Leben ab. Wie kommt einem jetzt so manches palastartig vor, von dessen blosser Beschreibung mir früher schon gegraust hätte, und worin ich es physisch auszuhalten nicht für möglich gehalten hätte, z.B. in der von Ungeziefer starrenden Hütte zu leben oder in einer Höhle zu übernachten, in der die Eiszapfen einem über den Kopf hängen. Und doch: wie gut verträgt man das alles! Ja unsere ganze Stellung gilt mit Recht als so bevorzugt, dass wir uns vor jedem Tausch fürchten. Ich bin nicht fürs Militär geboren. Sehr grosse Dienste werde ich kaum leisten. Freilich war bisher auch nicht die geringste Gelegenheit auch mir zu den allerbescheidensten Leistungen. Ein kleinzügiges schläfriges Leben, wie es

es der moderne Stellungskrieg zuweilen mit sich bringt. Käme morgen der Frieden, so würde diese ganze Zeit wie ein kurzer Traum spurlos versinken. Trotzdem _will_ ich dabei sein. Mir kam es ja lediglich darauf an, irgendwie mitzuhelfen im Bereich der Kugeln. Behandelt werde ich übrigens sehr gut und stets als „Professor." – Vielleicht hätte ich mich auch heute noch nicht zu diesen wenigen Zeilen aufgerafft, wenn nicht gestern Ihre unerhört schöne und süsse Sendung gekommen wäre. Wenn ich in meiner vorigen Karte an Ihren Mann von der Gier des Kriegers im Gegensatz zu der Kontemplativen Poetisierung der Mahlzeiten auf Reisen (wie weit das wirklich kontemplativ sei dahingestellt) schrieb, so muss ich das angesichts so schöner Liebesgaben wie der Ihrigen zurücknehmen. Auch hier vollzog sich die herrlichste Poetisierung. Die mir bisher ganz unbekannte Schokoladenmarke ist vornehm wie ein alter Wein. Von den Feigen war allerdings die Gier nicht ganz zu trennen. Aber sie waren prächtiger wie mir scheint, ~~wie mir scheint~~, als irgendwelche, die ich je gegessen. „Strümpfe allerdings lassen sich schwer poetisieren," so hätte ich eben beinahe geschrieben, muss es aber wieder zurücknehmen. Die ganze Sendung kam wunderbar zur richtigen Zeit, fand die allergrösste Empfänglichkeit bei mir vor und eine ebenso grosse Ergriffenheit und Dankbarkeit. Was für eine Fürsorge und Mühewaltung und liebevolle Auslese steckt dahinter. Aber all dies hat seinen Weg zu mir gefunden. „Über das ganze Deutschland hinüber," Bitte bestellen Sie Ihrem Mann Glückwünsche zu den Neuauflagen. Dass Ihre Söhne nicht hinaus müssen, finde ich selbstverständlich.

Mit tausend herzlichen Grüssen und innigstem Dank an Sie und Ihren Mann

Ihr Lask.

Brief (Abschrift) von Emil Lask an Sophie Rickert (Frau von Heinrich Rickert), 19. III. 1915

Letter (transcription) from Emil Lask to Sophie Rickert (Heinrich Rickert's wife), March 19, 1915

"I was not born for the military"

19 March 1915

Dear Frau Professor!

Thank you very much for your kind and upbeat letter. I wanted to write you at the very least a very brief word every day. But it was absolutely impossible. Even today, I can only find time for a few very fleeting lines, written on a postcard on sheets of notepaper. The situation has gotten slightly more precarious for us. We are in an heightened state of combat readiness, and more shots are banged-out than usual. And above all: the small duties of service, all the little worries concerning clothes, etc., permeate the entire day. And when we're actually down here in our quarters as I am while now writing these lines, I'm sitting here in a small miserable room with about 15-20 people, together with 7 little lambs and 2 kid goats – not to mention everything else. I just can't find any leisure even for the shortest letter. How much less time to reflect on the war and my present life or even on other philosophical considerations. So your question is answered, whether a new spring has arrived. On top of that, I've become more exhausted physically. The service has not been exhausting thus far, but this whole life here has become somehow very invasive and gnawing at the health. Or maybe it will get better. For the present requirements, things are sufficient. But how will things become, once things start up again?

We've been sitting here the entire time in the same position, North-East from Alexander Ypsilanti's high tower on the ridge of the Carpathians. In the trenches, in the shelter, in the Punja hut,* life goes on. How things now appear for one as being more palatial, the mere description of which I had earlier grumbled about, and for which I had never imagined that I could endure it mentally, for example, to live in a vermin-infested hut or sleep in a cave with icicles hanging over your head. And yet: how well one can endure all of this! Indeed, our entire position is rightly considered as privileged, that we fear just about any exchange. I was not born for the military. I will most surely not achieve anything great. Of course, not the slightest opportunity has thus presented itself for me to achieve even the most modest of accomplishments. A small sleepy life, as the modern war of positions sometimes brings with it. If peace would come tomorrow, all that time would sink like a brief dream without a trace. Nevertheless, I just wanted somehow to help where the action is, within the range of bullets. Incidentally, I am treated very well and always as a "Professor". – Perhaps even today I would not have been able to send-off these few lines, had yesterday your peerless beautiful and sweet letter parcel not arrived. When in my earlier [post]-card, I wrote to your husband of the greed of the warrior as opposed to the contemplative making of poetry from meals while traveling (how far that is really contemplative, not to mention), then I must take it back in the face of such beautiful gifts of love as yours. Here, too, the most glorious poeticisation took place. An hitherto completely unknown chocolate brand is as distinguished as an old wine. With the figs, however, the greed was not entirely avoided. But they were more gorgeous, it seems to me, than any others I have ever eaten. "Stockings, however, are difficult to turn into poetry" I almost wrote, but I have to take it back. The whole show came wonderfully at the right time, found the utmost sensitivity in me and an equally great emotion and gratitude. What kind of care and solicitude and loving concern stands behind it. But all this has found its way to me. "Over the whole Germany and beyond", please extend to your husband congratulations for the new editions. It goes without saying that your sons do not have to go out there to the front.

With a thousand warm regards and profound gratitude to you and your husband.

Your,
Lask

* Translator's note: a common expression for a typical Balkan hut.

„Nicht ganz verständlich ist uns, warum wir Ihnen nichts weiter schicken sollen"

"It is not completely understandable to us why we should not send you anything else"

Freiburg, 3 June 1915

Dear Lask,
Thank you very much for your letters of May 20 and 22. This time, the Post did not take that much time to send us the news. The manner in which you reported to us about your slight wound has greatly amused us, in spite of the seriousness of the matter, so that we had to laugh. Hopefully, it's really as harmless as you write. In the meantime, your whole situation will probably have changed again; in the area where you seem to stand, great things are now happening. There is no point in asking for further details as everything would be out-dated when it reaches you. I just wish that we will get back to you soon and hear that you are well. In the meantime, nothing has changed here, and since I have recently written to you in detail, I want to end for today with these few lines. It is not completely understandable to us why we should not send you anything else. If you have more than you need, surely there will be people who will be glad if you can give them something, and we are happy in the thought that we can do at least one such little thing for those who are out there risking their life and limb for us. The desired chocolates will of course be sent to you from my wife with pleasure. We both greet you many times. Be well and take care of yourself as much as the circumstances allow.
As always your old friend,
Heinrich Rickert.
From Windelband we have better news. He lies in bed and sleeps a lot, but he is mentally clear, and there is no danger at the moment.

Feldpostbrief von Heinrich Rickert an Emil Lask, 3. VI. 1915 (an Rickert zurückgesandt, da Lask am 26. V. gefallen war). Handschriftlicher Zusatz am Schluss des Briefes: „Wie immer Ihr alter Freund Heinrich Rickert. Von Windelband sind bessere Nachrichten. Er liegt zu Bett und schläft sehr viel, aber er ist geistig völlig klar, und Gefahr soll augenblicklich nicht bestehen."

Feldpost letter from Heinrich Rickert to Emil Lask, June 3, 1915. Returned to Rickert since Lask was killed on May, 26.

„Daß der Tod vielleicht nicht einwandfrei festgestellt worden ist"

Postkarte von Berta Jacobsohn (Schwester von Emil Lask) an Sophie Rickert (Frau von Heinrich Rickert), 24. VI. 1915

Postcard from Berta Jacobsohn (Emil Lask's sister) to Sophie Rickert (Heinrich Rickert's wife), June 24, 1915

Liebe Frau Rickert!
d. 24. 6. 15
Nachdem eine größere Anzahl von Päckchen u. Briefen mit der Aufschrift „Auf dem Felde der Ehre gefallen" zurückgekommen waren, kam gestern ein <u>später</u> abgesandtes Päckchen mit der Aufschrift „verwundet?" und heute kamen drei Päckchen mit der Aufschrift „vermißt" zurück. Aus der Meldung des Feldwebels ohne Datum u. ohne jede nähere Angabe hatten wir also mit Recht geschlossen, daß der Tod vielleicht nicht einwandfrei festgestellt worden ist. Mein Mann fährt in einigen Tagen nach Galizien. Vielen herzlichen Dank für Brief und Bild. Ihre
Berta Jacobsohn

"That perhaps death was not ascertained properly"

Dear Frau Rickert!
24 June 1915
After a larger number of packages and letters with the inscription "Fallen in the Field of Honor" were returned, there arrived yesterday a later dispatched small package with the inscription "wounded?" and then today came back three small packages with the inscription "missing." From a message by a Sergeant without a date and further details, we justly inferred that perhaps death was not ascertained properly. My husband is going to Galicia in a few days. Many thanks for letter and picture.
Your,
Berta Jacobsohn

„Welch ein Opfer der Krieg gefordert hat, und was die deutsche Philosophie mit ihm verliert"

<…> Anfang und Ende, Ausgangspunkt und Ziel liegen daher in keiner anderen Wissenschaft <wie in der Philosophie> so weit auseinander.

Hieran muss man denken, um die Bedeutung des Mannes zu würdigen, dem diese Zeilen gewidmet sind, und zu ermessen, welche Wunde die Vernichtung seines Lebens durch den Krieg uns geschlagen hat. Emil Lask ist am 25. September 1875 geboren. Er stand im vierzigsten Lebensjahr, als die feindliche Kugel ihn traf, und zwei Jahrzehnte intensivster Arbeit lagen hinter ihm. Trotzdem war sein Name über den Kreis seiner Fachgenossen und Schüler nicht hinausgedrungen. Das konnte nicht anders sein, denn was er schrieb und lehrte, verlangte schwierige Mitarbeit und schien auf ein „besonderes Fach", auf Logik und Erkenntnistheorie, beschränkt, das nur die Fachgelehrten etwas angeht. Der Fernerstehende hat daher in Lask wohl meist einen Spezialisten gesehen. Und doch ist er gerade dies nie gewesen. Alles in ihm drängte zu umfassendster Systematik, und nur die außerordentliche Gründlichkeit und Gewissenhaftigkeit seiner Person, verbunden mit der angedeuteten fachlichen Eigenart des im besten Sinne modernen Denkens hat es bewirkt, daß in seinen Büchern von dem, was jede echte Philosophie als letztes Ziel erstrebt, nur Ansätze zu finden sind. Seine Freunde und Fachgenossen, die imstande waren, seinen schwierigen Gedanken zu folgen, wußten seit langer Zeit, daß hier eine lebendige Kraft am Werke war, von der man das Größte erwarten durfte; ja, einige von uns haben Hoffnungen auf ihn gesetzt wie auf keinen zweiten seiner Generation, und zwar Hoffnungen nicht nur für die Durchführung von logischen und erkenntnistheoretischen Untersuchungen. Die hatten ja bereits angefangen, intensiv zu wirken. Sondern Hoffnungen gerade auf die Schöpfung einer Weltanschauung, die allen Seiten des Kulturlebens gerecht wird und zugleich den Sinn unseres Daseins einheitlich auf wissenschaftlicher Basis zu deuten unternimmt. Nun sind diese Hoffnungen vernichtet. Was hier im Wachsen war und sich besonders in den letzten Jahren immer kräftiger entfaltete, ist in sich zusammengesunken, ehe es die allen zugängliche Gestalt gefunden hat. Niemand wird imstande sein, den Sinn seines Lebens ganz zu deuten; ja, sein Ende, so bewunderungswürdig und erhebend es persönlich anmutet, steht vor uns als eine trostlose Sinnwidrigkeit. Für den, der weiß, wie Lask war, bleibt nur übrig, anderen zu sagen, welch ein Opfer der Krieg gefordert hat, und was die deutsche Philosophie mit ihm verliert.

"What a sacrifice the war has demanded, and what has been lost with this sacrifice for German philosophy"

[...] The beginning and the end, the starting point and the goal are therefore in no other science [as with philosophy] so far apart.

One must think about this statement in order to appreciate the significance of the man to whom these lines are dedicated and to gauge what kind of injury has been inflicted upon us by the war with the destruction of his life. Emil Lask was born on September 25, 1875. He was forty years old when an enemy bullet struck him, and two decades of intense work lay behind him. Nevertheless, his name had never extended beyond the circle of colleagues and students. This could not be otherwise, since what he wrote and taught demanded difficult participation and seemed to be restricted to a "special discipline," to logic and to theory of knowledge, which only concerns specialized scholars. Even the most far-sighted could only mostly see Lask as a specialist. And yet, he in fact was never just this. Everything in him urged him to an encompassing system, and only the extraordinary thoroughness and conscientiousness of his person, combined with the specialized technical uniqueness in the best sense of modern thinking, caused his books to offer mere approaches for what every true philosophy strives for as a final goal. His friends and colleagues, who were able to follow his difficult thoughts, knew for a long time that here was a living force at work, from whom one could expect the greatest things; indeed, some of us had placed our hopes in him like as with no other of his generation and hoped not only for the development of logical and epistemological investigations. He had already begun to work on these intensively. Our hopes were rather for the creation of a Weltanschauung, which would do justice to every facet of cultural life, and at the same time which would attempt to interpret the sense of our existence in an unified manner on a scientific basis. It is these hopes which are now destroyed. What was here growing and, in particular, unfolding even more powerfully in the last years has capsized before it could find its accessible form. No one will be able to fully interpret the sense of his life; yes, its end, as admirable and uplifting as it may seem personally, stands before us as an inconsolable absurdity. For the person who knew who Lask was, all that remains is to inform others what a sacrifice the war has demanded, and what has been lost with this sacrifice for German philosophy.

Titelblatt von Heinrich Rickerts Nachruf auf Emil Lask (Frankfurter Zeitung, 17. Oktober 1915, 1. Morgenblatt). Hier wird der Schlussteil des Nachrufes (S. 4) wiedergegeben.

Title page of Heinrich Rickert's obituary for Emil Lask (Frankfurter Zeitung, October 17, 1915, 1st morning sheet). Here, the final part of the obituary (page 4).

Aus einem Brief von Husserl an Heinrich Rickert, 5. XI. 1915:
Ihren schönen Nachruf für Emil Lask habe ich mit innigem Antheil gelesen. Der Tod dieses ungewöhnlichen und – wie jede seiner Schriften erwies – um die höchsten philosophischen Ziele ringenden Mannes hat auch mich tief ergriffen. Eine der schönsten Hoffnungen der deutschen Philosophie ist mit ihm dahingegangen. Ich bedaure es sehr, ihn nie persönlich kennen gelernt zu haben. – Die unerhörte Verwüstung geistiger Kräfte, die dieser unselige Krieg mit sich bringt, erfüllt mich mit schwerer Sorge. – <…>

Gestatten Sie, daß ich schließlich zeitgemäße gute Wünsche für Ihre w<erte> Familie beifüge, insbesondere für Ihren Sohn Heinrich, dessen ich noch mit herzlicher Sympathie gedenke. Meine beiden Söhne, von denen der eine seine schwere Verwundung gut überstanden hat, kämpfen an der Westfront: ich habe also allen Grund dem Schicksal dankbar zu sein.

From a letter from Husserl to Heinrich Rickert, 5 November 1915:
I read your beautiful obituary for Emil Lask with heartfelt sympathy. The death of this unique man (as each of his writings demonstrated), who struggled towards the highest philosophical goals, has affected me profoundly. One of the most beautiful hopes of German philosophy has passed away with him. I regret it very much that I never met him personally. The unprecedented devastation of spiritual powers brought about by this disastrous war fills me with profound sorrow.

Allow me, finally, to add my present good wishes for your dear family, especially for your son Heinrich, who I still remember with heartfelt sympathy. My two sons, one of whom has survived his severe injury well, are fighting on the Western Front: so I have every reason to be thankful to fate.

Aus einem Brief von Heinrich Rickert an Richard Kroner, 2. VII. 1915:
Es besteht leider Grund anzunehmen, daß Lask ein Opfer dieses Krieges geworden ist. <…> Was dieser Verlust für mich bedeutet, wissen Sie. Lask war nicht nur einer meiner liebsten Freunde, sondern seine wissenschaftliche Arbeit war mit der meinigen so eng verwoben wie die keines anderen Menschen, und so ist für mich sowohl persönlich als auch sachlich eine Lücke entstanden, die nie wieder ausgefüllt werden kann. Mir ist manchmal, als wüßte ich jetzt überhaupt erst, was dieser Krieg bedeutet.

From a letter from Heinrich Rickert to Richard Kroner, 2 July 1915:
Unfortunately, there is reason to assume that Lask has become a victim of this war. [...] What this loss means to me, you know. Lask was not only one of my dearest friends, but his scientific work was as closely intertwined with mine as with no other human being, and so for me both personally and intellectually, a gap has been torn that can never be filled. Sometimes I feel as if it is only now that I understand at all what this war means.

Adolf Reinach (1883-1917)

Adolf Reinach (Aufnahme aus dem Jahr 1904)

Adolf Reinach (photo from 1904)

Adolf Reinach: geb. 23. 12. 1883 in Mainz, gef. 16. 11. 1917 in Dixmuiden (Belgien). – WS 1901/02 Beginn des Studiums in München (Philosophie, Psychologie, Rechtswissenschaften und Geschichte); dort 1904 Promotion bei Theodor Lipps („Über den Ursachenbegriff im geltenden Strafrecht"). Ab SS 1905 Studium bei Husserl in Göttingen. Juni 1907 Abschluss des rechtswissenschaftlichen Studiums in Tübingen (1. Staatsexamen), danach Weiterführung des Studiums der Philosophie bei Husserl in Göttingen, dann vom WS 1907/08 an wieder in München. Mitglied der Göttinger Philosophischen Gesellschaft, der Vereinigung der Schüler Husserls. 1909 Habilitation bei Husserl („Wesen und Systematik des Urteils"), danach Privatdozent in Göttingen. Herausgeber (mit Husserl, Geiger, Pfänder, Scheler) des „Jahrbuchs für Philosophie und phänomenologische Forschung" (1913-1930). Zu Kriegsbeginn Meldung als Kriegsfreiwilliger, aber zunächst wegen seiner schlechten Augen abgelehnt. Schließlich kommt Reinach doch zur Ausbildung nach Gonsenheim bei Mainz und später mit einem Artillerieregiment an die Westfront. Zeitweise ist sein Bruder Heinrich sein Vorgesetzter. Von Oktober 1916 an ist Reinach als Zugführer bei Soissons im Norden Frankreichs in der Picardie stationiert. Während seines Fronteinsatzes entstehen Vorstudien zu einem religionsphilosophischen Buch und Manuskripte mit den Titeln „Phänomenologie der Ahnungen" und „Das Absolute". – Der Nachlass von Adolf Reinach befindet sich in der Bayerischen Staatsbibliothek München.

Adolf Reinach: born on December 23, 1883 in Mainz, killed in combat on November 16, 1917 in Dixmuiden (Belgium). 1901-1902, studied philosophy, psychology, law, and history in Munich; graduation in 1904 with Theodor Lipps ("Over the Cause Concept in Valid Criminal Law"). 1905, studied with Husserl in Göttingen. 1907, completion of studies in law in Tübingen (1st state examination), and continued studies in philosophy with Husserl in Göttingen; 1907-1908, continued studies in Munich. Member of the Göttingen Philosophical Society. 1909, habilitation with Husserl ("The Nature and System of Judgment"). Privatdozent in Göttingen. Editor (with Husserl, Geiger, Pfänder, Scheler) of the "Yearbook for Philosophy and Phenomenological Research" (1913-1930). With the outbreak of the war, volunteers for military service, but initially rejected due to poor eye-sight. Enters service with an artillery regiment on the Western Front (where he serves with his brother, Heinrich, his commander.) From October 1916, stationed as a platoon leader at Soissons in northern France in Picardy. During his service at the front, sketches preparatory studies for a book on religious philosophy and writes manuscripts "Phenomenology of Foreboding" and "The Absolute." – The papers of Adolf Reinach are housed in the Bavarian State Library Munich.

Baltzer-Jaray, K.: Doorway to the World of Essences: Adolf Reinach and the Early Phenomenological Movement. Saarbrücken 2009. – Conrad-Martius, H.: Einleitung. In: Reinach, Adolf: Gesammelte Schriften. Hg. von seinen Schülern. Halle 1921, V-XXXVII. – Burkhardt, A.: Soziale Akte, Sprechakte und Textillokutionen. A. Reinachs Rechtsphilosophie und die moderne Linguistik. Tübingen 1986. – Schuhmann, K. und Smith, B.: Adolf Reinach: An Intellectual Biography. In: Mulligan, K. (ed.): Speech Act and Sachverhalt: Reinach and the Foundations of Realist Phenomenology. Dordrecht 1987, 1-27.

„Ich brauche unbedingt meine Militärpapiere"

Lieber Conrad!
Ich komme mit einer dringenden Bitte an Sie, von der <u>sehr viel</u> für mich abhängt. Ich brauche unbedingt meine Militärpapiere, die aber zur Zeit an einem mir nicht zugänglichen Ort sich befinden. Ich muss also eine Abschrift haben und die ist nur auf dem Bezirkskommando München* zu haben. Auf schriftliches Ersuchen erfolgt in diesen Tagen keine Auskunft – <u>bitte</u>, <u>bitte</u> gehen Sie für mich hin und verlangen Sie sie. Man wird Ihnen entweder das Papier ausstellen oder Sie an eine and[e]re Stelle verweisen, die diese Dinge jetzt besorgt. Die Sache ist von entscheidender Wichtigkeit für mich – ich bin Ihnen von tiefstem Herzen dankbar für diesen Dienst.

   Ich habe mich 1907 in München gestellt, u. bin dem Landsturm überwiesen worden, so viel ich weiss, Landsturm <u>ohne</u> Waffe. Vielleicht telegraphieren Sie mir, wenn Sie dort waren.

   Es ist tief in der Nacht – wir erwarten die Mobilisierung. Verzeihen Sie, wenn ich heute nacht nicht mehr schreiben kann, Ihre Frau soll sich nur ruhig Zeit nehmen, vor Mitte August drucken wir – falls sie Sie nicht früher fertig sein sollte – nicht.

   Leben Sie recht wohl und seien Sie herzlichst gegrüsst von Ihrem dankbaren
Reinach.

* war wohl früher auf der Kohleninsel, wo L<and>st<urmamt> jetzt ist, ist mir unbekannt.

"I absolutely need my military papers"

Dear Conrad!
I come to you with an urgent request, on which very much depends for me. I absolutely need my military papers, which at the moment are not in an accessible place for me. I must therefore have a copy, and this can only be obtained at the District Headquarters in Munich. Written requests have not produced any results in these past days. Please, please, could you go there for me and ask for these papers. You'll either receive the paper or be sent to another office, where these things are now handled. This issue is of decisive importance for me – I'm grateful to you from the bottom of my heart for this service.

   I presented myself in 1907 in Munich and was transferred to the Landsturm, but as far as I know, Landsturm without weapons. Maybe you could send me a telegraph, when you're there.

   It's late at night – we're waiting for mobilization. Forgive me, if I'm not able to write anymore tonight, your wife should take her time, we'll not push forward until mid-August, just in case she should not finish earlier.
Be well and sincere greetings to you from your grateful
Reinach.

* was earlier on the coal island**, the location of office for the Landsturm is not known to me.

** Translator's note: *Kohleninsel* – an older name for the island in Munich before the construction of the German Museum (*Deutsches Museum*) in 1903.

Brief von Adolf Reinach an Theodor Conrad, wohl August 1914

Letter from Adolf Reinach to Theodor Conrad, most likely August 1914

„Wir wurden mit Erde förmlich überschüttet u. die Granatsplitter flogen und pfiffen um uns herum"

24. XI. <1914>
Liebe Freunde, wie viel Freude haben Sie mir mit Ihrer lieben Sendung und Ihren lieben Worten gemacht! Die Zigarren sind tadellos angekommen und schmecken über alle Begriffe gut. Es geht uns immer noch famos. Gestern zwar sassen die schweren feindl. Artillerie ganz bedenklich nahe – wir wurden mit Erde förmlich überschüttet u. die Granatsplitter flogen und pfiffen um uns herum – aber an so etwas gewöhnt man sich unglaublich rasch. Die Gegend, in der wir liegen, ist wundervoll – ich darf jetzt am Scherenfernrohr beobachten, und das macht mir sehr viel Freude. Es ist schon tüchtig kalt, aber wir haben einen kleinen Ofen in unserem Loch, und wenn er auch spauzt u. raucht, so wärmt er doch.
Viele herzliche Grüsse Ihr R.
Viele Grüsse an Rosenblum.

Feldpostkarte von Adolf Reinach an das Ehepaar Conrad, 24. XI. 1914

"We were literally showered with earth and the shrapnel flew and whistled all around us"

Field postcard from Adolf Reinach to the Conrads, 24 November 1914

24 November [1914]
Dear friends,
Your lovely parcel gave me so much joy along with your precious words! The cigars arrived in perfect condition and they tasted beyond comprehension. We're doing splendid here. Yesterday, we sat precariously close to heavy enemy artillery – we were literally showered with earth and the shrapnel flew and whistled all around us – but one gets used to such things so incredibly quickly. The area where we are positioned is wonderful. I am allowed to observe with the telescope [Scherenfernrohr], and this gives me great pleasure. It is already fairly cold, but we have a small stove in our hole, and even if this stove only spits and putters, it still gives heat.
Many greetings Your R.
Many greetings to Rosenblum.

„Dass Ihnen Schelers Buch gefallen hat, freut mich"

17. IV. 15.

Hochverehrter lieber Herr Professor,

haben Sie vielen Dank für Ihre liebe Karte. Wie schön, dass es Wolfgang wieder gut geht und wie herrlich, dass er das eiserne Kreuz erhalten hat! Ihm und Ihnen die herzlichsten Glückwünsche. Aus Ihrer Frage, ob ich Ihren Brief seinerzeit erhalten habe, muss ich entnehmen, dass mein Antwortschreiben auf diesen Brief, der mir so unendlich viel Freude gemacht hat, verloren gegangen ist. Das tut mir leid; und so bald es mir irgend möglich ist, werden Sie, lieber Herr Professor, eine ganz eingehende Schilderung unsres Lebens und Treibens erhalten. Wir hatten es eine Zeit lang nicht sehr gut – damals, als die wilden Kämpfe in der Champagne waren. Jetzt ziehen es die Herrn Franzosen offenbar vor, sich zwischen Mosel und Maas die Köpfe einzurennen. Durchkommen werden sie doch nicht! Mir persönlich ist es die ganze Zeit über sehr, sehr gut gegangen. Nette Kameraden und nette Vorgesetzte, der Dienst nicht allzu anstrengend und oft überaus interessant. Seit etwa 7 Wochen bin ich bei zwei „Sturmgeschützen", die unter dem Kommando meines Bruders stehen. Dass es Sturmgeschütze sind, besagt, dass wir nur in Momenten, in denen es drauf ankommt, in Tätigkeit zu treten haben, sonst aber uns mäuschenstill verhalten müssen – solche Geschütze stehen sehr weit vorne.

Dass Ihnen Schelers Buch gefallen hat, freut mich. Mir kam um die Weihnachtszeit herum ein Aufsatz von ihm über den „Genius des Krieges" in die Hände, der in seiner saloppen, undisziplinierten und grosssprecherischen Art sehr abstossend auf mich gewirkt hat. Undeutscheres lässt sich nicht wohl denken. Dass er das Jahrbuch wiederum im Stich lässt, kann nach den bisherigen Erfahrungen nicht Wunder nehmen. Es ist mir schrecklich, lieber Herr Professor, Sie in so grosser Zeit durch so widerwärtige und kleinliche Dinge belästigt zu wissen. Könnte ich die Durchsicht des Martius'schen Manuscriptes nicht übernehmen? Die Zeit würde ich erübrigen können. Was mich schreckt, ist nur die Gefahr eines

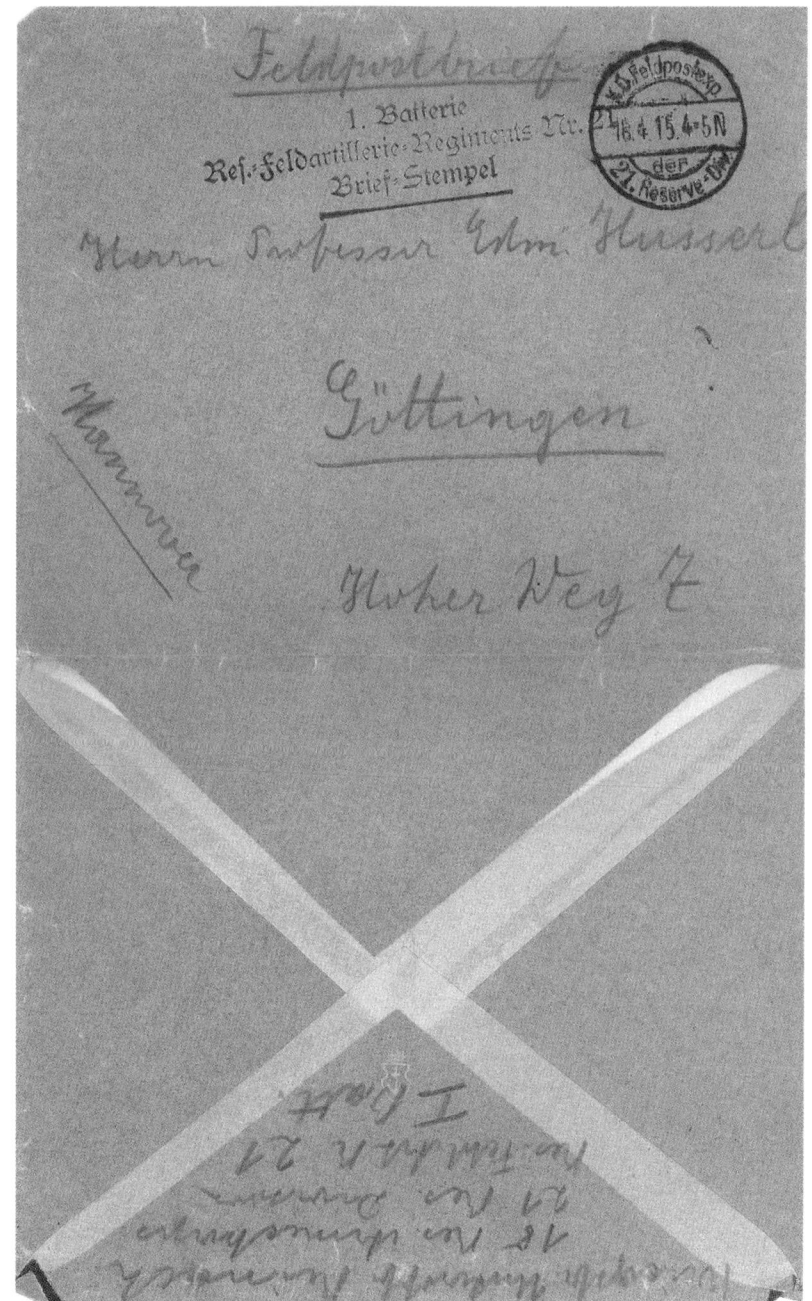

Umschlag eines Briefes von Adolf Reinach an Husserl, 17. IV. 1915

Envelope of a letter from Adolf Reinach to Husserl, 17 April 1915

Verlustes durch die Feldpost. Oder giebt es da einen sicheren Weg? Natürlich wäre es für mich eine grosse Freude, Ihnen diese Last abnehmen zu dürfen. – Ich habe Vorlesungen für das nächste Semester angekündigt – aufs Geradewohl und ein bischen wehen Herzens. Denn halten werde ich sie ja doch nicht. Möge Gott uns bald den Sieg und endgültigen Frieden schenken, den wir alle hier aus tiefstem Herzen ersehnen.

Leben Sie wohl, liebster Herr Professor, Ihnen und Ihrer Frau Gemahlin und den Kindern die herzlichsten Grüsse von

Ihrem treu und dankbar ergebenen

Adolf Reinach

"I am pleased that you liked Scheler's book"

17 April 1915
Esteemed, dear Herr Professor!

Thank you for your lovely card. How nice that Wolfgang is well again and how wonderful that he has received the Iron Cross! Heartfelt wishes to you as well as to him. Regarding your question whether I have since received your letter at that time, I must conclude that my letter in answer to this letter, which gave me so much joy, has gotten lost. I'm very sorry, and as soon as it becomes possible for me, dear Herr Professor, you'll receive a thorough portrayal of my life and doings. For some time now, things were doing not so well for us – back then, during the ferocious fighting in the Champagne. It now appears that the French gentlemen are preferring to run their heads against each other between the Mosel and the Maas [rivers]. They wouldn't however make it! For me personally, this entire time has been very, very good to me. Nice comrades and nice superiors, with duties not all too demanding and at times even interesting. Since around 7 weeks, I am serving with two "assault guns" under the command of my brother. That these are assault guns means that we only have to enter into action in those moments that matter, but otherwise we've been quiet as mice – such guns are placed very far ahead.

I am pleased that you liked Scheler's book. I got from him into my hands around Christmas time an essay about the "Genius of War," which, in his sloppy, undisciplined, and grandiose style made a very repulsive effect on me. Something as unGerman would be impossible to imagine. That he once again abandons the Yearbook is not any wonder given previous experiences. It's for me frightful, dear Herr Professor, to know that you have to be troubled by such repulsive and petty things during such immense times. Could I not take over the review of the Martius manuscript? I would be able to make the time. What scares me is now the danger of its being lost by the field-post. Or might there be a more secure way? Of course, it would be a great pleasure for me to relieve you of this burden. I have announced my lectures for the next semester – on the straight and narrow, and with a bit of aching heart. Since I shall not be able to give them after all. May God soon grant us the victory and the final peace that we here all long for from the bottom of our hearts.
Best wishes, dearest Professor, to you and your wife, and warmest greetings to the children,

Your loyal and thankfully devoted,

Adolf Reinach

„Sehr betrübt hat mich Lask's Tod"

21. August 1915.

Hochverehrter lieber Herr Professor!

Lange habe ich nichts von mir hören lassen – es sind ja nun wieder zwei ereignisschwere Monate seit dem schönen Aufenthalt in Göttingen verstrichen. Bei uns ist es militärisch recht still in dieser Zeit gewesen. Die Kämpfe in den Argonnen zwangen uns zwar stete Alarmbereitschaft auf, und von der Höhe unsres Schützengrabens aus konnten wir fast allnächtlich hinabblicken in die vom Aufblitzen der Geschütze taghell erleuchteten rasenden Kämpfe des tapfren 16. Armeekorps. Aber selbst verwickelt wurden wir in diese Kämpfe nicht. Wir liegen da und warten – warten auf den ersehnten Augenblick, in dem die Reihe an uns kommt vorzubrechen. Immer wieder erstaunt uns die Untätigkeit der Franzosen. Mässiges Artilleriefeuer – hie und da Minenwerfer – sonst nichts. Nach Aussagen von Gefangenen und Überläufern herrscht Mutlosigkeit und Überdruss im französ<ischen> Lager. Man glaubt nicht mehr daran, dass die Deutschen zurückgedrängt werden können und man ist von Abneigung, ja Hass gegen die Engländer erfüllt. Ohne ständige Überwachung durch Offiziere würden – so versichern die Gefangenen allgemein – zahllose Soldaten überlaufen. Man versichert ihnen immer wieder, sie würden als Überläufer von den Deutschen ohne weiteres erschossen werden. Gar nichts mehr erhoffen sie von Italien. Der Fall Lembergs und Warschaus ist ihnen bekannt.

Sehr betrübt hat mich Lask's Tod. Er war wohl einer der besten. Linke – um das Gegenstück gleich zu nennen – hat mir mit einigem Triumph geschrieben, dass er „seit längerer Zeit" von einem Augenleiden befallen ist. Ich denke, Deutschland vermag auf seine Hilfe zu verzichten. Conrad scheint noch in Wörishofen zu sein. Die Arbeit von Frau Dr. C<onrad>-M<artius> ist inhaltlich durchaus durchgearbeitet und druckfertig. Ich hoffe, dass der Setzer mit dem äusserlichen Gewand fertig werden wird und will ihr – unsrer Verabredung und dem Briefe Ihrer Frau Gemahlin an meine Frau gemäss – schreiben und eine Abschrift dieses Schreibens Ihnen übersenden.

Brief von Adolf Reinach an Husserl, 21. VIII. 1915

Letter from Adolf Reinach to Husserl, 21 August 1915

Von ganzem Herzen hoffe ich, dass es Ihren Söhnen recht, recht gut geht – von Wolf habe ich eine liebe Karte bekommen. Leben Sie recht wohl, liebster Herr Professor, lassen Sie mich bitte bald wissen, wie es Ihnen und Ihrer Arbeit geht und seien Sie und die lieben Ihren auf das herzlichste gegrüsst von
Ihrem dankbar und treu ergebenen
Adolf Reinach

"Lask's death saddened me greatly"

21 August 1915.
Esteemed, dear Herr Professor!
It has been some time now since I last wrote and it has been two eventful months since the beautiful stay in Göttingen has passed. It has been a very quiet time for us in the military. The fighting in the Argonne forced us to always be in a state of preparedness, and from the heights of our trenches we could look down almost every night with the illumination of artillery fire at the raging combat of the brave 16th Army Corps. But we ourselves were not engaged in these struggles. We're lying down here and waiting – waiting for the desired moment when it becomes our turn to attack. Time and again, we are astonished by the inactivity of the French. Moderate artillery fire, here and there mortars, otherwise, nothing. According to prisoners and defectors, despondency and weariness prevails in the French camp. One no longer believes that the Germans can be pushed back and one is filled with aversion, even hatred for the English. Without constant surveillance by officers, as our captives generally assure us, countless soldiers would flee. They are always assured, however, that they would be shot dead by the Germans as defectors. They expect nothing more from Italy. The capture of Lemberg and Warsaw is known to them.

Lask's death saddened me greatly. He was indeed one of the best. Linke – to get right to a counter-point – has written to me in some triumph that he has "suffered for a long time" from an eye illness. I think Germany could get on very well without his help. Conrad seems to be still in Wörishofen. The work of Frau Dr. Conrad-Martius is contentwise very well developed and ready for publication. I hope that the type-setter will be finished with the external form. I will send her a letter and a copy of this letter to you (in accordance with our agreement and the letter of your wife to my wife).

With all my heart I hope that your sons are doing very, very well. I received a lovely card from Wolf. Be well, dearest Herr Professor, and please let me know soon how you and your work are doing and warm greetings to you and your beloved ones.
Your grateful and faithful,
Adolf Reinach

„Es waren oft furchtbare Stunden, in denen man mit diesem Leben abgeschlossen hatte"

5. XI. 15
Liebe Freunde!
Etsch! Jetzt haben wir den Brief. Eigentlich ist er ganz nett, nicht? Ich weiss nicht, warum ich mich so sehr davor gefürchtet habe. Husserl soll leider recht krank sein. Es heisst Nikotinvergiftung, es geht aber auch das Gerücht von einem Schlaganfall. Jedenfalls liest er sein grosses Kolleg nicht. Ich hoffe von ganzem Herzen, dass er bald gesund sein wird.

Mir geht es arg gut. Ich bin so seelenvergnügt, als ob es keine Franzosen und keine schwere französ. Artillerie gäbe. Wir sind noch in unsrer alten Stellung. D. h. bei der Batterie; vorher waren mein Bruder und ich ja mit 2 Geschützen auf der Höhe 191. Höhe und Geschütze sind verloren gegangen. Aber wir haben die Geschütze erst verlassen, als unsre Infanterie schon hinter uns war und wir in Gefahr gerieten, von der eigenen Artillerie beschossen zu werden. Und als wir auf dem Weg zur Batterie an einer anderen deutschen Batterie vorbeikamen, deren Kanoniere schon fort waren, da haben wir uns an die fremden Geschütze gesetzt und auf die anrückenden Franzosen geschossen, bis die Nacht hereinbrach. Es waren oft furchtbare Stunden, in denen man mit diesem Leben abgeschlossen hatte. Aber es ist doch die stolzestes Zeit meines Lebens gewesen. Und darum bedeutet mir mein eisernes Kreuz, das ich für eben diese Tage erhalten habe, in der Tat sehr viel.

Das Manuscript wird meine Frau an Niemeyer schicken. Leben Sie recht wohl u. denken Sie manchmal an
Ihren Reinach.
Vielen Dank für das schöne Buch. Die früheren haben die Franzosen.

Adolf Reinach auf der Vorderseite einer Postkarte, die er im Februar 1917 an Theodor Conrad und Hedwig Conrad-Martius schickte

Adolf Reinach on the front of the postcard, which he sent in February 1917 to Theodor Conrad and Hedwig Conrad-Martius

Brief von Adolf Reinach an Theodor Conrad und Hedwig Conrad-Martius, 5. XI. 1915

Letter from Adolf Reinach to Theodor Conrad and Hedwig Conrad-Martius, 5 November 1915

"There were often terrible hours in which one could have been finished with this life"

5 November 1915
Dear friends!
Fiendish delight! We now have the letter. He's actually very nice, no? I do not know why I was so afraid about it. Unfortunately, Husserl is apparently quite ill. It's called nicotine poisoning, but there's also the rumor of a stroke. Anyway, he's not giving his large lecture. I hope with all my heart that he will soon be well.

I'm doing very well. I'm so thoroughly happy as if there would be no French and no heavy French artillery. We are still in our old positions, in other words, with the artillery battery. Before that, my brother and I along with two artillery pieces on Hill 191. The hill and the artillery pieces were lost. But we only abandoned the pieces when our infantry was already behind us and we found ourselves in danger of being shot by our own artillery. And we passed another German battery on the way to the battery, whose gunners had already left, we sat down at the abandoned guns and fired at the approaching Frenchmen until night fell. There were often terrible hours in which one could have been finished with this life. Yet, it was the proudest day of my life. And that is why my Iron Cross, which I just received for these days, means a great deal to me.

My wife will send the manuscript to Niemeyer. Take care of yourself and please remember
Your Reinach.
Thank you for the nice book. The French now have the earlier ones.

„Gott schütze Ihre Kinder in den Stürmen, die nun einsetzen werden"

"May God protect your children during the storms that are soon to begin"

5. III. 16.

Hochverehrter lieber Herr Professor,

wir sind hier so sehr in Spannung und Tätigkeit, und die ganzen Verhältnisse sind derart, dass ich Ihnen von mir und meinem Ergehen kaum etwas berichten kann – es sei denn, dass ich mich sehr wohl befinde. Aber tausend Dank muss ich Ihnen doch sagen – für Ihre rührend liebe Fürsorge und Tätigkeit für mich. Ich bin fest überzeugt, dass Ihr Eintreten für mich meine künftige Stellung in Göttingen wesentlich befestigen wird. Wie freue ich mich darauf in Ihrem Zeichen dort zu wirken.

Für Freiburg von ganzem Herzen alles Gute. Gott schütze Ihre Kinder in den Stürmen, die nun einsetzen werden. Ihnen und den Ihren die innigsten Grüsse von
Ihrem treu ergebenen
Adolf Reinach

5 March 1916

Esteemed dear Herr Professor,

We are in the midst of so much tension and activity, and the entire circumstances are such, that I can hardly tell anything about me and my life, other than that I am doing very well. A thousand thanks I must express to you, for your touching and loving concern and activity for me. I'm firmly convinced that with your commitment on my behalf, my future position in Göttingen will be essentially secured. How I am looking forward to working there in your spirit.

From all of my heart, all the best for Freiburg. May God protect your children during the storms that are soon to begin. With all good wishes to you and yours,
Your loyal,
Adolf Reinach

Brief von Adolf Reinach an Husserl, 5. III. 1916

Letter from Adolf Reinach to Husserl, 5 March 1916

"Phänomenologie der Ahnungen" – Embagneux, 26. Juli 1916

"Phenomenology of Foreboding" – Embagneux, 26 July 1916

In my half sleep I heard the talk of men resting during a pause from artillery firing. A young officer had fallen the day before; briefly before the ride [left], from which he never returned, he had, as he otherwise never did, given his fellow (officer) his trunk key, put his classified documents in order and written a farewell letter. He had therefore a foreboding of his own death. This story is tied to others. One was remarkably out of sorts and funereal before the grenade struck him; another one had his will and testament made; it is reported of many that they had said directly before their deaths that they would no longer be alive the following day. None of the infantryman doubted it, that there is (such a thing as) foreboding that lets us foreknow the future with certainty.

A young staff sergeant breaks into the conversation. I hear him, how he – a bit condescendingly – argues, how little it had to do with cases of foreboding. Certainly everyone assumes before a dangerous mission that perhaps or probably he will die. If this supposition comes true (fulfills itself), then its result is mysteriously foreboding; supposing it doesn't fulfill itself, then nobody remembers it. No, there are no forebodings; only reasonable calculations are possible that acknowledge themselves with more or less probability. The young staff sergeant becomes all the more scientific, and all the more quieter it becomes around him: foreboding are matters/things of dispositions (moods). If I am sad or ill-tempered, the world appears darker to me, and misfortune seems (to me) impending.

Perhaps such a misfortune really occurs. Then the number of mysterious forebodings is increased by one. Or it does not occur, then nobody talks about the affair. The realization of gloomy dispositions are particularly frequent in wars, whom should that surprise? For this reason, the numerous "forebodings" in this time, therefore there are also a large number of such forebodings before (the battle of) Verdun or at the Somme (in France) than at any quiet period on the front. It is sad enough that in our time one still believes in such things.

Who could dispute these words thrown out with the strength of higher education and reasonable intelligence (enlightenment)? Concerned silence quieted the infantryman. And probably it lasted for a full minute before their spokesperson begins a new story of a cousin, who not only spoke of but also wrote of his own death. But that response to the preceding conversation is not sufficient as a scientific claim. Shrugging, the young sergeant turns away.

However, in me a world ascends, for a long time, long immersed in anything but the suffocating activity of the soldier in war. What are proper forebodings/foresights? That they are justified in themselves was just now denied. And the contradiction has increased to the claim that there would be no forebodings. Now this was certainly quite an unscientific mistake on the part of the scientific staff sergeant: to put into question the proper essence of a thing, whose essence he precisely acknowledges through the fact that he negates its own inner truth and that he tries to explain genetically its frequent occurrence. But we do not discredit him for that which is found often enough in still more scientific people than him.

Whether foreboding/foreseeing carries justice or truth in itself, I do not have the means to say; it is impossible to say before I know what the proper essence of foreboding/foreseeing is. I do not know it yet. However, already the desire of the phenomenologist is awakened in me, to single out a structure from the fullness of the appearance, to seize it, to submerge oneself in it, what so far only acknowledged in the meaning of the word, henceforth it is to achieve intuitively the essence itself.

That every foreseeing as such necessarily requires a related content – the "foreseen" as such – so far stretched is the boundary of its possible contents here. Not only, for example, temporally but even future forebodings can refer to something. Within a scientific investigation a foreseeing of the result can rise up within me; here something forms apparently timeless (atemporal) – a more or less determinate proposition [*Satz*] or state of affairs [*Sachverhalt*] – the related content of a foreseeing. But not this foreseeing content, it being also identical with the content of a judgment or an apprehension, but rather the foreseeing as such – not the noematic, but the "noetic" side, to which Husserl speaks about, presents the real problem. If we avail ourselves of the division, in itself quite limited but sufficient for our purposes, of the psychic world [*seelischen Welt*] into "spheres of feeling – willing and thinking", then, since the foreseeing is certainly no volition, one will only be able to be undecided as to whether it could be taken as a feeling in such claims. Indeed it appears to have good sense to speak of felt foresights, of the aspect of being felt of any foreseeing. All the same, it is readily apparent that foreseeing – for example of a future event – is no feeling like joy or sorrow, no set of ego states (no state of being of the I), not in one way or another being a condition of the ego (the I).

Nevertheless the foreseeing adds something new to the total wealth of knowledge – in the broadest sense of knowledge spoken; the subject here appears to grasp by means of foreseeing, correctly or incorrectly remains to be seen, something from the river of future events, which was previously not accessible to him prior. What is meant by the words "aspect of being felt of the foreseeing" cannot be clarified until a more in-depth analysis occurs. Already here, however, we are allowed to include foreseeing, like everything that allows certain states of affairs to appear to the subject as subsisting now or in the future or in general, in the domain of knowledge and therefore of thought, in the sense of that threefold division. What clearly stands out from foreboding is the horror of future fortunes, which as a feeling springs from this forsightful grasp, as does all aspirations and reluctance, willing and not willing, which is rooted in this feeling and knowledge [*Wissen*].

Certainly "knowledge" [*Wissen*] is taken here in the widest sense; in a narrow and proper sense one can contrast foresight and knowledge against each other. So, after this first superficial orientation, closer determinations are vital. In this sphere, we make the fundamental and far-reaching distinction between grounding and grounded structures. I have already pursued knowledge in the narrower sense in an earlier work. (Munich Philosophical Treatises, *On the Negative Judgment*). Let us take knowledge [as cognition; *Erkennen*] in the stricter sense as the act in which a state of affairs comes to givenness for us, in which it illuminates for us and the corresponding proposition is understood by us, then the conviction that develops for us on the ground of this understanding distinguishes itself in all clarity from the state of affairs. We designate the first as knowledge [*Erkennen*], the second as judgment (in one of the many possible meanings of this term). Without further analysis both contrast one another clearly enough, if one considers that the case of cognition [*Erkennen*] concerns a temporally punctual act, which cannot endure any more or less, whereas we can live with a conviction for any length of time, and that furthermore a set of convictions can be maintained in ourselves without grounding themselves in an act of cognition or at any time having been grounded. From this point there is no doubt that we have to account for the grounding structures it has, not the grounded ones – i.e., those which by their essence are open to a grounding. Through foreboding/foresight we grasp – or rather we believe that we grasp – something that was previously concealed. And a conviction can also be grounded in the foreboding, which in strength and inner certainty itself need be in no way inferior to the conviction based upon knowledge [*Erkennen*]. From the foreboding of immanent death arises the certain conviction of having to die soon. As knowledge [*Erkennen*] and foresight/foreboding stand on equal rank in this relation, the task of identifying fundamental differences between the two becomes all the more urgent.

(translated by Kimberly Baltzer-Jaray; in: Brian Harding, Michael R. Kelly (ed.): Early Phenomenology: Metaphysics, Ethics, and the Philosophy of Religion. London (Bloomsbury), 25-28)

Typoskript von Adolf Reinachs Manuskript „Phänomenologie der Ahnungen", das er während seines Fronteinsatzes am 26. Juli 1916 in Embagneux (Frankreich) geschrieben hat.

Typed manuscript of Adolf Reinach's "Phenomenology of Foreboding," which he wrote during his service at the front on 26 July 1916 in Embagneux (France)

"Immer gewaltiger wird das Heer der Todten"

Hinterzarten Schwarzwald 25. XI. 17

Lieber Herr Doktor!

Wir sind in große Trauer versetzt – nun ist auch der treffliche Reinach dahingegangen, er ist am 17. d. <Monats> bei Dixmuiden gefallen. Immer gewaltiger wird das Heer der Todten, immer mehr zieht es die Besten, denen das Werk der Zukunft anvertraut war, sie die uns eine leuchtende Hoffnung waren, an sich. Wie sicher war er im Aufstieg, wie hoch hatte er seine Ziel gestellt, wie liebte er die Phänomenologie, fest überzeugt, daß sie das wahre Zukunftsland der Philosophie sei. Mit welcher Begeisterung bethätigte er sich in ihr als Pionier u. wie wußte er als Lehrer die Jugend für sie zu gewinnen u. in eifriger Mitarbeit sich selbst zu erhöhen. Wie hatte ich ihn mir als Nachfolger in G<öttingen> gewünscht, er schien wie berufen in Göttingen die Tradition der „Göttinger Schule" fortzusetzen u. den wohlbearbeiteten Boden in steter fruchtbarer Cultur zu erhalten. Leider hatte die G<ötting>er Fakultät hier wie sonst allzuwenig Interesse für den Bestand der G<öttinger> Schule u. so konnte ihm diese letzte große Freude nicht zu theil werden. Wie schmerzt es mich, daß diese Hauptstütze für meine Bestrebungen gesunken ist. Es ist um diese ausgezeichnete junge Kraft, deren Gleichen so selten sind, jammerschade. Gewiß werden Sie mit mir trauern. Ich bin seit 2 Tagen hier im Schwarzwald mich ein wenig zu erholen u. meine innere Erregung zu dämpfen. Morgen halte ich wieder Logikcolleg – freilich ein trauriges Colleg vor leeren Bänken, da nun auch die Damen, die sonst so treu u. eifrig die neue Kunde der Phä<nomenologie> aufgenommen hatten, in die Munitionsfabriken gegangen sind. Ich war 2 Ferienmonate in großer Arbeit im Bernauer Hochthal u. habe bis jetzt an der Phän<omenologie> der Zeit fortgeschafft, unterstützt von meiner trefflichen Assistentin, Frl. Stein. Alle Lebenskraft wende ich an die Ausführung meiner alten Entwürfe, in der Welt der Ideen entbinde ich mich von den schweren Lasten des Irdischen u. errette mich von den seelenlähmenden Erregungen der Kriegszeit. Was könnte ich sonst fürs Vaterland Besseres thun? Doch nicht politisieren über Kriegsziele, Parlamentarisierung usw. Jemand muß doch die großen Ewigkeitsprobleme fest im Griff, in Auge und Arbeit erhalten u. da die Jugend in Waffen u. Kämpfen lebt, muß das Alter die Kulturtraditionen, um die doch gekämpft wird, in lebendiger Kraft u. That erhalten. Wie geht es Ihnen, l<ieber> Herr Doktor? Oft denke ich an Sie u. Ihrer überall sich bewährenden Tüchtigkeit. Ihre Mittheilungen a. d. Felde sind mir allzeit eine besondere Freude. Also erfreuen Sie mich wieder! Von Herzen Ihr EHusserl.

Ausschnitt aus der „Deutschen Verlustliste", Liste Preußen 1036, S. 22429, 12. Januar 1918: „Reinach, Adolf, Ltn. d. R., – 23.12. Mainz – gefallen". – Reinach war am 16. XI. 1917 bei Dixmuide (Westflandern) gefallen. Aus einem Brief von Jean Hering an Friedrich Neumann, 24. XII. 1917: „Vor ein paar Wochen erhielt Frau Reinach das Telegramm, vor dem wir alle schon lange bangten. Möge sein Geist unserer Gemeinde die Einheit erhalten, die stets gefährdete, um die er sich lebend stets so erfolgreich mühte! Dass auch der junge Rickert fiel, erzählte mir sein Vetter Keibel."

Extract from "List of German Causalities," Prussian Lists 1036, p. 22429, 12 January 1918: "Reinach, Adolf, Lieutenant in the Reserves, 23.12 Mainz, killed in combat." Reinach was killed in combat on November 16, 1917 near Dixmuide (West Flanders)
From a letter from Jean Hering to Friedrich Neumann, December 24, 1917: "A few weeks ago, Frau Reinach received the telegram that we long feared. May his spirit sustain the unity of our community, which was always endangered, and for which he always struggled [to sustain] so successfully! That also the young Rickert fell in combat, was told to me by his cousin Keibel."

"The army of the dead grows ever more powerful"

Hinterzarten Black Forest

25 November 1917

Dear Herr Doctor!
We find ourselves in profound mourning – the excellent Reinach is now gone; he was killed in combat on the 17th of the month in Dixmuiden. The army of the dead grows ever more powerful, and more and more of the best of those who were entrusted with the work of the future have been surrendered to this army. How confident he was in ascending, how high had he set his goal, how he loved phenomenology, firmly convinced that it was the true future-land of philosophy. With what enthusiasm did he act as a pioneer and how he knew how to win the younger generation and to elevate himself through zealous collaboration. How I had wished for him to be my successor in Göttingen, since he seemed to be called to continue the tradition of the "Göttingen School" in Göttingen and keep the well-cultivated soil in a constant condition of fertile culture. Unfortunately, the Göttingen faculty here, as elsewhere, had too little interest for the important continuance of the Göttingen School, and so this last great joy could not be given to him. How painful it is for me that this mainstay of my endeavours has fallen. It's such a pity that this excellent youthful force, so rare, died. Surely you will mourn with me. I am here for 2 days in the Black Forest to recover a little and dampen my inner disturbances. Tomorrow, I'll be back teaching my course on logic; of course, it will be a sad course in front of so many empty benches, since now even the ladies, who are so loyal and excited to absorb the new message of phenomenology, have gone to the munitions factories. I was for 2 months deep within my work in the high valley in Bernau and have up to now worked on my phenomenology of time, [and was] supported by my excellent assistant, Fräulein Stein. All of my life energies I am applying to the execution of my old plans; I can release myself from the heavy burdens of evertyhing earthly and save myself from the soul-paralyzing disturbances of the war in the world of ideas. What else could I do better for the Fatherland? But let us not politicize about war aims and become parliamentarians. Someone must master the great problems of eternity, keep an eye on them and do real work [on them], and since the youth live with weapons and fighting, the older ones must preserve the cultural traditions, for which they are fighting, in living force and deed. How are you, dear Herr Doctor? I often think about you and your demonstrated mastery. Your communications from the front are always a special pleasure. So, please me again!
Sincerely,
Your,
EHusserl

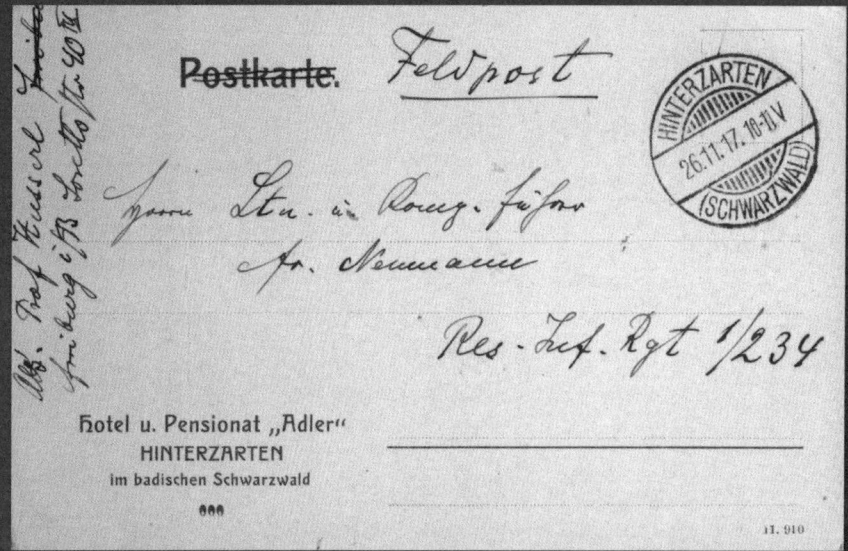

Feldpost von Husserl an Friedrich Neumann, 25. XI. 1917

Field post from Husserl to Friedrich Neumann, 25 November 1917

„Die feindliche Kugel traf den in sich Beruhigten, mit sich und Gott völlig Einigen"

Durch Adolf Reinachs frühen Tod hat die deutsche Philosophie einen schweren Verlust erlitten. Er war zwar noch durchaus im Werden, als der Krieg ausbrach und er voll Begeisterung als Freiwilliger auszog, der vaterländischen Pflicht zu genügen. Aber schon die ersten Arbeiten gaben Zeugnis von der Selbständigkeit und Kraft seines Geistes sowie von dem Ernst seines wissenschaftlichen Strebens, dem nur gründlichste Forschung genugtun konnte. <...> Im letzten Jahre vor dem Kriege beschäftigte sich Reinach mit Grundproblemen der allgemeinen Ontologie, und speziell über das Wesen der Bewegung glaubte er entscheidende phänomenologische Einsichten gewonnen zu haben. Es besteht die Hoffnung, daß wertvolle Stücke aus seinen literarisch unvollendeten Entwürfen der Öffentlichkeit zugänglich gemacht werden können. Im Kriege selbst widmete er seine Kräfte in nie versagender Freudigkeit dem Vaterlande. Aber zu tief war seine religiöse Grundstimmung durch die ungeheuren Kriegserlebnisse betroffen, als daß er in Zeiten eines relativ ruhigeren Frontdienstes nicht hätte den Versuch wagen müssen, seine Weltanschauung religionsphilosophisch auszubauen. Wie ich höre, rang er sich in der Tat zu einer ihn befriedigenden Klarheit durch: Die feindliche Kugel traf den in sich Beruhigten, mit sich und Gott völlig Einigen.

Anfangs- und Schlussteil des 1918 von Husserl in den Kant-Studien veröffentlichten Nachrufs auf Reinach (am 6. XII. 1917 war ein Nachruf Husserls in der "Frankfurter Zeitung" erschienen)

Beginning and closing parts from Husserl's 1918 obituary for Reinach in Kant-Studien (Husserl published another obituary in the "Frankfurter Newspaper" on 6 December 1917)

"The fatal bullet struck down a man who was fully at peace with himself and God"

German philosophy has suffered a heavy loss as a result of Adolf Reinach's early death. He was of course still very much in the process of developing when the war broke out and he left, full of enthusiasm, to enlist as a volunteer and fulfil his duty for his country. But even his first writings bore witness to the independence and power of his mind as well as to the seriousness of his striving for knowledge, which was able to be satisfied by only the most thorough kind of investigation. […] In the last years before the war, Reinach was occupied with basic problems of general ontology and especially with the essence of motion, where he felt that he had attained important phenomenological insights. There is hope that valuable fragments of his incomplete drafts will be published. During the war, he never faltered in the joy with which he served his country. But his religious nature was so deeply stirred by the overwhelming experience of the war that he could not help attempting, in times of relative quiet on the front, to develop his basic understanding of reality by turning to the philosophy of religion. I am told that he in fact made his way to clear convictions: the fatal bullet struck down a man who was fully at peace with himself and God.

Heinrich Rickert jr. (1891-1917)

Heinrich („Heini") Rickert: geb. 25. 12. 1891 in Freiburg, gef. 8. 8. 1917. – Zweitältester Sohn von Sophie und Heinrich Rickert. Ab SS 1912 Studium der Mathematik und Physik in Göttingen und Besuch der Lehrveranstaltungen von Husserl und Reinach. Mitglied der Göttinger Philosophischen Gesellschaft, der Vereinigung der Schüler Husserls.

Heinrich ("Heini") Rickert: born on December 25, 1891 in Freiburg, killed in combat on August 8, 1917. Second oldest son of Sophie and Heinrich Rickert. Since 1912, studied mathematics and physics in Göttingen and attended the lectures of Husserl and Reinach. Member of the Göttingen Philosophical Society.

Heinrich Rickert jr., etwa 1912 (Ausschnitt aus einem Gruppenphoto der „Göttinger Philosophischen Gesellschaft")

Heinrich Rickert, Jr, around 1912 (section from a group-photo of the Göttingen Philosophical Society)

„Darf ich bei Gelegenheit anfragen, wie es Ihrem Sohne Heinrich, dessen ich mit Sympathie gedenke, ergeht? Steht er im Felde, ist er heil geblieben?"

"May I on this occasion inquire about how things are doing with your son, Heinrich, who I keep in my thoughts with sympathy? Is he at the front, did he remain safe?"

Göttingen 26. 6. 15
Sehr geehrter Herr College!
Herzlichen Dank für die gütige Zusendung der neuen Auflage Ihres Werkes „Kulturw\<issenschaft\> u. Naturw\<issenschaft\>". Ich brauche nicht zu sagen, wie sehr willkommen mir diese Gabe ist, zumal Sie nun auch auf die neueren kritischen Einwände eingehende Rücksicht genommen haben. Darf ich bei Gelegenheit anfragen, wie es Ihrem Sohne Heinrich, dessen ich mit Sympathie gedenke, ergeht? Steht er im Felde, ist er heil geblieben? Haben Sie noch einen zweiten Sohn im vaterländischen Dienste? Von meinen beiden Söhnen, die von Anfang an vor Ypern nebeneinander kämpften, ist der Ältere unverwundet durchgekommen und steht noch bei seinem alten Reg\<imen\>t. Der Jüngere schied in Folge einer schweren Lungenverwundung für einige Monate aus und kämpft jetzt vor Verdun.
   Mit kollegialen Grüßen und besten Wünschen für Ihr Haus
Ihr Sie aufrichtig hochschätzender
EHusserl

Göttingen 26 June 1915
Dear Herr colleague,
Many thanks for the kindly dispatch of the new edition of your work "Science of Culture and the Natural Sciences." I don't need to say how much I appreciate this gift, especially since you have taken full account of recent critical objections. May I on this occasion inquire about how things are doing with your son, Heinrich, who I keep in my thoughts with sympathy? Is he at the front, did he remain safe? Do you have a second son in the service of the Fatherland? Of my two sons, who fought side by side at the front in Ypres from the beginning, the eldest one pulled through without a scratch and remains with his old regiment. The younger one was taken out for some months due to a serious lung-injury and is now fighting at Verdun.
With collegial greetings and best wishes for your household.
Your truly appreciative,
EHusserl

Postkarte von Husserl an Heinrich Rickert, 26. VI. 1915

Postcard from Husserl to Heinrich Rickert, 26 June 1915

Heinrich Rickert jr.

„Das verstärkt seinen Wunsch, an die Front geschickt zu werden"

<…> Unser Heini, dem es körperlich ja durchaus gut geht, und der noch immer im Lande ist, leidet unter seiner Umgebung sehr schwer. Er ist jetzt in Rastatt und kommt nicht mit einem einzigen Menschen aus unsern Kreisen und aus unserm Bildungsniveau zusammen, und das verstärkt seinen Wunsch, an die Front geschickt zu werden. Bisher ist ihm das aber noch nicht gelungen. Es kommt vor, daß ein jüngerer Arzt ihn für felddienstfähig erklärt, aber bei einer erneuten Untersuchung ist das jedes Mal wieder rückgängig gemacht worden. Die Aerzte sagen dann immer, er würde mit seinem Herzen den Anforderungen, die man heute an die Infanterie stelle, nicht gewachsen sein. Er bemüht sich, zu einer andern Truppe als zur Infanterie zu kommen, aber das hat bisher keinen Erfolg gehabt. So muß er abwarten. Uns ist es natürlich lieb, ihn außer Gefahr zu wissen, und wir können uns diesem Gefühl um so ruhiger hingeben, als niemand behaupten wird, daß Heini versucht habe, sich zu drücken. Ich gewinne sogar den Eindruck, daß der große Eifer, den er an den Tag legt, um an die Front zu kommen, die Aerzte bei den Untersuchungen ganz besonders vorsichtig sein läßt, denn man ist heute sonst gar nicht wählerisch und schickt Leute hinaus, die wohl sicher besser zu Hause blieben. Ueber die Pfingsttage hatte Heini Urlaub bekommen, und es war sehr nett, ihn wieder einmal hier zu haben. <…>

Heinrich Rickert über seinen Sohn Heinrich („Heini"). Auszug aus seinem Brief an Emil Lask, 28. V. 1915

Heinrich Rickert about his son Heinrich ("Heini"). Excerpt from a letter to Emil Lask, 28 May 1915

"That strengthens his desire to be sent to the front"

[...] Our Heini, who is physically very well, and who is still in the country, suffers very hard in his surroundings. He is now in Rastatt, and does not get together with a single person from our circles and our level of education and that strengthens his desire to be sent to the front. Thus far, he has not succeeded. It just so happened that a younger doctor declared him as unfit for field service, but with re-examination, this has been reversed every time. The doctors then always say that with his heart he would not be up to the demands made on the infantry today. He tries to get into another unit other than the infantry, but has not been successful thus far. So, he has to wait. Of course, it is nice to know that he is out of danger, and we can abandon ourselves more securely to this feeling, and no one will claim that Heini tried to shirk away. I even have the impression that the great eagerness which he shows in order to get to the front leaves the doctors particularly careful with their examinations, because today one is not at all picky and sends out people who should probably better stay home. Heini had been on holiday over the Whitsun days, and it was very nice to have him here again. [...]

„Was vor Wochen Ihr Innerstes am schwersten getroffen hat – den Verlust Ihres Sohnes Heinrich"

Freiburg i. B. 19. XI. 17.
<...> Hochverehrter Herr Geheimrat! Auch jetzt scheue ich mich fast noch mit dürren Worten das zu berühren, was vor Wochen Ihr Innerstes am schwersten getroffen hat – den Verlust Ihres Sohnes Heinrich. Ihre Anzeige — die schlichteste, die mir je begegnete – hat auf mich so gewirkt, daß ich es unterlassen mußte, mit der umgehenden pflichtmäßigen Teilnahmebezeugung mich einzudrängen. Ich tat es in der Überzeugung, daß Sie meiner aufrichtigen Anteilnahme gewiß sind. Diese Zeilen sollen es nur äußerlich bestätigen. Zugleich darf ich Sie, Herr Geheimrat, bitten, Ihre Frau Gemahlin meiner und meiner Frau Teilnahme zu versichern.
In aufrichtiger Verehrung
Ihr stets dankbarer
Martin Heidegger

Schlusszeilen eines Briefes von Martin Heidegger an Heinrich Rickert, 19. XI. 1917 (veröffentlicht in: Martin Heidegger/ Heinrich Rickert. Briefe 1912 bis 1933 und andere Dokumente. Aus den Nachlässen herausgegeben von Alfred Denker. Frankfurt am Main 2002, S. 44)

Final lines from a letter from Martin Heidegger to Heinrich Rickert, 19 November 1917

Heinrich Rickert (1863-1936)

"That which struck your heart the hardest a few weeks ago – the loss of your son Heinrich"

Freiburg, 19 November 1917
[...] Honored Herr Privy Councilor! Even now, I remain most hesitant to touch with such barren words that which struck your heart the hardest a few weeks ago – the loss of your son Heinrich. Your obituary – the simplest I've ever encountered – had such an effect on me, that I had to refrain from imposing myself with the immediate and compulsory expression of sympathy. I did so in the conviction that you are assured of my sincere sympathy. These lines should only confirm it externally. At the same time, may I ask you, Herr Privy Councilor, to communicate to your wife my and my wife's sympathy.
In sincere esteem,
Your always grateful,
Martin Heidegger

Heinrich Rickert jr.

Hermann Ritzel (1880-1915)

Hermann Ritzel, etwa 1914

Hermann Ritzel, around 1914

Hermann Ritzel: geb. 14. 5. 1880 in Bierstadt bei Wiesbaden, gef. 17. 5. 1915 in Galizien. – Frühjahr 1898 bis Herbst 1899 Studium der Philosophie, Kunstgeschichte, Archäologie und Literaturgeschichte in München. Herbst 1899 bis Herbst 1900 einjähriger, freiwilliger Militärdienst; anschließend Mitarbeit in dem Geschäft seines Bruders. Herbst 1901 bis Frühjahr 1904 Fortsetzung des Studiums in München. Während des Studiums Engagement im „Akademischen Verein für Psychologie", einer (1895 gegründeten) Vereinigung der Schüler des in München lehrenden Philosophen und Psychologen Theodor Lipps. Wegen gesundheitlicher Probleme muss Ritzel das Studium unterbrechen und kann es erst im Herbst 1908 wieder aufnehmen (zunächst Studium der Volkswirtschaft, dann der Philosophie u.a. bei Alexander Pfänder). Mitte Juli 1914 reicht Ritzel seine Dissertation („Über analytische Urteile. Eine Studie zur Phänomenologie des Begriffs") ein; wenig später meldet er sich freiwillig zum Militärdienst. Wegen seines frühen Todes (er fällt im Mai 1915 in Galizien) kann Ritzel nicht mehr die mündliche Promotions-Prüfung ablegen. Er wird von der philosophischen Fakultät der Universität München posthum mit seiner in Husserls „Jahrbuch für Philosophie und phänomenologische Forschung" (1916) veröffentlichten Arbeit promoviert. – Der Nachlass von Hermann Ritzel befindet sich in Familienbesitz.

Hermann Ritzel: born on May 14, 1880 in Bierstadt near Wiesbaden, killed in combat on May 17, 1915 in Galicia. 1898-1899, studied philosophy, art history, archeology, and history of literature in Munich. 1899-1900, one-year voluntary military service; worked in his brother's business. 1901-1904, continuation of studies in Munich. Engaged in the "Academic Association for Psychology" (founded in 1895), an association of students around the teachings of the Munich philosopher and psychologist Theodor Lipps. Due to health problems, curtailed studies; resumed in 1908 (economics, philosophy, with Alexander Pfänder). In July 1914, Ritzel submits his dissertation ("On Analytical Judgments: A Study on the Phenomenology of Concepts"); volunteers for military service. Due to his premature death (he is killed in combat in May 1915 in Galicia), Ritzel never sits for his oral doctoral examination. He received his doctorate posthumously from the Faculty of Philosophy of the University of Munich with his dissertation published in Husserl's "Yearbook for Philosophy and Phenomenological Research" (1916). – The papers of Hermann Ritzel are family owned.

Ritzel, H.: Über analytische Urteile. Eine Studie zur Phänomenologie des Begriffs. In: Jahrbuch für Philosophie und phänomenologische Forschung 3 (1916), 253-344. – Salice, A.: The Phenomenology of the Munich and Göttingen Circles. In: The Stanford Encyclopedia of Philosophy (Winter 2016 Edition), Edward N. Zalta (ed.), URL = <https://plato.stanford.edu/archives/win2016/entries/phenomenology-mg/>. – Schuhmann, K.: Die Dialektik der Phänomenologie I: Husserl über Pfänder. Den Haag 1973, 71. – Spiegelberg, H./Avé-Lallemant, E. (Hg.): Pfänder-Studien. The Hague/Boston/London 1984, 137.

„Dass mein lieber Freund, unser Hermann Ritzel am 17. Mai in Galizien gefallen ist"

München d<en> 6. Juni 15
Lieber Herr Daubert!
Gestern erhielt ich die mich tief betrübende Nachricht, dass mein lieber Freund, unser Hermann Ritzel am 17. Mai in Galizien gefallen ist. Ich weiss, dass auch Ihnen der Tod dieses braven Menschen nahe gehen wird. – Er selbst empfand, als er ins Feld zog, es als eine grosse Freude, dass er, der bisher neben dem Leben hergegangen sei, endlich einmal an einer grossen Sache selbst mittätig sein dürfe. – Wie geht es Ihnen? Mit herzlichem Gruss!
Ihr Brunswig

Feldpostkarte von Alfred Brunswig an Johannes Daubert, 6. VI. 1915

Field postcard from Alfred Brunswig to Johannes Daubert, 6 June 1915

"That my dear friend, our Hermann Ritzel, was killed in combat on the 17th of May in Galicia"

Munich, 6 June 15
Dear Herr Daubert!
Yesterday I received the profoundly saddening news that my dear friend, our Hermann Ritzel, was killed in combat on the 17th of May in Galicia. I know that the death of this brave person will also affect you closely. When he went to the front, he himself felt that it was such a great joy that he, who had hitherto walked alongside of life, was finally allowed himself to participate in a great cause. How are things with you? With kind regards!
Your Brunswig

„Sehr betrübt hat mich die Nachricht, daß Ritzel am 17/V in Galizien gefallen ist"

G<öttingen> 6/6 15.
Lieber Freund!
Wie geht es Ihnen? Schreiben Sie mir wieder! Ich mache mir sonst Sorgen. Momentan ist Reinach hier zu kl<einem> Urlaub, prächtig aussehend und ganz erfüllt von Eifer für seine krieg<erischen> Pflichten (U<nter>off<izier> d<er> Feldart<illerie>). Es ist mir eine große Freude ihn hier zu haben, er hat sich schön entwickelt u. ich habe mein Vertrauen zu ihm voll wiedergewonnen. Sehr betrübt hat mich die Nachricht, daß Ritzel am 17/V in Galizien gefallen ist. Eine gediegene Abh<andlung> von ihm über „analyt<ische> Urtheile", die in München als Diss<ertation> eingereicht war, liegt bei mir u. soll im Jahrb<uch> gedruckt erscheinen. Dieses stockt, da sonst alles mich im Stich gelassen hat. Doch hoffe ich demnächst den Druck wieder beginnen zu können. Wolf (d<er> Jüngere), wiederhergestellt, rückt Mitte d.M. wieder ins Feld. Der Ältere noch vor Ypern, gesund. Mein Befinden besser.
Herzlichst grüßt
Ihr
EHusserl
Desgl. m<eine> Frau.
Dr Geiger ist eingezogen, wird ausgebildet als Inf<anterist>

"I was very saddened by the news that Ritzel was killed in combat on 17/V in Galicia"

Göttingen, 6 June 1915
Dear friend!
How are you? Write me again! For otherwise I'm worried. For the moment, Reinach is here on vacation, splendid-looking and full of zeal for his warlike duties (non-comissioned officier in the field-artillery). It's a great pleasure for me to have him here, and he has developed nicely and I have regained my confidence in him. I was very saddened by the news that Ritzel was killed in combat on 17/V in Galicia. A solid treatise from him on "analytic" judgments, which had been submitted in Munich as a dissertation, is here with me and should be published in the Yearbook. I'm stuck on this, because everything else has left me hanging. But I soon hope to start printing again. Wolf (the younger), healthy once again, goes back to the front, the eldest one is at Ypres, doing well. My health is better.
Sincerely,
your
EHusserl
Also from my wife
Dr Geiger has been enlisted, is training as an infantryman

Feldpostkarte von Husserl an Johannes Daubert, 6. VI. 1915

Field postcard from Husserl to Johannes Daubert, 6 June 1915

„Ein edles, aber nur zu schweres Opfer in diesem großen Kampfe um unsere nationale Erhaltung"

6.6.1915

Es war für mich also eine nicht geringe Freude, als er mir im vorigen Herbste einen sehr sympathischen Brief schrieb und eine Abschrift seiner Dissertation einschickte, in die ich mich mit steigendem Interesse vertiefte und die einen ausgezeichneten Eindruck auf mich machte. Meine Erwartung waren übertroffen. Es ist eine durchaus gediegene Arbeit, Produkt eines voll ausgereiften, gründlichen, ehrlichen Forschers, also weit hinausragend über eine normale akademische Dissertation. Da mein Jahrbuch gerade dazu da ist, grundlegenden Abhandlungen der phänomenologischen Philosophie eine Stätte zu bieten, bat ich ihn, mir diese Arbeit zu überlassen. Es ist für mich ein großer Schmerz, dass er, der nun in meinen Augen die schönsten Zukunftshoffnungen berechtigte, dessen redlicher Forschersinn aus jedem Satze hervorleuchtet, dessen Denken so beherrscht, so methodisch strenge, so sicher auf klare Gründe gestellt war – dahingehen musste, ein edles, aber nur zu schweres Opfer in diesem großen Kampfe um unsere nationale Erhaltung.

Infolge mit dem Kriege zusammenhängende Störungen ist der laufende Band meines Jahrbuchs noch nicht gedruckt. Herzlich gerne würde ich auch jetzt die Arbeit Ihres Bruders aufnehmen; und gerade inmitten dieser Sammlung phänomenologischer Arbeiten würde sie die beste Wirkung üben, und sicher nicht übersehen werden.
E. Husserl

"A noble, and yet too heavy of a sacrifice in this great struggle for our national survival"

6 June 1915

It was for me nothing less than a great joy, when in the previous autumn, he wrote to me a very sympathetic letter and sent a copy of his dissertation, in which I deepened myself with growing interest, and which made an excellent impression on me. My expectations were exceeded. It is a very solid work and the product of a mature, thorough, and honest researcher, much beyond the level of a normal academic dissertation. Given that my Yearbook exists precisely to offer a home for fundamental treatises in phenomenological philosophy, I invited him to give me this work. It is for me such a great suffering that he, who in my eyes possessed the brightest horizons for the future, and whose honest sense of research emanated from every sentence, and whose thinking was so mastered, so methodically strict, so surely based on clear reasons – that he was taken away, such a noble, and yet too heavy of a sacrifice in this great struggle for our national survival.

As a result of disturbances from this war, the current volume of my Yearbook is not yet printed. I would like to include the work of your brother now as well; and just among this collection of phenomenological studies, it would surely have the best effect, and certainly would not be overlooked.
E. Husserl

Brief von Husserl an den Bruder von Hermann Ritzel, 6. VI. 1915 (Abschrift)

Hermann Ritzel beim Zeitunglesen (ca. 1914)

Letter from Husserl to Hermann Ritzel's brother, 6 June 1915 (copy)

Hermann Ritzel, reading a newspaper (around 1914)

München, 7. VII. 1915

Ich habe Ihren Herrn Sohn wegen seines überaus gediegenen, reichstes Wissen und regen Forschergeist mit rührender Bescheidenheit vereinenden Wesens vom ersten Anfang an, wo er mir näher trat, überaus hoch geschätzt, und verliere an ihm einen meiner allerbesten Schüler, von dem ich mir noch Bedeutendes versprach.

Seine Arbeit – für deren Druck schon Bestimmungen getroffen waren – ist eine der besten, die ich zu zensieren hatte, und der ich in meinem Votum für die Fakultät reiches Lob gespendet habe.

Dr. Baeumker

Munich, 7 July 1915

From the first time he approached me, I had always esteemed your son highly for his extremely solid and rich knowledge as well as for his energetic spirit of research with touching modesty, and lost with him one of the best among my students, from whom I assured myself that something important [would come].

His work, for which preparations were already made for publication, is some of the best that I have ever graded, and to which I have given rich praise in my vote for the faculty.

Brief von Clemens Baeumker an den Vater von Hermann Ritzel, 7. VII. 1915 (Abschrift). – Ritzel hatte bei dem katholischen Philosophen und Philosophiehistoriker Clemens Baeumker (1853-1924) in München studiert.

Letter from Clemens Baeumker to Hermann Ritzel's father, 7 July 1915 (copy). Ritzel studied with the Catholic philosopher and historian of philosophy Clemens Baeumker (1853-1924) in Munich.

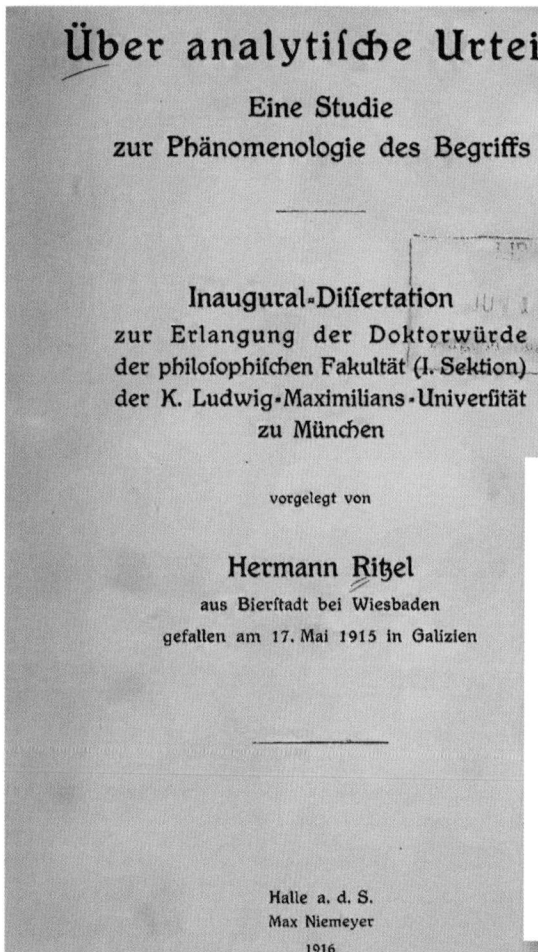

Hermann Ritzel war vor Abschluss des Promotionsverfahrens am 17. Mai 1915 gefallen. Das Manuskript seiner Dissertation („Über analytische Urteile. Eine Studie zur Phänomenologie des Begriffs") hatte er Ende 1914, bevor er an die Front ging, an Husserl gesandt. 1916 wurde die Arbeit im „Jahrbuch für Philosophie und phänomenologische Forschung" (III, S. 253-344) und separat veröffentlicht. Ritzel wurde posthum von der philosophischen Fakultät in München promoviert.

Hermann Ritzel was killed in combat before the completion of his PhD on May 17, 1915. The manuscript of his dissertation ("On Analytic Judgements. A Study on the Phenomenology of Concepts") had been sent to Husserl at the end of 1914 before he went to the front. His dissertation was published in 1916 in the "Yearbook for Philosophy and Phenomenological Research" (Vol. III, 253-344) as well as published separately. Ritzel was awarded his PhD posthumously by the philosophical faculty in Munich.

Select Bibliography

Avé-Lallemant, Eberhard: *Die Nachlässe der Münchener Phänomenologen in der Bayerischen Staatsbibliothek*, (Wiesbaden: Otto Harrassowitz, 1975).

Bernet R./ Kern, I. / Marbach, E. (eds.): *Edmund Husserl. Darstellung seines Denkens*, (Hamburg: Felix Meiner Verlag, 1996).

Besslich, Barbara: *Wege in den „Kulturkrieg": Zivilisationskritik in Deutschland. 1890-1914*, (Darmstadt: Wissenschaftliche Buchgesellschaft, 2000).

de Warren, Nicolas: "The First World War, Philosophy, and Europe," in: *Tijdschrift voor Filosofie,* 76, IV (2014): 715-737.

Embree, L. / Behnke, E. et al. (eds.): *Encyclopedia of Phenomenology*, (Dordrecht / Boston / London: Kluwer Academic Publishers, 1997).

Flasch, Kurt: *Die geistige Mobilmachung. Die deutschen Intellektuellen und der Erste Weltkrieg. Ein Versuch*, (Berlin: Alexander Fest Verlag, 2000).

Fries, Helmut: *Die große Katharsis. Der Erste Weltkrieg in der Sicht deutscher Dichter und Gelehrter*, Volume I: Die Kriegsbegeisterung von 1914: Ursprünge-Denkweisen-Auflösung; Volume II: Euphorie-Entsetzen-Widerspruch: Die Schriftsteller 1914-1918, (Konstanz: Verlag am Hockgraben, 1994/1995).

Hoeres, Peter: *Der Krieg der Philosophen: die deutsche und britische Philosophie im Ersten Weltkrieg*, (Paderborn: Verlag Ferdinand Schöningh, 2004).

Husserl, Edmund: *Briefwechsel, Husserliana Dokumente III*, in Verbindung mit Elisabeth Schuhmann hrsg. von Karl Schuhmann, (Dordrecht / Boston / London: Springer, 1994), vol. I-X (vol. I: *Die Brentanoschule* / vol. II: *Die Münchener Phänomenologen* / vol. III: *Die Göttinger Schule* / vol. IV: *Die Freiburger Schüler* / vol. V: *Die Neukantianer* / vol. VI: *Philosophenbriefe* / vol.VII: *Wissenschaftlerkorrespondenz* / vol. VIII: *Institutionelle Schreiben* / vol. IX: *Familienbriefe* / vol. X: *Einführung und Register*) [= Hua Dok III/1-9].

Husserl, Edmund: *Gesammelte Werke. Husserliana*, vol. I-XLIII, (Dordrecht / Heidelberg New York / London et al.: Springer et al., 1950-2018, [= Hua].

Husserl, E. / Geiger, M. / Pfänder, A. / Reinach, A. / Scheler, M. / Heidegger M. (eds.): *Jahrbuch für Philosophie und phänomenologische Forschung,* vol. I-XI, (Halle / Saale: Niemeyer Verlag, 1913-1930).

Lübbe, Hermann: *Politische Philosophie in Deutschland*, (München: DTV Deutscher Taschenbuch Verlag, 1974).

Luft, Sebastian: "Germany's Metaphysical War. Reflections on War by Two Representatives of German Philosophy: Max Scheler and Paul Natorp," *Themenportal Erster Weltkrieg* (2007), URL: http://www.erster-weltkrieg.clio-online.de.

Luft, S. / Overgaard, S. (eds.): *The Routledge Companion to Phenomenology*, (London / New York: Routledge, 2012).

Luft, S. / Wehrle, M. (eds.): *Husserl-Handbuch: Leben – Werk – Wirkung*, (Stuttgart: J. B. Metzler Verlag, 2017).

Metzger, Arnold: *Phänomenologie der Revolution. Frühe Schriften. Mit einem Nachwort von U. Sonnemann*, (Frankfurt am Main: Syndikat, 1979) [= AMPR].

Moran, D. / Parker, R.: "Resurrecting the Phenomenological Movement", in: *Studia Phaenomenologica*, XV (2015), 11–24.

Münkler, Herfried, *Der Große Krieg: Die Welt 1914 bis 1918*, (Berlin: Rowohlt, 2013).

Neiberg, Michel: *Dance of the Furies: Europe and the Outbreak of World War I*, (Cambridge: Belknap Press, 2011).

Salice, Alessandro, „The Phenomenology of the Munich and Göttingen Circles". In: *The Stanford Encyclopedia of Philosophy* (Winter 2016 Edition), Edward N. Zalta (ed.), URL: https://plato.stanford.edu/archives/win2016/entries/phenomenology-mg/.

Schuhmann, Karl, *Husserl-Chronik. Denk- und Lebensweg Edmund Husserls. Husserliana Dokumente I*, (Den Haag: Springer, 1977).

Schwabe, Klaus: *Wissenschaft und Kriegsmoral: Die Deutschen Hochschullehrer und die politischen Grundfragen des Ersten Weltkrieges*, (Göttingen: Musterschmidt Verlag, 1969).

Sepp, Hans Rainer (ed.): *Edmund Husserl und die Phänomenologische Bewegung. Zeugnisse in Text und Bild*, (Freiburg / München: Alber, 1988).

Sepp, H. R. / Embree, L.: *Handbook of Phenomenological Aesthetics*, (Dordrecht / Heidelberg / London / New York: Springer, 2010).

Sieg, Ulrich: *Aufstieg und Niedergang des Marburger Neukantianismus: die Geschichte einer philosophischen Schulgemeinschaft*, (Würzburg: Königshausen & Neumann, 1994).

Sieg, Ulrich: *Geist und Gewalt: Deutsche Philosophen zwischen Kaiserreich und Nationalsozialismus*, (Ulm: Carl Hanser Verlag, 2013).

Smith, B. / Smith, D. W. (eds.): *The Cambridge Companion to Husserl*, (Cambridge: Cambridge University Press, 1995).

Spiegelberg, Herbert, *The Phenomenological Movement. A Historical Introduction*. Third Revised and Enlarged Edition, with the Collaboration of Karl Schuhmann, (The Hague / Boston / London: Springer, 1982).

Stein, Edith: *Aus dem Leben einer jüdischen Familie und weitere autobiographische Beiträge*. Neu bearb. u. eingel. von Maria Amata Neyer (*Edith-Stein-Gesamtausgabe* 1), (Freiburg: Herder Verlag, 2002) [= ESGA 1].

Stein, Edith: *Selbstbildnis in Briefen III. Briefe an Roman Ingarden*. Bearbeitet von M.A. Neyer OCD und E. Avé-Lallemant (*Edith-Stein-Gesamtausgabe* 4), (Freiburg: Herder Verlag, 2001) [= ESGA 4].

Stein, Edith: *Life in a Jewish Family: An Autobiography, 1891-1916*. Translated by J. Koeppel. *The Collected Works of Edith Stein*, vol. 1, ed. L. Gelber and Romaeus Leuven OCD, (Washington, D.C: Institute for Carmelite Studies Publications, 1986) [= CWES 1].

Stein, Edith: *Self-Portrait in Letters. Letters to Roman Ingarden*. Translated by Hugh Candler Hunt; editing and comments by Maria Amata Neyer, O.C.D. *The Collected Works of Edith Stein*, vol. 12, (Washington, D.C: Institute for Carmelite Studies Publications, 2015) [= CWES 12].

Verhey, Jeffrey: *The Spirit of 1914. Militarism, Myth and Mobilization in Germany*, (Cambridge: Cambridge University Press, 2000).

Zahavi, Dan (ed.): *The Oxford Handbook of Contemporary Phenomenology*, (Oxford: Oxford University Press, 2012).

Additional bibliographical information for each individual philosopher is provided within the volume.

List of Sources

Abbreviations (see additional abbreviations in the bibliography)

BSB = Bayerische Staatsbibliothek München; EAM = Erzbischöfliches Archiv München; HA = Husserl-Archives Leuven; IfZ = Institut für Zeitgeschichte München; SUB = Niedersächsische Staats- und Universitätsbibliothek Göttingen; UAG = Universitätsarchiv Göttingen; UBF = Universitätsbibliothek Freiburg; UB Heidelberg = Universitätsbibliothek Heidelberg; ULB = Universitäts- und Landesbibliothek Bonn; UBM = Universitätsbibliothek Marburg.

Bold numbers refer to the page numbers of the present edition, followed by the indication of the source from which the documents originate. Documents published in Husserl's correspondence (Hua Dok III) or in Husserl's Collected Writings (Husserliana = Hua) are given with volume and page reference.

12-14: UBM Ms 862 (Hua Dok III/3, 404); **15-17**: HA; **18-19**: HA (Hua Dok III/9, 288); **21**: HA (copy); **22-23**: HA (Hua Dok III/9, 293); **24**: HA (Hua Dok III/9, 518); **25**: HA; **26**: HA (Hua Dok III/6, 302); **27**: wikipedia "Hugo Münsterberg"; **28**: HA (Hua Dok III/6, 300; Hua XXV, S. 293); **29-31**: HA; **32-34**: HA (Hua Dok III/9, 157); **36-37**: HA (Hua Dok III/9, 518); **38**: HA (Hua XXV, 267); **39**: HA; **40**: ULB, Hss. u. Rara, Signatur 2827, NL Dyroff (Hua Dok III/6, 67); **41**: UBF; **42-43**: HA; **44-45:** HA (Hua XXVII, 3-4); **46-47**: HA (Hua XXVII, 94-95); **48**: HA; **49-50**: HA (Hua Dok III/9, 340); **51**: HA (Hua Dok III/9, 342); **52**: HA; **53-56**: HA; **57**: HA; **58** HA; **59-69**: HA; **70**: HA (Hua Dok III/9, 297); **71**: HA (Hua Dok III/9, 299); **72-73**: HA (Hua Dok III/9, 301); **74-75**: HA; **76**: HA (copy); **77**: HA (Hua Dok III/6, 71); **81**: HA (Hua Dok III/6, 71); **82**: HA; **83**: HA; **84a**: C. Reid, Richard Courant 1888-1972. Berlin, Heidelberg, New York 1979, 19; **84b:** SUB Cod. Ms. D. Hilbert 773; **85-86**: SUB Cod. Ms. D. Hilbert 773; **87**: HA; **90**: HA (Hua Dok III/9, 301); **91**: HA (Hua Dok III/9, 211); **92-93**: HA; **94-97**: SUB Cod. Ms. D. Hilbert 773; **98**: HA (Hua Dok III/7, 249); **99-101**: HA (Hua Dok III/9, 159); **102-103**: HA (Hua Dok III/9, 172); **104-107**: SUB Cod. Ms. D. Hilbert 773; **108**: HA (copy); **109**: HA (copy) (Hua Dok III/1, 55); **110-111a**: HA (Hua Dok III/5, 121); **111b**: wikipedia "Paul Natorp"; **112-113**: HA (Hua Dok III/5, 122); **114a**: HA (copy) Pfänder photo; **114b**: HA (Hua Dok III/2, 153); **115a**: HA (copy) wikipedia "Georg Simmel"; **115b**: HA (Hua Dok III/6, 410); **116**: BSB München/Bildarchiv; Signatur: Daubertiana C.I.5 Photographien; **117**: BSB München/Bildarchiv; Signatur: Ana 378.C.II.2 Philos. Gesellsch. Göttingen. 21; **118**: HA; **119**: Mt. Allison University Archives – 6501/17/2/1; **120-121**: wikipedia "Studentenkarzer (Göttingen)"; **122**: Mt. Allison University Archives – 6501/1/20/ No.1 (Hua Dok III/3, 3); **123**: Mt. Allison University Archives – 6501/17/6/4.2; **124-128**: Mt. Allison University Archives – 6501/1/20/ No.2 (Hua Dok III/3, 4); **129**: BSB München/Bildarchiv Conrad-Martiusiana D.I.8.b; **131**: BSB München/Bildarchiv; Signatur: Ana 378.C.II.1 (41) (Conrad in uniform) & BSB Ana 378.C.I.4; **132**: HA (copy); **133**: BSB Conrad-Martiusana C.I.5 (advertisement post-card) & BSB Conrad-Martiusana D.I.3 (marriage ring) & BSB Ana 378.C.I.4; **134**: HA (copy); **135**: HA (Hua Dok III/2, 71); **136**: BSB Daubertiana B.II. Nr. 4; **137**: TU Darmstadt Berufspädagogisches Institut; **138**: BSB Daubertiana B.II. Nr. 10; **139**: HA (Hua Dok III/2, 72); **140**: HA (Hua Dok III/2, 72); **141-143**: BSB Daubertiana B.II. Nr. 11 + 11a; **144**: HA (Hua Dok III/2, 75); **145-146a**: BSB Daubertiana C.I.3 (roll call & application for lieutenant); **146b**: BSB Daubertiana B.II. Nr. 1 (Gallinger to Daubert); **147**: HA (copy); **148-150**: BSB Ana 347.E.I.2; **151**: BSB Ana 347.B.I.4; **152**: HA (copy); **153**: HA (Hua Dok III/9, 291); **154**: HA (copy); **155**: HA; **156**: Bildarchiv Foto Marburg Bilddatei-Nr. fmz32370; **157**: Martin-Heidegger-Archiv Stadt Meßkirch; **159:** Martin-Heidegger-Archiv Stadt Meßkirch; **160**: HA (copy) (Hua Dok III/4, 129); **161**: HA (Hua Dok III/4, 130); **162**: HA (Hua Dok III/4, 135); **164**: Image courtesy Archives & Special Collections, University of New Brunswick - Jean and Gustav Hubener fonds, UA RG 362, Series 6, File 2; **165-167**: BSB Ana 315.E.II; **168**: HA (copy); **169-170**: HA (Hua Dok III/3, 337); **171-172**: HA (Hua Dok III/3, 339); **173**: HA (Hua Dok III/3, 343); **174**: HA; **176**: HA (copy); **177a**: HA (engagement notice); **177b**: HA (copy); **178-179**: HA; **180**: BSB München/Bildarchiv, Signatur: Ana 507.C.III Photographien; **181**: HA (copy) (Hua Dok III/3, 383); **182**: BSB Ana 507.C.III. Photographien & BSB Ana 507.C.II (certificate); **183**: BSB München/Bildarchiv, Signatur: Ana.378.C.II.2.19; **184**: HA; **186**: HA (copy); **188**: HA (copy); **189**: HA (copy); **190**: Bildarchiv Foto Marburg, Neg.-Nr. B 24. 289/5; **191**: UBM Ms 862 (Hua Dok III/3, 401); **192-193**: UBM Ms 862 (Hua Dok III/3, 403); **194**: UBM Ms 862 (Hua Dok III/3, 407); **195-196**: HA; **198-199**: UBM Ms 862 (Hua Dok III/3, 413); **200**: Arnold Metzger: "Phänomenologie der Revolution. Frühe Schriften". Mit einem Nachwort von U. Sonnemann. Frankfurt am Main 1979, 163 (= AMPR); **201-203**: AMPR, 167; **204-205**: AMPR, 170; **206**: HA (Hua Dok III/4, 407); **209**: Voit Collection; **210**: SUB Cod. Ms. F. Neumann 1 : 1,189; **211**: Landesarchiv Saarbrücken; **212-213**: SUB Cod. Ms. F. Neumann 1 :

1,186; **214-215**: SUB Cod. Ms. F. Neumann 1 : 1,189; **216a**: SUB Cod. Ms. F. Neumann 1 : 1,189; **216b**: Landesarchiv Saarbrücken (photo Neumann); **217**: UAG, Kleine Sammlungen Y. 431 – Y. 437 Nachlass Neumann, Friedrich; **218**: HA (copy); **219**: HA (Hua Dok III/2, 223); **220**: HA (Hua Dok III/2, 225); **221**: HA; **222-223a**: BSB Ana 315.E.II; **223b**: Universitätsbibliothek der Humboldt-Universität zu Berlin, Porträtsammlung Hans Driesch; **224a**: BSB Ana 315.E.II; **224b**: EAM (photo Michael v. Faulhaber); **225**: HA (copy); **226-227**: Edith Stein Archiv, Karmel "Maria vom Frieden"; **229**: Archiwum rodzinne Krzysztofa Ingardena foto Archiwum K. Ingardena; **231**: M. Heidhues (Göttingen); **232**: Ana 378.C.II.2 Philos. Gesellsch. Göttingen. 23 (section from a group-photo); **233a**: SUB Cod Ms F C Andreas 1 65 Beil; **233b**: HA; **234**: SUB Cod Ms F C Andreas 1 65 Beil; **236**: HA; **237**: HA (Hua Dok III/5, 98); **238**: HA; **240**: Ana 378.C.II.2 Philos. Gesellsch. Göttingen. 23 (section from a group-photo); **241**: HA (copy); **242**: UB Heidelberg Heid. Hs. 3820, 258; **243**: UB Heidelberg Heid. Hs. 3820, 34; **244-245**: UB Heidelberg Heid. Hs. 3820, 502; **246**: UB Heidelberg Heid. Hs. 3820, 235; **247**: UB Heidelberg Heid. Hs. 3820, 249; **249a**: HA (copy) (Hua Dok III/5, 176) (Husserl to Heinrich Rickert); **249b**: UB Heidelberg Heid. Hs. 3820, 257 (Rickert to Kroner); **249c**: UB Heidelberg Heid. Hs. 3820, 260a (Rickert's obituary); **250**: BSB München/Bildarchiv Signatur Ana 378.C.II.2 (24); **251**: BSB Ana 379; **252**: BSB Ana 379; **253-254**: HA (Hua Dok III/2, 196); **255-256**: HA (Hua Dok III/2, 198); **257**: BSB Ana 379; **258**: HA (Hua Dok III/2, 202); **259-261**: HA (copy); **262a-263**: UAG Cod. Ms. F. Neumann 1 : 1,189; **262b**: HA (copy) (list); **262c**: Cod. Ms. F. Neumann 1 : 1,170 (Hering to Neumann, 1917); **264-265**: HA (Hua XXV, 296-303); translated by John F. Crosby: Philosophy of Law, in: Aletheia. An International Journal of Philosophy, vol. III, 1983, p. xi-xiv; **266**: Ana 378 C.II.2.23a (section from a group-photo); **267**: HA (copy) (Hua Dok. III/5, 175); **268**: UB Heidelberg Heid. Hs. 3820, 234; **269**: UB Heidelberg Heid. Hs. 2740 I A – 3 (Rickert Photo); **270**: Nachlass Familie Nataly Ritzel; **271**: BSB Daubertiana B.II. Nr. 8; **272-273**: HA (Hua Dok III/2, 73); **274-275**: Nachlass Familie Nataly Ritzel

Index of Names

Listed here are only the names of individuals who are important for an understanding of the documents in this volume. More detailed biographical information regarding individuals in this volume is presented at page references in bold.

A

Albrecht, Gustav (1858-1943), lifelong friend of Edmund Husserl, studied together with him in Berlin   82, 92-93

Albrecht, Elisabeth ("Elli"), Gustav Albrecht's eldest daughter; Edmund Husserl's godchild   92-93

Andreas, Friedrich Carl (1846-1930), German scholar of Iranian language and cultures, husband of Lou Andreas-Salomé   232, **233**

B

Baeumker, Clemens (1853-1924), German historian of philosophy   **275**

Baligand von, Karl (1893-1916), Husserl's student in 1914   170

Bell, Winthrop P. (1884-1965), Canadian philosopher, student of Husserl, and historian of Nova Scotia   26-27, 116, 118, **119-128**, 170

Bertholet, Alfred (1868-1951), Swiss theologian   77-78

Bolza, Oskar (1857-1942), German mathematician, studied together with Husserl in Berlin   42-43

Brandi, Karl (1868-1946), German historian   210-211

Brentano, Franz (1838-1917), German philosopher, psychologist, and priest, teacher of Husserl   108-109

Brunswig, Alfred (1877-1927), German philosopher   **136**, 271

Burkamp, Wilhelm (1879-1939), German philosopher and psychologist   170-172

C

Chandler, Albert R. (1884-1957), American philosopher, student of Husserl in summer 1912   118

Clemens, Rudolf (1890-1914), Husserl's student in Göttingen   116-118, 181, 212-213, **232-235**

Conrad, Theodor (1881-1969), German philosopher and student of Husserl   116-118, **129-133**, 226, 251-252, 255-257

Conrad-Martius, Hedwig (1888-1966), German philosopher and student of Husserl   116-118, **129-133**, 226, 252-257

Conrad, Waldemar (1878-1915), Husserl's student in Göttingen   116, **236-239**

D

Daubert, Johannes (1877-1947), German philosopher   114, 116, **134-146**, 271, 273

Darkow, Flora (1867-1942), cousin of Edmund Husserl, since 1891 living in the US   32-35, 99-103

Darkow, Marguerite (1893-1992), daughter of Flora Darkow, studied mathematics   32-34, 102-103

Dessoir, Max (1867-1947), German philosopher, psychologist and theorist of aesthetics   239

Driesch, Hans (1867-1941), German philosopher and biologist   **223**

E

Ebbinghaus, Hermann (jr.), son of the German psychologist Hermann Ebbinghaus (1850-1909) and brother of the philosopher Julius Ebbinghaus (1885-1981)   81, 215

Ettlinger, Max (1877-1929), German psychologist, philosopher, pedagogist   114

Eucken, Rudolf (1846-1926), German philosopher, Nobel Prize for Literature in 1908   171-172, 198, 200, 218

F

Faulhaber von, Michael (1869-1952), Roman Catholic Cardinal   224-225

Fischer, Aloys (1880-1937), German philosopher, founder of modern pedagogic studies   **137**, 138, 141-143

Foerster, Friedrich Wilhelm (1869-1966), German educationist, pacifist and philosopher, known for his public opposition to Nazism   166-167

Frankfurther, Fritz (1889-1914), Husserl's student in Göttingen   116, 118, 169-170, 181, **240-241**

G

Gallinger, August (1871-1959), German philosopher and doctor **146**

Geiger, Moritz (1880-1937), German philosopher 116, **147-151**, 156, 186, 198, 218, 250, 272,

Göppert/ Goeppert, Friedrich (1870-1927), German physician and pediatrician 49-50, 74-75

Gündell von, Erich (1854-1924), German General 54-55, 77-78, 104, 106, 116, 146, **152-155**

H

Hamburger, Siegfried (1891-1975), member of the Göttingen circle of phenomenology 117-118, 213

Heidegger, Martin (1889-1976), German philosopher 116, 147, **156-163**, 186, 218, 269

Henkel, Franz (1868-1936), grammar school teacher of Wolfgang Husserl, during wartime his superior (Captain) 54-55, 79, 85, 87, 104-107, 155

Hering, Jean (1890-1960), theologian, member of the Göttingen circle of phenomenology 117-118, 129-130, 213, 262

Hilbert (née Jerosch), Käthe (1864-1945), wife of the mathematician David Hilbert; she had a close relationship to Husserl's son Wolfgang, who often called her "aunt" 84, 94-97, 106

Hildebrand von, Dietrich (1899-1977), Roman Catholic philosopher and theologian, member of the Göttingen circle of phenomenology 118, 213, 219

Hippel von, Ernst (1895-1984), German legal philosopher 74, 75, 77, 78

Hübener, Gustav (1889-1941), German scholar of Milton 116-118, **164-167**, 213

Husserl (née Back), Clotilde (1866-1934), Heinrich Husserl's wife 15, 52, 57, 153-154

Husserl, Edmund (1838-1959), studied astronomy, mathematics, and philosophy; the founder of the Phenomenological movement **16-47** et passim

Husserl, Elisabeth ("Elli") (1892-1981), Edmund Husserl's daughter, studied history of art 13-15, 18-19, 49-57, 60-61, 82-83, 92-93, 97, 99, 101, 110-111, 113, 135, 140, 153-154, 206-207, 230

Husserl (née Tammann), Else ("Dodo") (1903-1992), Gerhart Husserl's wife 15, 102, 103

Husserl, Gerhart (1893-1973), Edmund Husserl's son, German legal scholar and phenomenological philosopher 12-15, 18-19, 33, 35, 51, 53-55, 57-58, 60-69, 71, 74-75, 80, 82, 90-93, 97-99, 101-103, 112, 140, 210-211, 215, 230

Husserl, Heinrich (1857-1928), Edmund Husserl's brother, published several poems 15, 18, 22-23, 52, 57, 153-154

Husserl (née Steinschneider), Malvine (1860-1950), Edmund Husserl's wife 13-15, **48-52**, 70-75, 85-87, 90-97, 99, 101-108, 135, 140, 154

Husserl (Back), Trude, stepdaughter of Heinrich Husserl 52, 57

Husserl, Wolfgang (1895-1916), Edmund Husserl's youngest son 12-15, 18-19, 33, 35, 49-50, 52-55, 57, 59, 60-79, 82-97, 99, 101-107, 112, 114, 115, 140, 152, 155, 210-211, 233, 241, 253-256

I

Ingarden, Roman (1893-1970), Polish philosopher and student of Husserl 228, **229**, 230

J

Jacobsohn (née Lask), Berta (1878-1967), German poet and journalist, sister of Emil Lask 247

Jensen, Paul (1850-1931), close friend of Edmund Husserl 49-50, 68-69

K

Kaufmann, Fritz (1891-1958), German philosopher and student of Husserl 116, **168-175**, 227

Koyré, Alexander (1892-1964), French philosopher of Russian origin, member of the Göttingen circle of phenomenology 117-118, 129-130

L

Lask, Emil (1875-1915), German philosopher   116, 239, **242-249**, 255-256, 268

Lewin, Kurt (1890-1947), German psychologist   116, **176-179**

Lewin, Fritz (1895-1918), younger brother of Kurt Lewin   176-177

Leyendecker, Herbert (1885-1958), studied with Husserl, Scheler, and Pfänder, worked later as art dealer   118

Linke, Paul Ferdinand (1876-1955), German philosopher, psychologist, and phenomenologist   255-256

Lipps, Hans (1889-1941), German philosopher and psychologist   116-118, 129-130, **180-185**

Lipps, Theodor (1851-1914), German psychologist and philosopher, many of his students studied later with Husserl   130, 134, 136, 147, 209, 218, 236, 250, 270

Littmann, Enno (1875-1958), German orientalist, Wolfgang Husserl studied with Littmann in summer 1914   49-50, 68-69, 77-78, 84, 112

Löwith, Karl (1897-1973), German philosopher   116, **186-189**

M

Mahnke, Dietrich (1884-1939), German philosopher and student of Husserl   12-13, 116, **190-199**

Metzger, Arnold (1892-1974), German philosopher and student of Husserl   116, **200-208**

Mirbt, Carl Theodor (1860-1929), father of Heinz Mirbt   **76**

Mirbt, Heinz (1894-1915), son of Carl Theodor Mirbt   **76**

Misch, Georg (1878-1965), German philosopher   152, 198

Müller(-Rastatt), Günther (1890-1957), specialist for German studies, studied with Husserl in Göttingen   212-213

Münsterberg, Hugo (1863-1916), German philosopher and psychologist   26, **27**-28, 147

N

Natorp, Paul (1854-1924), German philosopher, educationalist, and cofounder of the Marburg school of neo-Kantianism   110-111, 113, 162, 198, 237

Neumann, Friedrich (1889-1978), German philosopher   116-118, **209-217**, 262-263

P

Perry, Ralph B. (1876-1957), American philosopher, leader of the school of new realism   26-27

Pfänder, Alexander (1870-1941), German philosopher and leading member of the Munich school of phenomenology   114, 129, 134, 137-138, 147, 156, 186, 189, 198, 218, 250, 270

R

Reinach, Adolf (1883-1917), German philosopher   49-50, 116-118, 129, 135, 147, 156, 164, 170, 180-181, 198, 209-211, 218-219, 226-227, 231, 240, **250-265**, 266, 272

Reinach (née Stettenheimer), Anna (1884-1953), doctor's degree in physics, wife of Adolf Reinach   226, 257, 262

Reinach, Heinrich (1888-1965), younger brother of Adolf Reinach, studied law and philosophy   250, 253, 257

Rickert, Heinrich (1863-1936), German philosopher, one of the leaders of the so-called Southwestern or Baden school of Neo-Kantianism   156, 158-159, 163, 242-244, 246-247, 249, 266-269

Rickert jr., Heinrich („Heini") (1891-1917), Heinrich Rickert's son   116, 118, 249, 262-263, **266-269**

Rickert (née Keibel), Sophie (1864-1951), wife of Heinrich Rickert   247, 266

Ritzel, Hermann (1880-1915), Husserl's student in Göttingen   116, 135, **270-275**

Rohrbach, Paul (1869-1956), German (born in Russia) political publicist and economist, interested in colonial politics   137-138

Rolland, Romain (1866-1944), French dramatist, novelist, essayist, Nobel Prize for Literature in 1915   42-43, 126, 128

Rosenblum, Alexander (1883-1950), Polish student of Husserl, member of the Göttingen circle of phenomenology   252

Royce, Josiah (1855-1916), American philosopher   26-27, 119, 147

Runge, Carl (1856-1927), German mathematician and physicist, studied together with Husserl   77-78

Runge (née Du Bois-Reymond), Aimée (1862-1941), wife of Carl Runge   51

Runge, Bernhard (1897-1914), son of Aimée and Carl Runge   63-64

S

Santayana, George (1863-1952), Spanish-American philosopher, essayist, and poet   147

Scheler, Max (1874-1928), German philosopher   116-118, 137-138, 147, 156, 165, 167, **218-225**, 232, 250, 253-254

Schickele, René (1883-1940), German-French writer   166-167

Schröder, Edward (1858-1942), Germanist and mediaevalist   209-211, 216-217

Schulze-Gaevernitz von, Gerhart (1864-1943), German economist and politician   98

Simmel, Georg (1858-1918), German sociologist and philosopher   115

Sombart, Werner (1863-1941), German economist and sociologist   137-138

Spranger, Eduard (1882-1963), German philosopher and educationalist   175, 200

Stein, Edith (1891-1942), German philosopher and Carmelite nun   13-14, 116, 120-121, 129-130, 171-173, **226-230**, 232, 240, 262-263

Stumpf, Carl (1848-1936), German philosopher and psychologist, teacher of Husserl   168, 176, 198

Sybel von, Alfred (1885-1945), German philosopher, psychologist, and phenomenologist; 1907-1912 student of Husserl   117-118, 129-130

V

Volkelt, Johannes (1848-1930), German philosopher   134, 198

W

Walther, Gerda (1897-1977), German philosopher and student of Husserl   **189**

Wendland, Paul (1864-1915), German classical philologist   171-172

Windelband, Wilhelm (1848-1915), German philosopher of the so called "Baden School" of neo-Kantianism   242, 246

Wirth, Wilhelm (1876-1952), German psychologist   238

Wundt, Wilhelm (1832-1920), German physician, physiologist and philosopher; the "father" of experimental psychology   134, 147, 168

Z

Zweig, Arnold (1887-1968), German writer and intellectual   **232**

The publication and research of this volume was supported by the European Research Council under the European Union's Seventh Framework Programme (FP7/2007 - 2013) / ERC grant agreement no. 61765911, GRAPH project "The Great War and Modern Philosophy."

© 2017 by Leuven University Press / Presses Universitaires de Louvain / Universitaire Pers Leuven. Minderbroederstraat 4, B-3000 Leuven (België)

All rights reserved. No part of this book may be reproduced, stored in an automated database, or published, in any form or by any means, whether electronic, mechanical, photocopying, recording or otherwise, without the express prior written permission of the publisher.

ISBN 978 94 6270 121 2
D/2017/1869/60
NUR: 730

Cover image: Kriegsfotos Walter Naumann
                Negativalbum Nr. 3, Fotos Nr. 201-300, item 66

Title page image: Excerpt from a letter from Edmund Husserl
                    to Fritz Kaufmann, 30 January 1916
                    (Husserl Archives)

Design and lay-out: Friedemann Vervoort

Every effort has been made to contact all holders of the copyright to the visual material contained in this publication. Any copyright-holders who believe that illustrations have been reproduced without their knowledge are asked to contact the publisher.

gutes Land. Versuche nicht u[…]
duld, denen gerade die frie[…]
dürfen. Ich weiß wie schwer […]
sine dura necessitas. Also […]
fort in Essen, in […]
eile! für einen Urlaub zu […]
keine Möglichkeiten. Ihn Dess[…]
[…] du nicht bereits etc. Hoff[…]
[…] – zu Frbg